IN THE SHADOW OF THE TEMPLE

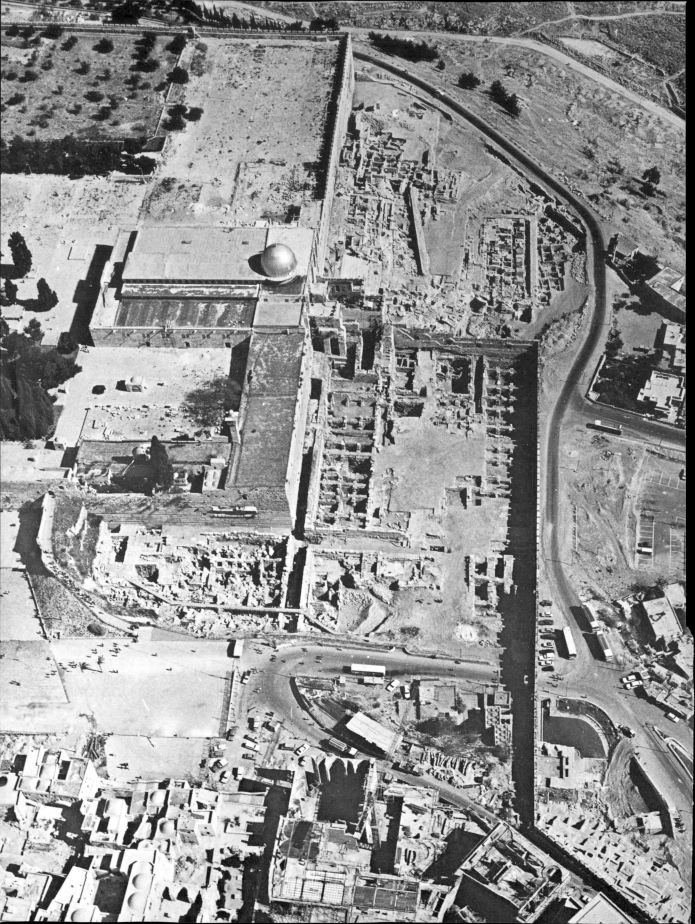

Meir Ben-Dov

IN THE SHADOW OF THE TEMPLE
OF THE TEMPLE

The Discovery of Ancient Jerusalem

Translated from the Hebrew by Ina Friedman

HARPER & ROW, PUBLISHERS, New York

Cambridge, Philadelphia, San Francisco, London

1817 *Mexico City, São Paulo, Singapore, Sydney*

This work was originally published in Hebrew in Israel under the title חפירות הר הבית.
Copyright © 1982 by Keter Publishing House Jerusalem, Ltd.

IN THE SHADOW OF THE TEMPLE. English translation copyright © 1985 by Keter Publishing
House Jerusalem, Ltd. All rights reserved. Printed in Israel. No part of this book may be
used or reproduced in any manner whatsoever without written permission except in the case
of brief quotations embodied in critical articles and reviews. For information address
Harper & Row, Publishers, Inc., 10 East 53rd Street, New York, N.Y. 10022. Published
simultaneously in Canada by Fitzhenry & Whiteside Limited. Toronto.

FIRST U.S. EDITION

Library of Congress Cataloging in Publication Data

Ben-Dov, M.
    In the shadow of the Temple.

    Translation of: Hafirot Har ha-Bayit.
    1. Temple Mount (Jerusalem) — Antiquities. 2. Jerusalem — Antiquities. 3.
Excavations (Archaeology) — Jerusalem.
I. Title. II. Title: Discovery of ancient Jerusalem.
DS109.28.B4613 1985   933   84-48639
ISBN 0-06-015362-8

85 86 87 88 89 10 9 8 7 6 5 4 3 2 1

Contents

Introduction

To excavate in the shadow of the Temple Mount in Jerusalem, at the foot of the monumental walls built by King Herod, is a gift, for it is far from a usual undertaking among archaeological excavations in Israel — or anywhere else, for that matter. Jerusalem has been a holy and royal city ever since King David declared it his capital and his son Solomon built the First Temple there. In antiquity it was the spiritual and cultural center of the Jewish people. Here the kings of Judah consolidated their rule, and here the prophets stood on the threshold of the house of the Lord and preached the doctrine of social justice. After the Babylonian conquest, the Temple was destroyed and Jerusalem lay in ruins, its inhabitants driven into exile; but they returned to the city a few decades later, drawn by their yearning to rebuild the Temple. And although the Second Temple was initially smaller and more modest than its predecessor, in the course of time both the Temple and the entire Temple Mount were rebuilt and refashioned in the height of splendor. During the final decades of the Temple's existence, building activity on the Temple Mount reached such proportions that the site grew into the largest holy place ever built by man. Little wonder, then, that after the soldiers of the Tenth Roman Legion destroyed the Second Temple and Jerusalem was again ravaged, restoring the Temple became the ultimate dream of Jews everywhere, and the Temple itself became a symbol of national and spiritual rebirth.

Jerusalem was rebuilt by the emperors of ascendant Christendom, who once again fashioned it as a holy city, though this time as a symbol of their new world view. Public works such as paving new streets, building a grand church, and constructing a densely populated residential neighborhood at the foot of the ruined Temple Mount characterized the period of Byzantine rule. But the Temple Mount itself remained desolate, for the destruction of the Temple was a cardinal tenet of Christian doctrine. The compound and its surroundings were not restored to a reflection of their former glory until the Moslem conquest of Jerusalem, when the retaining walls were rebuilt, holy buildings were erected on the Temple Mount, and the regime's secular buildings were constructed directly below it.

So it was that Jerusalem became holy to three monotheistic religions — Judaism, Christianity, and Islam — and was transformed into a beacon of their faiths. This is also the reason for the intensity of events related to Jerusalem and the Temple Mount, the spurts of monumental building followed by massive destruction in a pattern that recurred periodically over the centuries.

Our labors did not go unrewarded, and 3,000 years of history have been uncovered at the foot of the Temple Mount. They were buried in twenty-five distinct archaeological strata that covered twelve historical periods. Moving hundreds of thousands of square meters of detritus, revealing scores of destroyed buildings, and discovering thousands of everyday objects are among the results of our excavations in the shadow of the Temple Mount.

When I accepted the job of writing an interim report on the dig, I had no idea how difficult a task it would be. Imagine trying to sum up such an extensive excavation plus the array of discoveries and finds in a single volume. Even though my publishers extended the book's length to a third more than originally planned, it hardly sufficed to cover all that we found and tell of the historical events that have been illuminated by and in some cases totally reconsidered as a result of the finds.

In describing the dig I have chosen to write in reverse order of the discoveries themselves. Unlike the excavation proper, which begins with the most recent period and moves down into the depths of the earth to bring up remains from the ever more distant past, following the order of the archaeological strata, this book opens with the most ancient stratum and climbs upward and forward in history to trace events in the order they occurred. Thus from bedrock up through the remains of the most recent residential quarters, we are able to piece together a mosaic of the Temple Mount's history from the days of King Solomon, the first to build in this area in the tenth century B.C., to Suleiman the Magnificent, the Ottoman sultan who ruled the city during the sixteenth century A.D.

Sometimes the various strata of our excavations shed light on dark spots in history or yielded up remains that have elucidated certain chapters of the past in a new way. From the beginning of the history of man and his culture in the Mediterranean Basin, the rulers of the world have always taken a special interest in Jerusalem. It has therefore been necessary to expand somewhat on the historical background of the various periods or elaborate on certain events. In discussing our finds, I have placed stress on architectonic descriptions and kept the discussion of everyday objects and implements to a minimum because it is the architectural endeavor, public and private, that has always been the highlight of the Temple Mount and its surroundings.

It is only natural that many people took part in such a large excavation, each contributing to the success of the project in his or her own way. First and foremost I must cite the tens of thousands of volunteers from all over the world, without whose dedicated work in the blistering heat of summer and the bitter cold of winter the excavation could not possibly have succeeded. The laborers and building contractors who worked with us were likewise infected with a sense of mission, displaying a considerable measure of sensitivity and never complainig when their payment was delayed — as it was more than once. Many of the government ministries and public bodies operating in or near the site of the excavation lent a hand, and those who did not actually help out physically often aided us through their advice and good spirits — which were no less valuable during the difficult and occasionally turbulent times we experienced during the dig. I also wish to thank all those who contributed to the excavation fund, for without their donations it is doubtful whether the dig would ever have taken place.

I will not try to hide the fact that the number of hands extended in aid were frequently offset by a number of feet extended in an effort to trip us up or at least impede our work. Much patience and resourcefulness were required to circumvent the various parties that rallied their energies to halt our activity in the field. It is impossible to mention all those who helped or all those who hindered, though they will be dealt with at length in the final report on the excavation. I cannot close, however, without mentioning the members of the scientific and administrative staff, who were largely responsible for the achievements of this venture.

The field archaeologists who participated over the years were D. Bahar, A. Segal, M. Gelzar, S. Nisbet, D. Kafri, M. Megidon, V. Constantino, R. Gardiner, Y. Magen, A. Less, M. Ben-Eliezer, M. Fayer, K. Omhani, and Z. Shevach. The archaeologists who worked on classifying and studying the finds were E. Lefrak, D. Packman, M. Magen, L. Wertheim, A. Koren, A. Zidon. A. Davis, G. Aloni, A. Shefer, E. Ariel, and A. Hasson, who was responsible for the laboratory. Y. Meshorer, A. Berman, and D. Abrahami dealt with the coins. The measurements were done by M. Feist, E. Galveron, A. Orweider, B. Lelor, D. Sheehan, P. Loufer, L. Reitmeyer, K. Galancy, A. Leiblich, P. Admansky, and M. Gross. Artistic sketches were done by M. Ritmeijer and N. Cohen, and the drawings of the objects were done by E. Merhav, M. Saguy, and M. Eichelberg. The restoration work was done by R. Alon, K. Kalmer, and E. Osterman. M. Pan, Y. Guber and A. Glick handled the photography of the area and the finds, while S. Windsor and G. Stanley manned the photo laboratory. The labor foremen were Y. Cohen, M. Abadi, and V. Suri. A. Sheduli was responsible for the toolshed; Y. Rami and Y. Abadi handled the mechanical equipment; A. Mazar and M. Levi ran the office and administration; and H. Mizrachi and Abu Hussein were the chief laborers.

The sketches and ilustrations in the following pages were specially prepared for this book. All the measurements and drafts of the drawings and sketches were provided by the author; the artwork itself was commissioned from a first-class team: the illustrations on pages 40, 72, 98, 100, 125, 126, 129, 152, 247, 256, 305, and 370 are the work of Y. Rachlin, a new immigrant from the Soviet Union who is an architect and master draftsman. The illustrations on pages 92, 120, 210, 217, 231, 253, 254, 260, 297, 300, 314, 315, 350, 351, and 358 are the work of K. Himmelman, an artist and a recent immigrant from the United States for whom this was the first experience with architectural drawing. The illustration on page 255 was done by H. Puhlas and that on page 327 by V. Levros. All the rest of the plans and illustrations were done by M. Ritmeijer, a young Dutch woman who began working on architectural drawings during our excavations and became one of the best people in this field in the country. This is the talented team that prepared the plans and illustrations — all executed perfectly — and any fault therein is entirely my own, as I placed sketches at their disposal.

The photographs were also taken specially for this book. Half of them were shot by A. Glick, a master photographer who makes his home in Jerusalem and began working with us as the excavation's chief photographer; the other half were taken by the author.

I owe special thanks to my mentor and friend the late Munya Dunaevsky, who recommended me for my position with the excavation, and to Professor Benyamin Mazar, who placed the organizational and scientific administration of the dig in my hands and extended me much credit and independence in all matters of administration.

The Keter Publishing House, its director, E. Cohen, and its production manager, Y. Zoreff, spared no effort to accord this book its attractive appearance, for which they have earned my special appreciation. The book was designed by Alex Berlyne, who assumed a difficult task because of the limitations placed upon him, and who has my gratitude both for his fine work and for the many hours we spent working together.

Finally, my wife, Zippi — to whom this book is dedicated — has my deepest thanks for her unstinting cooperation all along the way, for bearing far more than her fair share of the responsibility for the house and the family, and for the many sacrifices she made so that I could devote most of my time to excavating and writing.

Meir Ben-Dov
June 1984

1 A Dig Is Born

The Temple Mount in Jerusalem

Five thousand years ago, Jerusalem was a small walled city built on a slope above the Gihon Spring with a bald rocky mountain rising to the north of it. Two thousand years later, at the time of King Solomon, it was on that mountain that the Temple was built. Known as the Temple Mount ever since, it has been a focus of the city's life. Hardly has a visitor come

right: Section of the bedrock from west to east

to Jerusalem and not been to that site; in fact, many of the countless thousands who have come to Jerusalem did so because of the Temple Mount. So it was in the days past; so it is in our own day: the Temple Mount is the heart of Jerusalem.

Our story begins with a deadly plague that broke out among the Israelites during the last years of King David's reign, claiming thousands of victims. To cure the people of this terrifying affliction, the prophet Gad was sent to see the king, and the tale of his mission is preserved in the Bible:

... And Gad came that day to David and said unto him, Go up, rear an altar unto the Lord in the threshingfloor of Aruanah the Jebusite. And David, according to the saying of Gad, went up as the Lord commanded. ... So David bought the threshingfloor and the oxen for fifty shekels of silver. And David built there an altar to the Lord ... (II Samuel 24:18–25).

David's deed — which the Bible, in characteristic style, treats tersely but dramatically — established Jerusalem's status and the future course of history for generations. For the corollary to the building of an altar on Aruanah's threshing floor was the construction of the Temple on that same mountain during the reign of David's son Solomon: "And it came to pass in the four hundred and eightieth year after the children of Israel were come out of the land of Egypt, in the fourth year of Solomon's reign over Israel ... that he began to build the house of the Lord" (I Kings 6:1). Solomon had just ascended the throne and was already preparing to fulfill his father's dream of building the Temple on the mountain north of the city. Seven years of arduous work executed with the aid of the kingdom's finest architects and artisans, together with professionals from Tyre and Sidon, Solomon's allies to the north, brought the venture to its conclusion. As the Bible tells it, "... and in the eleventh year, in the month of Bul, which is the eighth month, the house was finished throughout all the parts thereof and according to all the fashion of it. So was he seven years in building it" (I Kings 6:38).

opposite: The excavation south of the Temple Mount; aerial photograph, 1976

Ever since then, Jerusalem has lived in the shadow of the Temple Mount, which an ancient tradition of the Jewish people associates with one of the key events in its early history as a nation: the sacrifice of Isaac. The Temple built on that mountain became the focus of the nation's spiritual life, its holiest of holy places. It is from there that the prophets derived their inspiration and from there that tenets and doctrines that comprise the cornerstone of Jewish society first issued forth.

When Solomon's Temple — the First Temple — was destroyed by the armies of King Nebuchadnezzar of Babylonia in 586 B.C. and Jerusalem's inhabitants were exiled, the desire to restore the Temple and renew the life of the nation in its own land became a leitmotif for the Jews. The first exiles to return to Jerusalem restored the altar; in the generations to come, the Temple itself — the Second Temple — was built on the ruins of its predecessor, and the Temple Mount again knew days of glory. The Jewish people enjoyed religious freedom under the rule of the superpowers of the day, Persia and Greece, and developed a thriving spiritual and cultural life, of which the Temple and the Temple Mount were tangible symbols. Yet there were also aberrant episodes in those years of relative peace and liberty. Antiochus IV, king of Syria, was one of those flagrant exceptions in his determination to destroy the Jewish people and obliterate its culture. Opposing him was a guerrilla army under the leadership of the Maccabees, or sons of the Hasmoneans, who won their struggle against oppression and went on to found a dynasty that ruled the independent Jewish state for generations to come.

It was during the reign of the Hasmoneans that the Land of Israel (later known as Palestine), like all the other lands of the East, came under the rule of Rome, the new world power of the day. By then Jewish communities had sprung up and prospered throughout the civilized world, but they all continued to regard Jerusalem as their spiritual capital and the Temple as the hub of Jewish life. It was on and alongside the Temple Mount that the spiritual institutions and leadership of the Jewish people — the priesthood and the Sanhedrin — centered. The Temple was the lodestone for reformers, philosophers, and prophets of social and economic revival who dreamed of bringing salvation to a suffering world. As the Second Temple developed into an emblem of the uniqueness and strength of the Jewish people and its faith, it also became the prime target of the rulers who conquered the Jews, subjugated them, and strove to destroy them. In one of Israel's finest hours in antiquity, during the rule of King Herod and his successors, the Temple in Jerusalem was the largest and most impressive shrine in the world. Even the commanders of the Roman Legions who besieged and ultimately conquered the city were awed by the grandeur of the Temple and deliberated how to save it. After it was nevertheless destroyed in A.D. 70, the Temple lived on in the minds and hearts of Jews the world over who, generation after generation, awaited the opportunity to rebuild, seeing in its restoration a symbol of redemption and of the revival of the Jewish people as a sovereign nation. It was precisely in a desire to crush the remnant of the Jewish people and its hope for redemption that the Emperor Hadrian ordered the construction of a magnificent pagan temple on the Temple Mount, and his decision led to the Bar Kokhba revolt, one of the most desperate and bloody uprisings ever known by the Roman Empire.

Jerusalem under the rule of the Byzantine Empire, which flourished the banner of the new Christian faith, also developed in the shadow of the Temple Mount but in exactly the opposite way. The Byzantines built monumental structures in Jerusalem but took pains to preserve the desolation of the Temple Mount, for the destruction of the Temple and the metaphysical message it implied about the ignominious status of Judaism was a *sine qua non* of the Christian world view.

Eventually, however, a reversal occurred. After centuries of Christian rule, the city fell to the armies of Islam in A.D. 638. The new religion, which drew on the traditions of its predecessors, also gloried in Jerusalem as a holy city, and the Temple Mount became the setting of one of the most popular legends of the Moslem faith: the tale of the prophet Mohammed's ascent to heaven. Once the site became holy to Islam, too, the Temple Mount and its surroundings began to hum with activity again.

Then came the return of the Christian armies in the form of the Crusader knights, redeemers of the Holy Land and Jerusalem who emblazoned with the liberation of the Holy Sepulcher on their banner. The Crusaders conquered the Temple Mount and its mosques in 1099 and established one of their major headquarters there. When Saladin reconquered Jerusalem from them in 1187 and thereafter under the Mameluke caliphs of Egypt and the Ottoman sultans of Turkey, activity on the Temple Mount and its surroundings experienced a new revival. The mark of these events and activities can still be seen in the alleyways surrounding the compound.

No other place in the world has inspired such zealous activity for over 3,000 years. No other place in the world has had so much written about it — barbs of ridicule as well as songs of praise. No other place in the world has been so closely studied and scrutinized as Jerusalem, so that hardly a month goes by without at least one research paper being published on one aspect or another of the history of the Temple Mount. Nevertheless, despite all that had been written and done, a multitude of secrets still lay hidden in the belly of the earth. The archaeologist's spade had much to contribute to the study of the Temple Mount and deciphering secrets from its past. After fourteen years of work, we can definitely say that the excavations at the foot of the Temple Mount have yielded results we never dared dream of.

The History of Research

For generations the study of Jerusalem, and particularly research on the Temple Mount, was a subject of focal interest to historians and other scholars. Over the centuries Jerusalem has been the destination of countless pilgrims and travelers of all nations and faiths, and their writings still rank as a major contribution to the research on the city's past. But the study of Jerusalem received special impetus during the past 150 years, when the tools of research were considerably enhanced by appraisals of architecture, topography, and the outstanding landmarks in the area. Most of all, however, it was archaeology that generated this new thrust. A young field of research, just beginning to grope its way forward, archaeology contributed enormously to historical scholarship by adding an entirely new source of knowledge. Finds salvaged from the earth through systematic excavation began to reveal things that could not possibly have been known by any other means, for it is only natural that not every event of the past is mentioned by contemporary sources — and in fact few written sources have survived at all. The finds delivered up by the archaeologist's spade are usually of two kinds: the remains of buildings and various small objects used in daily life, complementing each other to enrich and enhance research. Sometimes, in addition to expanding the knowledge at our disposal, a find, whether great or small, enables us to ask

opposite, above: View of the area inside the city wall before the excavation, 1936

opposite, below: View of the area outside the city wall before the excavation, 1969

above: A hut on the excavation site outside the Old City wall
below: South of the Temple Mount before the excavations, looking eastward

new questions; and questions, even more than answers, are the building blocks of research.

It was therefore reasonable to assume that a major excavation in Jerusalem, particularly in the vicinity of the Temple Mount, was only a matter of time. But although the theoretical study of the Temple Mount continued, expanded, and assumed depth, and hundreds of books and virtually thousands of articles were written on the subject, the number of excavations carried out in the field could be counted on the fingers of one hand. One might imagine that the primary reason for this dearth of archaeological endeavor was an objective one, namely, that the vicinity of the Temple Mount was a densely built-up area, making it impossible to conduct a dig without damaging residential buildings. But the fact is there were no buildings whatever along the southern wall — or anything else that would preclude the execution of archaeological excavations. The same was true of the southern parts of the eastern and western walls. The failure to conduct excavations was due solely to the fervent opposition of the *waqf*, or Moslem religious trust, which was the nominal owner of the area. Determined to prevent any encroachment by scholars on their territory, the trustees of the *waqf* turned down repeated requests from both archaeologists and various scholarly institutions abroad.

This implacable resistance was anchored in two fears. One was that the excavations might turn up finds that contradicted the tenets of Islam. But far more decisive was the fact that the trustees knew the Temple Mount had been built over the foundations of an infrastructure from the Second Temple period and that excavations in this area might well reveal who had preceded the Moslems in the area. Because it would probably unearth additional testimony to Jewish life in Jerusalem and on the Temple Mount in particular, any dig, the men of the *waqf* reasoned, would be a disservice to their own institution and cause. This was the real reason why the trustees of the *waqf* wanted to avoid any association with a venture of this sort.

Mixing politics and science produces a wicked brew, regardless of which side is stirring the cauldron. Yet this stalemate prevailed for over a century, and only twice did British expeditions succeed in overcoming the taboo on excavating in the area. The first was a series of research expeditions funded by the Palestine Exploration Fund and headed by two young engineering officers named Charles Warren and C. W. Wilson. Their pioneering work, carried out under highly adverse conditions, is considered the cornerstone of research on the Temple Mount, both because of the great ability reflected in their results, and because no other team operated in the area until our day, and in the absence of anything better, the old research was still the best we had. The second expedition to excavate in the vicinity of the Temple Mount was led by Miss Kathleen Kenyon. Its main focus was on the City of David, well south of the Temple Mount, for at that time (the 1950s) King Hussein of Jordan wanted to build a school in the open area there and asked the expedition to conduct a trial dig to establish whether there were any valuable antiquities in the area. Miss Kenyon's dig was a microcosm of an excavation, and its results were accordingly meager. Until the Six-Day War in 1967 — which by a quirk of history was also the 100th anniversary of the Palestine Exploration Fund's expedition by the Temple Mount — despite (or perhaps because of) the great success of this expedition, the Temple Mount and its surroundings remained an enigma waiting to be unraveled.

The Palestine Exploration Fund

In 1865 a group of men met in the Jerusalem Room of Westminster Abbey to proclaim the establishment of the Palestine Exploration Fund. Though remembered for its pioneering efforts, the new institution was in fact the successor of an earlier group, the Palestine Association, which had already dispatched a team of two scholars on an expedition to Palestine and Jerusalem. The venerable scholars never got beyond Malta, however, for upon being apprised of the perils awaiting them should they attempt to undertake investigative work in Jerusalem, they promptly returned to London. Undaunted, however, the new society considered the study of Palestine and Jerusalem as the alpha and omega of its work, especially since British Military Intelligence had come to the conclusion that scientific research of this sort was also of military value. Working through the auspices of the fund would make it possible to chart the country, study its geograpy and population, and simultaneously obtain valuable intelligence under the guise of a scientific interest in antiquities. This is essentially why the first and subsequent expedition were manned mostly by officers from Her Majesty's Army, particularly the Royal Engineers.

The first expedition was headed by a young officer named Charles Wilson. Thanks to his talents and to the bold and youthful character of his team, Wilson returned to England with a good deal of new information, despite the many obstacles placed in his path by local residents and Ottoman officials. Wilson's success prompted the members of the fund to dispatch a second expedition to Palestine, this time with the objective of conducting special archaeological research on Jerusalem, and its crowning achievement was the study of the Temple Mount. Composed of officers and men from the Royal Engineers and commanded by a twenty-seven-year-old officer named Charles Warren, the expedition departed for Palestine in 1867, exactly a century before our own undertaking began. Upon arriving, however, the engineers faced a battery of difficulties, the most irksome being their inability to obtain permission to excavate on the Temple Mount proper. Consequently, Warren focused his work outside the confines of the Temple Mount but close to its walls. The expedition's opening gambit was to bribe the local religious functionaries and the officials of the Ottoman regime — quite generously, I might add. But financial difficulties, limited manpower, and the restricted license provided by those authorities kept it from working beyond a very small area.

The members of the Warren expedition identified the most important spots surrounding the Temple Mount and proceeded to dig narrow vertical shafts close to the walls and at other key points not occupied by structures. Each shaft was about one square meter but reached all the way down to bedrock, which was sometimes as deep as 25 meters. Where the detritus was unstable, the shafts were shored up by wooden boards; and once the excavation was completed, most of these shafts were refilled with dirt. We managed to locate some of them in our excavation, including a few whose sides were still lined with wooden boards that, though rotted by now, were still *in situ*. It was a special treat for us to uncover the remains of the expedition that had preceded us by a century and was a milestone in the study of the Temple Mount.

Excavations employing this method of sinking shafts demanded unusual skill and daring, both of which the British teams had in generous supply. In one case the engineers failed to obtain permission to dig a shaft alongside the eastern wall of the Temple Mount. Having caught on to the game being played by the Ottoman officials and *waqf* authorities, they knew that the purpose of the prohibition was to force them into conducting negotiations and ultimately extort money from them in return for a license to dig. But due to a chronic shortage of funds — and an extraordinary sense of pride — they refused to submit. Instead they pulled back from the wall and dug first a standard vertical shaft and then a gallery that reached the wall anyway. For many years an illustration of this operation was reproduced on the title page of all of the Palestine Exploration Fund's publications.

Even though its work was limited to only a few sites, the importance of the fund's excavations was unsurpassed in terms of advancing the study of the Temple Mount. Yet we must keep in mind that the great value of this research derived from its exclusivity. For a century the results of the Warren expedition's efforts served as the sole basis of scholarship on the Temple Mount. Yet the amount of information obtained by these two expeditions was far from sufficient to answer contemporary demands. To put it in more colorful terms, one could say that the fund's two expeditions managed to diagnose the problem, but the operation still lay ahead. Warren's dig was a peek into the unknown, but it would take excavations on a much broader scale to derive true insight into the structures built alongside the Temple Mount. Moreover, the work done by the Palestine Exploration Fund supplied information only on the Second Temple period, which was the chief interest of the expedition's members, whereas life had gone on alongside the Temple Mount for 3,000 years.

From a Dream to Reality

In June 1967, a century after the Palestine Exploration Fund began its work alongside the Temple Mount, a very different atmosphere prevailed in that area. The Jordanian Arab Legion had positions scattered all along the Temple Mount's walls, and when war broke out between Israel and Egypt on the morning of June 6th, the Jordanian army soon found itself actively involved in what subsequently became known as the Six-Day War. Jerusalem was involved in a bitter and complex battle — one of many in its history. Ironically enough, the city whose name contains the word "peace" and is perceived by three religions as the City of Peace has from the dawn of history been touched by every war that has afflicted this region.

In 1967 I was called up as a reservist, and my unit was posted to the north of the country, facing the Golan Heights. I can still recall the army spokesman's announcement informing the nation that the Israel Defense Forces had opened a counterattack on the Jordanian positions that were raining artillery fire down on Jewish Jerusalem. The operation culminated two days later in the encirclement of the Old City and its surrender to Israeli troops. This conquest was unique in Jerusalem's history, for it ended without destruction or even appreciable damage to the city and its holy places. Especially moving was the announcement about the I.D.F.'s entry into the Old City, the gathering of forces on the Temple Mount, and the prayers that Jews held at the Western (Wailing) Wall for the first time since 1948, when the city was divided in two.

Meanwhile, the war had moved on to our sector, as fighting broke out on the Golan Heights. Obviously I was completely steeped in the demands and perils of combat. But I was demobilized shortly after the fighting ended, and then my thoughts went first and foremost to Jerusalem. Even before going to the Wailing Wall — via a route that had been cleared especially for this purpose before the rest of the Old City was open to visitors — I paid a visit to the Archaeological Institute of the Hebrew University to find out about my colleagues serving in other reserve units. There I ran into the archaeologist - architect Munya Dunaevsky, who was on the teaching staff of the institute, and he asked if I would be interested in taking part in an envisioned archaeological dig alongside the Wailing Wall. It took barely a split second for me to reply that I would be delighted to participate in the venture. Then he invited me to come along to Professor Benjamin Mazar's office.

Professor Mazar, one of Israel's veteran and venerated archaeologists, told me that as soon as he heard about the capture of East Jerusalem and the Old City — meaning that the Wailing Wall was in Israel's hands — he began thinking about undertaking a dig in the area. "The dream of every archaeologist is within reach," Mazar exulted. "When I talked to Munya Dunaevsky about putting together a team, he brought up your name, and here you are! What do you think?"

"When do we start?" was my immediate answer.

"Yesterday!" he quipped with his favorite reply.

Needless to say, there was boundless enthusiasm for the idea in many quarters, and in my mind's eye I could already see the workers carrying tools into the area of the Temple Mount. That was, as I've said, before I visited the site. It was only after my chance meeting with Munya and that chat with Professor Mazar that I actually went to the Temple Mount to see what was involved, and it didn't take me long to realize that the operation would be far more complex than any other excavation I had ever worked on. The road ahead before the first pickax touched earth was going to be a hard one.

After a considerable delay — a number of months, in fact, during which I managed to finish excavating the Crusader fortress of Belvoir overlooking the Jordan Valley — I returned to Jerusalem and we began organizing our team and making initial plans for the dig. The administration of the dig included Professor Mazar, its head; Yosef Aviram, the director of the Archaeological Institute and secretary of the Israel Exploration Society, who was responsible for mobilizing and managing our funds; and myself as field director, which meant that I was responsible for organizing the team and managing the work itself. Nine months passed before Professor Mazar's dream became an excavation — nine long months filled with hard work, frustration, and no few misgivings. Day after day went by, but the excavations never got started. The idea had seemed so popular; to those of us directly connected with the project, it looked like a natural. Yet nothing was happening. You are probably assuming that the universal gremlin, financial problems, was the major obstacle in our path, but in this case it wasn't so. True, the capital for the excavation fund had not been raised yet, but we had a commitment from Mayor Teddy Kollek that once the dig began, he would make available to us an initial grant of 50,000 Israeli pounds (equivalent to about $12,500) — a not inconsiderable sum, for starters. The mayor's one condition was that the dig would start on a Sunday. Yet each week Sunday came and Sunday went and the initiation of the dig was postponed for another seven days.

The delays arose because the government had made its permission to dig conditional upon the agreement of the chief rabbis; we were, after all, talking about an excavation by the holy place most sacred to Jews, the Wailing Wall. Professor Mazar duly took it upon himself to meet with the rabbis — individually, of course, since deep-seated rivalries made it out of the question to meet with them together — and we knew that more often than not they contradicted one another's views, making everything dependent upon which of them was consulted first. *Our* case, however, was one of the few on which the two rabbis were in absolute agreement: they both turned us down flat. The Sephardi chief rabbi, Rabbi Nissim, explained his refusal by the fact that the area of our proposed dig was a holy place. When asked to elucidate his answer further, he intimated that we might prove that the Wailing Wall is not in fact the western wall of the Temple Mount. Besides, what point was there in taking the chance and conducting a dig for scientific purposes when they were irrelevant anyway. On the other hand, the Ashkenazi chief rabbi, Rabbi Unterman, agonized over the halakhic problems (questions of Jewish law). "What will happen," he mused aloud, "if, as a result of the archaeological excavation, you find the Ark of the Covenant, which Jewish tradition says is buried in the depths of the earth?" "That would be wonderful!" Professor Mazar replied in all innocence. But the venerable rabbi told the good professor that *that* was precisely what he feared. Since the Children of Israel are not "pure," from the viewpoint of Jewish religious law, they are forbidden to touch the Ark of the Covenant. Hence it is unthinkable to even consider excavating until the Messiah comes!

For lack of choice, we began to entertain the idea of excavating at the foot of the Temple Mount's southern wall. (In retrospect, this proved to be an excellent idea, for the southern wall was the front of the Temple Mount and contained the main gates.) But Rabbi Nissim stuck to his guns in insisting that no excavation should be allowed along either the western or the southern wall — or at any distance from them. He further made it clear that if any such excavation was inaugurated against his will, he would instigate mass demonstrations and carry on a fight to the finish against it. Clearly the Rabbinate was dead set against a dig of any kind, though its reasons were somewhat far-fetched, or at least not very convincing. The rabbis with whom I spoke in the ultra-orthodox Meah Shearim quarter told me that the *halakhah* is not explicit on the question of whether or not an archaeological excavation is permissible alongside the Temple Mount. They, too, objected to the idea on theoretical grounds, because they found fault with the very essence of archaeology. Still, they did not believe there was any specific halakhic prohibition against a dig, so that, strictly speaking, it was permissible to excavate as long as the "honor" of the Temple Mount was preserved.

Convinced that he could persuade the rabbis to favor us with their permission to dig, Professor Mazar kept up his trek between Rabbi Nissim's office and Rabbi Unterman's house, between drinking steaming Turkish coffee and quaffing glasses of hot tea with home-baked cakes. I meanwhile was the target of the mayor's wrath because the excavations had not begun yet. And so it was that between tea and coffee, between one bawling out and the next, most of the winter of 1968 went by.

Dig We Must: The Stratagem

At the beginning of the 1960s, the Jordanians had built a girls' school south of the Temple Mount. It was a structure put up without any logic, for, as we were soon to reveal, it was built over remains from the early Moslem period with enormous importance for the study of the history of Islam in Jerusalem. Be that as it may, after the Six-Day War the school was moved into another building, because the vicinity of the Wailing Wall had again become a prayer site and the structure built by King Hussein was slated to be demolished. It was not torn down immediately, however. Instead, the Jerusalem Municipality temporarily placed it at the disposal of the Rabbinical High Court, which occupied only about half its rooms. As fate would have it, the court was presided over by Chief Rabbi Nissim.

Each day I made a habit of touring around the Temple Mount's walls both to plan our excavation and to keep an eye on what was going on there. One of my chief concerns was to prevent irregularities and violations of the Antiquities Law, especially since the chief rabbi's associates had repeatedly attempted to dig up the area around the walls on their own. Their aim was to prepare the area south of the Temple Mount as a prayer site, even though worshippers showed no interest in coming to pray there; the religious community was faithful to the centuries-old tradition of praying by the Wailing Wall and would have no other wall beside it. But the chief rabbi wanted to establish a *fait accompli* that would block any possibility of an excavation in this southern area. I met with Rabbi Nissim's representatives a number of times and tried to feel them out on whether we would be able to obtain the use of a few rooms in the former school building once our excavations were approved. When I saw how strong their resistance was to this idea, it occurred to me that the building might indeed be the key to getting the dig going. We had a license from the Municipality and the Department of Antiquities in our pocket; the government had no objection to the dig but, for the sake of good order, wanted the approval of the rabbis; while the rabbis would not hear of it. So my new strategy was to try to shift their attention away from the struggle against the archaeological dig to another issue, namely, use of the building now serving the Rabbinical Court. Placing my trust in the adage about possession being nine points of the law, I set to work.

First, I asked Teddy Kollek, the nominal "landlord" of the building, for permission to use some of its empty rooms, and when he agreed we decided to begin the excavations at 7 A.M. on Wednesday, February 29, 1968 — come what may! On the appointed day I arrived at the area south of the Temple Mount with fifteen laborers, an array of excavating equipment, and a full measure of hope. I marked out a number of squares and began to brief the laborers, who lacked experience in archaeological excavations, while a few members of the staff began to organize the office and the toolshed inside the school-turned-rabbinical court. We got the key from a cleaning woman on the basis of a note that Teddy Kollek had scrawled on a chit of paper!

At 8 o'clock sharp the court secretary arrived at work and, seeing that the excavation had begun and that we were already busy organizing the office and the various storerooms in the building's unused wing, he frantically summoned Rabbi Nissim. The rabbi turned up in a matter of minutes, firmly ordering us to vacate the rooms. Before long the civil altercation between us had burgeoned into a full-blown dispute. Yet I was keenly aware that the rabbi had not said so much as a word about the excavation going on before his very eyes; all his energies were channeled into getting us out of that building posthaste. He was outraged by the incursion onto what he regarded as "his rooms" and by the blow to his prestige in the eyes of his employees, the other rabbis, and the laborers at the dig. When he failed to get his way, Rabbi Nissim stomped off in high dudgeon — but not before warning me that he would teach me a lesson for defying a chief rabbi!

Almost instantly, it seemed, the minister of religious affairs was looking for me in person. He was followed by a stream of officials from the Municipality, including the director of East Jerusalem and Old City affairs, and from various ministries. All were chastened by the rabbi's rage and eager to mollify him at any cost; all had but one request: that the rooms be vacated and turned over to the Rabbinate. No one breathed a word about the dig. But since I understood that the fate of the excavation depended on holding on to those rooms for a few days — until we could get our work going as a *fait accompli* — I decided to stand my ground against all pressure. (And I must say, an incredible amount of pressure had suddenly materialized on all sides.) In the meantime, we stepped up the rate of the work and within a few days had eighty people in the field. We also began to use the first volunteers. In anger at our refusal to yield on the building issue, the Municipality now reversed itself and suspended its financial support of the dig. To our surprise donations began to pour in from private sources, and the Labor Ministry did its part by sending over more and more workers every day.

As the days wore on and the number of meetings with government ministers and other intermediaries mounted, the excavation itself became an incontrovertible fact: all along the western-half of the Temple Mount's southern wall, meaning the section inside the Old City wall, an archeological dig was going on without the least interference. Rabbi Nissim's threats over the issue had vanished; it appeared that he had given his tacit agreement to the excavation, though he never spoke of it publicly. Consequently, I too relented and returned two of the four rooms we occupied to representatives of the Ministry of Religious Affairs, who in turn assigned them specifically for the use of the rabbinical court. Even so, Rabbi Nissim rarely visited the disputed building after that, and except for a few special cases we didn't see him again, so infuriated was he over the incident.

Before the excavation had fully established itself as a going concern, however, a new front opened against it. This time our antagonists were the Moslem notables in Jerusalem: the *mufti*, the *qadi*, and the members of the Higher Moslem Council, all of whom regarded any excavation as the contravention of a long-standing tradition in the area. They justified their opposition on two grounds. The first, reminiscent of the reason cited earlier by the Jewish sages, was that the excavation might produce finds

opposite, above: Aerial photograph of the area taken after a few months of work, 1968

opposite, below, right: Aerial photograph of the excavation soon after it had begun, looking westward

opposite, below, left: Aerial photograph of the first squares, looking eastward

The Moslem Notables Have Their Day

right: A visit by Rabbi David Mintzberg of the Meah Shearim quarter
left: A visit by the Russian Orthodox patriarch and his entourage

contradicting hallowed religious tenets. (In essence, the very notion of submitting historical affairs to scientific scrutiny was unacceptable to them.) The second reason was political: the Moslem leadership feared that the dig would yield "Jewish" discoveries designed to show who the original "owners" of the site were. The validity of this claim was no less questionable, as the purpose of the dig was to investigate Jerusalem's history over the ages, not to traffick in politics or prove any long-antiquated "ownership." The truth of the matter is that many of our discoveries contributed to an appreciation of the glory of Jerusalem under Moslem rule, making this objection seem almost self-defeating in retrospect. When all else failed, an ostensibly pragmatic complaint was drummed up: "The excavations are not in fact a scientific venture; their Zionist objective is rather to undermine the southern wall of the Temple Mount, which is likewise the southern wall of the Al Aqsa Mosque, as a way of destroying the mosque." Need I add that this charge was as unfounded as its predecessors?

Fortunately, it was not long before a large and very impressive structure not mentioned in any of the written sources began to emerge from under the heaps of detritus south of the Temple Mount. Together with similar buildings uncovered later on, it dated to the early Moslem period — about which relatively little is known, so that any additional data gleaned from archaeology is of unusual value for all students of Jerusalem's past. I invited the Moslem notables to visit the excavation and proudly showed them our discovery. During the tour they could see for themselves that our workers took pains to preserve every wall they uncovered and that the sensitive area along the wall under the Al Aqsa Mosque was receiving special treatment.

As I had hoped, this visit dispelled most of their fears and led the trustees of the *waqf* to reconsider their position on the excavations. I wouldn't go so far as to say that they supported our work, but at least they no longer swallowed the propaganda about the excavation damaging the Al Aqsa Mosque, deliberately or otherwise. The tour also put an end to their concern that we were digging in order to find "proof" of any thesis. Thus for all intents and purposes, their objections were withdrawn. Even though, officially speaking, a standard letter of protest continued to be sent to the prime minister and the secretary-general of the United Nations every month, the substance of these letters was purely political, rather than pertinent to the matter at hand. Members of the Higher Moslem Council returned for additional tours, and on one of these occasions I happened to overhear one of the notables remark to another, "What's all this nonsense coming from Jordan about the mosque being destroyed by the excavations? Look at the discoveries from the Moslem period. They're truly gems!" Then I understood what the real source of the complaints was.

One summer, while on a visit to his family in the West Bank, the deputy director of the Jordanian Department of Antiquities, Mr. Rafiq Dajani, was invited to the dig. Dajani was the scion of the most noted Arab families in the country, and as an archaeologist he took great interest in the excavations and displayed enormous appreciation for what we were doing. "If we could leave politics to the politicians, I would heartily congratulate you on your work, revealing finds from periods of which we knew very little up until now," he confided in me, adding somewhat awkwardly, "The finds from the early Moslem period are thrilling, and

The author introduces Professor Mazar to the Moslem *qadi*, Sa'ad a-Din Al-Almi

frankly I'm surprised that Israeli scholars have made them public." A foreign correspondent who happened to be along on that tour saw to it that the world was apprised of Mr. Dajani's statemet — after first obtaining his permission to broadcast it. Much to our regret, Dajani's attempt to separate politics from science was a naive and futile gesture. Two weeks later, when he returned to his country, he was summarily dismissed from his post. Later on the man died in his prime, probably of despair.

Over the months and years, the opposition of the Moslem sages gradually died out altogether. When UNESCO saw fit to voice its denunciation of the excavations, its rallying cry no longer aroused a spirit of resistance among the Moslem leadership in Jerusalem. After becoming acquainted with the dig and its results, though they had not exactly become its leading advocates, at least their objections had become solely perfunctory.

The Christian View

As we shall see, the chief importance of the Temple Mount for Christianity during the early Byzantine era was the fact that it lay in ruins — vindication of Jesus' prophecy that the Temple would be destroyed and symbolic testimony to the withering of Judaism and the growth of the new doctrine of Christianity in its stead. The Christian world's primary interest in Jerusalem centered on the holy places that memorialize the outstanding events of Jesus' life, such as the site of the last Supper on Mount Zion, the Church of the Holy Sepulcher, and the site of the ascension on the Mount of Olives. This approach obtained throughout the ages with the exception of the twelfth century, when the Crusaders captured Jerusalem, took over the Islamic buildings on the Temple Mount, and converted them into both secular and religious institutions of their own. In recent decades, however, a return to studying Jewish history of both the First and Second Temple periods as background to Jesus' life and works has led Christian scholars to take up research on the Temple Mount. These scholars include clergymen who helped lay the foundations of modern academic inquiry. In fact, a number of schools of archaeology in Jerusalem that grew out of religious institutions have produced some of the leading scholars of Palestine's history — including the history of the Jews up to the destruction of the Second Temple.

When we first began excavating, scholars from the Christian community refrained from visiting the site, and it was difficult to comprehend their reservations about the dig. Some of our people ascribed their guardedness to the political ramifications of the excavations and their desire to appear neutral. Others explained it by citing practical considerations: the Christian scholars were afraid of jeopardizing their ties with or prejudicing their work in Jordan and other Arab countries. But there were those who speculated about the fears that may have lurked in the hearts of these scholars, all men of the cloth. Perhaps they suspected that the purpose of the excavation was to lay the groundwork for building the Third Temple and the whole business about an archaeological venture was just a cover for an invidious plot. All I can say is that until you actually hear these rumors with your own ears, they sound like the product of a demonic imagination. Yet more than once — whether in jest or otherwise — people whose exceptional intelligence and abilities as historians and archaeologists are beyond question have come straight out and asked me, "Don't you intend to reinstitute the Temple? Isn't this project essentially a replay of what happened during the time of the Emperor Julian or King Khosrau II

Volunteers and laborers at work

of Persia, when the Jews began to rebuild the Temple?" In short, "Is this *really* a purely scientific venture?"

For all that, the scholars of the Christian community kept their distance only during the early stages of the dig. Slowly but surely, scientific curiosity overcame whatever misgivings they may have had, and many of them began to frequent the site — whether openly in their clerical garb together with their students or alone after work hours and in mufti. These visits were highly fruitful to both sides, for scientific work, by its nature, must stand up to criticism and grapple with challenges to its basic premises; that is how its conclusions are tested. In our case, the longer the dig lasted and the more renowned it became for its discoveries, the more it became accepted by the various religious parties involved. The more that Jews, Moslems, and Christians saw for themselves that our aim was truly to unearth chapters from the past and corroborate facts, the more the initial standoffishness dissolved. I should add that this change of heart was most welcome and contributed enormously to the excavation, the archaeologists, and the world of research as a whole.

On the Work and the Workers

Feeding off sheer determination, we threw the dig into high gear, though the question of a budget continued to plague us. The till was chronically empty, and accelerating the pace of the excavations required considerable resources. On the other hand, since echoes of our initial struggle had been heard over the mass media and even penetrated the Cabinet room, it was not very difficult to attract government ministers and other public figures to the site. Some had come to see our initial finds; others were drawn by curiosity about why the rabbis and Moslem notables were in such a lather. From the outset we worked at a fevered pace by the southern wall, so that by the end of a week it was possible to show off a substantial section of this wall, with its monumental ashlars, as well as the remains of an imposing structure from the early Moslem period.

These discoveries did the trick, and soon the Ministry of Labor was supplying us with an additional 150 workers who had previously been employed in afforestation. The trouble was that many of these laborers regarded the pickax as more of a camp stool than a tool of honest labor, and frankly we had little hope for them. Nevertheless, I took it upon myself to give them a fair try and talked to them before they were sent off to face the layers of packed earth awaiting removal. I spoke of the challenge of working at the foot of the Temple Mount and told them that here their work was really needed; this was no benign social-service project dreamed up to mete out a welfare allotment under the guise of a day's hard-earned pay. I tried to stress that working in this particular place was a privilege, rather than a chore, and my words fell on sympathetic ears. When supervisors from the Labor Ministry paid us a visit a week later, they thought we had hired new laborers. The pace, the determination, and the enthusiasm was phenomenal. Simply stated, the joy of doing something meaningful restored the self-respect of these men and improved their attitude toward work as a whole.

As to the volunteers, we never made an appeal for them. We simply never had to. On the contrary, appeals and pressure came from hundreds of people who wanted a hand in our venture. Still, we hesitated at first because we were not organized to handle volunteers, having neither places to lodge them nor a budget to cover their expenses. So we set down a simple rule: whoever wanted to work with us was welcome

on condition that he stay on for a week and cover all his own expenses.

Archaeological excavations in Israel are usually conducted during the summer, but since we wanted to conclude this dig in our own generation, we extended the season into the winter as well. There were far fewer volunteers in the cold months, but they still amounted to quite a work force. The first winter, 1969, did not go badly at all; only six work days were lost due to bad weather (including two days of heavy snow). Invariably I would get up at 6 A.M. to see that it was raining outside and ask myself whether there was any point in going to the dig. Yet as soon as I got to work there would be a lull in the rain, only to have it start again when 3 o'clock came round. Incredible as it may sound, the days went on like that for ten successive winters, and we lost an average of only six or seven work days a year, since it had a way of raining mostly at night. Even more uncanny was what Josephus Flavius, the first-century Jewish historian, had to say about this phenomenon: "When they built the Temple, our fathers tell us, it only rained in Jerusalem at night." Josephus believed that this was the hand of Providence helping the operation along. Perhaps that was so, or perhaps this is merely a quirk of Jerusalem's climate. Either way, it was as true now as it had been two millennia ago.

Working at an accelerated pace produced an appreciable amount of earth and fill that had to be disposed of. For this purpose we called in a bulldozer — after checking through the detritus by sinking a number of investigatory shafts — and thus saved precious time. A bulldozer is the last thing an archaeologist would normally expect to find at a dig, but the experience I had acquired excavating the Belvoir fortress taught me that if its operator is graced with a sensitive soul, and if an archaeologist is stationed permanently beside its scoop, it can be a very helpful instrument. As time went on a quiet revolution took place, and today you can see bulldozers working at many sites where it is necessary to remove large quantities of earth and debris. By the end of five years of excavation, we had moved over 300,000 cubic meters of detritus. (I believe this is a world record and doubt it will be broken very soon.) Some of it underwent

above, right: The conclusions of the initial investigation: a bulldozer can be used

above, left: The detritus is removed by hand and mechanical wheelbarrows

opposite: The first squares for investigating the area

Ben-Gurion visits the dig

Kathleen Kenyon engaged in an archaeological debate

careful winnowing by hand and yielded up more than 25,000 coins, in addition to thousands of other small artifacts from various periods.

The unique site of our dig required us to employ some unconventional methods from the scientific viewpoint as well. Excavations are usually held during the summer months, while during the winter the archaeologists turn their attention to studying the finds and preparing for the next season. As we could not afford the luxury of halting our field work for six months out of the year, we devised an alternate system by working in parallel teams: a field team to handle the supervision of the excavations and a workshop team to handle the treatment of the finds, prepare plans and photographs, and decipher and study the discoveries. The teams were composed of archaeologists, engineers, architects, photographers, surveyors, draftsmen, artists, and restorers. Some of them worked for seven or eight years, others spent less time with us. Their energy and talents are what crowned our efforts with success despite the difficulties of the day-to-day work and the lackluster that is typical of an archaeological dig. The test of this book is the saga of that success and the people who made it possible.

A Royal City and a Nation's Temple

Jerusalem started out as a small city built on a low rise above a spring. It was surrounded by higher mountains on all sides: the Mount of Olives to the east; what became known as the Temple Mount to the north; a hill later known as the Upper City to the west; and the mountain that now houses the village of Silwan to the south. About 10 acres large, it had a population of approximately 4,000 inhabitants, mostly farmers who made their living by working the land in the surrounding valleys and supplemented it by hosting the commercial caravans that passed by the outskirts of the city. This was the Jerusalem founded some 5,000 years ago, and so it remained for two millennia — a small settlement on a rise above the Gihon Spring in the Kidron Valley — until King David conquered it.

Jerusalem was among the few Canaanite cities mentioned in Egyptian documents from the second millennium B.C. as a settlement of distinction prior to the Israelite conquest. Its importance stemmed from its role in Egypt's military disposition, which was the controlling factor in Canaan at that time. Egypt's primary interest in Canaan focused on the main axes of transport that crisscrossed the region from the south toward the domain of the "superpowers" in the north along the Tigris and Euphrates rivers. One of these major axes — the road that traversed Canaan from west to east and linked up to the north–south routes — ran close to Jerusalem. The city was again mentioned some 3,400 years ago in the correspondence between the Egyptian kings who then ruled Canaan and some of the governors of the Canaanite cities. Preserved in the archive uncovered during the excavations at El Amarna in Egypt, this correspondence shows that even though it remained a small city, Jerusalem was of prime importance.

So on the eve of its conquest by David, Jerusalem was still a small but free and open city whose Jebusite inhabitants managed to maintain their independence though they were wedged in between the veteran Canaanite population and the Israelite newcomers — along the lines of an ancient Switzerland tucked in between the Israelite tribes to the north and south and the Canaanites and Philistines to the west. After David captured it at the beginning of the first millennium B.C., however, Jerusalem was transformed from a small city of mostly local import to the capital of the greater Israelite kingdom. And as a result of its new and enhanced status, the city experienced a spell of unprecedented growth and expansion. The principal government institutions, army headquarters, and the center of religious ritual were transferred to the new capital, and soon Jerusalem proved too small to contain the influx of the new establishment and the population that went along with it (especialy since the indigenous Jebusite inhabitants remained in the city and even served the new regime). It was therefore imperative to provide a new land for the city's growing needs.

More than all else, Jerusalem's status for generations to come was forged by the decision to move the Ark of the Covenant to the city, thus establishing it as the religious center for all the Israelites. King David did not content himself with transferring the ark to Jerusalem, however. He wanted to place it in a permanent structure and drew encouragement for

Interior of a tomb from the First Temple period. The opening in the center was made by grave robbers

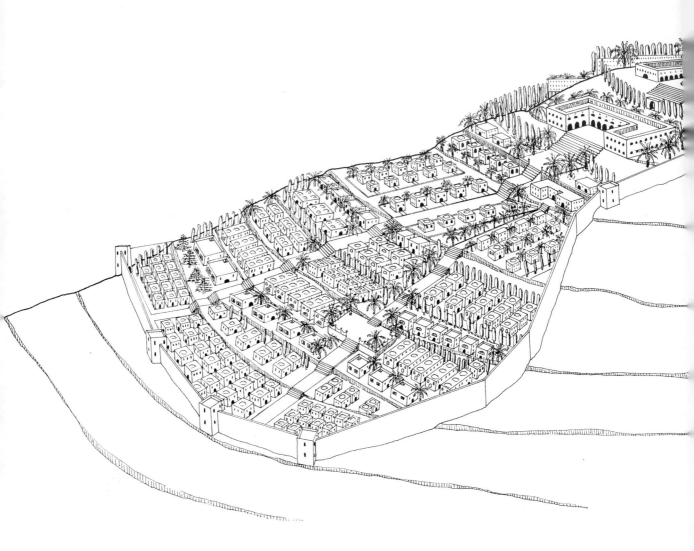

this plan from the prophet Nathan, as we learn in the Second Book of Samuel:

> And it came to pass when the king sat in his house, and the Lord had given him rest round about from all his enemies; that the king said unto Nathan the prophet, See now, I dwell in a house of cedar, but the ark of the Lord dwelleth within curtains. And Nathan said to the king, Do, do all that is in thine heart; for the Lord is with thee (7:1–3).

On further reflection, however, Nathan grasped the difficulties involved in carrying this plan out during David's lifetime. He therefore reversed himself, appeared before the king, and told David that the time was not yet ripe to build a permanent resting place for the ark and that the Lord did not regard David as the right man to build His Temple. Jewish tradition has it that God chose Solomon, rather than David, to carry out this holy task because the temple was a symbol of peace, and David's struggle for power and wars with the enemies of Israel had been marked by much

The city, the Ophel, the government quarter above it, and the Temple above all

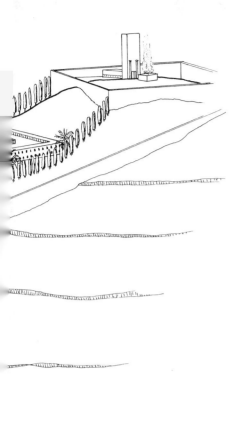

bloodshed, making the popular monarch and founder of the dynasty an unsuitable candidate for building the Lord's house.

In David's waning years a lethal plague broke out among the Israelites, and in his desire to obtain relief for his people the king consulted with the prophet Gad, who told him to build an altar to the Lord in the threshingfloor of Araunah the Jebusite. David bought the site from Araunah for 50 shekels of silver and built an altar there; the plague duly subsided and passed (II Samuel 24: 18–25). Jewish tradition has it that Araunah's threshingfloor was the site on which Abraham, the founding father of the Jewish people, had earlier built an altar in preparing to sacrifice his son Isaac. Obviously, David was interested in highlighting this tradition as a way of encouraging all the tribes of Israel to accept the sanctity of the site.

When Solomon succeeded David, he took it for granted that he would have to build a temple in Jerusalem, and in his desire to create a center around which the spiritual and ritual life of the entire nation would revolve, he envisioned a building that would house the Ark of the Covenant and contain an altar, the most important ritual symbols of the people of Israel. Solomon's choice of a site naturally fell on the mountain his father purchased from Araunah the Jebusite. Aided by his allies to the north, the kings of Tyre and Sidon — who were partners in managing international trade and other commercial activities of the day — Solomon approached the task with the boundless energy that characterized his building ventures throughout the kingdom, though nowhere more than in Jerusalem. Builders and craftsmen invested years of diligent work under the king's watchful eye, and when the job was done the First Temple stood in all its splendor. It made an enormous impression on the members of Solomon's generation and those to come, but even stronger than its physical grandeur was its influence on the spiritual life of the people: the Temple became a beacon of faith and morality that long outlasted its own existence.

Built as it was on the original site of David's (and Abraham's) altar, the Temple was located on the mountain to the north of the Jebusite city (known since the time of its conquest as the City of David) and was separated from the city by a gap of about 100 × 250 meters. Consequently, this open space was incorporated into the bounds of the city and effectively became one huge building plot. Wedged in between the city and the site of the Temple, the area came to be known as the Ophel, meaning high or lofty (in the Bible it is also called the Millo) and most of the royal buildings were constructed there. To prepare the ground for this constellation of palaces and other royal structures, it was necessary to build retaining walls and fill them in with earth and detritus (hence the term Millo, meaning fill). Within a few years Jerusalem had truly become the capital of the country, from both the religious and political standpoints, for it contained the "house of the Lord and the king's house," as the Bible puts it.

Solomon's city plan remained in force for more than 350 years. The borders of the kingdom expanded and contracted, but Jerusalem always remained the capital, and the seat of government continued to be located on the southern slope of the Temple Mount. In the course of time, the Temple and its courts were enlarged, and considerable portions of the Ophel were buried under subsequent construction (primarily during the Second Temple period). Nevertheless, we harbored hopes of finding remains that would enhance our knowledge of the First Temple period, especially because information on that era based on hard facts is relatively meager.

Exactly where was Jerusalem of the First Temple located and what were its boundaries? These questions are among the most basic and long-standing issues of Jerusalem scholarship; even the historian Josephus Flavius addressed himself to them some 1,900 years ago. Josephus believed that the hill to the west of the Temple Mount lay within the city limits in the First Temple period. The view most commonly endorsed and clearly articulated by modern scholars is that the original city was located *only* on the slope of the southern hill, meaning the area of the original Canaanite and subsequent Jebusite cities with the addition of the Ophel and the Temple Mount. Few scholars believed that Jerusalem had spread up the slope of the western hill (into the area of the present-day Jewish Quarter) as far back as the days of the kings of Judah — though the Bible speaks of unwalled suburbs to the west of the city, especially at the end of the era.

Kathleen Kenyon's excavations in the 1960s were the first to touch upon this problem. Pottery shards from the First Temple period had been found in various parts of the city, but the prevailing view was that they reached the western hill in the fill carted there during the Second Temple period to level out the area before construction began. An alternative theory posited that a few isolated buildings may indeed have been located on the western hill even though it was outside the city proper. Yet because Miss Kenyon's excavation was conducted by means of narrow shafts, no remains of structures were found, and the conclusions drawn from her work were misleading.

Since 1967 archaeological excavations have been going on in various places in Jerusalem and the finds have been astonishing. They include discoveries that considerably enhance our knowledge of the First Temple period and cast light on the scope of the city's boundaries during that era. The fact is that finds from the First Temple period have turned up all over the western hill: near the citadel by the Jaffa Gate, in a number of places in the Armenian Quarter, on Mount Zion, and within the Jewish Quarter. Especially revealing was the dig conducted in the Jewish Quarter, for it brought to light a fortified tower and sections of a wall from the First Temple period. These structures show that a line of fortifications ran between the Temple Mount and what is today the Jaffa Gate. Consequently, a good part of the western hill must have been included in the fortified city of Jerusalem at that time. Also uncovered in the Jewish Quarter was a section of a thick wall dating to the First Temple period, but it is still not clear whether it was part of the city wall or of some internal fortification. Either way, though, it proves that by the end of the First Temple period organized settlement extended to the western hill. We are therefore able to state with confidence that the city covered the broad area suggested by the minority of scholars. Equally important is the lesson to be learned about Josephus Flavius' writings, namely, that they should be treated far more seriously and studied far more carefully before we pass any drastic judgments on them.

One question that remains unanswered is when the process of expansion began. Did the spread westward date back to the days of David and Solomon or was it the product of a later age? The process of delineating an era with the aid of archaeology is based primarily on the dating of

The Boundaries of Jerusalem

pottery — in this case from the time of the kings of Judah — to within a quarter of a century. On the basis of pottery finds, some archaeologists believe that it is possible to date the expansion of Jerusalem to the end of the eighth century B.C., the days of King Hezekiah. I, however, do not subscribe to the view that pottery can provide us with so precise a determination of time. Not only must the span of dates be broader, for our purposes here a less rigid approach that takes into account historical as well as archaeological evidence seems to be far more serviceable. So the question remains: which of the kings of Israel was behind the new, expanded fortification of Jerusalem? And is it possible to come up with an historical explanation for his fortification campaign?

It seems to me that the best answer — albeit wanting in precision — is that the expansion of the city's fortifications could have taken place anywhere from the reign of King Uzziah close to the beginning of the eighth century B.C. up to the reign of King Manasseh during the seventh century B.C. Each of these two kings, or any of those who ruled between them, could definitely have initiated the process. How the excavations by the Temple Mount provided some clues for dating the expansions of the city westward is a subject we will elaborate upon below.

Finds in the Crevices of the Rock and in the Fill

While excavating close to the southern wall of the Temple Mount, on a street whose paving stones had been dismantled back in antiquity, we decided to deepen the excavation to get a look at the courses of the wall from the Second Temple period. To help establish dates of construction, we made it a habit to collect the fill in an area and carefully strain it for small artifacts and coins. A veritable haul emerged from this fill, and following our standard procedure we marked the finds with tags noting the area and stratum from which they had been retrieved. Then all the material was transferred to the work area, where the pottery shards were washed and sorted. Some were preserved for further study, others tossed into the scrap heaps. One morning the two archaeologists responsible for registering and studying the material, Ellen Lefrak and Daliah Packman, excitedly told us that they had finally identified pottery which differed from what we had been finding up till then. "We have regards from the First Temple period!" was how they put it.

The trove was quite an interesting assortment of finds from the days of the First Temple: typical shards, pottery figurines of animals, a statuette of the goddess Astarte, and jug handles stamped with impressions in Hebrew characters. Some of these handles had the Hebrew word "to the king" stamped on them, others bore the personal seals of court officials.

Needless to say, we were absolutely delighted, for our excavations had hardly begun and here we seemed already to be touching Jerusalem of the First Temple period. Everyone's attention shifted to the area in which these finds had been unearthed. After a few days, however, artifacts from the First Temple stopped turning up, and in their place came shards and coins from the Hasmonean era, almost 1,000 years later. It was a topsy-turvy world; the earlier period was higher up and a later period further down. Yet as soon as we expanded the area of the excavation somewhat and dug further down, the enigma was cleared up. It turned out that we were digging inside a structure that had been built in Herod's day to support the street above it. For the fill, detritus had been hauled in from various parts of the city and especially from the areas that Herod had demolished in order to expand the Temple Mount. The lowest layer of fill was naturally from the stratum of the Hasmonean period, being the closest to Herod's time and the uppermost level of debris. The laborers of Herod's day then reached the debris of the First Temple period under the remains of the Hasmonean stratum and poured it over the initial layer of fill. So the problem of the topsy-turvy world was solved: we had, in fact, discovered a wealth of finds from the First Temple period, but they were contained in fill that had been carted in from other sectors of the city. As for structures from the First Temple period, which could provide even more details and enhance our knowledge of that era, we had yet to discover any and could only hope for better luck in the future.

Later on during the dig we again unearthed pottery shards from the First Temple period in the vicinity of the western wall and the rocky slope that rises up toward the Jewish Quarter. This time the finds were discovered in crevices in the bedrock. Actually, they were more like natural pits filled with red soil — terra rossa. Embedded in this soil we found pottery shards, as a rule. Occasionally, however, whole objects such as oil lamps, cruses, and figurines from the early part of the First Temple period (the tenth–twelfth centuries B.C.) emerged from it intact. We also found shards from the Middle Canaanite period (the eighteenth–seventeenth centuries B.C.).

As we continued to work, this phenomenon of pits filled with shards and artifacts buried in red soil became a frequent find wherever we reached bedrock. It indicated that at a certain time during the First Temple period, as the city expanded westward, fill was carted in from destroyed buildings (perhaps from the City of David) to level out the area slated for construction. Hence the contents of the fill must date back prior to the time when the city expanded in this direction. This was our first hint that the expansion process did not begin until after the ninth century B.C., but the question of exactly when it did begin remains unanswered.

Our discovery of both Canaanite and Israelite pottery in fill used for leveling out an area before commencing construction also shed light on an odd conclusion reached by Kathleen Kenyon when she excavated on the slopes of the City of David. One of Miss Kenyon's most important finds on the eastern slope of the City of David was a wall from the First Temple period, or, to be more exact, from the eighth–seventh centuries B.C. She apparently dated this wall on the basis of the red soil below it and the pottery shards found in crevices in the bedrock. Yet here, too, an operation was undertaken to fill up and level out the depressions before any structures were built. Miss Kenyon posited that the wall dated to the beginning of the Middle Canaanite period — which is curious in itself, since the survival of a wall over such a long span of time is so unusual as to be quite unknown in antiquity — but never explained how she arrived at this conclusion. In an attempt to reconstruct her line of thinking, we may assume that it was based on her discovery of Canaanite pottery in depressions in the bedrock. The interpretation we are proposing here probably never occurred to Miss Kenyon. Instead, she associated the pottery that was undoubtedly hauled in from elsewhere as part of the fill with the buildings themselves. The experience taught us that carefully studying our finds and trying to determine the significance of their presence in any one area are absolutely vital.

While conducting a search for remains of masonry some 40 meters west of the western wall, in the bedrock we found the remains of cisterns and

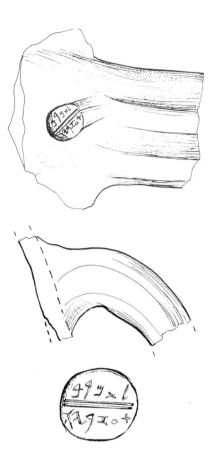

An impression that reads: "To Tamar, daughter of Azriah"

ritual baths from the Second Temple period. Among them was an oddly shaped cistern — or rather what must have served as a cistern at one stage during the Second Temple period, when the opening at its side was blocked and its walls were plastered. When we removed the accouterments that had turned it into a cistern, however, we came up with a most peculiar item: a pool with a hole in its side. The puzzle of this particular carved cistern teased us for weeks, especially because two others were found nearby. We took every visiting archaeologist to see it in the hope that one of them might have come across a similar structure elsewhere, and ultimately it proved to be a profitable technique.

One day when Professor Mazar's nephew Ami was visiting the dig, we took him to the mystery structure. Ami was then an archaeology student, and in response to Mazar's challenge — "Well, what do you have to say about this strange creature?" — the novice scholar replied, "What's the problem? It's a tomb. I've excavated tombs like this in the Western Galilee with the district archaeologist, Moshe Prausnitz." We asked Moshe to come as quickly as possible, and he brought along the plan of the tombs they had excavated in the area of Achziv, north of the coastal town of Nahariya. The resemblance was striking, though unlike the tombs here in Jerusalem, which were devoid of human bones or any other finds, those in Achziv had been sealed and contained human skeletons and objects belonging to their occupants.

The carved structure we found resembled a chamber over 3 meters long and 2.5 meters wide and high. A square opening had been carved in its southern wall to serve as an entrance, and it led onto an open court (likewise carved out of stone) about 3-square-meters large. Above the opening was a carved niche that may have had an inscribed tablet set into it. Tombs of this type are known to us from burial customs in the Mediterranean Basin. They all have an enclosed entry court with an opening in one wall leading to the burial chamber, and all are carved out of rock. But one unusual element shared by tombs in Jerusalem and Achziv (and common to other tombs in Phoenicia) was a vertical shaft in the ceiling. We called it a "chimney" because of its location. Tombs without any shaft of this sort are routine finds in Palestine, but those sporting such a "chimney" are relatively rare, and we were the first to uncover them in Judah, Jerusalem in particular (we went on to find "chimneys" in seven other carved structures identified as tombs, some of them twice the size of that first presumed cistern). According to their excavators, the Achziv tombs dated to the tenth–ninth centuries B.C., a determination based upon the wealth of finds within them. If we extend this dating to the tombs in Jerusalem, we may conclude that what we had found, entirely by chance, was a deluxe cemetery of individual tombs that, judging by their architectural style and burial ritual, were identical to Phoenician burial tombs.

At an early stage of his development, man began to bury his dead rather than abandon them like waste in the field. The act of burial was an expression of the world view found in the Bible — "Dust thou art, and unto dust shalt thou return" — while the notion of an afterlife in the presumed Next World led to the awareness that a distinction must be drawn between the body and the soul. Just as the body, the epitome of corporeality, returns to the earth from which it came, so the soul rises upward to the source of the true life in the Next World, or Heaven. To illustrate this belief, a stone was placed on the grave. The corpse was

A tomb from the First Temple period
showing the hole made by grave
robbers and above it a recess for an
inscribed tablet

right: A tomb from the First Temple
period showing the entrance and the
"chimney"

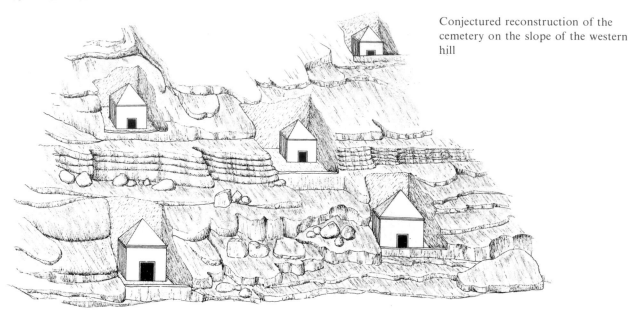

Conjectured reconstruction of the cemetery on the slope of the western hill

interred within the earth or the carved rock and covered over, while the stone — or the *"nefesh"* in the language of the day — was placed above it as a sign of the soul's ascendance. In the course of time, the shape of the *"nefesh"* changed to resemble a pyramid, like the roof of a house. Thus the place for interring the body was equivalent to a house — the grave dug in the earth or carved into rock — while the habitation of the soul was between the ceiling and the roof. (This notion, that the souls of the dead dwell between the ceilings and roofs of houses, is found in the folklore of many peoples.) In time a third element was added to this system, namely, the passage connecting the burial chamber with the dwelling place of the "soul." This link was effected by carving a small vertical shaft, otherwise known as our "chimney."

To the degree that tombs of this sort are found in the lands of the Mediterranean Basin (and they are relatively rare), they are known from Phoenicia and lands in the Phoenician sphere of influence and date to the tenth–ninth centuries B.C. Thus we come full circle, for in the ninth century B.C. Jerusalem and Judah maintained close ties with the northern Kingdom of Israel and both these kingdoms maintained close ties with the Phoenicians. Bonds of marriage were the formal framework of these alliances, but their real substance was expressed in economic and commercial ties. King Ahab of Israel and Jehoshaphat of Judah, Queen Jezebel in the north and her daughter Queen Athaliah in Judah, together with their households, were the leading advocates of these ties. The economic association of the two peoples, marital affiliations, the exchanges of envoys, and joint projects, primarily in the field of seafaring, eventually led to the spread of religious and cultural influences, mostly to the northern kingdom, but as far south as Judah, too.

The strong resistance to these influences by the faithful of Israel, headed by the prophet Elijah, are documented in the Bible. Nevertheless, they penetrated to at least a certain stratum of Israelite society. Burial rites, the nature of beliefs about the Next World, and even the shape of tombs are part of the cultural heritage of every people; so that when we find a cemetery in Jerusalem built in the Phoenician style, it is strong evidence of the weight of this foreign cultural influence. Later on, when

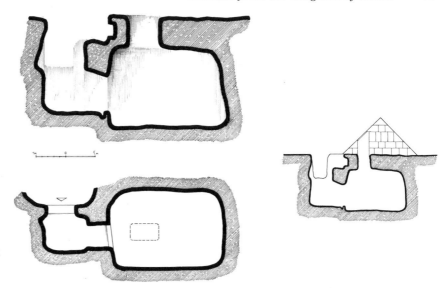

The monument of a tomb carved out of rock — plan, section, and reconstruction

Queen Athaliah was defeated and Judah was purged of all traces of the Phoenician rite, this burial tradition disappeared from Jerusalem. Indeed, the many other graves discovered in and around the city differ from these "chimney" tombs in a variety of ways.

At the time of their carving, these tombs were located outside the city limits on the slope of the western hill facing the royal palaces and the Temple. Both their location and the immense physical effort involved in carving them leads us to conclude that they must have been tombs of the local aristocracy. From the eighth century onward, the cemeteries of Jerusalem's upper classes were located southeast of the city, among the houses of what is now the Arab village of Silwan. Some of these tombs can still be seen in the village, and a burial inscription from the eighth century B.C. has also been found there. Tombs of the Silwan type have been uncovered all over Jerusalem: near the Damascus Gate, on the slope of Mount Zion, and near the railway station. But no tombs of this sort have been found within the confines of the Old City or on Mount Zion, that is, within the bounds of Jerusalem at the close of the First Temple period.

It is clear that with the possible exception of the tombs of the kings of Judah (which have yet to be found), there were no cemeteries in Jerusalem, as the Israelites were not in the habit of burying their dead within the city limits. Hence the cemetery containing the "chimney" tombs was a glaring exception to the rule. Its location within the city may be explained by one of two theories. The first possibility is that it was a royal burial ground deliberately established inside the city limits. The cemetery's placement in the vicinity of the royal palaces tends to support this premise, though a decisive determination regarding such an important matter requires more definitive proof. (In any event, this premise is no less plausible than an earlier hypothesis which located the tombs of the Davidian dynasty in the southern portion of the City of David within a network of caves that hardly seem to be burial caves at all.) More likely is the suggestion that this cemetery dates to the ninth century B.C., that it served the Jerusalemite aristocracy, and that it was located outside the city. As we have seen, Jerusalem did not expand westward until the eighth century

B.C., when burials ceased to take place in this area and the cemeteries were removed from the city, in its broadest sense.

The existence of this abandoned cemetery within the bounds of Jerusalem deeply perturbed the later prophets Jeremiah and Ezekiel — for whom the laws of ritual purity were highly important — and they ascribed many of the tragedies that befell Jerusalem to its presence. Yet the cemetery was not completely eliminated until the Second Temple period, during the rule of the Hasmonean and Herodian dynasties (a point that has been corroborated by the finds we removed from the graves). It may also be that Josephus Flavius' tales about the treasures removed from the Davidic tombs by the Hasmonean king John Hyrcanus and by King Herod are references to the evacuation of the tombs of local patricians. One way or another, there is no doubt that what we have here is a fascinating discovery that illuminates a critical point about Jerusalem's boundaries during the First Temple period.

As our excavation spread eastward beyond the Old City wall, we reached an area that all agree was within the boundaries of Jerusalem during the First Temple period. This had been the Ophel, the city's Acropolis or the compound where the royal palaces and public institutions were concentrated. At first we were brimming with hope that it would yield remains of some kind from the First Temple period, but as we became better acquainted with the area we were able to appreciate the grave damage that had been inflicted on it by construction in the Herodian, Byzantine, and Moslem periods. Since the engineers in each of these three periods had their laborers dig to bedrock, our hope of turning up any remains from the days of the kings of Judah grew weaker from day to day. If it were necessary to reconstruct the history of this part of Jerusalem solely on the basis of archaeological finds, without benefit of any historical account from the Bible, we would "lose" a few hundred years of the city's history. For so extensive was the damage and the removal of the original detritus that the area failed to produce a single find — not even pottery shards!

In the summer of 1972 we were joined by a volunteer from Iceland who wanted to work for a number of months but found that the oppressive heat of the Jerusalem summer wore him down. Worse yet, he was laboring at the foot of the southern wall, which absorbs the sun's warmth and reflects it back down on the people at work. It was difficult for us to watch this youngster suffer so, but he refused to yield. To make things a bit easier for him, we put him to work in the drainage canals in the vicinity of the Triple Gate (whose excavation and cleaning was originally scheduled for the winter). These canals had been carved out of the bedrock and were a haven for mosquitos; but the shade and moisture were a boon, and our young volunteer soon found true happiness in cleaning out the tunnels.

Working at a brisk pace, within a few days he had reached the point where the canals run under the Temple Mount's southern wall, and there he discovered a plastered cistern. The plaster was of a kind we had not come upon in cisterns of either the Second Temple or Byzantine eras. It was pale yellow in color and inferior in quality to what we were accustomed to finding in that it was rather brittle, though still waterproof. On the floor of this cistern were some fifteen pottery vessels that had evidently fallen into the pool while it was still in use. They dated to the First Temple period (tenth–eighth centuries B.C.), providing us with our first remains of

The First Evidence of Construction in the Ophel

A water cistern (left in photo) from the First Temple period found under the Triple Gate of the Temple Mount's southern wall that long-sought-after city. It saddened us to discover that all that remained of the residential building which had once stood here was the bottom half of a cistern carved out of the rock; the rest of the pool and the structure that had housed it had been totally destroyed by Herod's builders. But even though it was merely the bottom of a cistern, this discovery, made after four years of excavation, kindled new hope in us. I am glad to be able to report that our hope was not disappointed.

A Huge Structure

The remains of the cistern and the pottery found within it suggested that we could definitely expect to find important discoveries from the First Temple period. I also sensed that the farther away we moved from the Temple Mount, the more likely we were to enter areas upon which man's hand and the ravages of time had wreaked less damage, and chances were good that we could find substantive remains. One such area was on the upper slope of the City of David, near the road that exists from the Dung Gate and links up with the main road to Jericho. Kathleen Kenyon's expedition had excavated one square of its own there. Miss Kenyon wrote little about that square in her book on Jerusalem, but she did claim that remains from the First Temple period had been found in it. From the meager material published about the dig in that area — including two

photographs and a bit of description — it was clear that she had erred in identifying the structures. According to Miss Kenyon, the wall found in the vicinity of her square was a remnant of the city's southern wall from the Second Temple period. One thing was beyond doubt, however: the pottery shards she found there were from the period of the kings of Judah.

Because of what her finds augured for further research, I took great pains to get an excavation going in that area. First I had to reach an arrangement with the owner of the property, who lived on it in a dilapidated building. Then I had to convince Professor Mazar, who feared that we were extending the dig over too large an area. But, because I knew that deep in his heart Mazar was yearning for some finds from the First Temple period, I decided to proceed with my plan. We began digging with a large number of volunteers, since a considerable amount of earth had to be removed and we were working over a larger area than is customary in such excavations. Once again we were confronted by the usual difficulties of excavating in Jerusalem. First we uncovered a wall whose dimensions are impressive even by today's standards: 3 meters thick and still 4–5 meters high. It proved to be the city wall from the early Byzantine period (fourth century A.D.). Built into this wall was a watchtower, and it was the lower courses of this tower that Kathleen Kenyon identified as being from the Israelite period — not entirely without reason, I must add, since the dressing of the lower stones was crude and resembled the ancient technique. True to our ways, however, we excavated the entire tower and the rest of the fortification, only to find that the tower's western wall (likewise built of stones with an "Israelite"-style of dressing) was built on top of a huge structure from the Second Temple period. This building contained several ritual baths, stone arches and domes, and an array of finds on the floor — for the most part coins and vessels that were still intact. Altogether it pointed to an impressive building that had been devastated on the 9th of the Hebrew month of Av in the year A.D. 70, the day Titus destroyed Jerusalem.

I could see a look of disappointment reflected in the eyes of the team, but it did not last long. For soon we could see that this structure was built over yet an earlier one and had made use of its remaining walls. In contrast to the Second Temple building, whose dressed stones were of soft, white limestone, the earlier structure had been built of undressed hard stones of a reddish hue. The construction using undressed stones was "dry," meaning that no mortar was used between the stones, whereas during the Second Temple period construction was effected with the aid of a special mortar and the building's walls were also plastered. Thus a strong, imposing structure had stood in this spot at some time prior to the Second Temple period, and the remains of its well-preserved walls had been used as the foundations for a building constructed during the Second Temple period.

Apart from the fact that it preceded the Second Temple period, what was the date of this building? A response to this query was not long in coming. The answer to this question was readily found once we uncovered a beaten-earth floor in one of its rooms. Lying on the floor was a mixture of ash, burned beams, and large pottery pots facing downward. Clearly we were in a storage room that had been outfitted with wooden shelves to hold clay pots. A fire had broken out when the building was destroyed, and the shelves collapsed and became fuel for the flames. The vessels —

Vessels *in situ* in a plastered cistern from the First Temple period

dating to the First Temple period — were characteristic of the eighth–seventh centuries B.C.

Could this be tangible evidence of the destruction of Jerusalem in 586 B.C. by King Nebuchadnezzar's troops? We could easily posit that here on the side of the road, deep in the belly of the earth near the Temple Mount, a part of Jerusalem's tragic past was revealed before our eyes in the form of a huge building that had been destroyed by Nebuchadnezzar and served as the foundation for a public building of unusual dimensions, in the Second Temple period, and was likewise destined to be destroyed — this time by Titus and his Roman legionnaires. (We found other cases in which remnants of masonry from the First Temple period were used as the foundations and reconstructed sections of buildings in the Second Temple period, attesting to the high quality of the construction in the earlier age.) The hand of fate must have been behind the fact that the building from the Second Temple period began to show through the earth on the 17th of Tammuz, the date of a fast commemorating the breach of the city walls by the Romans, and the pottery vessels in the First Temple structure were found on the 10th of Av, a day after the date on which the Temple was destroyed.

This discovery imbued us with a whole new spirit, for after five years of digging in the vicinity of the Temple Mount we had finally succeeded in uncovering an impressive structure from the First Temple era in the Ophel. We poured all our energies into excavating the entire area over the winter of 1975/76 and the following summer, and it was while working a site not far from the large building that we came upon an equally fascinating find: a small room (c. 3 × 2.5 meters) filled with layers of broken pottery vessels piled one on top of the other. In all, we found more than 100 broken vessels in this room, most of them large storage jars whose shards were subsequently pieced together to restore them. All the vessels were misshapen or otherwise flawed ("seconds," in modern parlance).

After the shards had been taken off to the work area for restoration, we discovered that the vessels had not originally belonged to that room. Our restorer at that time, Eva Osterman, devoted most of her time to working on these vessels and was very good with them. As a standard archaeological procedure, whenever we reached the floor of a room we cleaned it thoroughly. I should point out that the floors of that period were usually of pressed or beaten earth, and it is very difficult to distinguish between the floors themselves and the detritus above them that has been compressed and hardened by natural circumstances. When we assumed that we had reached the bona fide floor of the room in question, we decided to continue digging to see what finds were hidden below it.

The fact is that we found more pottery shards below the floor as well. They too were taken off for restoration, and a number of vessels were wholly reconstructed. This work had barely been completed when the "experts" were already busy finding differences between the pottery found above the floor and below it; some were even quick to draw chronological and even historical conclusions about the room having an earlier period and a later one. But while the pottery shards of the "lower level" were spread on the restorer's table, she noticed that a number of them looked as if they belonged to vessels from the "upper level" — and she was right. A few vessels from the so-called upper level had missing pieces that turned up among the shards in the lower one and pieced together into a single unit. Thus the notion of two distinct strata was an error that stemmed

The southern wall of the large building from the First Temple period showing the cisterns and ritual baths built into it during the subsequent era

overleaf: Pottery jars from the end of the First Temple period found in the rooms of the large building

A pot as it emerged on the burned floor

A vial for purgative spices imported from Assyria

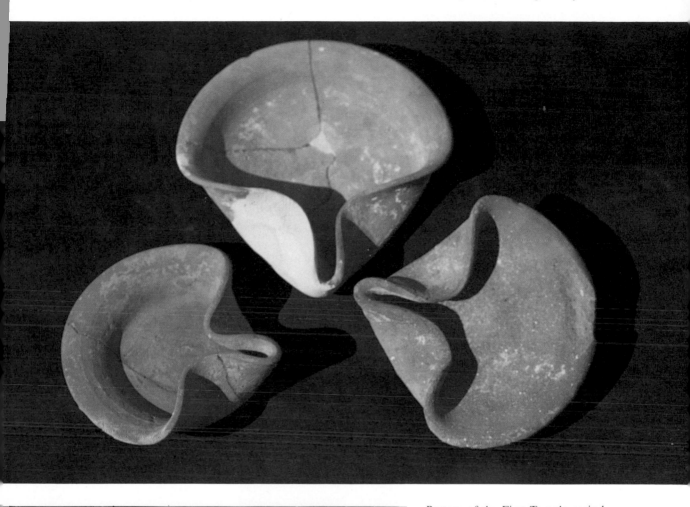

Pottery of the First Temple period
found in the ruins of the large
building

Oil lamps, pots, and bowls

from the over-precision, technically speaking, of the excavation in that particular room. The contents of the entire room, right down to the bedrock, were in fact a single concentration of broken vessels. How they got there was elementary: during the Second Temple period, when the builders had cleared away the ruins of the previous age to start new construction, one of the rooms was earmarked for fill, and all the pottery shards and other remains collected in the area were shoveled into it.

What we had before us, then, was a room from the First Temple period with all the finds therein — and we're talking about 100 vessels — dating to the same period, or, to be more precise, to the eighth–seventh centuries B.C. It was not these finds that enabled us to date the building, for they had been placed in the room during the subsequent era. By the same reasoning, the contents of the fill could have come from any period prior to the time of the new construction work. We were overjoyed about

A dividing wall of the large building

A section of the southern wall of the large building

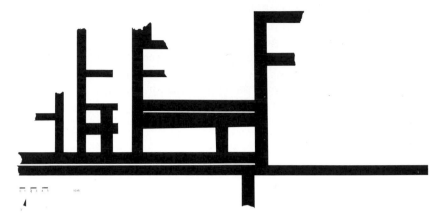

Plan of the large building from the First Temple period

the haul of intact vessels, for 100 pieces of pottery from the First Temple period are hardly a run-of-the-mill find in Jerusalem. The experience also taught us how difficult it is to determine the degree of contemporaneity and the connection between a structure and the finds within it, and this served as a warning to all those who were in a hurry to draw conclusions from pottery shards, even when they come from the same era and are found in the same place.

The date of the building before us was determined by the intact pottery vessels found *in situ* on the floor of one of the rooms, which is the only accurate indicator in archaeology. The rest of the building could be dated to the same period if it should prove to be archaeologically consistent both in its layout and construction. We therefore began to study the building's construction almost as soon as we started excavating it.

Before long we were able to conclude that the construction was unique. The walls were built of particularly hard stones of a reddish hue, and an absolute minimum dressing had been invested in them. The main walls run the length of the building parallel to the slope of the Kidron Valley, which veers in a northeast–southwest direction here. They are divided by walls running the width of the building to create rooms. The thickness of the walls is 1.4 meters and they are built of two façades with fill sandwiched in between. The layers of stones were aligned by placing small undressed stones between the larger ones. Because of their thickness, as well as the technique of construction and the fact that their foundations are built on rock, these walls are quite strong. Yet at some point one of them was undermined and began to buckle outward; as a means of supporting it, a parallel wall, also 1.4 meters thick, was built up against it on the outside.

Piecing together the data gathered to date, we find that the nature of this building still eludes us. We simply lack sufficient details about its plan and its relationship to the city's wall and fortifications. For example, we cannot say whether it stood inside the city wall as an independent unit or was part and parcel of the network of fortifications to the east, on the slopes of the Kidron Valley. Professor Mazar's suggestion that this building is the Millo House warrants serious attention, even though it is somewhat problematic because we do not really know what that name meant. The Millo House is mentioned only once in the Bible — in the context of the rebellion against Queen Athaliah — and the events related there undoubtedly occurred close or within the palace, which was located north of the building in question.

Artifacts from the First Temple period

above: A semiprecious-stone seal with the figure of a griffon

right: A seal impression on the handle of a jug: "Save them, Haggai"

opposite, above: A faience figurine of an Egyptian goddess

opposite, below: Head of a pottery figurine

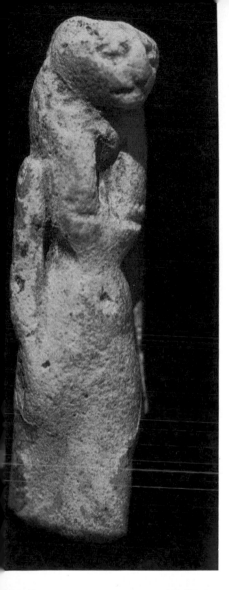

Another question deserving of scrutiny is whether we can date the building with any greater precision. One way of doing so is to take the path of historical deduction. The premise that this building was demolished when Jerusalem fell to the Babylonians in 586 B.C. is a reasonable one, making 586 B.C. its upper (or latest) date. Determining its lower date, or the time of its construction, is a far more complex affair, as the building was constructed on bedrock and there are no earlier structures below it. Some scholars believe that the lifespan of a building of this type can be 100–150 years and determine the date of its construction accordingly. But this system of calculation is less than reliable, as a study of the foundations of many buildings show that a structure is capable of standing for centuries. In this case we found that the ruins of the building continued to serve as a firm foundation for 400 years after its destruction, and in other places we were able to identify remains, particularly of public buildings, that prevailed for even longer. If anyone were to postulate that the structure under examination here dates back to Solomon's building campaign in the Ophel, we would be hard put to refute the theory, especially as it was the first structure to be built in the area without taking recourse to earlier remains.

Finally, it is pertinent to query the significance of the building's thick sandwich walls. As I have mentioned, at one point a process of structural deterioration began to affect one of these walls. To save the building, a new and equally thick wall was built up against the exterior side of the buckled area as a means of support. One explanation for this deterioration may be the massive earthquake that struck Jerusalem in the middle of the eighth century B.C., during the days of the prophet Amos. Despite the building's essential sturdiness, it suffered enough of a shock to require structural repairs, particularly a reinforcement of the walls and their supports. If this premise is correct, the building must have predated Uzziah's reign and may in fact have been built during the days of King Solomon, as suggested above. It would then have been 350 years old at the time of its destruction, which is not unusual for a public building in Jerusalem — especially a structure with such solid foundations. Whatever the case, our study of this particular building promises that far more is likely to be written about it — and hopefully about other discoveries from the First Temple period — in the near future.

3   The Persian and Hasmonean Eras

From Ezra and Nehemiah to Herod

For fifty years Jerusalem and the Temple lay in ruins, not to be redeemed from their ignominy until Cyrus the Great rose to power in Persia in the middle of the sixth century B.C. Early in his reign Cyrus conquered Babylonia, absorbing its territories into his dominion, and he rightly deemed it politic to cultivate allies on the marches of his expanding empire. Since he regarded Egypt as a potential rival and threat to the stability of Persian rule, he paid special attention to buttressing the states south of his kingdom. Judah took pride of place among them and, coupled with the Persians' great religious tolerance, this policy enabled the exiled Jews of Babylonia to return to Jerusalem. Clearly, their first order of priority was to rebuild the Temple, and Cyrus proved more than amenable to their wishes, as we read in the Bible: "Thus saith Cyrus king of Persia, The Lord God of heaven hath given me all the kingdoms of the earth; and he hath charged me to build him a house at Jerusalem, which is in Judah" (Ezra 1:2). A more detailed royal proclamation on this subject stated:

Let the house be builded, the place where they offered sacrifices, and let the foundations thereof be strongly laid; the height threescore cubits ... and let the expenses be given out of the king's house and also let the golden and silver vessels of the house of God, which Nebuchadnezzar took forth out of the temple which is at Jerusalem, and brought into Babylon, be restored and brought again into the Temple ... (Ezra 6:3-5).

Buoyed by the king's patronage and generosity, the first Jews to return to Zion were filled with enthusiasm, though they faced no few difficulties. For on top of the tendency of local Persian officials to stymie their efforts was the opposition of the other inhabitants of Judah — Samaritans and Arabs — to the reconstruction of Jerusalem and the Temple, as a flagrant violation of the status quo established with Nebuchadnezzar's conquest. Work therefore proceeded slowly, one step at a time.

The first stage was to reconsecrate the altar and reinstitute sacrifices, while the construction of the Temple proper went on at a halting pace that was further punctuated by countless snags. So it went until the arrival of Nehemiah, an exile imbued with extraordinary nationalist fervor. Nehemiah was both a senior minister in the Persian court and a pious Jew who was anguished by the knowledge that Jerusalem still lay in ruins and the Temple had not been restored in its original format. Possessed of both power and connections, he managed to get himself appointed governor of Judah and, thus endowed with the prerogatives of rule, Nehemiah arrived in Jerusalem and began to rebuild the city in earnest. Working alongside him to resurrect the community as well as the city was one of the leading Jewish intellectuals of the day, Ezra the Scribe. What Nehemiah accomplished in the realm of policy, organization, and performance, Ezra complemented in terms of the community's spiritual and cultural life by reorienting the Jewish nation and the Jewish faith toward the Temple in Jerusalem. Their work was far from easy, especially since the offspring of the Jews who had remained behind in Judah had, ironically enough, grown distant from Judaism and found it hard to cope with the new

opposite: The Acra pool after removing the ritual bath from the Herodian era

overleaf: Aerial photo of the area excavated at the foot of the Temple Mount, 1976

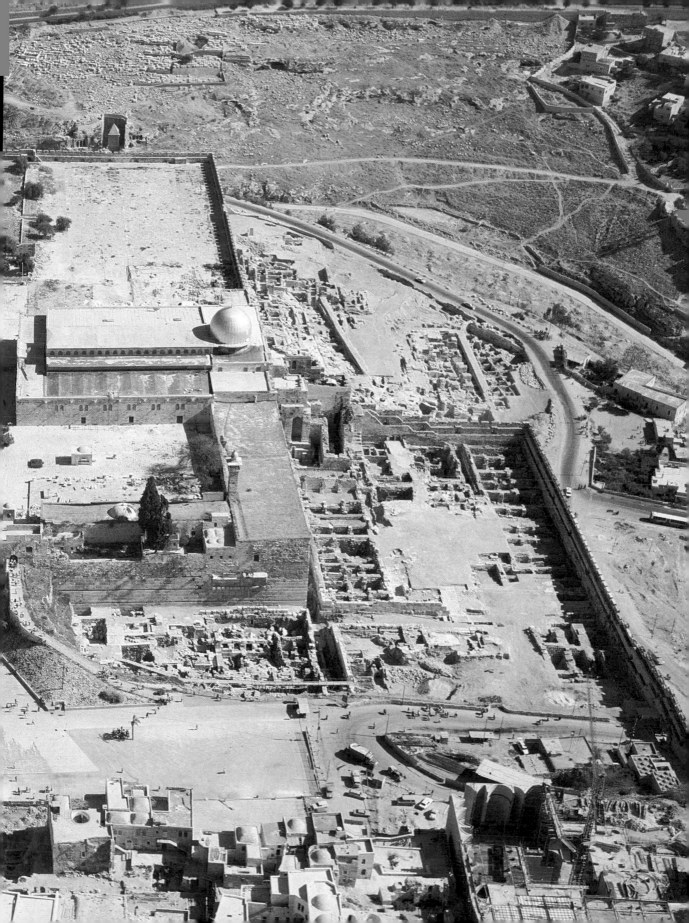

demands of daily life as Jews. Thus it was not for naught that these two men were accorded a special place of honor in Jewish history for building the land and the Temple and for imbuing the people with a new spirit.

Under Persian rule Judah and Jerusalem experienced a revival and flourish as in days past. We know from the Bible that it was Nehemiah who repaired the walls of Jerusalem and refortified the city. Subsequent sources in the form of plans, maps, and studies dealing with the history of Jerusalem inform us that for the most part the course of the walls reconstructed by Nehemiah followed that of the City of David, meaning the city in its smallest format. This conclusion was based on the premise (established back when scholars generally agreed that Jerusalem's fortifications in the First Temple period covered a minimal area) that few of the Babylonian exiles returned to Jerusalem at the time, and only a small number of masons and squads of laborers took part in the work of restoring the walls. But today we know that the city's walls in the First Temple period encompassed a broader area than was originally believed, including the western hill. So if the walls reconstructed by Nehemiah followed a course similar to the walls at the end of the First Temple period, they must have embraced both the southern hill (the City of David) and the western one. What's more, that such a project could be accomplished relatively quickly is further testimony to the fact that it entailed restoration work, not building from scratch. Although Jerusalem had been laid waste by the Babylonians, enough of its walls apparently survived for repairs alone to render them serviceable.

While Jerusalem and the Temple enjoyed two centuries of prosperity under Persian rule, a revolution began to overtake the east with the spread of Hellenistic influence and hegemony. In 333 B.C. it reached Palestine when Alexander the Great conquered the country en route to Egypt. Some traditions have it that Jerusalem surrendered to him without a fight, but in any case he must have been impressed by his meeting with the High Priest, for he granted the Temple in Jerusalem a special status.

Brief spells of persecution notwithstanding, the Hellenistic period was an age of religious tolerance. Then again slowly but surely Hellenism was absorbed and embraced by the peoples within the Greek sphere of influence, and from this standpoint Judah was no different from any other country; many of the Jews were quite taken with this new world view. But as often happens in an encounter between cultures, the peoples of the East, including the Jews, adopted mainly the trappings of the new lore, not its deeper substance and ethos. Only a minority apprehended the essential content of Hellenism and were able to maintain their identity as Jews while selecting only the choice elements from their new cultural milieu. Architecture is a case in point. Hellenism's greatest contribution to civilization was in the realm of aesthetics and external form, and it left its deepest mark on things physical, especially on architecture. In Judah construction underwent a revolution in terms of both technical accomplishments and form. The tombs in the Kidron Valley, for example — popularly known as Absalom's Tomb, Zechariah's Tomb, and so forth — are striking testimony to the artistic achievements of the period.

Considering Hellenism's strong appeal, especially among the upper classes, it is not surprising that the tug of war between the Hellenists and the purists in the Jewish community sometimes grew so fierce that the authorities had to intervene to restore calm. By the time the Seleucid emperor Antiochus IV (Epiphanes) ascended to the throne in 175 B.C., this struggle was at its height and he was determined to decide it — though not out of any concern for Jewish solidarity. The new emperor deemed it politicaly expedient to gather all his subjects under the mantle of a single culture both as a means of guaranteeing the stability of his rule and because he was profoundly convinced of Hellenism's superiority over every other culture in the world. For the most part, Antiochus succeeded in imposing this monocultural design on his subjects; only one "stiff-necked" people resisted him: the Jews.

It was on his return from a campaign against Egypt that Antiochus first passed through Palestine, where rumors were afoot that he had been killed in the Egyptian action and many were glad of it. When word of this mood reached the emperor, he was forced to concede that all his efforts to unite the minorities in his empire around the predominating rite were a vain dream. Gripped by frustration and anger, he vented his wrath on the Jews. Antiochus marched on Jerusalem and began to destroy the city, perpetrating a brutal massacre on its defenseless population and pillaging the treasures of the Temple. As a final humiliation and symbol of his determination to be obeyed, the emperor built a mighty fortress to the south of the Temple. Called the Acra, it housed the garrison left behind to keep an eye on the proceedings in the Temple and make sure it did not become a hotbed of rebellion. Nevertheless, the situation continued to deteriorate, and by 168 B.C. relations between the Seleucids and the Jews had reached the breaking point when the Temple was desecrated, a statue of Antiochus was placed in its court, and the Jewish rites brought to a halt. For all intents and purposes, the Temple in Jerusalem, which had hitherto weathered all the storms that had swamped the other peoples and cults of the religion, now ceased to function. Yet the emperor's ruthlessness proved to be his downfall, for it accomplished exactly the opposite of what it was meant to.

Oppressed beyond sufferance by the latest decrees, a small, elite group of guerrillas in the provincial town of Modi'in raised the banner of revolt against the Greeks. Led by Mattathias the priest and his five sons, their rebellion quickly mustered support and grew into a war of national and religious liberation. At the start it was a struggle of the few against the many, but by using unconventional tactics the guerrillas were able to foil the Greek armies and eventually liberate Jerusalem from foreign domination and reinstitute the Jewish rite in the Temple, after cleansing the building of all traces of the Greek presence and ritual.

This period and the century that followed are known as the Hasmonean or Maccabean era in Jewish history, after the family that led the resistance movement. Following their victory, the Hasmoneans took up the scepter of rule in Judah. At first they exercised their power through the office of High Priest (which they promptly arrogated to themselves), but their progeny crowned themselves kings — though they did so warily, knowing that tradition in Judah called for the king to be scion of the family of David. The early Hasmonean monarchs proved to be very astute statesmen and were adept at exploiting the political vacuum caused by the bitter wars of succession between contenders for the Seleucid throne. Masters at finessing their way through the labyrinth of rivalries and intrigues, they eventually obtained imperial recognition for their religious autonomy and authority — and finally for their political liberty as well. Jerusalem and the Temple were the heart and emblem of their regime, and as a mark of their independence the Hasmoneans razed the

Acra fortress, thereby obliterating the final reminder of alien rule in the city.

With their well-honed political senses, even the earliest of the Hasmoneans was alert to the signs of a new empire rising in the West and soon to be knocking at the gates of history. Their response was to send delegations to Rome in a bid to weave a network of political and military alliances with the power of the future. This far-sighted policy proved itself as soon as Rome conquered the East and succeeded the Greeks as the rulers of the region, for it enabled the Jewish kings to preserve the independence of the Temple and thus protect the religious liberties of people of Judah (now known as Judea). In the course of time, however, the Hasmoneans suffered the fate of the Seleucids before them as internecine wars of succession undermined their independent rule in Judea. Finally the Romans bestowed the crown upon Herod, a Jew by religion and a native of the country but also a man after their own hearts who could be depended on to serve the best interests of the Roman Empire.

above: A horse's head from a pottery figurine of the Persian period

opposite: A woman's head from a pottery figurine of the Hellenistic period

Even before embarking on their campaigns to forge an empire, the Romans had been strongly influenced by the intellectual culture of Greece, though the disposition of the indigenous Roman culture was fundamentally materialist and excelled particularly in the spheres of architecture, engineering, and the like. Judea's encounter with Rome, following its earlier one with Hellenism, again injected a refreshing spirit into the country's architecture, particularly in Jerusalem. The firm economic standing of the Hasmoneans, who were well integrated in the contemporary network of international trade, bespoke a substantial income. And drawing on the capital that had accumulated in their coffers, plus the knowledge of engineering they had acquired from Rome, they instituted an accelerated process of building and development that changed the face of Jerusalem. Both the western hill and the courts of the Temple became the focus of public and private building. In essence, Jerusalem's glory in Herod's day was an outgrowth of the Hasmonean dream on an even grander scale.

During the Hasmonean era the western hill and Mount Zion became residential quarters inhabited largely by the aristocracy, their homes being among the most attractive buildings in the city. In the 500 years since the Return to Zion, the Temple Mount and the slopes of Mount Zion had become the prestigious areas of the city — symbols of the "good life" that Jerusalem had enjoyed during most of that period. What finds were awaiting us from this long and fascinating period? We faced that question eagerly, even though the experience of past excavations in Jerusalem did not bode well for us on this score.

Archaeological Finds

The 500 years between Cyrus' proclamation enabling the Jews to return to Zion and Herod's reconstruction of the Temple were among the most turbulent and eventful in the history of the Jewish people in its homeland. Three mighty empires — Persia, Greece, and Rome — each very different in character and political, social, and religious outlook, had ruled Palestine in succession. Under their aegis, the people of Judah experienced intervals of self-rule and political liberty and for almost the entire period they enjoyed religious freedom as well. These were five centuries about which our historical knowledge of Jerusalem, the Temple Mount, and the Temple itself is relatively abundant. But the lion's share of the information comes to us from written sources alone, for no archaeological excavation prior to the Six-Day War yielded any more than a paucity of finds from this rich period. In fact, anyone attempting to reconstruct the history of Jerusalem through archaeological means would find himself in very difficult straits when it comes to this span of half a millennium. The only material available is common artifacts, all of them small objects; architectural finds — meaning the remains of buildings — are almost entirely absent. Of course, we hoped that our own dig would change this sorry situation, but our hopes went unfulfilled. Neither our excavation below the Temple Mount nor any of the other digs carried out in the Old City after the Six-Day War uncovered any architectural remains. A few artifacts from that period did, of course, turn up — bits here and there — but the actual remains of buildings were nowhere to be found, leaving our problem unsolved.

On further thought, it is possible to understand the reason for this dearth of remains. The most impressive archaeological finds that turn up in excavations are usually "courtesy of" destruction and ruin — destruction by man's hand and the ruin caused by natural disasters. But in a city that has been spared these disruptions and renewed itself through organized development projects, all the older structures were usually demolished, sometimes clear down to the foundations, to make way for new construction. That is why nothing of them remains for posterity.

This explanation not only accounts for the absence of architectural remains from the above-mentioned periods, it may also explain the dearth of small finds. Although artifacts and objects that were in daily use are uncovered from time to time, they are usually found buried in the fill and rubbish heaps of the day. No objects have ever been found *in situ* because the remains of the buildings have been removed. In this context I should mention that coins from the Hasmonean period, especially from the reign of Alexander Jannaeus, are usually found in abundance at excavation sites in Jerusalem, but they cannot teach us very much about the era because their use as legal tender extended until the end of the Second Temple period.

One indication of the scarcity of buildings from the Persian and Hellenistic periods throughout the country is literally illustrated in books on the history of Palestine. In describing the various periods, the authors generally try to avail themselves of illustrated material, mainly photographs, and we naturally expect to find refreshing and different illustrations in each new volume. Yet when it comes to the chapters dealing with these two periods, almost every book includes the same photographs of the tombs in the Kidron Valley, essentially because these are the only remains that have been found in Jerusalem. More than once I have come upon a despondent photographer who has been desperately searching for a new and different site from the Persian or Hellenistic periods only to find himself standing by those same old tombs and hoping at best to shoot them from a new angle. Actually, there is one other salient remain from the Hasmonean period in Jerusalem — a substantial section of the eastern wall of the Temple Mount — but today most of it is covered by the earth that comprises the city's main Moslem cemetery.

Occasionally we find mementos of Persian or Hellenistic Jerusalem under the ruins of structures built in Herod's day. I must immediately qualify this statement, however, by explaining that because Herod's builders always penetrated down to bedrock, the only earlier remains are appurtenances that were carved into the rock: plaster-coated cisterns, ritual baths, drainage canals, and the like. When uncovered far from the Temple Mount, in the Jewish Quarter or outside the Turkish wall, remains of this sort are always described by the same general formula: "Dating from the late Second Temple period to the destruction in A.D. 70." The determination of this date is based upon the finds uncovered within the structures and is valid regarding the time of their destruction; more difficult to determine is the date of their construction, as some of them may belong to the decades immediately preceding the destruction of the city and others may go back much earlier. In any case, it is clear that the remains found under the Herodian construction predate Herod's reign and are the first evidence we have of the extensive building that took place during the Hasmonean era.

The Acra   We have already noted that after Antiochus conquered Jerusalem in 168 B.C., he built a formidable fortress close to the Temple Mount to ensure the stability of his rule with the aid of a permanent garrison and a comple-

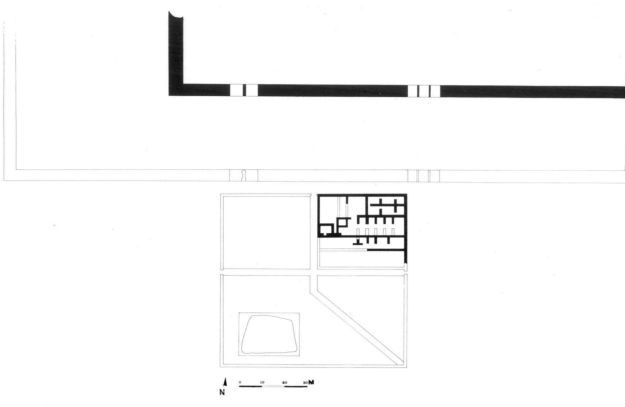

The remains of the Acra south of the Hulda Gate

ment of pro-Hellenist Jews. Testimony to this effect is found in the writings of Josephus Flavius:

And [Antiochus] burned the finest parts of the city, and pulling down the walls, built the Acra (citadel) in the Lower City: for it was high enough to overlook the temple, and it was for this reason that he fortified it with high walls and towers, and stationed a Macedonian garrison therein. None the less there remained in the Acra those of the people who were impious and of bad character, and at their hands the citizens were destined to suffer many terrible things (*Jewish Antiquities*, XII. 253).

The Hasmoneans liberated Jerusalem in 164 B.C., but the Acra — that despised symbol of Greek rule — continued to be occupied by foreign troops until 141 B.C., when Simon the Hasmonean captured and destroyed it. He could, of course, have left the citadel intact and exploited it for his own needs. Yet he chose to raze it because although he accurately assessed the weakness of the Seleucid rulers, he knew that in days to come they might recover their might and reclaim title to the fortress, in which case he would have no choice but to yield it to them. It was to obviate this prospect that he utterly obliterated the structure. Josepus adds the detail that to be absolutely sure no trace of the Acra would remain, the demolition team bore right down into the bedrock.

The problem of fixing the location of the Acra fortress goes as far back as the inception of modern research on Jerusalem and still remains unsolved. On the face of it, this should be a rather simple task: the Acra is to be sought south of the Temple Mount, as Josephus states quite explicitly. Indeed, the early scholars, who always followed Josephus, placed the Acra south of the Temple Mount in the City of David. Yet this straightforward solution proved to be problematic because the site they established is about 60 meters lower than the Temple Mount platform. Add to this the height of the Temple Mount's southern wall and you have a difference of at least 75 meters. In order for it to have been possible to see into the Temple's courts from the Acra, as the sources describing the fortress maintain, Antiochus would have had to build a virtual skyscraper, at least 85 meters high — which was an all but impossible task in those days. To overcome this difficulty, some scholars hold that this detail about being able to see onto the Temple Mount was something of an exaggeration and probably meant that it was possible to see the Temple Mount's gates from the Acra. Others contend that the citadel was located on the city's western hill — even though Josephus explicitly stated that the Acra was south of the Temple Mount — and explain this contradiction as a scribal error that crept into Josephus' text somewhere along the way. Support for this theory was even adduced from the fact that it was possible to see onto the Temple Mount from the Hasmonean palace subsequently built on the western hill, prompting advocates of this view to propose that the Acra was undoubtedly destroyed to make room for the palace. Both these schools shared the distinction of having to "correct" the historical sources to make them conform with their theories.

The most recent hypothesis establishes the site of the Acra by identifying a prominent architectural feature in Jerusalem as one of its walls. This theory posits that the section of the Temple Mount's eastern wall beginning slightly south of the Golden Gate and extending up to the "seam" 32 meters north of the wall's southeast corner is none other than the eastern wall of the Acra. To understand the thinking behind this conclusion, I should explain that the eastern wall of the Temple Mount is composed of two parts: the major section of the wall runs from the northeast corner down to a point 32 meters from the southeast corner; appended to it is a second, 32-meter stretch of wall built when the Temple Mount was extended by Herod. The point where the two walls join is called the "seam," in archaeological parlance, and is easy to discern because the two sections of the wall were built by different methods, though both are constructed out of unusually large stones. It is beyond question that the whole length of this wall served as the eastern wall of the Temple Mount in Herod's time. Moreover, the premise accepted in scholarly literature is that the section running from the "seam" northward was the eastern wall of the Temple Mount in the Hasmonean era.

The difficulty arises when we try to equate a section of this wall with the eastern wall of the Acra. We know that the western wall of the Temple Mount was a product of Herod's extension of the compound. If we assume that its eastern wall was originally the eastern wall of the Acra, there wouldn't have been any room for the Temple Mount itself in the Hasmonean era. Even more to the point is the fact that this section of the wall rises to a height of at least 30 meters, and it is impossible to reconcile the testimony about the Acra being razed to its foundations with the fact that such high walls still remain standing today. Another, no less serious drawback in identifying the eastern wall of the Temple Mount with that of the Acra is the sober fact that the citadel was built by Antiochus, an enemy of the Jews and a nefarious defiler of the Temple. Who could possibly have had the unmitigated gall to use any structure built by this infamous 'anti-Semite as part of the Temple Mount?

Where, then, was the Acra? A find that turned up quite incidentally has led us to conclude that we have found the remains of that elusive fortress. Most important, perhaps, this discovery does not require us to correct any ancient source; on the contrary, it is entirely congruent with the sources and their descriptions of the events related to the Acra.

It all began with a group of young volunteers from the United States sponsored by the organization of Conservative synagogues. Every summer groups of youngsters from this organization tour Israel. As part of their program they travel the length and breadth of the country, become familiar with Jerusalem, and work on an agricultural settlement. When we were approached to engage these groups at the dig for a three-day stint, we found ourselves in something of a bind. As a rule we did not take on volunteers for only three days; on the other hand, these youngsters amounted to an appreciable work force, since twenty groups came every summer and each consisted of dozens of teenagers. In the end, we were persuaded by the thought that the experience would have profound significance for these young people, not to speak of its educational value. It was also easy to reach an understanding about the work arrangements since our talks were held in the winter, which is generally an off-season for volunteers and was at any rate months before their scheduled arrival.

All this planning notwithstanding, on the day we received a call informing us that the first group would show up the following morning, it came like a bolt out of the blue. How would we integrate another eighty volunteers among the more than 400 already working on the site? Where would we find enough professional manpower to brief them on the work and supervise them? After all, at the end of three days they would be gone and a new group would arrive in their place! Once the initial panic subsided, we solved both these problems by assigning the youngsters to areas that required strenuous physical labor but an absolute minimum of professional training: they were sent to haul off detritus from heavily damaged or totally destroyed areas.

One area that was "tailor-made" for these teenagers was located about 40 meters south of the western Hulda Gate in the Temple Mount's southern wall. The structures there had been mutilated beyond recognition, as the area had been used in the Middle Ages as a stone quarry for building the city wall nearby. We decided to clear the entire area of the quarry and check whether any remains of earlier periods could be found on its periphery. As matters turned out, the quarry contained remains from the early Moslem, Byzantine, and Second Temple periods. Horren-

A reconstruction of the Acra — suggestion for the smaller format

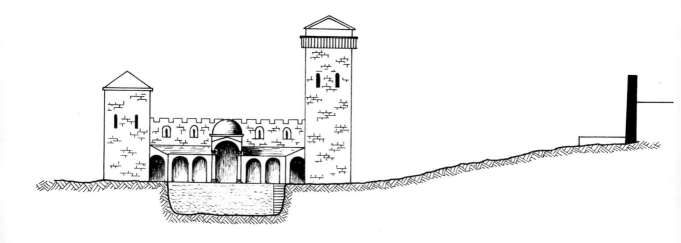

dous damage had been done to them all, but we nevertheless acquired important information by excavating and cleaning the area.

To our great surprise we discovered a mikvah (ritual bath) from the Second Temple period, an adjacent network of cisterns, and the remains of what were evidently public buildings, such as sections of plastered walls and the parts of delicate mosaic floors. But our astonishment was all the greater when we realized that these remains had been built over the ruins of a large plastered pool that probably dated to the same period. Its dimensions were c. 20 × 15 meters and it had been carved deep into the rock on the northern, eastern, and southern sides. Thereafter pottery shards characteristic of the third–second centuries B.C. were also uncovered among its ruins. They included seal impressins on jar handles and impressions in Hebrew mentioning the words Judah and Jerusalem that some scholars believe were the regime's stamp on vessels produced on its behalf. Judah's name during the period of Persian and Greek rule was the province of Yahud, and this term continued to be employed well into the reign of the Hasmoneans and even of Herod and his successors.

Together with these finds we discovered seal impressions on jar handles that are known in the scholarly literature as Rhodian seals, indicating that the provenance of these vessels must have been the island of Rhodes. The jars were used to transport fine wines to Judah, and their handles bear the seal of the producer and the pertinent date, but it is still unclear whether the seals were the hallmarks of the potters or the vintners. (If the latter proves to be the case, then citing the year of vintage is not a French innovation.) In any event, the date of these jars — the middle of the second century B.C. — is beyond doubt. Similar finds that have cropped up in this area or to the south of it, in excavations past and present, can be classified as refuse — vessels that were simply discarded after use.

Northeast of the large pools were remnants of a multi-roomed building whose basement or lower floor had been carved out of the bedrock. The rooms were arranged one next to the other with joining doors between them, and their walls were coated with an attractive white plaster. Two phases of construction are evident in the ruins of this building. In the first, a number of ritual baths and related cisterns had been carved into the center of the rooms, rendering the remainder of their area useless. Thereafter the houses containing these ritual baths and cisterns were evacuated and destroyed to make way for the street paved south of the Temple

A reconstruction of the Acra — suggestion for the larger and more likely format

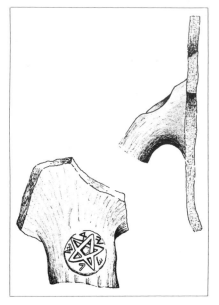

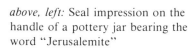

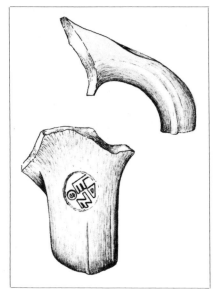

Pottery jar from Rhodes bearing seal impressions on its handles

above, left: Seal impression on the handle of a pottery jar bearing the word "Jerusalemite"

below, left: Seal impression on the handle of a pottery jar bearing the word "Yahud"

Mount. Plans of similar multi-roomed buildings constructed around an enclosed courtyard are well known to us. The court essentially served as a pool for collecting water and was covered by a roof that doubled as the floor of the courtyard. Another popular form was the multi-roomed building that enclosed a roofed-over pool designed either for recreation or decorative purposes. This second layout was closer to what we found in the field and more typical of the Hellenistic lifestyle of the period.

By drawing on these finds, we are able to propose the following reconstruction of the history and post-history of the Acra fortress: built south of the Temple Mount, the Acra was demolished down to its foundations by Simon the Hasmonean and a neighborhood of private homes, replete with ritual baths and cisterns, was built on its ruins. In the following stage, Herod expropriated this area to pave the streets and squares fronting the Temple Mount. This Herodian phase dates to the first century B.C., plac-

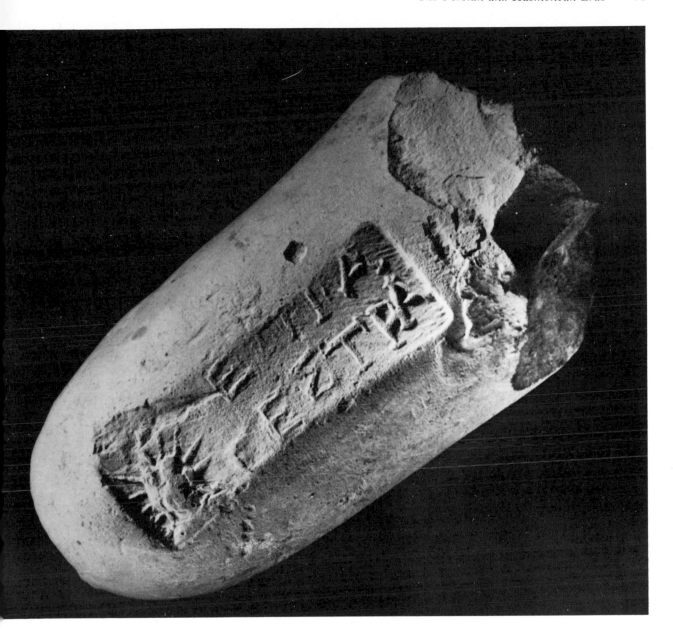

Seal impression on the handle of a wine jug of the "Rhodes" type

ing the previous one (in which the baths and cisterns were carved into the bedrock) at some time during the latter half of the second century B.C.

The fortress must therefore have stood at a reasonable distance from the Temple Mount's gates — some 40 meters south of the southern wall of the Hellenistic period. Building the Acra's towers there to a height of 20 meters made it possible to see into the Temple's courts, as described in the sources. Thus the Acra could have had two possible formats: it was either a small citadel or a larger structure of which the plastered pool was a part. One way or the other, our unexpected finds were as close to the discovery of the lost Acra as anyone is likely to get.

4   Herod's Monumental Enterprise

The Temple Mount in All Its Glory

The Second Temple and the Temple Mount were remodeled and rebuilt by King Herod during the last quarter of the first century B.C. and destroyed by Titus toward the end of the first century A.D. Perhaps the best way to obtain a sense of their magnificence is to begin at the end, just before they were destroyed by the Romans. By A.D. 70 Titus' siege of Jerusalem was at its height, the culmination of a four-year war that began as a revolt by the Jews against increasingly intolerable, and incompetent, Roman rule. The Romans had conducted their siege operation slowly but with a sure hand. Within the city, frustration ate away at the beleaguered Jews as hunger stalked them and a pall of a failure hovered over their strongholds. Still, no one considered surrender even during the early days of the month of Av, after months of investment and attrition, though it was clear that the fall of the city was only days away, a week at most. As the end approached, Titus summoned his General Staff, the commanders of the Legions, to discuss how to proceed once the Roman forces had broken into the city. Their consultation was apparently held on the Mount of Olives, with the Temple Mount laid out at their feet in all its glory. An account of this discussion is preserved in the works of Tacitus, one of the greatest of Roman historians: "It is said that Titus, who called the council, declared that the first thing to decide is whether or not to destroy the Temple, one of man's consummate building achievements. A few of [the officers] felt that it would not be right to destroy a holy building renowned as one of the greatest products of human endeavor . . ."

That hardened army officers at the end of a brutal war were troubled by the question of how to proceed after their conquest is an eloquent tribute to the unparalleled majesty of the Temple and the Temple Mount. It was a custom of the age to punish rebellious nations by destroying their temples, and one would expect this rule to apply all the more so in the case of the Jews, whose defiance and obstinacy stemmed from a religion, philosophy, and national outlook in which the Temple and the Temple Mount played a central role. However, the Temple had earned itself a reputation as one of the greatest cultural attainments of all time, and such distinction had to be taken into account, lest Rome come to rue that its legions had not parted with convention in this case. Raised as they were in materialist culture that placed great value on architectural achievement, the Roman officers displayed unusual sensitivity regarding this matter.

Testaments to the glory of the Temple and Temple Mount designed and built by Herod are naturally found in contemporary Jewish sources as well. "Whoever has not seen Herod's building has never seen a beautiful structure" is one of the sayings of the sages of Israel — Jewish intellectuals who had seen many lavish edifices and were familiar with such cities as Rome, Alexandria, Antioch, and Athens. Most of all, however, a sense of the Temple Mount's magnificence emerges from the descriptions and impressions of the Jewish historian of the war against Rome, Josephus Flavius. Josephus, who lived at a time when the Temple was at the acme of its splendor, was also a witness to its destruction. As a native of

A reconstruction of the façade of the Temple in Herod's day

Jerusalem and the son of a priestly family, he knew the Temple and the Temple Mount down to the last detail and devoted whole chapters of his works to describing them. These accounts provide us with so astonishing and detailed a picture of the structure's power and grandeur that in many cases they sometimes strike the reader as the product of an overactive imagination. In summing up a series of descriptions praising the Temple, for example, Josephus tells that "The external façade of the Temple had all that it takes to excite wonder in the eye and the heart." He provides so many details about the architecture and construction methods that he almost seems to have taken part in the building venture, for only a man intimately acquainted with the subject could present us with so cogent a picture of a structure we have never seen. Nevertheless, most scholars were indisposed to accept these descriptions at face value, treating them instead as oriental flights of fancy or hyperbole, at best. With a measure of condescension, one scholar attempted to defend these ostensible exaggerations by saying that Josephus undoubtedly suffered a lapse of memory as a result of his distance from the Temple and his being distracted by the hustle, bustle, and pleasures of life at the Roman emperor's court, where he lived while penning his books.

Now, on the basis of the finds uncovered in our archaeological investigations, we are able to say that the details given in Josephus's works are not only far from exaggerations, they correspond amazingly to what has been uncovered in the field. As a matter of fact, the degree of precision in the factual information Josephus imparts to us is quite remarkable — though one may well take issue with his analyses and conclusions, and in some cases it is only natural to do so.

Why Was the Greatest of Temples Built in Jerusalem?

The question of why the greatest temple of all times was built in Jerusalem was asked by the earliest scholars of the city's history; and in view of the fact that the man responsible for this undertaking was King Herod, their answer was simple. To a man, they perceived Herod as a hard-hearted despot who was more interested in immortalizing his name than in serving the best interests of his subjects. It was for this reason, they believed, that he invested most of the kingdom's resources into his monumental building project in Jerusalem, confident that it would bring him eternal fame. Jewish sages of the past also grappled with this question and came to the conclusion that Herod felt the need to repent for his sins and built the Temple Mount as an act of contrition. Yet in delving into the deeds of political figures, one must be wary of personalizing motives to arrive at simple answers. As we have come to see it, the motive for undertaking this ambitious construction project was far less personal and more prosaic, if you will. It stemmed from the needs of the hour and was an attempt to solve a constellation of problems created by the mass movement of pilgrims to and from the Temple Mount. Put simply, Herod was out to relieve his city of a monstrous traffic jam.

Ever since first being built by Solomon, the Temple stood at the top of a hill that came to be known as the Temple Mount. The summit of this mountain was a relatively small area that sloped off on a steep gradient on the west, south, and east. To the north a flat extension continued for a few dozen meters practically level with the summit and then began to slope moderately toward the saddle connecting this extension with the ridge to the north of it. As a result of this topography, the masses that streamed to the Temple were forced to crowd into the small area of the summit, most of which was occupied by the Temple itself. The first builders of the Temple Mount dealt with this problem by constructing retaining walls on the slopes to support an esplanade around the Temple and make it possible for more people to take part in the events centering on it. This same solution was adopted by Herod and his engineers in enlarging the Temple Mount to its present dimensions.

One obvious question is why the whole matter came up in Herod's day. At the time of Herod's ascension to the throne in Judea, most of the Jews were concentrated in Palestine. But even then large and important Jewish communities existed throughout the civilized world. A diversified and flourishing Jewish community whose members descended from the Babylonian exiles was scattered throughout the Parthian Empire between the Tigris and Euphrates rivers, and other important communities were to be found in Syria, Phoenicia, and Anatolia, as well as the rest of the lands bordering on the Mediterranean: Egypt and North Africa, Spain, Italy, Greece, and the islands in the sea. Most renowned for its power and eminence, in fact, was the Jewish community of Rome itself. The Jews of the Diaspora held important positions in public administration, international trade, and other branches of economic life and certainly left their mark on the culture of their countries of residence.

Considering this unparalleled dichotomy, the Jews of Palestine grappled with the question of how to relate to their co-religionists in the Diaspora. Should they be considered fellow-Jews in every way, or were Jews to be defined only as people who live in the land of Judea? Clearly, from both the emotional and the political and economic standpoints, the more a sense of national unity was maintained among the dispersed communities, the better it would be for all concerned. The problem was how to translate this sentiment into action, and one answer was by placing stress on the absolute exclusivity of the center of Jewish ritual in Jerusalem: the Temple. All efforts, together with the longings of the people in dispersion, had to be channeled toward that site.

Toward this end, the pilgrimage to Jerusalem on the Jewish holidays and festivals was actively promoted and soon became the goal of Jews everywhere. This custom brought crowds of pilgrims from abroad and within the country as well. Some scholars have estimated the number of pilgrims during the Roman period at 80,000–100,000 people on each festival. This swarm of visitors turning up on the holidays presented the city fathers with a major logistical headache. Above all it was imperative that this huge congregation be able to visit the Temple Mount at one and the same time. Jerusalem was then one of the largest cities in the world with a population of 150,000–200,000. Add to this number the tens of thousands of pilgrims from outside the city and you have a constituency of over 200,000 people massed together in one spot. An equivalent volume of traffic to a single site is rare even in our day. Thus the extension of the Temple Mount was designed to host this formidable crowd on an esplanade so that it could witness the ritual ceremonies performed in the Temple's courts.

Herod's Address to the Nation

When Herod decided to rebuild the Temple Mount so as to accommodate the mass pilgrimage to Jerusalem, he knew that he would have to overcome opposition from various quarters. This resistance was born of suspicions about the King's real intentions, and considering the fact that Herod was in the good graces of the Roman emperors, it was only natural that such misgivings should arise. Herod therefore decided to address the leaders of the people and apprise them of the details of his plans. His speech is preserved for us by Josephus, who evidently copied it from the court archive. Here is what Herod told his subjects:

So far as the other things achieved during my reign are concerned, my countrymen, I consider it unnecessary to speak of them, although they were of such a kind that the prestige which comes from them to me is less than the security which they have brought you. For in the most difficult situations I have not been unmindful of the things that might benefit you in your need, nor have I in my building been more intent upon my own invulnerability than upon that of all of you, and I think I have, by the will of God, brought the Jewish nation to such a state of prosperity as it has never known before. Now as for the various buildings which we have erected in our country and in the cities of our land and those of acquired territories, with which, as the most beautiful adornment, we have embellished our nation, it seems to me quite needless to speak of them to you, knowing them as you do. But that the enterprise which I now propose to undertake is the most pious and beautiful of our time I will now make clear. For this was the temple which our fathers built to the Most Great God after their return from Babylon, but it lacks 60 cubits in height, the amount by which the first temple, built by Solomon, exceeded it. And yet no one should condemn our fathers for neglecting their pious duty, for it was not their fault that this temple is smaller. Rather it was Cyrus and Darius, the son of Hystaspes, who prescribed these dimensions for building, and since our fathers were subject to them and their descendants after them to the Macedonians, they had no opportunity to restore this first archetype of piety to its former size. But since, by the will of God, I am now ruler and there continues to be a long period of peace and an abundance of wealth and great revenues, and — what is of most importance — the Romans, who are, so to speak, the masters of the world are [my] loyal friends, I will try to remedy the oversight caused by the necessity and subjection of that earlier time, and by this act of piety make full return to God for the gift of this kingdom (*Jewish Antiquities*, XV, II. 382–387).

This speech, following the stock formula of a ruler showing deference to his subjects, must have achieved its aim, because we do not hear of any pockets of resistance to Herod's plan. On the contrary, enormous forces were rallied to execute the task. But local support was not enough. After taking care to defuse potential opposition at home, Herod still had to obtain a "building permit" from Rome.

Rome Yields — After the Fact

Extending the area of the Temple Mount required the construction of massive retaining walls to bear the weight of the structures above them. Jewish religious law *(halakhah)* regarding the entrance to the Temple Mount demands that it contain two gates, and this restriction on access accorded the area the appearance and properties of a fortification. The fact is that during the Jewish revolt that culminated in the destruction of the Temple, a group of Zealots barricaded themselves on the Temple Mount and held out there for quite a while. How was it, then, that the Roman authorities permitted Herod to build a complex that could conceivably become an obstacle to them in governing Jerusalem?

No known source contains Herod's request for permission to rebuild the Temple Mount. Neither does any source suggest that the Romans made any attempt to foil the operation. But a talmudic legend based on the Baba Batra Tractate 4:71 tells that Herod had a healthy fear of the Romans and therefore consulted with a sage by the name of Bava, who advised him as follows:

Send an envoy [to Rome to request permission for the project] and let him take a year on the way and stay in Rome and take a year coming back, and in the meantime you can pull down the Temple and rebuild it. [Herod] did so, and received the following message [from Rome]: If you have not yet pulled it down, do not do so; if you have pulled it down, do not rebuild it; and if you have pulled it down and already rebuilt it, you are one of those bad servants who do first and ask permission afterward.

We cannot know whether or not this legend contains a kernel of historical truth and the deed preceded the authorization. Yet it is entirely possible that things happened just this way, though we could equally well assume that Herod's keen political instincts guided him in "packaging" and "selling" his idea to the powers that be and that he knew how to worm his way into the hearts of the Roman rulers and extract their permission to build. Herod built a strong fortress near the royal palace in Jerusalem, for example, and there is no evidence that Rome interfered with that project in any way. Neither do we have any reason to believe that he met any difficulty in obtaining authorization to build any of his other projects, and many were the fortifications and fortresses he built throughout the kingdom.

The Dimensions of the Temple Mount

The dimensions of the Temple Mount in Jerusalem, the largest site of its kind in the ancient world, were as follows: the southern wall, the shortest of the retaining walls, is 280 meters long; the eastern wall is 460 meters; the western and longest wall of the retaining walls is 485 meters; and the northern wall is 315 meters. The Temple Mount is therefore a trapezoid covering 144,000 square meters. Twelve soccer fields — bleachers included — would fit into the area!

The retaining walls rose 30 meters above the paved avenues at the foot of the mount — to about the height of a ten-storey building — while the towers at their corners soared at least 35 meters above street level. In some places the foundations of these retaining walls reached down as far as 20 meters below the street, making the walls there a total of more than 50 meters high. (All these measurements relate to the actual architectural finds, not the halakhic dimension of the Temple Mount.)

A Jewel in Its Setting

The retaining walls served to support the spacious plaza or esplanade built around the Temple but also furnished the solution to two other major architectural problems. In the early phase of the Temple's existence, during the reign of Solomon and his successors, the Temple Mount towered above the other sections of the city. It was higher even than the Ophel, which contained the royal palaces and other public buildings. The inhabitants of the city lived on the slopes of the holy mountain, and Jerusalem's topography satisfied the requirement that the Ark of the Covenant and the Lord's house rise above all the other buildings in the city. But in the latter part of the First Temple period, and with increasing frequency during the Second Temple period, particularly during the Hasmonean era, this convention was violated. Jerusalem's population steadily mounted, and the City of David proved too small to accommodate it all. As the city cried out for additional land, the first area to be exploited was naturally the hill west of the City of David (today's Jewish Quarter and Mount Zion), for its summit and eastern slope face the Temple Mount. The problem was that this hill is a few dozen meters higher than the Temple Mount, creating an unacceptable situation. David established the location of the Temple, and Solomon immortalized it through divine inspiration. Had we been dealing with one of the other religions of the ancient East, the problem would not have arisen at all, for if any change occurred in the city's plan the temple could be moved to a higher or otherwise more suitable location. In this case, however, the site itself was sacrosanct, making it unthinkable to move the Temple elsewhere.

To further complicate the matter, the size of the Temple was codified by law and could not be altered so much as an inch. Solomon's Temple was an imposing public building in the age of the kings of Judah, but in Herod's day, 900 years later, its dimensions were closer to those of a standard house. Its length, for example, was 60 cubits — equivalent to about 30 meters. Considering the advances in construction that had been attained by Herod's day, it was possible to build a wall that long using just three or four stones: Yet here again, as in the case of the location, the dictates of size were hallowed, and it was out of the question to deviate from them in any way. One could try to improve the appearance of the Temple — plate it in gold and precious stones or otherwise adorn it in splendor — and that was indeed done; but it had to remain exactly the size Solomon established when he first built it. The solution to these difficulties lay in a marvelous architectural concept that was related to the structure of the retaining walls.

As we have seen, the retaining walls were 30 meters high on their exterior side with broad avenues paved below them and low-ceilinged shops (only 3 meters high) fronting them. The city's new residential quarters were constructed a fair distance from the walls (on the slopes of the western hill) and appeared to be stacked upon the incline house by house, giving the city the look of a theater with its seats sloping upward. That, at least, is how the view from the southwest corner of the Temple Mount struck Josephus, for he wrote, ". . . the city lay opposite the Temple, being in the form of a theatre and being bordered by a deep ravine along its whole southern side" (*Jewish Antiquities*, xv. 410). The view from the city toward the Temple had exactly the opposite effect: as you stood between the low houses looking eastward, a colossal wall rose up before you. Even though in objective terms you might be standing at a point level with or even higher than the Temple Mount esplanade, the towering walls created the optical illusion that the Temple compound was higher still. The further you descended toward the street bordering the Temple Mount, the greater the sensation of its height: as you walked down, the mountain seemed to grow higher before you. The southern and western walls could thus be compared to a pair of enormous hands raising the Temple Mount heavenward.

The very enormity of these retaining walls helped to balance out the relatively modest proportions of the Temple itself. There was no halakhic limit on the size of the support walls, and indeed they were the longest, highest, and most impressive of any shrine in the ancient world, though they were constructed simply and in maximum coordination with the Temple above them. Other walls surrounded the Temple proper — the *hayl* and the *soreg* — but they were low structures, though also built in a simple style to complement the Temple. This rule of building for compatability created a singular and consistent architectural whole, and the public grew accustomed to viewing the Temple and the Temple Mount as a unit; whether calling it the Temple or the Temple Mount, everyone meant the entire complex when referring to it as the largest temple in the world. It resembled a precious-stone ring crafted by a master jeweler. The final product of a true artist will be a beautiful ring, not a precious stone and a setting but a precious-stone ring.

This was the great achievement of the Temple Mount's architect: creating the setting of retaining walls and dividing walls with the precious stone — the Temple — crowning them all.

Wrecking in Order to Build

The plan to extend the Temple Mount affected primarily the southern and western slopes of the holy mountain. At the time the project was conceived, these slopes were covered by residential housing huddled up against the Temple Mount in its Hasmonean format, so that to carry out the expansion project the houses had first to be cleared away. One can almost see the look of vindication invading the faces of those who persist in the belief that Herod was a villain: here is additional proof that he was a heartless tyrant who dispossessed helpless people from their homes for the sake of his ostentatious building schemes. The problem with this reading is that it was impossible to expropriate land at that time without the owner's consent, not even by order of the king.

I do not dispute that Herod was a strong and aggressive monarch, but there definitely was a limit to the king's power over his subjects. To illustrate how strict were Jewish laws of land ownership, it is sufficient to cite the story of King Ahab's brush with Naboth. To expropriate Naboth's vineyard in Jezreel, Ahab was forced to go so far as staging a treason trial and had to maneuver his way through some rather intricate machinations. As to Herod, it was imperative that his building program have the support of the people and their spiritual leaders, for otherwise he could not have embarked on such an ambitious operation. Hence the king must first have reached an accommodation with the landowners in the area; the various pressure groups in Jerusalem were simply too powerful for even an imposing figure like Herod to ignore (and there is evidence that a number of royal plans were derailed by such pressure groups). We can therefore assume that the reason we do not hear about any problems regarding the evacuation of these homes is that no problems arose, and the operation was carried out smoothly. Undoubtedly the owners of the land and houses received ample financial compensation.

Our excavation has provided a wealth of information confirming the premise that the residential areas at the foot of the Temple Mount were systematically evacuated and transformed into a building site following Herod's masterplan. Remains of residential buildings from the Hasmonean era and the early years of Herod's reign turned up wherever we excavated or conducted a standard check under the stratum of the Herodian era. Among these architectural remains were buildings, support walls, the foundations of houses, and plastered cisterns and ritual baths carved out of the rock in the cellars of the houses. All were found in a state of wholesale ruin as a result of Herod's building activities. For the most part, the evacuation operation went off smoothly as plots were systematically purchased for the new building venture, for the residents of Jerusalem understood that it would be impossible to live a normal life in the city unless the area of the Temple Mount were developed properly. The whole mechanism of pilgrimage was marred by disruptions so severe that they might have jeopardized its future had it not been for Herod's initiative, and many of the residents of Jerusalem made their livelihood from the tourist trade that was inevitably associated with pilgrimage.

Nevertheless, there were occasional hitches. The complexity of buying up the land adjoining the Temple Mount, even for so worthy a cause, is illustrated by one of the more curious finds we came upon our work. On

the western side of the Tyropoeon Valley, northwest of the Temple
Mount, we uncovered a broad, stone-paved street running north–south.
Down past the compound's southwest corner, this street suddenly veered
eastward, turning back a few dozen meters later to resume its original
course southward. We learned of this detour from the drainage system
constructed under the street, though as far as we could see it wasn't
justified from a purely topological point of view — or any other, for that
matter. On the contrary, it appeared to be a deliberate deviation for which
there was no logical reason. But it could be explained by the fact that the
builders came up against a stubborn landowner who refused to compromise, so the street had to be rerouted to bypass his property. Such incidents
are hardly unexampled. Talk to any mayor today and you'll hear similar
stories, for human nature is much the same the world over, and history
has a way of repeating itself.

A Grandiose Plan

We have established that the redesign of the Temple Mount was undertaken to solve the problem of accommodating the thousands of pilgrims
and Jerusalemites who frequented the area on the high holidays. The
plan would not be complete, however, without redesigning the immediate
vicinity of the Temple Mount to ensure aesthetic coordination between
the compound above and the area below. Obviously it was not sufficient
to enlarge the esplanade if the streets that channeled the flow of tens and
thousand of people to and from the Temple Mount remained narrow
alleyways. It would be equally senseless to leave the entry gates and the
squares fronting them in their former state. As we shall illustrate in the
coming chapters, before Herod was done the entire constellation of structures outside the Temple Mount had been rebuilt, every last detail in
coordination with the masterplan. Long, broad, shop-lined streets were
paved at the foot of the mount (these were the markets that furnished the
pilgrims with merchandise of every kind), and spacious plazas were laid
out at appropriate intervals. The first overpasses in history were built to
regulate and ease the press of traffic, while huge entry gates were fashioned with grandeur. And under it all a drainage system was dug and
plastered against leakage — one of the most efficient systems to be built in
the country to this day.

Financial Resources and Manpower

The *pièce de résistance* of Herod's building program was the construction
of the new Temple Mount, but it was certainly not the only project he
undertook in the capital. On the contrary, the king embarked on an orgy
of construction that included a new royal palace near today's Jaffa Gate,
the adjoining citadel with its three famous towers (Phasael, Hippicus, and
Miriamne), the Antonia Fortress, the repair and restoration of the walls,
cultural arenas such as a theater and a hippodrome, and a number of
markets. What's more, Herod did not restrict his building activities to
Jerusalem; his entire kingdom underwent a striking architectural transformation. Caesarea changed from an anonymous fishing village into the
largest port in the eastern Mediterranean Basin (larger even than Piraeus),
and Sebaste (Samaria) was enhanced by new walls, markets, a theater,
and other imposing structures — to mention just two of these remodeling
schemes. At the same time, the king developed the Jordan Valley by
establishing a vast agricultural farm there, in addition to building palaces
and fortifications in Jericho, Cypros, Terrex, Geba, Heshbon, and Masada. He rebuilt and expanded the Hasmonean fortresses of Alexandrium,

Hyrcania, and Macherus and carried out many other projects throughout the country. And Herod's passion for building was not restricted to his own kingdom; he donated funds to erect markets and other public structures in a number of cities in both the East and West, far from the borders of Judea. In short, the man just loved to build. But public building on such a grand scale took more than love to accomplish. Untold sums had to be produced to finance it, not to speak of the manpower — tens of thousands of laborers — needed to execute it. As the fourteenth-century Moslem historian Ibn-Khaldun wrote of the building works of the ancient world:

Yet you must know that these construction enterprises of the ancients were possible only thanks to architectural planning, the organization of the laborers, and the maximalization of working hands. Only thus was it possible to construct the buildings and the temples (*Muqaddamah*, Part 3, Chapter 18).

The obvious question is where did Herod get the capital and manpower for all these building projects. Here again, the prejudice of earlier scholars held their minds in thrall: the capital, they believed, came mostly from the heavy taxes he imposed on the inhabitants of the country, and a good part of the manpower came from slave labor. As is usually true of simplistic answers, however, these suffered from superficiality and a remoteness from the truth, and a more penetrating investigation of the subject produced very different insights into the origin of those resources.

As Herod explained to his people in the address quoted by Josephus, "there continues to be . . . an abundance of wealth and great revenues," and it was with the aid of these riches that he intended to execute his plans. If Herod's income had derived solely from taxes, it is doubtful that he would have had either the backing of the masses for rebuilding the Temple Mount or the audacity to appear before his subjects and deliver the speech he did. Moreover, if we examine the country's sources of income as an agrarian economy, even if we calculate all the income from agriculture as if it were a tax, there wouldn't have been nearly enough money to finance Herod's building spree.

Logically, then, he must have had other sources of income. Foremost among them was his toll from controlling the international trade routes of what was known, rather inappropriately, as the "spice" or "luxury" trade and proved to be a lucrative source of profit for all associated with it. The main beneficiaries of this bounty were the Arab tribes and the Nabateans living on the marches of Judea. The Hasmoneans had tried unsuccessfully to cash in on this flourishing branch of commerce, but Herod succeeded where they had failed. The "spice trade" was undoubtedly the real motive behind his wars, the regional friction, and Herod's ties with the Nabateans. It also explains Herod's territorial expansion into the districts of Batanean (Bashan) and Trachonitis to the north and east. Though the ostensible reason for this annexation of territory was to protect the Jewish pilgrims coming from Babylonia, in retrospect it was more like an outstretched fist that dominated the commercial route from Damascus, making it impossible to bypass Herod's kingdom. This was also the reason for Herod's penetration into Moab (Transjordan) and the fortification of Heshbon. As a matter of fact, the construction of the large harbor at Caesarea should also be seen in the same light, as the small harbors of Jaffa, Gaza, and Ashkelon were swamped by the volume of trade.

The second major source of income for Herod's coffers was the development of special agricultural farms in the Jordan Valley. The entire area north and west of the Dead Sea (Jericho, Phasaelis, Archalais, and Ein Gedi) and east of the Jordan (Beit Haram and other sections) was transformed into a gigantic hothouse for the cultivation of spices, medicinal plants, and dates. Herod mobilized hydraulic engineers to get spring water flowing to these plantations over many miles. The dry, warm climate did its part, and the income from the yield proved to be enormous. Jericho dates, for example, were renowned for their quality throughout the Roman Empire; one strain was even named after Nicholas of Damascus, the Greek historian who was Herod's friend and a denizen of Augustus' court. The value of dates to the Judean economy derived from the fact that they served as the principal sweetener in those days, before the lands of the Mediterranean discovered the pleasures of sugar cane. Neither was this elaborate operation kept secret. When Mark Antony wanted to give Cleopatra a special gift and told her to choose any place in the East (within the Roman Empire), she asked for Herod's farm in Jericho. Since she lacked the manpower to run it, however, she leased it back to Herod, who calculated that even with the added expense of rent, it would still be a lucrative operation for him. (Incidentally, Augustus subsequently returned the farm to Herod.)

As to where the second major element — labor — came from, we have noted that Palestine was essentially an agrarian country whose Jewish inhabitants made a livelihood from working the land. Their encounter with the Roman world introduced them to new technologies, such as hydraulic engineering and forging metals, and the Jews were quick to apply them to the sphere of agriculture. Hydraulics, which made it possible to conduct water over great distances in aqueducts, was originally developed in Rome to enhance urban architecture through the construction of public fountains and heighten the emperor's pleasure by the spectacle of water games. In Palestine, however, it was harnessed to serve the needs of agriculture through irrigation. Forging iron was developed in Rome to augment the power of the Roman army — the main prop of the empire — by equipping it with the best weaponry; the Jews of Palestine learned the techniques from the Romans but used them to make such agricultural tools as plows, pruning hooks, and spades. These technologies, coupled with the cultural sophistication of the Jews of Palestine, greatly boosted the level of agricultural productivity. In practical terms, these improvements meant that the individual farm required fewer working hands to generate an appreciable yield. Augustus' long reign was an age of peace for the Roman Empire, and natural increase rose as a matter of course, so that before long this combination of factors had generated pockets of unemployment due to the sheer excess of working hands.

It was a combination of the abundance of capital in the royal coffers and this surplus of working hands throughout the country that sparked the great surge in construction in Herod's day. In fact throughout history, whenever we come across an extraordinary spasm of building, these same two factors are lurking in the background. Certainly they were salient economic features of Herod's age.

Josephus tells us that when Herod completed his address to the people of Jerusalem, they were aghast at the magnitude of the task he had proposed. Most of all they feared the king would tear down the existing Temple and that circumstances might then prevent him from rebuilding

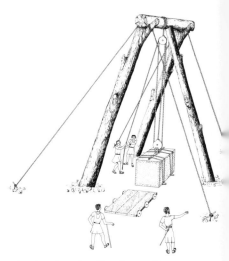

A tripod and pulley for lifting stones in construction work

The Workers and Construction Technologies

Technologies for transporting and building in stone:

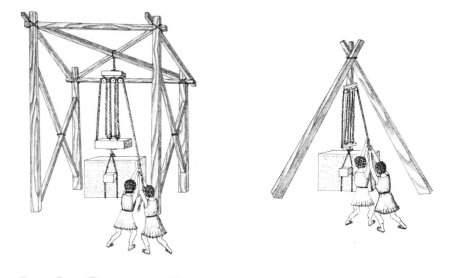

Hoisting stones with the aid of a tripod

Transporting stones with the aid of oxen

Attaching wooden wheels to a stone block in order to transport it

Hauling stones with the aid of oxen

it. But Herod, who was well versed in building lore, assuaged their fears by explaining that first he intended to train laborers and stockpile the raw materials, and only when everything was ready would he initiate the task of demolition and construction. "The king spoke encouragingly to them, saying that he would not pull down the Temple before having ready all the materials needed for its completion", Josephus sums up. "And these assurances he did not belie" (*Jewish Antiquities*, xv. 389).

Before embarking upon this bold operation, Herod prepared 1,000 wagons for transporting stones, selected tens of thousand of highly experienced construction workers, and purchased robes for the 1,000 priests who were slated to build the Temple itself. These priests were meticulously chosen, painstakingly trained, and groomed in all the spheres of construction and craftsmanship — so thoroughly was Herod determined to honor Jewish law and avoid any friction with the religious community. The other laborers were engaged to build the rest of the Temple Mount.

Herod's masons invested eight years in preparations alone — quarrying, dressing, and transporting stones to the building site — before the king gave the green light for actual construction work to begin. Another three years passed between the initiation of work and the dedication of the Temple, with lavish ceremonies that included the sacrifice of hundreds

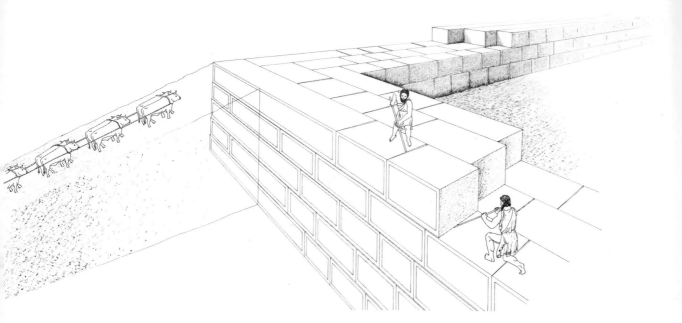

of offerings. The Temple itself was built by the priests over a period of eighteen months.

Carrying stones to the top of the wall on an earth embankment and setting a block of stone in place on the wall

Throughout those eleven years, Josephus informs us, it rained in Jerusalem only at night, so as not to interfere with the construction work. A talmudic legend that refers to this same phenomenon adds that at dawn "the wind blew and the clouds dispersed, the sun shone so that the people were able to go out to their work, and then they knew they were engaged in sacred work" (Jerusalem Talmud Berachot 1:8; Babylonian Talmud, Ta'anit 23:71). Before our dig this colorful description may well have appeared to be an exaggeration, but now, at the end of fourteen years of excavation, with thirteen winters behind us, we can confirm this detail as a realistic one. As I mentioned earlier, throughout this period we lost an average of only five workdays a year due to rain and snow, as most of the precipitation fell at night.

The stone used for building the Temple Mount came from quarries near the bulding site. Jerusalem stone is found in natural strata about a meter high, making that the height of most of the courses of the Temple Mount's walls. To free the stone from the bedrock, holes were drilled delineating the size of the blocks desired by the builder. Then wooden pegs were inserted into these holes and they were filled with water. When the wood absorbed the water, it expanded and cracked the stone, releasing it from the bedrock. Once the block of stone had broken away, it received its initial treatment in the quarry and was then transported to the building site over the dirt roads cut especially for that purpose. The usual transport vehicle was an ox-drawn wagon, though in some cases wagon wheels were attached directly to the block of stone and it was rolled to the building site itself before the blocks were set in place on the walls.

In the course of the construction work, pulleys based on multiple gears were used to hoist and manipulate the building materials. The stones were hauled up to the topmost course over gently sloped earth embankments, then placed on rollers that moved over the thick walls. Each massive block was planed down and set flush against the next one with polished precision; no adhesive material was used between them.

Great effort and enormous energy were invested in this construction venture, but more than physical exertion it required impeccable organization and planning. Even after having the methods of transport and elevation explained, all who lay eyes on those monumental stones find it hard to credit the construction process of the time. Because our generation is not accustomed to manual labor, the overall project looks highly complicated to us. I myself had an interesting experience in this connection when restoration work was being carried out in the Church of the Holy Sepulcher. To reconstruct the columns of the church's rotunda, blocks of stone weighing 5–10 tons were transported to the church by a small group of workers who hauled them over a few hundred meters, through the alleys of the Old City, in simple carts. Once they arrived at the rotunda, these stones — bases, columns, and capitals — were raised and set into place using hand-operated cranes (simple gear pulleys). I was able to see for myself that organization and expertise count far more than the brawn usually associated with this kind of work.

Thus the conventional explanations for Herod's success in meeting the challenge of his massive building enterprise — that he used slaves or imported forced labor — are quite groundless. The question is not how he overcame a shortage of labor, for labor was in surplus right at home. The success of such a venture is explained, rather, by the level of sophistication, technical knowledge, and the will to succeed. And these requirements, in turn, call for first-class engineers and construction technicians, talented foremen, and motivated workers of a high professional standard. Slaves and forced laborers would simply have not passed muster, and had Herod resorted to them he would not have been able to attain anywhere near the accomplishments of the Temple Mount project.

5   The Walls of the Temple Mount

The Retaining Walls

The walls surrounding the Temple Mount were built to support the large esplanade paved around the Temple proper. We should recall that the Temple stood on the relatively narrow crest of a small mountain north of the original City of David. The technique of using high retaining walls to extend the level area around the sanctuary was chosen because it provided solutions to a number of construction and aesthetic problems. Whoever examines the Temple Mount's walls as they have been exposed by our archaeological excavations is amazed by the high quality of their construction. Two thousand years have passed since these walls were built, yet they are still as solid and sturdy as if they had been built rather recently. All the more striking is the fact that they were built by the "dry" method of construction, meaning that no concrete, cement, or mortar of any kind was spread between the stones as an adhesive element. Sometimes cracks are visible in the ashlars, but they result from the quality of Jerusalem stone — which is not particularly known for its strength, has many natural veins and cracks, and is susceptible to changes in weather from dampness to dryness and back again. Yet if we examine the spots where the stones meet, we can see that they have not moved at all, not even so much as a millimeter. In fact they are so stable that were it not for the dressing around the edges, we would sometimes be unable to distinguish between one stone and the next. And all this after 2,000 years. How can we account for this remarkable durability? There are three explanations for the phenomenon: the way in which the foundations were laid and built, the weight of the stones, and the way of handling the problem of fill on the inside of the retaining walls.

Foundations on Bedrock

The secret of the strength of these retaining walls lies first and foremost in their remarkable foundations, which were always built on bedrock. Sometimes the masons dug down only 2 meters before reaching bedrock, sometimes they had to go down 7–10 meters. Occasionally the wall's foundation extended 20 meters below street level, for that is how deep the bedrock was and there was absolutely no exception to the rule that the wall's foundations was to be built on the natural rock. The face of the bedrock was planed down and prepared to take the stones of the first course, on which the subsequent layers were built. Then these lower courses were covered with the same fill used under the streets.

The foundations of the Temple Mount, like the visible part of the walls, were crafted on a scrupulously high level. Their ashlars are large and dressed, some smoothed down with the characteristic marginal dressing, others with only the marginal dressing and the raised area in the center left in its natural, rough state. In the latter case it is easy to understand the builders' thinking: it was pointless to invest time and effort in dressing stones that were destined to be buried underground anyway. Nevertheless, some sections of the foundations contain stones that are dressed both around the edges and in the raised areas in the center, and it is difficult to explain this phenomenon on architectural grounds. One possibility is that these were ashlars — excess pieces left

above: the southern section of the western wall

below: The marginal dressing on the stones

over in the inventory — for they had all been prepared in advance — and were therefore used for the foundations. However, this hypothesis is admittedly farfetched, considering the fact that the foundations were built first. Another possible explanation is simple human error: an order may have been given to dress all the stones before one of the foremen realized that it was really unnecessary to invest all that work in foundation stones. Yet another possibility is that stone contractors and labor foremen were engaged in shady dealings, since a much higher fee was paid for the perfectly smooth blocks. Eventually one of the more responsible managers probably caught on to the scheme and limited the dressing to only what was absolute necessary, meaning the edges or margins. One way or another, dressing of both types is found in the foundations of the retaining walls.

The sturdiness of the Temple Mount's retaining walls is also a function of the extraordinary weight of their stones. The smallest of these blocks — and the majority of the stones used in the walls — weighed 2–5 tons. Many others weighed 10 tons or more, and some stones (particularly at the corners) exceeded even that weight; the southwest corner of the Temple Mount contains ashlars that weigh about 50 tons a piece! The length of such a stone is 12 meters, and its height is 1 meter, and its thickness is 2.5 meters. A number of massive stones were also uncovered in the western wall, north of Wilson's Arch. Unequalled in size anywhere in the ancient world, one of these blocks is 12 meters long, 3 meters high, about 4 meters thick, and weighs close to 400 tons! The use of such monumental stones solved the problem of stability and is responsible for the fact that the walls still stand in our own day, 2,000 years after being built.

Stones Weighing Tens of Tons

Yet it is questionable whether stability was the sole reason for building with such mammoth blocks of stone. Sturdiness could have been achieved even if the walls had been built with small stones, but that would have ruled out the possiblity of employing the "dry construction" method, making it necesary to use mortar or cement as an adhesive material. That was how buildings were constructed in Rome, for example. Sometimes the mortar was made out of loam with a low lime content, and in the course of time it would begin to flake and cause a wall to buckle or crumble. In their desire to construct sturdy buildings that would stand up to years of wear, the Roman builders used a mortar that resembled cement. Once it dried and became hard, it joined the stones into a single unit. This mortar was constantly improved over the years until an excellent cement was achieved — the proof being that some of the walls built with it are still standing.

This high-grade mortar was made out of a mixture of 50 percent lime and 50 percent river silt or gravel with the addition of soil. The production of lime required a considerable output of energy, and the main source of energy at the time was wood — trees from forests and groves. The amount of cement needed for building with small stones was equal to half the volume of a wall, making the necessary amount of lime equal to a quarter of the volume of a wall! Production of the lime necessitated running ovens for a full day and night, sometimes two full days and nights, as the process entailed burning blocks of limestone at high temperatures. There was no shortage of trees in Rome and the rest of the countries north of the Mediterranean. Much to the contrary, the great struggle of the day was to turn forest land into agricultural land, and man made a

above; The stones of the southern wall set on the bedrock

below: Stones weighing 50 tons apiece

point of cutting down trees to expand the area available for cultivation. The favored method of construction in these countries used baked bricks, whose production required even more energy. Thus in addition to the creation of arable land, the clearing of forests brought in an income from the sale of wood for energy needs.

In the lands of the East, however, and particularly in Palestine — which was a heavily populated country — the demand for wood proved to be a major problem in the Second Temple period. Wood was prized both as a source of energy and as the main raw material in construction, crafts, and industry. It was used to make tools, plows, sickles, furniture, scaffolding, doors, and ceilings, not to mention its common use as a fuel for running ovens and to produce the coals used for cooking and household heating. Wood therefore played a focal role in man's life.

The trees of Palestine during that period were mostly pines, oaks, and terebinths. Due to the warm climate and meager amount of annual precipitation, it took many years to replace trees that had been cut down. Sensitive to this problem, the sages of the Mishna and Talmud went so far as to forbid the raising of small cattle, particularly goats, which were (and continue to be) the scourge of the forest. Whenever the country was dominated by foreign rulers, however, little consideration was given to the quality of life of its inhabitants, and it was then that the forests were exploited to the point of depletion, without any thought for the future. Anyone who wanted to build could simply hack down trees to his heart's content, whether for quality timber or for the wood needed to produce lime. Obviously this led to the exhaustion of energy sources and, as a consequence, to an appreciable decline in the standard of living.

For all these reasons, saving on the consumption of wood was an imperative in Palestine. Any responsible regime was obliged to pursue an intelligent policy regarding both the felling of trees and the development of new approaches to saving on wood, including the use of alternative sources of energy, raw materials, and building techniques. The stone dome, for example — a construction technique imported from Rome — proved to be an excellent means of economizing on wood. Instead of building roofs and ceilings out of timber beams, as was then the custom, the houses were topped off with domes built of local stone. This solution called for expertise in stonecutting and a high level of construction skills, but it led to a saving of countless square meters of timber. "Dry construction," which accounted for a great saving in lime, likewise spared the wood needed to produce it.

One should not conclude, however, that lime was not produced in abundance in Palestine. For instance it was a common practice to plaster walls, especially in cisterns, and lime is a primary component of plaster. Yet wherever it was possible to economize, the saving was welcomed. Building walls without cement or mortar as an adhesive element called for an immense investment in dressing the stones, planing them down, and meticulously working them into a shape that would enable them to adhere to the stones laid around them. Moreover, the construction of high, massive walls like those of the Temple Mount required not only hewing the stones and dressing them properly but starting off with huge blocks that had to be transported to the building site. The extra effort was worth it, however: an initial calculation shows that building the Temple Mount's retaining walls by the dry-construction method saved 100 square kilometers of forest that would otherwise have gone into the production of lime.

The ability to build well with massive stones is, above, all, a matter of knowledge, organizational ability, and teamwork. Experience was gained in the course of work, and after transporting a few of these monumental blocks and setting them in place, the team of laborers learned to overcome initial difficulties and insecurities and the work became simpler and more routine. Building with large stones also made it possible for the project to proceed at an incalculably faster pace. When a 12-meter-long stone was set in place, the structure advanced by 12 meters in a single stroke! Hence, using large ashlars was also a way of saving time. In fact, we can hazard a conjecture that the building time was cut by more than half. When it comes to public construction, builders are usually in no rush to complete their work, and the pace is determined by the rate at which contributions and public funds come in. Sometimes a project can go on for generations, as was true of many of the cathedrals built in Europe. Yet just the opposite was true in the case of the Temple Mount. As we have seen, Herod was playing a dangerous double game with his overlord in Rome, and he feared the consequences if the emperor denied him permission to build before he had established the new Temple as a *fait accompli*. Clearly, then, it was vital to complete the project as quickly as humanly possible.

To these pragmatic reasons for using huge ashlars, we should add the majestic appearance they accorded to the long, high walls of the Temple Mount and the strength and awe they bestowed upon their surroundings. The use of massive stones answered all the needs of the hour and place.

Stacked Vaults

The concept of using retaining walls to support a plaza implies that they will be fully visible on the outside but covered on the inside by the earth fill that underlies the esplanade. Modern construction demands that the ratio between the height of a support wall and its thickness be 4:1 in order for it to withstand the pressure of the fill. The height of the Temple Mount's retaining walls at its southeast corner are c. 20 meters (they are topped by an additional 13 meters of masonry comprising the exterior wall of the porticoes). If Herod's masons had studied modern engineering, they would have built the walls to a thickness of 5 meters; but since they did not have access to the textbooks we consulted, we were obliged to ascertain how thick these walls actually were to determine whether or not we would have to use supports during our work. Fortunately, we found a spot in one of the upper courses of the eastern wall where a stone was missing, and it happened to be one of the original stones from the Second Temple period. With the approval of the *waqf*, we cleared away the detritus at that spot and penetrated the wall to discover that it is precisely 5 meters thick and is built of three rows of stones that firmly adhere to each other. The problem was that our dig was at the foot of the western and southern walls, not the eastern one; and we had to be absolutely sure that the thickness of the walls in question was the same 5 meters. Here our luck ran out, in a sense, since not a single stone was missing from either of those two walls.

We decided to appeal to the engineers at the Haifa Technion for help, and they suggested drilling a small hole at the point where two stones meet. They even displayed an admirable knowledge of *halakha* by informing us that we should use a diamond drill head, rather than a steel one. I raised this issue before the Halakhah Committee of the Ministry of Religious Affairs, which was appointed to deal with problems of this sort, and

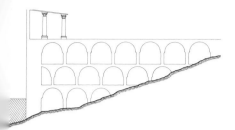

A section of the void under the Temple Mount esplanade showing the form of construction using layers of vaults

the committee passed the ball on to the Chief Rabbinate. After meeting for a number of sessions to consider this rather unusual matter, the Rabbinate finally issued a halakhic ruling that the drilling operations would be permissible if it served the needs and the good of the Wailing Wall. Only after we were well into the preparations to begin drilling did the rabbis inform us that an archaeological dig did not qualify as serving the good, and certainly not the needs, of the Wailing Wall: since there was no need to excavate, it was quite unnecessary to ascertain the thickness of the wall. We spent another week trying to persuade the rabbis otherwise, dabbling in such esoterica as "What is the good of the Wailing Wall?" But our efforts were futile; they simply would not be moved. It was then that a team from Israel's Geological Institute came to our rescue. They happened to be working on the development of a geo-electrical system designed to ascertain the thicknes of rock by a technique that resembles radar. After two days of painstaking investigation, their results indicated that the thickness of the western and southern walls was 4.8 meters. Now we could announce, with wholly anachronistic pride, that Herod's engineers had passed the test of the Technion!

The irony of our discovery was that although Herod's engineers followed the rules of advanced architectural doctrine, they did not have to build the walls that thick at all. For these support walls were not subject to the pressure of earth behind them; the inside of the retaining walls faced onto a void. Instead of filling the area within the support walls with earth and building the esplanade above it, Herod's architects constructed layers of vaults in the open space between the mountain's natural slope and the projected plaza. At the outer end, adjoining the retaining walls, there were three stories of vaults; at the other end, close to the mountain's summit, the number of stories was reduced to one, as dictated by the gradient. Over the vaults on the upper story came the paved plaza. In effect, then, the Temple Mount was constructed out of vaults covered, at the desired height, by an open plaza. This approach also made it possible to use the ample space provided by the vaults for storage and similar needs.

Yet it was not for reasons of economy or space, nor even for security considerations, that the Temple Mount was built in this way. Jewish ritual law is the real motive behind this style of construction. Here is how the pertinent issue is articulated in the Mishna: "Beneath both the Temple Mount and the Courts of the Temple was a hollowed space for fear of any grave down in the depths" (Parah 3:3). We know that the Jews of antiquity were scrupulous about observing the laws of ritual purity. But what did these laws have to do with the vaults below the Temple Mount?

According to the *halakhah*, entering a cemetery leaves a Jew ritually unclean and is totally forbidden to the priestly class. The definition of a cemetery was any place where gravestones were cordoned off by a fence. But what about graves that could be anywhere but because they are unmarked are unknown to the casual passerby? These were referred to as "graves down in the depths" (*kivrey tehom* in Hebrew), or hidden graves, and did not render one ritually unclean, for it was impossible to know where and whether they existed. If such hidden graves also contaminated a Jew, it would be impossible to go anywhere at all.

When it came to the Temple Mount, the rabbis wanted to be absolutely sure that there was no risk of encountering even these innocuous unmarked graves, especially as the Temple rituals were conducted by priests.

This extra precaution was evidently prompted by some hard evidence in the form of human bones that were uncovered during one of the early building operations or while digging the foundations. Talmudic legends make reference to a debate over whether Adam was buried on this site or the bones were the earthly remains of Araunah the Jebusite, from whom David bought the mountain. Earlier we noted that in digging by the southern part of the western wall, we uncovered tombs from the First Temple period. Their contents had been removed not long before the retaining wall was built, and perhaps other graves were still present in the area.

Jewish law prescribes the construction of vaults over graves as a way of "neutralizing" their ritual impurity, and this was the method adopted at the Cave of the Patriarchs in Hebron, where tradition has it that the forefathers of the Jewish people are interred. In order to enable a congregation — including its priests — to visit the site, a structure was built out of vaults to create a void above the cave (and therefore above the graves it contained). Then a floor was laid above the vaults and paved with large stones; over that another structure was built to serve as a prayer room. The same solution was used in the Temple Mount, which is constructed of layers of vaults to eliminate the possibility of ritual contamination.

The Height of the Retaining Walls

During the Second Temple period, the western wall was about 32 meters above the street near the point where it met the southern wall. How is it possible to reconstruct its height as 32 meters when the wall at that spot today is only 23 meters high and just 14 of those 23 meters are of the original Herodian masonry?

The walls of the Temple Mount served both as retaining walls for the esplanade and as the exterior walls of its porticoes. The lower portion of the western wall, which was designed to support the plaza, was almost 19 meters high — a measure that is readily calculated with the help of Robinson's Arch (located near the southern end of the western wall and about which we will have much more to relate further on). The point at which the arch begins to curve out from the western wall is 11 meters above the street. We know that the arch's diameter was 13 meters. Thus its radius, or half that figure, added to 11 meters, brings us to the maximum height of the interior of the arch — 17.5 meters above street level. To this we must add another 1.5 meters representing the height of the arch's stones, and we reach a total of 19 meters above the paved street. Nineteen meters is therefore the level of the Temple Mount's esplanade and of the section of the wall that served as a retaining wall. The addition built above the 19-meter mark was the exterior wall of the western portico. According to Josephus, the porticoes were 25 cubits or close to 12.6 meters high. Add this figure to the height of the retaining wall and we arrive at the total height of the western wall: c. 31 meters.

Even though the porticoes were totally destroyed, we can also reconstruct their height with the aid of an archaeological find. Josephus describes the girth of the columns in these porticoes by telling us that it took three men holding hands with outstretched arms to compass their circumference. We uncovered the remains of columns from the porticoes and found that they were 1.5 meters in diameter. But we uncovered only parts of these columns. How, then, is it possible to know how high they were?

The doctrine of classical architecture placed great importance on the ratio between the height of a column and its diameter, which was established as 6:1. Thus a column whose diameter is 1.5 meters must have been 9 meters high. To this we must add the height of the capital above it (1 meter) and the base below it (1 meter) for a total of 11 meters. If we add to this the thickness of the ceiling and the roof (1 meter), we reach a figure that corresponds to the equivalent of Josephus' 25 cubits.

The architect of the Temple Mount wanted to distinguish visually between the lower part of the walls, which served for support, and their upper part, which comprised the exterior wall of the porticoes. He did so by building the retaining wall flat and adorning the portico wall with stone projections that resembled pilasters. In the seventh century A.D., the Temple Mount's walls were destroyed down to the point where the pilasters began. So how do we know they were built that way? First of all, at the northern end of the western wall (today within the confines of a building), we found a section of the original wall that contains parts of the pilasters *in situ*. Second, in order to fashion the pilasters the stones were dressed in a special way, and we uncovered examples of this unique dressing among the debris at the foot of the western and southern walls. Some of these stones turned up in the rubble created by Titus' soldiers in A.D. 70, others were found among the ruins from the late Byzantine era, when Jerusalem was recaptured from the Persians by the Emperor Heraclius in A.D. 628. We will deal with both of these instances in later chapters.

Each of the corners of the Temple Mount was graced with a tower whose main purpose was to enable guards to monitor what was going on in the Temple's precincts and head off the build-up of crowds. The northwest corner even boasted a military fortress, called the Antonia Fortress, which served Herod's troops and, in days to come, the soldiers of the

A reconstruction of the overpass built over Robinson's Arch and the southwest corner of the Temple Mount

The inscription on the head cornerstone

Roman Legions. The other three corners of the Temple Mount had standard towers manned by lookouts and guards of the priestly class, who were responsible for the Temple's security and personnel. (We should also note that the state treasury was kept in the Temple, as was customary in temples throughout the ancient world.) Above and beyond the corner towers, the considerable length of the eastern and western walls required the construction of additional towers somewhere around the middle of these walls.

When our dig had reached down to the level of the paved street that skirted the Temple Mount at the southeast corner, we came upon a stone that could well have been the cornerstone of the tower above. It was dressed on three sides, which indicates that it was not only a cornerstone in the literal sense of the term but the topmost stone of that corner. Some scholars have interpreted the term "the head cornerstone" to mean the foundation stone laid at the start of a structure, but here we had incontrovertible evidence that the stone was located at the top of the building, as its name implies. Evidently our ancestors held their dedication ceremonies when the last stone of a building was laid, whereas we dedicate a building by laying the foundation stone (and in many cases all work ceases thereafter). In any event, the importance of this stone lay in the opportunity it provided to study the contour of the top of the Temple Mount wall, and it hogged the attention of the entire archaeological team.

Once the initial fuss died down, Ron Gardiner, one of our archaeologists, decided to come over and have a look at the stone. As usual, Ron preferred to examine it alone, avoiding the hubbub that usually arises when a crowd observes a find. Suddenly we heard shouts of joy coming from his direction. Ron is a level-headed Welshman who first came to this country as a policeman in the mid-1940s, toward the end of the British Mandate, and has returned from time to time to join archaeological expeditions. It's not every day that you can see him succumb to excitement, and shouts were a sure sign that he had discovered something. And a delectable something it was. "There's a Hebrew inscription engraved on the stone!" he called up to us. The inscription was easily deciphered because its letters were clear and deeply engraved, and we soon realized that it was incomplete. It read: "To the trumpet-call building to pr ...." At that point the stone was broken, and the rest of it could not be found. "What a pity!" was the universal response. I suppose it's human nature to moan over what we lack rather than rejoice over what we have.

After we recovered from the excitement, we set our minds to figuring out the missing part of the inscription and establishing the significance of the stone being found at that particular spot. One suggestion was that the inscription originally read: "To the trumpet-call building to pr[oclaim.]" But what would have been proclaimed there? None of the sources at our disposal — neither Josephus' descriptions of the Temple Mount nor the mishnaic sources — seemed to touch upon this subject. Then I recalled a piece by Josephus that mentioned the towers in a completely different context:

> They, moreover, improved this advantage of position by erecting four huge towers in order to increase the elevation from which their missiles were discharged: one at the northeast corner, the second above the *xystus*, the third at another corner opposite the lower town. The last was erected above the roof of the priests' chambers, at the point where it was the custom for one of the priests to stand and to give notice, by sound of trumpet, in the afternoon of the approach, and on the following evening of the close, of every seventh day, announcing to the people the respective hours for ceasing work and for resuming their labors. (*The Jewish War*, IV, IX, 12, pp. 574–582)

Josephus assumed that anyone familiar with Jerusalem was able to identify the towers easily, so he stressed that the outermost tower was the one from which the trumpets proclaimed the start and the end of the Sabbath. The southwestern corner was the most suitable one for this purpose, since it rose above the Lower Market, Jerusalem's main commercial center.

What did the inscription mean? The Hebrew prefix consisting of the letter *lamed* (ל) can mean "to" or "toward," indicating direction as in "to Jerusalem." In the case before us, an inscription beginning with the word "to" could have graced a signpost directing the priest to the place where he was to blow his trumpet. On the other hand, the inscription was engraved at the top of the tower, so that by the time the priest got up there he no longer needed directions. Another possibility is that the letter *lamed* connoted association or possession, as in "belongs to" the trumpet-call building. It took three years to build the Temple Mount's walls and eight before them to prepare the stones and other raw materials for the operation. Perhaps during that time certain stones were keyed with inscriptions or markings indicating to the foremen where they should be placed in accordance with the architect's blueprint. This is a common practice in construction, but the problem with the theory is that such markings were usually abbreviations or initials, never so elaborate a rendition as we have here.

The final possibility is that we had before us a dedication stone. While the Temple Mount was being built, many people made donations to the project. The standard contribution was apparently a building stone — not the actual stone, of course, but a sum equal to the cost of one stone or a portion thereof. An ancient legend tells that one of the sages of the period was so wretchedly poor that he couldn't affort a donation to the holy enterprise. But he was aided by Heaven, took heart, and carried a stone on his back all the way from the Judean Desert. This tale alludes to the custom of "donating stones" to the Temple Mount. The system apparently worked like the contemporary custom of planting trees, whereby the donor doesn't actually furnish or purchase a specific tree but contributes the cost of having a tree planted for him. If a man has the means and the desire to donate an entire forest, he will surely want to have a sign or plaque posted at the entrance acknowledging his generosity or perhaps even have the forest named in his honor. Our cornerstone may have represented a similar convention: a man of means had donated a tidy sum for the entire wing of the trumpet-call building, and his generosity was duly immortalized by a dedication stone. If that were indeed the case, the full inscription probably read: "For the Trumpet-Call Building, to Proclaim the Sabbath, Donated by John Doe" — or, rather, the Hebrew equivalent of his time. Similar instances are known to us from dedicatory inscriptions found in ancient synagogues throughout the country. We even have a precedent from the Temple itself: the Nicanor Gates were donated by a man named Nicanor. Beyond offering this conjecture, however, we can only hope that the broken part of this stone will turn up in the future so that the puzzle will be solved.

The Mark of Herodian Stonework?

The dressing of the stones used in the Temple Mount's walls was of the highest quality, with the ashlars being worked to a smooth surface on five of their sides and placed next to and above one another in perfect alignment. This consummate construction, coupled with the smooth surface of the stones, created the look of a massive stone wall whose individual components were invisible to the naked eye. Each wall appeared to be an evenly textured, consistently white, plastered surface. At the same time, the architects' intent was to create the sensation that the walls were a composite of stones — and they succeeded in that, too. For anyone who views the Temple Mount from a distance is able to see that its walls are built of distinctively individual blocks. The walls are not a monolithic surface but a patchwork that is manifest because of the special dressing executed on their stones. Scholars call it marginal dressing, and its purpose is to create a frame or margin around the block. After the stone's outer face was smoothed down, the masons chiseled a frame 1 or 2 centimeters deep around its edge. The length of the margin is of course identical to that of the stone; its width varies from 9 to 18 centimeters, a variance that obtains not only between one stone and the next but on the same block and does not seem to be guided by any method or consistency. The area of the stone's surface between the margins is referred to as the boss and is also completely smooth; yet the fact that it stands out some 2 centimeters more than the margins is sufficient to make each stone distinguishable from those around it.

This method of dressing stones was obviously meant only for the visible parts of a wall. The margins served as a guide for setting the stones in place with precision and were therefore required on all the stones of a wall. But the boss of those ashlars destined to be used in the foundations, and consequently covered with earth, did not have to be dressed. Indeed, when we uncovered the foundations of the southern wall, we found that the boss of the ashlars set below street level were left rough. The architects were undoubtedly interested in saving both time and money on the dressing work, and we can better appreciate their reasoning if we recall that the foundations sometimes extended 20 meters below street level. Yet even this rule had its exception. The stones in all nine courses of the foundation toward the northern end of the western wall were worked down to a smooth polish, in blatant contradiction to all logic. How can we explain this aberration? At best we must credit it to human failings — negligence or plain greed — as suggested earlier.

We have already noted that despite this method of highlighting the individual stones, the support walls retained something of a flat appearance. But the same cannot be said of the upper section of the walls, or exterior of the porticoes, which were adorned with pilasters. To further avoid the possibility of this upper section appearing flat, highly prominent square bosses were worked into the center of a number of stones. The dimensions of these protrusions were 20×20 centimeters in length and height, and they extended about 20–25 centimeters outward, like cubes attached to the center of the stones. Each of them cast a deep shadow on the area around it, creating a play of light and shade that de-emphasized the flatness of the wall. The stones bearing these cube-like bosses were scattered throughout the wall at random: sometimes they are found on two adjoining stones, sometimes considerably further away from each other.

The technique of marginal dressing took root as a building style and was copied on walls made of rough stone as well. These walls were treated to a coating of white plaster that completely covered their surface, so that no stones were visible on the outside. Then the coating was divided into strips by systematically etching 2 centimeters into the plaster along the entire length and height of the wall. The result was the impression of a stone wall worked in the style of marginal dressing. The plaster could be etched to resemble either the huge ashlars used in the Temple Mount's walls or smaller blocks. We believe that this fashion was an expression of identification with the Temple Mount. It was adopted in the royal buildings at Masada as well as the fashionable private homes built in the Upper City (the area of today's Jewish Quarter) during and after the reign of Herod. Plastered walls with imitation marginal dressing can also be found inside these buildings, whereas the interior façade of the Temple Mount's walls were built of completely smooth stone with no dressing on the margins.

A few scholars have referred to this marginal style of stonework as Herodian dressing, but it is definitely not typical of all the structures built during the Herodian period. The Temple Mount itself has walls whose stones are completely smooth, for example, on the inside of the Double Gate. Anyone who walks past these walls can see that they were built of individual stones, so there was no need to invest a special effort in working the margins. This observation also reinforces our original premise that the purpose of the dressing on the margins was to make the stones stand out. Buildings of later periods, all the way up to the Ottoman era, have likewise been found to have marginal dressing, evidently executed for the same reasons that motivated the Herodian architects. Marginal stonework strikingly similar to the effect achieved on the Temple Mount was also done prior to Herod's day. The palace of the Tobias family, located in Transjordan and built some 200 years before Herod's enterprise, contains walls with marginal dressing that is very similar to that of the Temple Mount. Thus the presence of marginal dressing is not in and of itself a criterion for the chronological classification of buildings.

The Esplanade

Anyone who visits the Temple Mount today can discern the two levels of the pavement: the upper level found in the vicinity of the Dome of the Rock and to the north of it; and the lower level (4 meters lower) found in

A reconstruction of the Temple
Mount viewed from the southeast

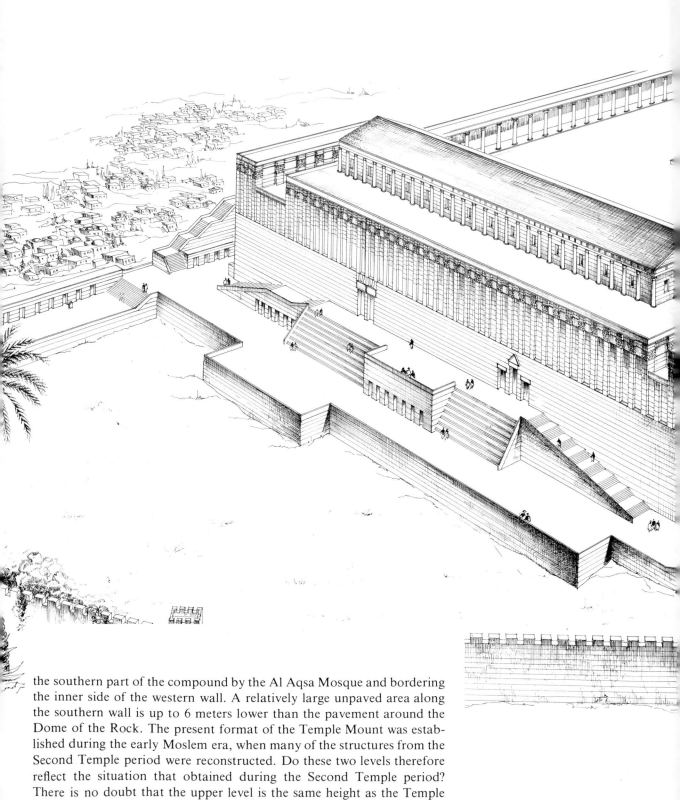

the southern part of the compound by the Al Aqsa Mosque and bordering
the inner side of the western wall. A relatively large unpaved area along
the southern wall is up to 6 meters lower than the pavement around the
Dome of the Rock. The present format of the Temple Mount was established during the early Moslem era, when many of the structures from the
Second Temple period were reconstructed. Do these two levels therefore
reflect the situation that obtained during the Second Temple period?
There is no doubt that the upper level is the same height as the Temple

Mount esplanade of the Herodian era, as it is built directly on bedrock. The same cannot be said for the level of the pavement to the south, east, and west. Yet we know that the purpose of building the Temple Mount in Herod's day was to accommodate a mass of people and enable them to witness the ceremonies taking place in the Temple's courts. If we set out from this premise, common sense dictates that the entire enclosure must have been paved on a single level.

We can obtain decisive proof for this assumption if we examine the

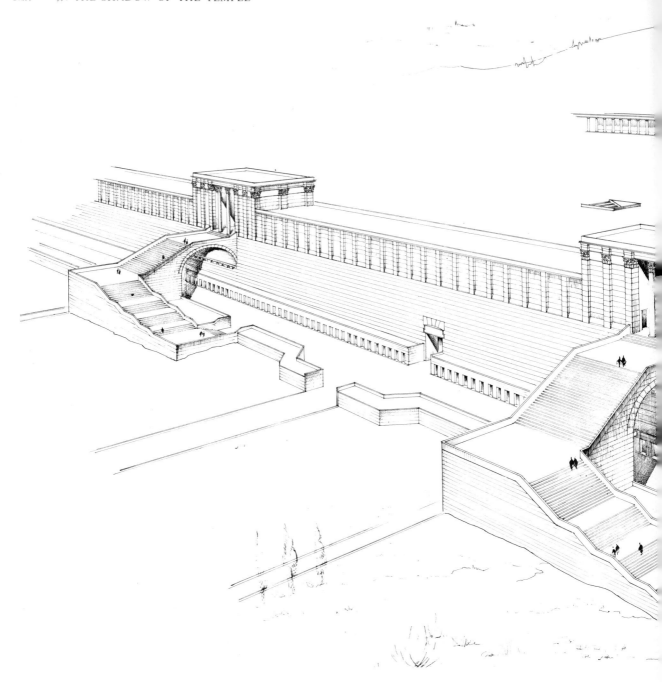

height of the aqueduct that carried water from Solomon's Pools, near Bethlehem, to the Temple Mount. The section of the aqueduct uncovered on the slopes of the Jewish Quarter, near the spot where it entered the compound, shows that the channel of flow was at precisely the level of the Temple Mount esplanade, just above the pedestrian pavement of Robinson's Arch. This leads us to conclude that the water must have entered the enclosure at the height of what is now the upper level of the pavement but was the only level in Herod's day. One last word about the pavement here: the grand esplanade was originally paved with large stones, like all the streets alongside the Temple Mount. North of the Temple, in places where

A reconstruction of the Temple Mount viewed from the southwest

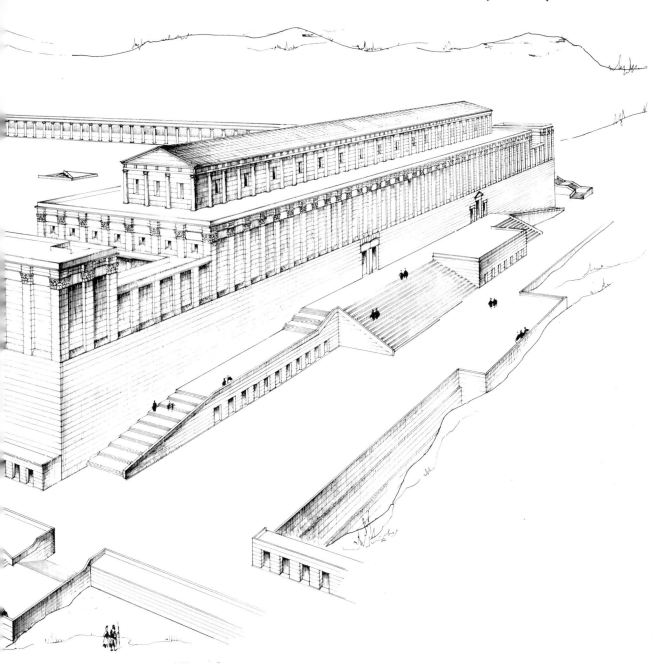

the natural rock was particularly high, it was planed down flat and etched with lines to accord it the appearance of a stone pavement.

The "Seam"

In the previous chapter we defined the so-called seam near the southern corner of the Temple Mount's eastern wall as the join between walls built in two different periods. From the "seam" northward, the wall is constructed of large stones with marginal dressing and inner areas that were smoothed down but not polished like the stones in the other walls. These inner areas stand out about 15–20 centimeters from the marginal frame and their stonework is generally simple, compared to the dressing on the

ΜΗΘΕΝΑΑΛΛΟΓΕΝΗΕΙΣΠΟ
ΡΕΥΕΣΟΛΙΕΝΤΟΣΤΟΙΠΕ
ΡΙΤΟΙΕΡΟΝΤΡΥΦΑΚΤΟΥΚΑΙ
ΠΕΡΙΒΟΛΟΥΟΣΔΑΝΛΗ
ΦΘΗΕΑΥΤΩΙΑΙΤΙΟΣΕΣ
ΤΑΙΔΙΑΤΟΕΞΛΚΟΛΟΥ
ΟΕΙΝΟΑΝΑΤΟΝ

above: A reconstruction of the *soreg*, or balustrade, which non-Jews were not allowed to pass

left: A stone-carved Greek inscription forbidding non-Jews to enter the area of the Temple

other walls. From the "seam" southward the stones are identical in every way to the ashlars in the rest of the walls. The length of this southern section is 32 meters, out of the eastern wall's total length of 460 meters. As we have said, the "seam" marks the spot where the eastern wall once ended. Herod apparently decided that this wall, built solidly during or sometime before the Hasmonean period, warranted inclusion in the structure he was planning. The strength and sturdiness of this particular wall, as opposed to the other walls of the Hasmonean Temple Mount, was among the reasons why Herod decided to expand the Temple Mount westward and southward toward the city, rather than eastward into areas that lay outside the city limits and would have obviated the need to evacuate residents and buy up settled property. Because of limited resources, the Hasmoneans devoted most of their care and attention to the eastern wall, which was both the retaining wall for the Temple Mount and the city wall in that area.

Before concluding this chapter we should take special note of the high degree of technical precision exhibited in the construction of the Temple Mount's walls and the detailed engineering calculations invested in them. For example, every course of the retaining walls is set about 3 centimeters further in than the one below it. Calculated over a stretch of 19 meters, this brings the top of the wall to a position some 60 centimeters further back than its bottom. This method of laying the courses was not adopted to make the walls stronger or sturdier but solely for aesthetic reasons: from a distance, the walls of the Temple Mount looked like the sides of a pyramid with its top lopped off. Then again, this gradual recess may have been effected to decrease the "dead area" at the foot of the Temple Mount from the viewpoint of the observer standing at the top of the wall. Either way, the meticulous attention to detail in such a monumental project is one of the factors that made the Temple Mount one of the most renowned wonders of the Roman world.

6   The Streets and Drainage System

Uncovering the Southern Street

It is in the nature of things that an archaeological dig uncovers the most recent strata first and then proceeds deeper down and further back into history. Our dig began to turn up many important finds almost from the start, particularly from the early Moslem period. We had decided to excavate over a broad area, rather than open up selected small squares, because the less restrictive method would enable us to define structures with a far greater degree of accuracy. Nevertheless, from time to time we did take recourse to opening up a small square and going down very deep. The purpose of excavating a small area in this way was to ascertain what we were likely to contend with in the lower strata, so that we could plan the dig accordingly. Yet, these "peeks into the future" sometimes spawned untold frustration. Three months into the dig, although we had invested an enormous amount of effort and the results were remarkable, we were still poking around in the upper, later strata. A look at the calendar showed us that in a few days' time our excavation would be 100 days old. Jerusalem Day fell at about the same time, and a major celebration was planned to mark the first anniversary of the city's reunification. In anticipation of this double event, it was only natural that we wanted to produce some remains from the Second Temple period, especially since the data of the Palestine Exploration Fund expeditions showed that we were pretty close to reaching them. We also knew that hitting upon finds from Herod's day would give us the shot in the arm we so badly needed from a budgetary standpoint, as the excavation's funds were running out at an alarming rate.

We knew from our reading that the excavators sent by the Palestine Exploration Fund had reached a section of the Herodian stone pavement close to the southwest corner of the Temple Mount by means of a one-square-meter shaft. So in the few days left before Jerusalem Day, we stepped up the pace of work in this area with the dim hope of repeating their achievement. The studies published by the Palestine Exploration

opposite: A section of the Second Temple street at the foot of the southern wall and the remains of the sewage system from the Roman period

right: The streets and staircases fronting the Temple Mount's southern wall

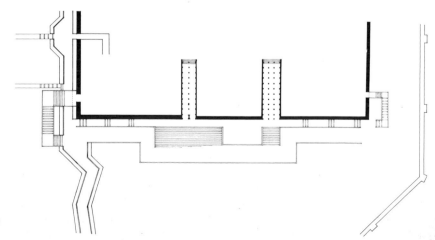

Fund indicated that the pavement was located at a height of 716 meters above sea level. On the eve of Jerusalem Day, I asked the strongest of our laborers, Yohanan (formerly a porter from the mountains of Kurdistan) and one of our veteran volunteers, Sylvie Nisbet of London (who had acquired previous experience at the Masada excavations) to stay behind with me at the end of the day and try to reach the pavement. We did so quietly to avoid creating expectations that would probably be disappointing, for the chances were even that we would not find the pavement through the shaft we were sinking. Perhaps the earlier excavators had not been precise in recording the pertinent details. After all, their dig in this area was limited to the space of a single square meter.

Despite the less than encouraging odds, given the time we had to complete our task, we threw ourselves into hours of hard labor. We were already down so deep that every additional basket of dirt had to be hauled up 8 meters. But the extra effort was more than worth it, for slowly the debris of monumental stones began to appear under the detritus. This was the first time we were privileged to see and touch the stones of the Temple Mount that had been smashed during the destruction of the Temple on the 9th of Av in A.D. 70. I knew that debris of this kind must be lying on some sort of pavement, so we carefully began to burrow between the stones, measuring as we went along, and at about 5 P.M. we reached down to 716 meters above sea level— the height at which the British expedition had hit upon a white stone floor. But we didn't hit upon anything, and the expression on Yohanan's and Sylvie's faces betrayed their keen disappointment. Sylvie seemed particularly disconsolate, as if she were carrying the full weight of British credibility on her shoulders. How could it be that the British excavators claimed to have reached a pavement at this level when there was no pavement to be seen? Was this a simple error, or had the excavators deliberately led the public astray? I found it difficult to ask my two partners to stay on for another half hour and try to get down a bit deeper, but they agreed that it was worthwhile trying. One more centimeter, 2 more centimeters went by, and at the end of 15 more centimeters — at a level of 715.85 meters above sea level — we began to get a glimpse of the beautifully dressed, large paving stones from the Second Temple period. (At that moment we easily forgave Warren and his men an error of 15 centimeters after having descended over 13 meters into a dark and narrow shaft.) Needless to say, our excitement knew no bounds. Imagine actually standing on a stone pavement from the Second Temple period, wedged in between the stones that had smashed down on the 9th of Av — and on the eve of Jerusalem Day, at that!

I sent Yohanan and Sylvie on their way and followed soon after, deeply moved by the experience. Near the entrance to the dig, I happened to meet two reporters from Israel Radio who were going to the Wailing Wall to cover the Jerusalem Day ceremonies. When I told them what we had just uncovered, they insisted on seeing the find for themselves. On the spot, they taped a report about reaching the Herodian stratum, and that evening the news bulletins opened with their taped story about the pavement that had waited centuries for this moment.

Next day the site was bustling with visitors — scientific colleagues, public figures, friends and acquaintances — all coming to see the pavement. Overnight our excavation had become a household word. Far more important, from our point of view, was the fact that various government agencies now opened their doors to us when we came to ask for financial assistance. Only a day or two earlier, we were calculating whether we would have to halt the excavation for lack of funds; now we had to organize quickly to move full speed ahead.

Streets and Plazas

The coming years were spent searching for the network of streets that had been paved at the foot of the Temple Mount. After discovering the pavement at the southwest corner, we expanded our excavation in all four directions, and now, at the end of more than a decade, we are able to present a blueprint of this network. The streets in the cities of antiquity were not usually very wide. As these were walled cities, they were not given to "urban sprawl," and the space inside their walls had to be conserved. The result is that narrow streets and alleyways with few, if any, open squares are typical of every "old city" in the world. Sometimes, to exploit the limited area more efficiently, arches were built over sections of the streets so that rooms could be constructed above them (though this option was not adopted in Jerusalem).

The city planners of ancient Jerusalem also had to address themselves to the layout of a city that attracted tourism. Imagine tens of thousands of pilgrims streaming toward the Temple Mount only to find that they would have to negotiate a maze of narrow streets and alleys. How would they ever find their way? Our discoveries confirmed that the planning of public space in the vicinity of the Temple Mount differed from what was common in other cities. Unusually broad streets were laid out, paved with large stones, delineated with curbstones, and occasionally extended outward to create squares. A design of this sort clearly catered to the needs of large crowds.

The paving stones ranged from about 1 to 18 square meters apiece, most being 2–4 square meters. A large stone that is 18 square meters (3 × 6 meters) and around 40 centimeters thick weighs close to 19 tons; the weight of a medium-sized paving stone is 5–10 tons. A number of factors accounted for the fact that these enormous stones were used to pave the streets. The first was an architectural-aesthetic consideration: since the walls of the Temple Mount were built out of large ashlars, paving streets with small stones would have destroyed the architechtonic consistency of the area. (This rule also applies to the present, so that the plaza fronting the Wailing Wall, recently repaved to accommodate the congregation of worshippers, also uses large paving stones.)

Another factor relates to the amazing durability of the stones. Even though huge boulder-like ashlars fell onto the street from the heights of the retaining walls, the pavement stone hardly cracked or was jostled out of place. This incredible soundness resulted not only from the great weight of the pavement stones but from the technique used to create the foundations under the streets. The depth of the foundations was an average of 6–7 meters but sometimes reached as much as 20 meters. One of two methods was used to construct them: sometimes the pavement was laid over stone vaults, just like the method used to construct the Temple Mount esplanade. This was the approach generally taken where the street was higher than the square fronting it, and the consequent void was exploited to house shops and other commercial enterprises facing on the square. The second method was to lay the street over a bed of detritus and earth as fill. A fill of this sort usually had to be stabilized, if it was to be expected to hold up, and for that purpose the engineers working on the Temple Mount developed the following procedure: they built stone walls along the length and width of the streets until they had achieved something resembling a chessboard arrangement of squares measuring about 3 square meters a piece. (The walls were about 80 centimeters thick and reached down to bedrock.) Then huge hauls of detritus and earth dug up in the course of the building operation were poured in between these walls. Once the "cubes" were filled and the paving stones were laid on top of them, the fill was about as solid as you could get.

A paved street ran along the entire length of the southern wall (for a distance of about 280 meters), and since its purpose was to serve as an access to the Hulda Gates, we shall call it Hulda Gates Street. It began in the west at Tyropoeon Valley Street, which was 6 meters lower than the threshold of the Hulda Gates, so that its planners had to compensate for the difference. They did so by means of steps. Five steps were built eight meters east of the junction with Tyropoeon Valley Street, to make up for a height of 1 meter. The street then continued on this new level, rising by means of steps at standard intervals along the 70-meter stretch from the southeast corner up to the western Hulda Gate. From there to the eastern Hulda Gate, a distance of about 80 meters, the street remained level, but beyond the eastern gate it began to descend again by means of interspaced steps until it met the street running along the eastern wall of the Temple Mount. Hulda Gates Street was 7 meters wide. Its eastern portion can be reconstructed with the aid of the vaults over which it was paved (though only their walls survived), because the fires that broke out in the vaults when Titus' armies destroyed the city left blisters and black stains on the stones of the southern retaining wall, making it easy to reconstruct them.

Fronting the Hulda Gates were staircases that connected the upper street (Hulda Gates Street) with the squares below (where the pilgrims gathered). Only heavily damaged sections of this staircase remain in the area of the western Hulda Gate. We do not know how far the square extended southward, but it is clear that it did not exceed 20 meters, for beyond that point the bedrock drops sharply. We can assume that the square was 13 meters wide, which was the rule for the plazas below the Temple Mount. Between the staircases leading up to the eastern and the western Hulda Gates, respectively, was another square built on the site of the Acra Fortress.

Hulda Gates Street

The Staircases to the Hulda Gates

The notion of excavating near the Hulda Gates seemed like more of a fantasy than an option for us because we had been digging within the bounds of the Old City, but to unravel the secrets hidden in the area of the Hulda Gates we would have to move outside the city wall. And that raised a problem bound up with the ticklish matter of possession. The areas we had excavated up to that point were in the public domain, but the sector outside the city wall belonged to the *waqf* and was leased out to individuals. Would the trustees of the *waqf* and the lessees agree to an excavation there? For decades the trustees had refused to give their blessing to excavations in Jerusalem, but perhaps now, after seeing the fascinating finds uncovered from the early Moslem period, they would make an exception and allow us to dig. Thus the real question was how the needs of a purely scientific venture would fare in a contest with political interests.

I embarked on some intelligence work to find out who the lessees were and how they felt about the issue. It turned out that quite a few people were involved but it would be necessary to convince only one key figure

The street at the foot of the western wall

The curbstones that delineate the western side of this street

Debris from the western wall on the pavement

Uncovering the stairs in front of the western Hulda Gate

A detail of the same staircase *in situ*

for the rest to concede that our operation was not at all sinister and could even be of benefit. At the same time, I tried to ensure that even if the *waqf* did not back our venture, at least it would not instigate the lessees against it. Once again we invited a number of Moslem notables to visit the excavations, and once again they were convinced that the finds relating to Islam, together with the rest of the discoveries enabling us to decipher the secrets of ancient Jerusalem, were of major import. They were also convinced that there was no political motive behind our work and that the

The stairs after their restoration was completed

charges about our desire to undermine the foundations of the Al Aqsa Mosque were totally unfounded. On the contrary, all the structurally weak points around the mosque, which had been neglected for years, were now receiving proper treatment. Many cups of savory coffee were downed during my subsequent talk with the trustees of the *waqf*, and the conversation rambled from one subject to another, in the best spirit of Oriental hospitality, before we got round to the matter of excavating south of the city wall. Here, again, we spent hours upon hours talking and drinking at

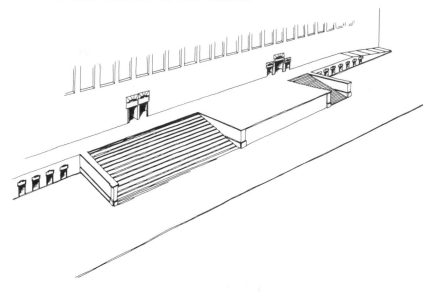

The staircases fronting the Hulda Gates and the shops below the upper street

a calm, leisurely pace before a contract was drawn up placing areas south of the Old City wall at our disposal for the purpose of excavation, reconstruction, and preservation of the remains.

Not that the matter ended there. After we began working on the site, certain parties that will here remain unnamed used the agreement as an excuse to vilify a number of Moslem religious dignitaries. One of the *qadis* who signed the lease with us was even forced to relinquish his post, though he honored his signature and obligations anyway. The judge in question came from one of the leading Palestinian nationalist families of the previous generation (he was a relative of the former *mufti* of Jerusalem, Haj Amin el-Husseini), and his traditional rivals seized on the opportunity to blacken his name in the local Arab press. Sometime later I met the ex-*qadi*, who lamented to me, "You see, my friend, there are those who sell their land to Jews and their souls to the Devil and no one says so much as a word. But when I lease land for the purpose of a scientific project whose discoveries tell us so much about the Moslem past in Jerusalem and of the kings and prophets whom we, too, venerate, see what happens. Still, you should know that I do not regret what I have done — not one whit. I am old, and in standing before God I am confident that what I did is for the best."

Hoping to vindicate such courage, we began to dig and the results were not long in coming. After working our way down 1 meter through dust and dirt, we came upon a structure built of stone. The quality of its construction and the size of its stones left no room for error: our find dated to the Second Temple period. As the excavation continued, we were able to confirm our initial hunch that what we had hit upon was one of the magnificent staircases connecting a public square with Hulda Gates Street. Since the Hulda Gates were the main entrance to and exit from the Temple Mount, these steps had once borne tens of thousands of pilgrims to the ceremonies in the Temple.

The patriarch of the Ethiopian Church happened to visit the dig soon after we had uncovered these steps. "Is it possible that Jesus and the Apostles walked up these stairs?" he asked. "There's no doubt about it," I told him. "This is the main staircase that led to the Temple Mount, and it was the only one used by pilgrims bound for the Temple." Upon hearing my answer, a wave of emotion swept over the patriarch and his retinue, and we paused so that they could offer up prayers on the spot.

The traffic to and from the Temple Mount in the south moved via the Hulda Gates. These were two distinct gates bearing the same name, one in the east, the other in the west; one for entry, the other for exit. The public ascended the stairs and entered the compound through the eastern gate, made a circuit around the Temple, and exited via the western gate. The staircase fronting the eastern Hulda Gate was 15 meters wide, while the one leading down from the western gates was 65 meters wide. It was taken for granted that the entry to and exit from the Temple area had to be done in a leisurely manner, as a Jew was coming to the holiest of holy places, which demanded that he be composed and not distracted in any way. Stairs, by their very nature, have a way of spurring a man to increase his pace as he ascends them. If we watch a man go up or down stairs, it's plain to see that he is moving faster than his normal gait, and the architects wanted to impede this natural tendency to speed up on the stairs. In the Acropolis in Athens, the builders took this mission to extremes by making each of the ascending steps more than half a meter high, forcing the climber to take measured steps. The solution adopted in Jerusalem was far more pleasant and required less exertion. The height of each step here is 18–25 centimeters and allows one to ascend or descend without any effort whatsoever. To slow down the pace, the *depth* of each step varied, one being 30 centimeters, the next 90 in an alternating pattern. Thus it is not necessary to invest physical effort into the climb, but the alternating depth of the steps makes it impossible to walk quickly — a satisfying solution indeed. I once overheard one of the Israeli volunteers explaining this concept to a group of high school students. "Two thousand years ago, the Greeks were an athletic people, while many of the Jews suffered from heart disease due to a lack of physical activity and too much time spent sitting and studying." The next day the youngsters rolled up their sleeves and worked at twice their usual pace!

Tyropoeon Valley Street and Its Bazaar

The main street at the foot of the Temple Mount ran parallel to the western wall and, like Hulda Gates Street, it was paved with large stones that accorded it a look of grandeur. The street was bordered on its western side by high curbstones that prevented rainwater from running into the shops. These curbstones were uncovered at a distance of 13 meters from the western wall, which is also where we found the pillar of Robinson's Arch. The point of this coincidence is clear: since the arch undoubtedly bridged the street, the street must have been 13 meters wide. The problem was that we turned up curbstones wherever we dug on the western side of the street but no sign of curb or pavement stones anywhere on the eastern edge of the street, bordering on the western wall. We archaeologists have ready-made answers for inconsistencies of this kind: "The stones must have been pillaged at some time in the past" is one of them. But this simplistic explanation, designed to gag a nagging conscience, did not satisfy us. I was determined to uncover the elusive eastern edge of the street, so we opened up a square about 4 meters from the Temple Mount wall and after a few days' work had the problem licked. For in that square the street turned up again, about 3 meters west of the wall, and this time it was lined with curbstones, just as on its western side. This find taught us that the street was 10, not 13 meters wide, and that it was lined with curbstones on both sides. We failed to find any signs of a street directly adjoining the western wall not because they had been pillaged but because they simply weren't there.

The reason why became clear later on in the dig. All along the western side of the street, we found a line of small structures built close together, and when we began excavating the eastern side we found the foundations of similar structures there, too. These were the remains of dozens of shops set along both sides of Tyropoeon Valley Street, which was Jerusalem's central bazaar during that period. Here is where the tens of thousands of visitors to Jerusalem strolled along at leisure and did their shopping. The price of a square meter of land along this street must have been among the highest in all Jerusalem, which was a very costly city as it was. Even the pillar of Robinson's Arch was exploited: because of its sheer bulk, no less than four shops were built into it. One of them yielded a cache of coins, stone storage jars, and stone weights (the latter including weights marked by municipal supervisors employed to maintain order in the markets and ensure fair trade practices). We followed the terminology of the Second Temple period in referring to this area as a market, but it would be more accurate to call it a commercial center, a place where you could find whatever your heart desired, from restaurants and grocery stores to perfumeries and spice stores, banks (for changing money), and clothing stores (precursors of the contemporary "boutique").

When the French film director Claude Lelouch came to see the dig in preparation for films on biblical themes, his comment was, "Why give it that strange name, Tyropoeon Valley Street? Let's call it call it the Champs-Elysée." And that is just what it was, a Second-Temple period version of the Champs-Elysée, the most prestigious commercial center in Jerusalem. Not far from here were the City Council buildings and the Jerusalem Archive, where documents and promissory notes, contracts, and the like were stored. Further on were the Chamber of Hewn Stone, where the Sanhedrin (or chief rabbinical council) met, and other public buildings.

Tyropoeon Valley Street is the name Josephus uses when referring to this thoroughfare (although in one place he calls it the Lower Market). As to the origin of this name, we know that in the First Temple period a narrow riverbed passed by here and was popularly referred to as "the valley." In the course of time, as the area developed, it was no longer possible to distinguish the valley from its surroundings, for it was "buried" under many structures; the only memento of it was the name of the street. (Incidentally, this is an ongoing tradition, for the street that descends from Damascus Gate toward the temple Mount today is called Valley Street in both Hebrew and Arabic.) The word *tyropoeon* means "cheesemaker" in Greek, and some believe the valley is so named because it was once a center of the cheese industry, though others posit that the valley took the name from the cheese stalls in the commercial center. Yet another possibility is that it was named after the owner of its lands. Tryphon was a Greek name that was absorbed into the pool of Jewish names during that period. In fact, Tryphon or Tarphon were common names at the time, and the Tyropoeon Valley may well have been the valley of the Tryphon family. In another combination of circumstances, the Tryphon family may also have been cheesemakers. Be that as it may, we do know that naming valleys and riverbeds after the owner of the property was not uncommon in Jerusalem, one example being the valley named after the Ben Hinnom family.

Tyropoeon Valley Stret extended the full length of the western wall and continued southward to the Siloam Pool. It was first uncovered, together with its curbstones and drainage system, in the 1920s by a British expedition working in the southern part of the City of David. As its northern end, the street continued up to the magnificent gate in the northern wall known today as the Damascus Gate.

The Street to the Upper City

In describing Jerusalem and the area of the Temple Mount, Josephus speaks of the gate above Robinson's Arch by saying that it "led to the other part of the city [i.e., to the Upper City], from which it was separated by many steps going down to the ravine [Tyropoeon Valley] and from here up again to the hill" (*Jewish Antiquities*, XV: 410). Whoever wanted to make his way to the Upper City or the western hill of Jerusalem — now the site of the Jewish Quarter, the Armenian Quarter, and Mount Zion, and in Josephus' time the site of the choice residential neighborhoods in Jerusalem — would have to follow the street crossing from the commercial center to the residential quarters. When we began to excavate west of the shops along Tyropoeon Valley Street, we found exactly what we expected: slightly north of Robinson's Arch, a paved street branches out from Tyropoeon Valley Street and climbs up in the direction of the western hill. It is 4 meters wide and is constructed of a number of stone steps followed by a small plateau, steps again and another plateau, and so on alternating repeatedly. The steps are built over vaults whose interiors were exploited for the drainage system.

This was the street that carried traffic from the Temple Mount to the residential and commercial areas on the western hill and on to the king's palace and citadel near today's Jaffa Gate. As a matter of fact, a number of such streets ran parallel to it from Tyropoeon Valley Street toward the Upper City. In the Upper City itself, a perpendicular street running north–south bisected Jerusalem from the present-day Damascus Gate to the top of Mount Zion. Like Tyropoeon Valley Street, this thoroughfare also had a commercial name — the Upper Market — and was one of the commercial centers serving residents of and visitors to the Upper City and the royal palace. Between these two main north–south avenues lined by scores of shops was a network of less imposing streets running in both directions, and this general layout of the city still remains in force.

The Eastern Overpass and the Scapegoat

Near the "seam" on the eastern wall are the remains of an arch that was similar to the Robinson's Arch in the west, and its discovery indicates the existence of an overpass that helped to regulate the flow of traffic on the street below and over the bridge above it. At the very least, it implies that a paved street ran under the arch — for our purposes let us call it the Eastern Street — and it must have been within the bounds of the city (meaning inside the city wall). But unlike the case with Robinson's Arch and Wilson's Arch on the western side of the Temple Mount, which led to the esplanade level of the enclosure, the overpass in the east led to the level of the vaults built under the platform. As we noted earlier, these vaults were used as storage areas, which allows us to surmise that the donations and sacrifices brought to the Temple by pilgrims — sheep, wheat, fruit, firewood, and the like — were delivered to the storage areas via this overpass.

The gate atop this eastern overpass also seems to have had another purpose, namely, the exit for the goats released into the desert — the

The remains of the overpass arch on the eastern wall near the "seam"

literal scapegoats. Thus, the overpass mentioned in the Mishna as the "Hairy Goat" may well be this one.

Barclay's Gate Square

One access to the Temple Mount, mentioned in the Midot Tractate of the Mishna as Coponius' Gate, was located in the western wall and is evidently to be identified with the impressive gate that now bears the name of the American scholar who first studied it, J. T. Barclay. When we were tracing the layout of the streets on the western side of the Temple Mount, we decided to open up an investigatory square north of Robinson's Arch. After completing the usual procedures and sketching and photographing the pavement from the early Moslem period, we began to remove the paving stones and continued digging down to the Herodian pavement. But there, under the Moslem pavement, we came upon a plastered cistern that apparently dated to the Byzantine era. To delve deeper into this matter, we cleared a spot just north of Barclay's Gate to dig another square, only to find that a great surprise awaited us. When we reached a depth of 4 meters under the floor of the Moslem structure, there before our eyes was the Herodian pavement. But even though we were on a straight line with the curbstones that bordered the street, no curbstones were found here, and the street appeared to continue onward in a westerly direction! This time we decided not to traffic in guesses and extended our square until we reached the end of the street moving westward and ascertained what it all meant. Enlarging our square by another 4 meters showed us that the street was still there and, as expected, was delineated by the same curbstones we had come upon earlier. The solution to the riddle was essentially simple: since we were standing before an entry gate to the Temple Mount where "traffic jams" were created at "rush hour" by the crowds gathered there, the Temple Mount's architects deemed it wise to create a plaza in front of the gate. This public square was a reflection of foresight and a profound understanding of city planning.

"The Invisible Wall"

Jerusalem's walls received a relatively detailed treatment by Josephus, but nowhere in his writings is there any mention of a wall that fortified the Upper City on the east. One of the greatest scholars of ancient Jerusalem, Professor Michael Avi-Yonah, believed that such a wall had to have existed, and here is what he wrote about it:

Inside the First Wall there had once been an "invisible wall" about which Josephus says nothing. The existence of such a wall was a necessary corollary of the historical situation, for the Upper City stood up to a siege [by the Romans] for an entire month from the 10th of Av until the 8th of Elul), even after the Temple Mount and the Lower City had fallen to the enemy. This stubborn resistance makes us believe that the Upper Cith [which we call the western hill] was also fortified on the east ("On Your Walls, Jerusalem," *Jerusalem Through the Ages*, 1969).

Many other scholars accepted this view, and if you look at a contemporary atlas of Second Temple Jerusalem, you will find that the wall mooted by Avi-Yonah winds across the slopes of the western hill overlooking the Temple Mount.

During various stages of our excavations, we spread out over all the slopes of the western hill, but neither in the course of our search for a royal bridge to the Upper City nor in the excavation outside the Dung Gate did we find any trace of a wall from the Second Temple period. On the other hand, we did find the remains of residential buildings that had been destroyed when the Romans captured the city. Thus we again had an opportunity to see for ourselves that Josephus' descriptions were highly reliable, and if he failed to mention something as important as a wall in this area, it was because no such wall existed. When the Romans invested Jerusalem, the city was divided up among the groups of Jewish defenders known as the Zealots. We can assume that they holed up in the Upper City by barricading the streets leading up from the Tyropoeon Valley with piles of stones. From a functional viewpoint, these barricades were essentially a kind of wall, though strictly speaking they were not. When I mentioned this reading of the situation to Professor Avi-Yonah, a scholar known for his uncommon magnanimity, he acknowledged its virtues and had a change of heart about his own theory. Unfortunately, he passed away before being able to retract it in print.

Drainage Systems

As Jerusalem is a city built on the edge of the desert, the supply of water has always been an issue of major concern to its inhabitants. This is the reason why the city was first settled on the hill above the Gihon Spring. In the Second Temple period, Jerusalem boasted a population of more than 150,000 people and hosted another 100,000 or so pilgrims during the holidays. Add to these human needs the demands of the Temple itself, which used an appreciable amount of water for ritual purposes, and we can begin to appreciate the magnitude of the problem confronting the city fathers and city planners. The Gihon Spring could not begin to provide water for such a large population, and home owners assumed responsibility for their own needs by carving cisterns out of the rock under their houses. These cisterns were well plastered so that the water from natural precipitation that collected in the winter could be saved for use in the dry summer months. The Temple and the king's palace were supplied by the springs near Bethlehem (Solomon's Pools), by means of an aqueduct that was an impressive engineering feat. Even so, the city required additional supplies of water for daily use and to maintain its reserves, for agriculture and the gardens on the slope of the Kidron Valley, and to meet the needs of many of the City's residents whose cisterns were not filled. The Siloam Pool was designed for just this purpose. Originally it had been a ritual bath built by King Hezekiah at the end of the eighth century B.C., but in the Second Temple period, after being enlarged, it served as a reservoir that held tens of thousands of cubic meters of water. To supply this reservoir, a sophisticated drainage system was created to catch every drop of rainwater that fell in the city's public areas — streets and squares —

left: A drainage canal south of the Temple Mount

right: A drainage canal west of the Temple Mount

and carry it to the Siloam Pool. This elaborate system, uncovered under Tyropoeon Valley Street near the western wall, was first investigated by the excavators of the Palestine Exploration Fund under the supervision of Charles Warren. They uncovered it while digging down to examine the pillar of Robinson's Arch. We decided to go in and examine it for ourselves, and in doing so we discovered some fascinating details.

Wherever we reached the pavement of the Second Temple period, we realized it was laid over a ramified network of drainage canals crafted out of stone. The ceilings of these canals were sometimes vaulted, sometimes flat, their height was 1 meter or more, compared to a width of 60–80 centimeters. Part of this drainage system was carved out of the rock; part of it had rock-carved sides but a ceiling consisting of a stone dome or flat-stone plaques. The system evidently originated in the area of the Damascus Gate and ended at the Siloam Pool. In a number of places its builders came across large chambers (ancient graves or pools) and integrated them into the network.

As we noted earlier, some of the streets branching out from Tyropoeon Valley Street and leading to the Upper City were paved over stone vaults, and a few of these vaults were utilized as control cells for the drainage network. If you walk through the streets of the city today, you can see municipal employees climbing down manholes into subterranean cubicles whence they have access to the sewers needing service or repair. The same was true in Jerusalem during the Second Temple period. Each of the vaults provided access to three different drainage channels of the upper system. If the channels became blocked or damaged, the workers would enter these cells to repair them. On the whole, the system was a paragon of advanced planning.

During the rainy season today, a cloud burst can sometimes swamp the streets of the new city of Jerusalem because its drainage system is unable to absorb the water quickly enough. Yet we never had this problem in the area of the excavation. There the water flowed swiftly through the underground channels, and no puddles ever developed. It appears that the drainage system built during Herod's day is still working efficiently, collecting and carrying the rainwater to its destination.

Excavating this drainage system was particularly hard work. The truth is that more time was spent measuring, photographing, and studying it than actually digging. Our progress was hampered by many technical difficulties, including poor lighting and the incredibly high humidity in the channels even at the height of summer. I can remember the fierce struggle between the volunteers for an assignment to the drainage system, though after a few days they understood their mistake and begged to be reassigned. What seemed at first glance like a haven from the merciless summer sun turned into a torture chamber of humidity. Needless to say, during the winter we couldn't work there at all. Removing the detritus is an impossible task, so we often found ourselves shifting it from one spot to another just to glean a few details. In order to work properly and thoroughly in the drainage system, it will be necessary to open up additional access routes and create bearable working conditions, but to date we have not been able to do so. Perhaps the future will bring new technologies and make the full exposure and investigation of this system a feasible goal.

The Largest Arches in the Classical World

In 1838 the dean of the Bible faculty of the New York Theological Seminary, Edward Robinson, visited Jerusalem as the realization of a childhood dream. Scholarly work that resulted from that pilgrimage was published in three volumes in 1841 and led to a major change in the study of the history and geography of Palestine. Many consider Robinson to be the father of modern research on these subjects — and with good reason. Among the salient and fascinating finds he uncovered in his work here were vestiges of a huge destroyed arch, which he first discerned from telltale signs in an otherwise undistinguished vegetable plot in Jerusalem. While touring around the Temple Mount's walls, Robinson spotted some very large stones protruding out of the western wall 12 meters north of its southern corner and immediately grasped that they were the remains of an enormous arch. Having brushed up on his Josephus, he assumed it was one of the arches supporting the bridge that led from the Temple Mount over the Tyropoeon Valley to the Upper City.

Naturally enough, the scholars who followed Robinson adopted his premise, and in 1867, when the Palestine Exploration Fund expedition arrived to conduct research surveys and excavations by the Temple Mount, it was taken for granted that studying this arch would be one of its major objectives. The custom of the day was to name a major architectural element after the first scholar to discover it. This one was christened Robinson's Arch and has been thus known in the literature, and by the public at large, ever since.

It was Charles Wilson, one of the leading excavators of the Palestine Exploration Fund, who followed Robinson by discovering another arch protruding from the western wall well north of Robinson's discovery. This one was unearthed below the houses of the Old City and was still intact! Over the years the name Wilson's Arch attached to it, and that is how it is still known today. Needless to say, it likewise served as an important object of inquiry for the Palestine Exploration Fund's excavations.

Since the location of Wilson's Arch coincided exactly with that of the bridge mentioned by Josepus, its discovery created something of a problem: two arches had been found in the field and they were assumed to be the remains of two bridges, but the historical sources made mention only of one bridge. It wasn't long before the plot thickened, for the remains of yet a third arch were discerned in the southern part of the eastern wall, near the "seam." Since this arch was not mentioned in any written sources, scholars came up with a convenient solution by arguing that a historian like Josephus would not have bothered to go into the architectural details of an area unless they happened to catch his eye or were directly pertinent to a point he was developing. Others believed the bridge that had once rested on Wilson's Arch was in fact a structure mentioned in connection with an event that occurred prior to Herod's reign, namely, Pompey's conquest of Jerusalem in 63 B.C. Josephus tells us that Pompey reached the Temple Mount over the bridge that connected the esplanade with the Upper City. But since we know that the western wall that sup-

A reconstruction of Robinson's Arch and the shops lining the street that ran under it

ported Wilson's Arch was built in Herod's day, the hypothesis that the arch held up the bridge crossed by Pompey necessarily falls by the wayside. Pompey could not possibly have crossed a bridge built over an arch that was supported by a wall built forty years after he captured the city!

To unravel the enigma of how many bridges there were and exactly where they were located, we must return for a moment to the excavators of the Palestine Exploration Fund. In a complex maneuver — like all of their operations in the area of the Temple Mount — the fund's teams excavated the sites of the two arches spanning out of the western wall. Being well versed in the rules of classical architecture, they knew that the arches of this period were rounded; thus if any section of the arch were to be found in the field, it could be used to calculate the diameter of the whole. A calculation of this kind done for Robinson's Arch revealed that the diameter of the arch's vault was 13 meters — exactly that of Wilson's Arch (which was found intact). Since Robinson's Arch had been totally destroyed, Charles Warren's expedition used this data to begin digging at a distance of 13 meters from the western wall in the hope of finding the arch's pier. Using a vertical shaft 1 meter square (the standard size of the shafts dug by that expedition), Warren's team began to work its way down into the earth, and sure enough, after reaching a depth of 8 meters, they came upon a massive stone structure identified as the arch's pier. The excavators also found the stone pavement of the Second Temple period and the drainage system beneath it.

Relative to its limited area, Warren's dig yielded a wealth of finds. Nevertheless, his team could not have known then all that we do now after systematically excavating the entire area. Once they had uncovered the pier of Robinson's Arch, following the widespread assumption that this arch was the last in a chain of several over which a bridge had been built, the British excavators continued to sink shafts at 13-meter intervals in search of the remains of other arches. What they uncovered in those shafts bore no resemblance at all to the remnant of Robinson's Arch. Still, they convinced themselves that the data they had acquired justified the conclusion that they had found the remains of additional arches that had supported the bridge linking the Temple Mount with the Upper City. This bridge, they posited, had been built over a total of seven arches and was more than 100 meters long and 15.2 meters wide — according with the length (from north to south) of Robinson's (and, we might add, Wilson's) Arch. Similarly, they assumed that the pedestrian level of the bridge coincided with the height of the Temple Mount esplanade, for that was the height of the arch. They further postulated that a staircase must have been built at the point where the bridge reached the Upper City, since the topography at that spot was a few dozen meters higher than the elevation of the Temple Mount and therefore of the bridge as well. In any case, the belief that Robinson's Arch was the last link in a series of arches built over the Tyropoeon Valley to support a bridge was universally accepted — though I should note that one of the outstanding scholars of that generation, Conrad Schick, did not take this theory at face value. Noting that the finds in the rest of the test shafts did not lend themselves to a reconstruction of piers like that of Robinson's Arch, he believed that only the final link in the chain was built of stone, while the rest of the bridge was a narrow wooden structure. Yet even Schick subscribed to the view that Robinson's Arch supported a bridge, and over the years his particu-

The Excavations of the Palestine Exploration Fund

Robinson's Arch above a vegetable plot before the excavations began, 1968

Robinson's Arch after being excavated, 1970

The western pier of Robinson's Arch

lar rendering of that bridge was forgotten; the conclusions of the British expedition became holy writ.

For what purpose could a bridge that was more than 100 meters long and 15.2 meters wide possibly have been built? The main accesses to the Temple Mount — the two Hulda Gates in the southern wall and Barclay's Gate in the western wall — were on street level, and it was through these gates that the public at large passed on its visits to the Temple's precincts. Who, then, was served by the gate built above Robinson's Arch?

For decades scholars have offered their answer as an open-and-shut case. The bridge was built to serve King Herod alone, and for this reason it was dubbed "the Royal Bridge" (to distinguish it from "the High Priest's Bridge," whose final link was Wilson's Arch). How did they arrive at this conclusion? First, they reasoned, who if not Herod would build himself such a unique and majestic entrance to the Temple Mount? Clearly this approach is consonant with the hostile attitude that most of the scholars displayed toward Herod, but as we have seen their harsh assessment of him as an incorrigible megalomaniac was quite unjustified. The second reason was based on the writings of Josephus, who stated that a grand hall was built in the southern part of the Temple Mount, extending across the compound from east to west, and it was approached through the gate above Robinson's Arch. This hall, which Josephus described in detail, was known as the Royal Portico or Triple Portico. The Greek term for a royal portico is a basilica and is derived from *basileus*, meaning king. This etymology led earlier scholars to believe that the king had royal offices in the southern part of the Temple Mount, and it was to reach these offices easily that he built a monumental bridge. The glaring contrast between the huge dimensions of the bridge and the small royal entourage that used it did not raise doubts among the researchers who propounded this solution. On the contrary, it merely confirmed their censorious view of Herod as an insufferable egotist. To get a feel for the imposing dimensions of this bridge, it is enough to note that its width, 15.2 meters, approximates that of a modern four-lane highway! Indeed, a man would need an ample measure of arrogance or be suffering from delusions of grandeur to build such a bridge for his private use.

In his description of the Temple Mount in *Jewish Antiquities*, Josephus stated that:

The fourth front of this [court], facing south, also had gates in the middle and had over it the Royal Portico, which had three aisles extended in length from the eastern to the western ravine ... It was a structure more noteworthy than any under the sun ... The height of the portico was so great that if anyone looked down from its roof-top ... he would become dizzy and his vision would be unable to reach the end of so measureless a depth. Now the columns [of the portico] stood in four rows, one opposite the other all along — the fourth row was attached to the wall built of stone — and the thickness of each column was such that it would take three men with outstretched arms touching one another to envelop it; its height was twenty-seven feet ... and the number of all the columns was a hundred and sixty-two, and their capitals were ornamented in the Corinthian style of carving, which caused amazement by the magnificence of its whole effect. Since there were four rows, they made three aisles among them, under the porticoes (xv. 411 ff.).

The Royal Portico was indeed unique in both its size and beauty for, as Josephus tells us, it was composed of three parts and its ceiling was

Why Was an Overpass Built?

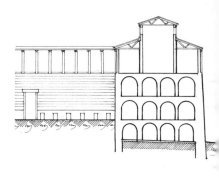

The Basilica in the South

supported by pillars. The two side halls, or aisles, were of equal width but narrower than the central hall, in addition to being about half its height. The southern side of the building was sealed by the southern wall of the Temple Mount, but its northern side had openings facing onto the Temple Mount esplanade and offering a magnificent view. A portico (or *stoa* in Greek) was usually a structure that extended from a blank wall on one side to a colonnade on the other. A more elaborate form, called the triple portico, was designed to roof over a broad area. Since the length of wooden beams was necessarily limited, additional supports were needed for the ceiling of such a structure. The resultant shape was a central hall and two side aisles. The central hall was built higher than the aisles to accommodate windows, for it was naturally the darker part of the building. Earlier we noted that this architectural mode had two names, a triple

A plan and section of the Royal Portico at the southern end of the Temple Mount

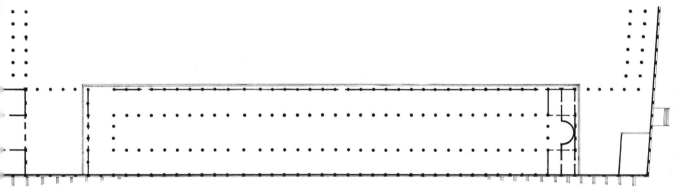

portico (from the obvious fact that it had three parts) and a basilica, or "royal hall," because it had an air of regal magnificence (compared with a standard portico). At any rate, the term was basically technical and in no way implies any association with the king. Incidentally, remains of a portico that was known as a basilica are to be found in the Agora in Athens, which served as the religious, commercial, and political center of the city. This portico was apparently built in the fifth century B.C., and in this case, too, the name derived solely from the elegance of the structure.

New Conclusions About Robinson's Arch

Our excavations began near the southern wall of the Temple Mount, and it wasn't until the work got into a steady routine that we found time to survey the area of the western wall, particularly by Robinson's Arch, and planned to start working there too. We knew that fascinating finds awaited us, for excavating the entire area could answer the question of how this vital sector of the Temple Mount was organized. But we could not possibly have foreseen that our word would change the prevailing view about Robinson's Arch, the bridge that it supported, and the purported arches to the west of it. All we wanted to achieve was a better understanding of how this massive bridge fit into the city's layout. It was not difficult to get work going in the area because it was still covered by a vegetable patch, just as it had been in Robinson's day 130 years ago. Once the problems of land ownership were settled, we embarked on a systematic excavation of the whole section west of Robinson's Arch.

After removing appreciable amounts of the upper detritus, our aim was to reach the arch's pier and use it as a point of reference for the rest of

One of the pillars in the Royal
Portico that took "three men with
outstretched arms touching one
another to envelop"

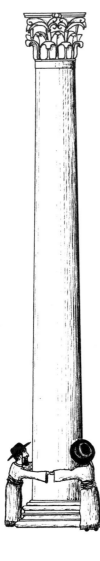

right: A reconstruction of the interior
of the Royal Portico

the dig. Hardly an hour had passed from the start of the excavation when
the archaeologist supervising that area, Vasily Constantino, summoned
me with cries of joy. Vasily, who hails from Salonika, Greece, came to
Israel after having read Leon Uris' novel *Exodus* and stayed on to study
archaeology here. He joined our team at the very beginning and was one
of its leading lights. We used to tease him that his work in uncovering the
glories of the area around the Temple Mount was a way of making

amends for Antiochus' nefarious deeds in Jerusalem. Vasily wasn't the type to let his emotions run away with him, so we were all very curious about what was causing those whoops of joy. It turned out that near what we presumed to be the northern part of the pillar, his team had dug up the remains of a wooden form approximately 1 meter square and consisting of boards in an advanced state of rot. It wasn't difficult to identify this find: what we had in hand was a memento of the British expedition's dig for the pillar exactly 100 years earlier. Then, as now, the excavation site was covered with crumbly detritus mixed with gravel. Every strike of the pickax could cause a rock slide, so the members of the British expedition shored up the sides of their shafts with wooden forms to prevent a hail of detritus and stones coming down on them. The sense of continuity evoked by this tangible link with the previous expedition — the first and last to dig in the vicinity of the Temple Mount until our arrival — is what prompted Vasily to carry on so. What's more, now we knew for sure that we would reach the pillar. The discovery of those wooden boards spurred on the volunteers, and a week after beginning to dig on that site we reached the top of the destroyed pier.

It took another few day's work before the entire pier was revealed, and what a magnificent structure it was: 15.2 meters long (from north to south) and 3.6 meters wide. This bulk was necessary for the pier to bear the weight of the arch. Considering that it had been destroyed at the time of Titus' siege of Jerusalem, the pier was in a remarkably good state of preservation. Its northern side still had five courses of stone, for a height of more than 5 meters, and it was 2–3 meters high on its other sides. Built out of the same monumental stones as the ashlars used in the retaining walls (and with the same stonework), the pier contained four voids with openings facing eastward. After a while we realized that these were four shops that had been part of the commercial center of Tyropoeon Valley Street, the Lower Market mentioned by Josephus. The fact that these shops were built into the pier indicates that the bazaar was conceived as a

The overpass of Robinson's Arch leading to the Royal Portico

single unit in the general blueprint of the Temple Mount area. We were able to certify that these hollow areas had indeed been stores by the stone weights, storage vessels, and abundance of coins found in one of them.

The third course of the pier was built out of extremely large stones that doubled as the lintels of the shop doors. To prevent these lintels from cracking or becoming otherwise damaged, or even destroyed, by the construction of additional layers of stone above them, the builders availed themselves of an engineering solution. They simply built the equivalent of mini-arches above the lintels to ease the burden above that particular course and then blocked up these arches with semicircular stones (which we found on the site). Once again we had tangible proof that a knowledge of engineering had been exploited to the full.

The pier of Robinson's Arch was uncovered at a distance of about 13 meters from the western wall, which supported the other end of the arch. At the point where the arch began to vault out from the western wall, we found a layer of smoothly dressed, oblong stones protruding from the wall to create the effect of a row of teeth (an architectural feature known, appropriately enough, as dentils). The pier also had these so-called dentils, all of which were found in secondary use in the wall of a Moslem building from the eighth century A.D. (This finds allowed us to reach the conclusion that the pier was still 11 meters high — the level of the dentils — at the onset of the early Moslem period.) Some scholars hold that these dentils played a role in the construction of the pier, while others believe they were supports for the wooden scaffolding that held the stones of the arch in place while it was being built. Since we were entertaining the idea of reconstructing the arch, we consulted one of the leading engineers in the country only to find that the mere creation of a form for building the arch was a complex problem. He told us to keep in mind that until all the stones of the arch are in place, culminating with the keystone, the form must bear their combined weight. In the case of Robinson's Arch, which was the largest in the world in its day, we're speaking about a collection of stones that weighed more than 1,000 tons. Naturally it took an unusually large and strong form to bear the weight of that mass.

Delving yet deeper into this technique, we discovered that the masons of antiquity, like the Arab builders today, made extensive use of earthen forms for building arches and domes. Simply put, they would pile up earth in the shape of a mound corresponding to the contour of the arch. This solution fulfilled the demand that the form be strong while saving on substantial quantities of wood in a country poor in timber. At the end of the construction process, when the keystone was laid, the mound of earth was simply cleared away, leaving a void. To build Robinson's Arch, a virtual hill of earth was required to constitute the form. This method of construction rules out the theory propounded by Warren (and adopted by his colleagues) that the arch caved in during the course of construction and had to be rebuilt, since there was no way that stones resting on a huge mound of earth could have collapsed. I mention this point because a large arch stone was uncovered in the water system, and the scholars of the British expedition explained it as debris from the arch that had collapsed during the building process. Assuming now that an earthen form was used, we must find another explanation for the presence of this stone between the ceiling of the water system and the earth fill under the street.

The arch on the eastern wall of the Temple Mount was built using the same style of dentils. Wilson's Arch is built differently, but we must keep in mind that its present form dates to a few centuries later (the original arch was destroyed, and its stones can be found on the pavement of the Second Temple period). Since these arches were built with the aid of earthen forms, the dentils found at the point where they began to curve outward from the wall and pier did not serve any role in their construction. Instead, they must have had an aesthetic purpose, namely, to draw attention to the spot where the arch begins to vault. Incidentaly, dentils are a fairly common element in piers from the Second Temple period and are found in mosaics and frescoes as well.

Once we had mastered all the data about the arch and its pillar, we decided to expand the dig and search for other signs of the conjectured bridge. To do so, we opened up the area to the west of the pier. Concrete details about the bridge and the arches supporting it were still obscure because the finds turned up by earlier excavators were both meager and tangential. We were disappointed but should not have been surprised that we could find absolutely no trace of a second or third pier where the long-standing premise held them to be. Finally we opened up an exploratory square close to the slope of the western hill, where the last in the series of piers should have been, but could find no evidence of one there, either. What we did find, instead, were the remains of buildings, ritual baths, and sections of a street dating to the Second Temple period, and that is when we realized that the apocryphal bridge surmised by the early investigators probably never existed. Some myths die hard, however, and despite the evidence before our eyes, the notion of a bridge held us in its thrall. We tried to justify the absence of piers by advancing the hypothesis that the bridge must have been supported by the roofs of buildings, Robinson's Arch (the final link) being the exception.

Proposal for a New Reconstruction

Then a very revealing architectural find turned up southwest of Robinson's Arch. After getting down past pavements and walls from the early Moslem period (the eighth century) and what was left of buildings from the Byzantine era (the sixth century), we began to uncover architectural remains from the Second Temple period — more specifically, from the era in which Herod's Temple stood. Slowly we grasped that these were the remains of vaults; then sections of arches began to turn up here and there. At first none of this appeared to be particularly special or propitious, for the arch and the vault were common structural elements in Herod's age. What's more, it was difficult to synthesize these elements into a single architectural picture, because remains from the Moslem and Byzantine periods were also scattered around the area and the vaults did not appear to have any visible connection between them.

But once we had finished excavating this area, it struck us that what had seemed to be a random collection of vaults and arches was actually a single, consolidated structure whose components bore an amazing degree of resemblance to elements in the pier of Robinson's Arch. First of all, the vaulted structures were contiguous, each being 15 meters deep (precisely the depth of Robinson's Arch) and about 5 meters wide. They were built to the west of and perpendicular to Robinson's Arch, beginning at the northern part of the pier and continuing southward for a distance of 35 meters. There were seven vaults in all, each one lower than the next, the highest being in the north and the lowest in the south. Even though the vaults were not found whole, we were able to reconstruct them exactly. Then a few dozen stone steps turned up in the ruins near these arches, including three steps that were still attached. Still later a number of steps were uncovered *in situ* above one of the vaults. That piece of the puzzle clued us to the fact that this multiple-arched structure was a staircase built to connect Tyropoeon Valley Street with the top of Robinson's Arch and its extension, the Royal Portico.

The picture that took shape from these finds was radically different from anything scholars had imagined until then. No longer was there talk of a bridge to ease the flow of traffic and shorten the route from the residential area of the Upper City to the Temple Mount. What we found instead was an elaborately conceived staircase for reaching the southern area of the esplanade (the Royal Portico) from Tyropoeon Valley Street. Later we also found that a complex of streets and stairs connected the area southwest of the Temple Mount with the Upper City. In essence, whoever approached the Temple Mount area from the Upper City used the steps leading to Tyropoeon Valley Street and, upon arrival, had the option of remaining in the Lower Market or ascending the staircase to the Royal Portico. If we turn to the written sources, we find that this is exactly how Josephus depicted the scene in this southwest corner. In writing about the four gates in the Temple Mount's western wall, he says of the southern gate (the one above Robinson's Arch): ". . . And the last [gate] led to the other part of the city, from which it was separated by many steps going down to the ravine and from here up again to the hill [Upper City] (*Jewish Antiquities*, xv. 411). What we have here is a straightforward and precise description: people ascended to and descended from the Temple Mount by a flight of steps. In retrospect, it is difficult to understand why the investigators (ourselves included) clung with such tenacity to the notion of a horizontal link, which is precisely the opposite of the written evidence.

A Public Thoroughfare

Once this picture became incontestably clear and the bridge theory collapsed, one question still remained: why was such an enormous effort invested in building Robinson's Arch? The explanation that it supported the king's access to the Temple Mount was not a very convincing one, on a number of counts. First, the traffic entailed first coming down from the Upper City, mostly via stairs, and then ascending another staircase to reach the Royal Portico — a rather arduous route for a royal personage. Second, this portico did not give access to the Temple itself, because the esplanade was divided by a low parapet or balustrade that did not block the view of the Temple and its courts from the basilica but absolutely prevented entry thereto. (This balustrade bore signs in Greek and Latin warning non-Jews against entering the Temple.) The main entrances to the Temple Mount were the Hulda Gates in the southern wall. If a separate entrance had been built for the king, we would expect it to lead him to the Temple, which this route emphatically did not. Moreover, separate royal access — and such a monumental one, at that — would surely have been noted by Josephus; after all, he wrote about the tunnel that Herod dug as an access to the fortress north of the Temple Mount. Equally important is the testimony of a non-Jewish traveler who visited Jerusalem before Herod's day and was amazed to see that the kings of the Jews entered the Temple Mount alongside the rest of the citizenry. They simply removed their shoes, like everyone else, and walked in with the crowd. The fact of the matter is that there was nothing extraordinary about this behavior: in the Second Temple period, the kings of the Jews regarded themselves — and were regarded by their subjects — as representatives of the people charged with running their affairs, not as rulers by God-given right. This approach was admittedly unusual among the nations of the day, but we have no evidence that any Judean king during the Second Temple period — Herod included — deviated from the egalitarian norm. In entering the Temple Mount, they evidently used the same gates as every other Jew.

Returning now to Robinson's Arch, its huge dimensions certainly do not suggest that it was designed to carry the sparse traffic of a royal entourage. It must therefore have served the public at large as an access route to the southern area of the Temple Mount, namely, the Royal Portico. In the classical world, public buildings meant to house banks, stock exchanges, and courts of justice were designed in the form of a basilica or triple portico, as described above, and basilicas of this kind were built alongside every urban commercial center or forum. As Jerusalem's commercial center was adjacent to the Temple Mount, on the main street that ran through the Tyropoeon Valley, a basilica was obviously called for there, too. Upon arriving in Jerusalem, visitors probably wanted to exchange money or deposit their cash or valuables for safekeeping, much as travelers do today. Moreover, various kinds of judicial hearings were conducted in the basilica, and the pilgrimage seasons were earmarked for precisely such sessions. Since the Temple Mount had grown to rather large dimensions, its southern section, which was not a holy place, was exploited for these purposes by building the basilica there. Conseqently there must have been a steady flow of traffic between the Lower Market and the basilica in the compound proper; and to avoid overcongestion or other snags, the complex centering on Robinson's Arch was devised. In effect, the arch was an architectural answer to the need to regulate the mass movement of pedestrians by means of an overpass. Today one can find its likes at many road junctions, but the overpass built onto the Temple Mount was the first of its kind. At the risk of belaboring a point, let me again stress that it was not the desire to build a monumental and spectacular structure that lay behind the planning and building effort involved in creating Robinson's Arch but the needs of the hour and a consideration for the public's comfort and the city's well-being.

Testimony to this effect can be found in sources written long after the destruction of the Temple. They tell of the wanderings of the Sanhedrin, the Supreme Court of its time. For reasons we cannot trace, the Sanhedrin moved house twice within Jerusalem, ". . . from the Chamber of Hewn Stone to the Shop, from the Shop to Jerusalem," before it left the city altogether and relocated in Yavneh. This reference to the "Shop" is none other than the basilica, a sobriquet that alludes to the building's commercial role before the Sanhedrin moved into it. Many Jews regarded the existence of commercial institutions in close proximity to the Temple as offensive, if not downright outrageous, and a good number complained and even demonstrated over this issue. Perhaps this is how we should understand Jesus' behavior in overturning the tables of the money changers on the Temple Mount, as related in the New Testament (Matthew 21: 12–13):

And Jesus went into the temple of God, and cast out all them that sold and bought in the temple, and overthrew the tables of the money changers, and the seats of them that sold doves, and said unto them, it is written, my house shall be called the house of prayer, but ye have made it a den of thieves.

The Destruction of the Overpass

Only a few score years passed between the time the monumental overpass was built over the series of arches culminating in Robinson's Arch and the date of its devastation. Our excavations revealed the results of the spree of destruction that claimed the arch. The structure's monumental stones fell from a height of 17 meters onto the street below and caused the pavement to sink a bit, cracking or breaking its stones. Still, the damage was relatively light because of the excellent quality of construction and the firm fill beneath the pavement. The original structure of Wilson's Arch was likewise destroyed during the Second Temple period, and its debris is found on the street below it. The arch we see today intact dates back to the Moslem period.

Our first impulse was to conclude that the Roman Legions, intoxicated with victory after burning the Temple, must have been responsible for wreaking this destruction. But the evidence at our disposal does not support that assumption at all. On the contrary, the results of our excavations show that the Temple Mount's walls continued to stand to a considerable height on the eve of the Persian conquest of Jerusalem in A.D. 614.

Who, then, was responsible for the ruin of the complex of arches and overpasses leading to the Temple Mount? It is a fair guess that this wanton destruction was perpetrated by the group of Jewish Zealots led by Simon Bar Giora who holed up on the Temple Mount during the Roman siege. Actually, the group first fortified itself on the Temple Mount during the period of internecine strife between the Zealots themselves, when Bar Giora's men took up quarters on the Temple Mount (especially the southern portion thereof) and a rival group led by John of Giscala fortified itself in the Upper City. To improve their defensive posture, Bar Giora's fighters probably destroyed the overpass, thus impeding access to the Temple Mount. Thus this highly sophisticated and wholly original enterprise was destroyed, as it had been created, by Jewish hands.

8   The Gates of the Temple Mount

How Many Gates Were There?

There were five gates to the Temple Mount: the two Hulda Gates on the south that served for coming in and going out; Coponius' Gate on the west, that served for coming in and going out; the Tadi Gate on the north, which was not used at all; the Eastern Gate, on which was portrayed the Palace of Shushan. Through this the High Priest who burned the [Red] Heifer, and the Heifer, and all that aided him went forth to the Mount of Olives (Mishna, Midot Tracate 1:3).

In this passage the Mishna informs us in the very clearest of terms about the number of gates on the Temple Mount, the direction they faced, their names, and the purpose they served. But Josephus' writings and archaeological and architectural research nevertheless raise questions about the number of gates. In describing the Temple Mount, Josephus speaks of four gates in the western retaining wall, and archaeological finds have confirmed the accuracy of his observations. And in the eastern wall there is at least one gate other than the Shushan Gate mentioned by the Mishna, namely, the gate providing exit from the area of the vaults known today as "Solomon's Stables." Is this an insoluble contradiction, or is it somehow possible to reconcile the conflicting testimonies from these separate sources?

The gates that Josephus mentions as being in the western wall (and that have been confirmed by archaeological research) are the two openings above the overpasses (Robinson's Arch and Wilson's Arch), Barclay's Gate (believed to be identical to Coponius' Gate), and Warren's Gate (to the north of Wilson's Arch). The two gates leading off the overpasses were used to gain entry to the area of the public institutions within the Temple Mount compound but not to the area of the Temple itself, which was sanctified according to Jewish law. If a person standing in the vicinity of these public institutions wished to reach the Temple's precincts, he had to leave the compound and re-enter it through one of the gates specifically designed for that purpose, since there was no direct access between these two sections of the Temple Mount. The Mishna, by its nature, deals only with the aspects of the Temple Mount related to *halakhah*, so the Midot Tractate mentions the five gates that led to the sanctified area. Josephus, on the other hand, described *all* the gates of the Temple Mount, not only those leading to the Temple's precincts. Hence the ostensible contradiction between these two sources.

The Two Hulda Gates in the South

From the Mishna we also know that "the two Hulda Gates in the south that served for coming in and going out" were the main gates to the Temple Mount. The natural question is why the entry and exit gates were built in the south — which determined that the façade of the Temple Mount would face southward — when most of the residential quarters of Jerusalem in the Second Temple period were in the Upper City, to the west of the Temple Mount.

A number of factors came into play in forging this decision, but foremost among them was tradition. Solomon built the First Temple to the north of the city, so that visitors entered its compound through gates in the south, and it was important, perhaps even essential, to preserve this

A capital of the Second Temple period representative of those in the Royal Portico tradition. Throughout the ages it was a standard practice to build temples in the highest spot in any given area, so that a visit to the holy site involved "ascent." The slope to the south of the Temple Mount was the longest and steepest of all the gradients surrounding it; only there was it possible to manifest the idea that the approach to the Temple Mount would be both impressive and steep enough to create the feeling of ascent. This also explains the call in the Bible, "Arise ye, and let us go up to Zion" (Jeremiah 31:6), not in its modern "Zionist" sense but quite literally; for it was addressed to the inhabitants of Jerusalem, most of whom were then living in the City of David, south of and below the Ophel.

The two gates in the southern wall are about 70 meters apart and served the pattern established for entry and exit: "Whoever it was that entered the Temple Mount came in on the right and went around and came out on the left, save any [who have suffered some tragedy], for he went round to the left. 'What aileth thee that thou goest to the left?' 'Because I am a mourner.' 'May He that dwelleth in this House give thee comfort'" (Midot Tractate 2:2).

The picture that emerges from this description has the majority of the public entering the compound via the eastern Hulda Gate, walking around the Temple, and exiting through the western Hulda Gate, while a person in mourning that year would walk around the Temple in the opposite direction, entering through the western gate and leaving through the eastern one. This was a fitting custom, for if a visitor to the Temple met anyone walking in the opposite direction — even a perfect stranger — he immediately understood that the man had suffered a tragedy, inquired about it, and comforted the mourner in his grief. In this way, a visit to the Temple was personalized and helped to cultivate a sense of national solidarity, which was not common to the temples of other peoples.

The Source of the Name Hulda Gate

Our ancient sources do not explain the derivation of the name "Hulda" for these two gates, but there are two theories on this subject. Some scholars believe it traces to the grave of the prophetess Hulda of the First Temple period, since legends have it that she was buried by the Temple Mount's southern gates; other traditions relate that she sat by these gates when she pronounced her prophecies. However, the Temple Mount was enlarged in the Second Temple period, and its gates from the First Temple period were located well to the north of the Hulda Gates as reconstructed by Herod. Moreover, to this day there are traditions claiming that Hulda's grave is on the Mount of Olives, to the east of the Temple Mount.

Following another track entirely, it may be that the etymology of the name is a function of the way in which the Temple Mount enclosure was reached through the gates. "Hulda Gates Street," paved at the foot of the southern wall, is 14 meters lower than the Temple Mount esplanade, and the threshold of the two gates is at street level. To get from the street to the esplanade, one walked through a sloping tunnel built into the vaulted space below the compound, ultimately emerging on the esplanade. Since this passage was reminiscent of the way a rat (*hulda* in Hebrew) emerges from its underground burrow, it's as good a conjecture as any that the name of the gates was inspired by this association.

On the Decorative Art of the Temple Mount

The tunnels ascending from the Hulda Gates to the esplanade were constructed out of a series of round stone domes supported by both the walls and sturdy pillars and embossed with delicate artwork that produced the effect of an enormous carpet suspended above the heads of the people passing through. More than a century ago, visitors and scholars were able to discern some of the ornamentation in this series of vaults. The decorations are found under the Al Aqsa Mosque in the tunnel of the western Hulda Gate, which the Arabs of our day call Al Aqsa al-Qadima (or the Ancient Al Aqsa) and consider a holy place. While digging outside the Hulda Gates, we came to the conclusion that a new study of these tunnels and their decorations would be of great value to us, and we asked the *waqf* for permission to enter the site. In view of the good relations we maintained with the secretary of the *waqf*, Hassan Tahboub, and his engineers, our request was readily granted, and we were even offered assistance in the form of lighting and ladders. In fact, we returned to the place a number of times to record the details of the decorations. Without actually seeing these domes and their ornamentation, it is impossible fully to appreciate Jewish art of the Second Temple period.

The walls of the tunnels are built of large ashlars, but unlike the ashlars of the Temple Mount's outer walls, with their characteristic marginal dressing, these stones were worked down to a smooth finish without margins. The domes that comprised the tunnels' ceilings were quite large, (more than 5 meters in diameter) and are among the earliest known to us in classical architecture. They were constructed of carefully laid stones embossed with a variety of decorations that, in accordance with the biblical prohibition against "graven images," were limited to geometric and floral motifs; there's not even a hint of a human or animal form among them. In the best oriental tradition, the artist left no open spaces, covering the entire dome with ornamentation — to the point where there's hardly room to squeeze the head of a match in between the designs. The floral motifs are of local plants and flowers, with vines and clusters of grapes featured prominently. We know that the entrance to the Temple bore a motif of fruited vines fashioned entirely of gold. The vine served as a symbol of blessing, happiness, and productivity, so that it is not surprising to find it as a key element in this art. Alongside the vines are an assortment of local flowers, such as the anemone, crowfoot, chrysanthemum, and tulip. The earliest scholars called these flowers rosettes but they actually represent a variety of floral species. Though carved in a stylized and rather geometric form, the rosettes give expression to the artist's deep familiarity with the world of flora. Finally, the flowers were painted in suitable colors, creating the impression of an exquisite Persian carpet embossed on the stone.

In the course of our excavation, we found about 300 stone fragments carved in this style. They apparently traced to the ruins of the eastern Hulda Gate, which was decorated in the same manner as the western one. Most of these fragments were found in secondary use in construction dating to the early Moslem period (the seventh century A.D.), some in walls, others in collections of building materials, and yet others as masonry rejects relegated to the fill under the floors of the Moslem structures. This find is additional evidence that major sections of the Temple Mount were still standing intact until the eve of the Moslem conquest and were apparently destroyed at the beginning of the seventh century during the bitter wars between the Persians and the Byzantines.

Today the Hulda Gates are known as the Triple Gate (the eastern gate) and the Double Gate (the western one), the reason being readily visible. The western gate is essentially constructed out of two adjoining

overleaf: Rock fragments that show the engraving work on the eastern Hulda Gate

apertures with the addition of a decorated lintel and pillars bearing capitals at the sides of each gatepost. Today only half of its right wing can be seen from the outside, the rest of the gate being located within a medieval building that rests up against the Temple Mount's southern wall. The format of a double gate is an exception to the rule in classical architecture — where single or triple gates were customary — making the western Hulda Gate one of the many innovations of Jewish architecture found in the Temple Mount.

The decorated domes at the gate's entrance, its inner walls, and its central pillar all date to the Second Temple period. The western gatepost is preserved to a height of 6 meters and is constructed of six courses of stone (some of which are now missing). The original eastern gatepost is slightly less than 3 meters high now and has only two courses, one 1.80 meters and the other 1 meter high. The gate's lintel, a single large stone, is probably the original one, having been salvaged at some point and put back lower than its original place. Above the lintel is an arch in the style of the Moslem period that was designed to ease the burden on it. Above the arch are teeth-like decorations (dentils) carved with floral and geometric designs. From the standpoint of the type of rock used, artistic style, and technical mode of creation, these motifs date to the early Moslem period and are highly reminiscent of the ornamentation on the Golden Gate. Thus the inside of the western Hulda Gate is the original Herodian gate but its façade was reconstructed by Moslem builders to replace the part apparently destroyed by the Christians at the end of the Byzantine era, when they recaptured Jerusalem from the Persians.

The Triple Gate is built on the ruins of the eastern Hulda Gate, which was the main entrance to the Temple Mount and which the New Testament (Acts 3:2) calls the Beautiful Gate, in testimony to its splendor. Other than its threshold and one of the stones of its western gatepost, not much of the original gate remains. After being destroyed during the Byzantine reconquest of Jerusalem in A.D. 628, this gate was rebuilt by the Moslems, though not in its original format. Three arches of equal height and width were built in its façade, giving the gate its name; all that remained of the original gate was the dimension of its width (which also applies to the gate's inner passage). Since the width of the gate — 15 meters — is far too large for a double gate, not to speak of a single one, it was probably originally a triple gate built according to a formula used widely in clasical architecture: a high central opening and two lower side archways flanking it. As noted earlier, most of the carved stones uncovered during our excavation turned up near this gate and evidently belonged to it. Many of them were found in masonry refuse of the Moslem period, at which time the builders must have collected the debris of the destroyed gate and dressed it to serve in the construction of the palace nearby.

The staircase leading to the Triple Gate (or eastern Hulda Gate) is only one third as wide as the parallel staircase leading to the Double Gate (or western Hulda Gate), making the access to the Temple Mount narrower than the exit route. If you think about it, this design is highly appropriate for a public structure, as the flow of traffic into public buildings was both continuous and controlled. After all, some people might have come early, either out of a desire to secure a better spot for viewing the ceremonies or simply because they lost patience with waiting. And all

visitors to the Temple Mount were checked to be sure that they had undergone a ritual bath prior to approaching the area (written confirmation to that effect was mandatory, though as the number of visitors to the Temple grew, this formal check was abolished and the punishment of transgressors was left to Providence). On the other hand, the exit from the Temple Mount at the end of the ceremonies was simultaneous and swift. At first glance the structure of the two gates would appear to contradict this hypothesis, for the entrance was a triple gate and the exit a double one. Yet this is only an ostensible contradiction, since the entry gate was essentially a single gate (the middle section of the triple gate); during the holidays only this central passage was opened, whereas the double exit gate had both its passages open during the festivals.

The side archways flanking the main opening of the triple gate must therefore have served another purpose. What could it have been? One possibility is that they were entrances for dignitaries such as priests or members of the royal entourage during the holidays. Another is that during most of the year the main gates to the Temple Mount were not open at all, and the side gates of the eastern Hulda Gate served for both entry and exit — the right side for entering and the left for leaving (the order of course being reversed for mourners). Whatever the case, it was the central of the three apertures that served primarily, if not exclusively, as the entrance to the Temple Mount, whereas both openings of the double gate were used as exits during the times of peak traffic.

Capital of a pillar supporting the dome of the western Hulda Gate

The Mishna informs us that "Coponius' Gate on the west [served] for coming in and going out," so that above and beyond the two Hulda Gates, another of the five gates to the Temple Mount gave access to the esplanade. We can tell that Coponius' Gate was not designed for the mass traffic that passed through the Hulda Gates; it was meant for selective entry and exit, and perhaps this was the gate used by the non-Jews who were allowed to visit specific areas of the Temple Mount compound.

Where was "Coponius in the west"? According to Josephus the western wall had four gates (testimony that has been confirmed by archaeological research). A gate discovered deep in the ground slightly north of Wilson's Arch and named after its discoverer, Charles Warren, could not have been Coponius' Gate because it led to the vaults under the esplanade, not to the esplanade proper. Neither could the two gates situated over Robinson's and Wilson's Arches, respectively, because they led directly to the secular public institutions on the Temple Mount, rather than the Temple area of the esplanade.

What remains is therefore the more southerly gate in the western wall or Barclay's Gate — named after its discoverer, J. T. Barclay, an American consul in Jerusalem at the end of the nineteenth century and one of the first scholars of Jerusalem. One promising sign of this correspondence is that a tunnel ran from the gate's entrance on Tyropoeon Valley Street up to the Temple Mount esplanade. The distance between its gateposts is 5.60 meters and its height from lintel to threshold is 8.80 meters. The lintel is a single stone 2 meters high and about 7 meters wide. Assuming that its minimal thickness is 1 meter, this stone must weigh close to 50 tons. If you scrutinize the Wailing Wall from the vantage of the women's prayer section, you can discern the northern part of the gate's lintel and the stones used to block its opening at the far right of this area. Barclay studied the gate from its interior side, which we were not able to do

Is Coponius' Gate Barclay's Gate?

because this was the one site the *waqf* refused us permission to enter and study. I believe this refusal was grounded in political motives, because of the gate's proximity to the Wailing Wall. It does appear, however, that Barclay's Gate should be identified as Coponius' Gate.

As to the gate's name, we can only surmise that it derives from the Roman proconsul who served in Palestine during the first century A.D. We know the gate was built in Herod's day, but its doors or some other section thereof may have been completed or decorated during the period of Coponius' rule, with his permission or on the basis of a donation from him. It is also possible that the name Coponius was that of a Jewish donor. There are instances of other gates on the Temple Mount, such as Nicanor's Gate, named in honor of the donor of their artistically fashioned doors.

The Dimensions of the Gates

"All the entrances and the gates ... there were 20 cubits high and 10 cubits wide ..." (Mishna, Midot Tractate 2:3). The Mishna appears to clarify for us the precise size of the Temple Mount's gates, and according to this version they were very imposing indeed. But the question is whether this description concurs with the evidence of our own eyes. To apply this formula to Barclay's Gate, for example, we must first establish the measure of a cubit — a task, it turns out, that is rather formidable. In fact, determining the length of a cubit has occupied the rabbis and sages for many a generation, especially because so many of the laws related to the Temple Mount are couched in terms of cubits.

In our search for the exact equivalent of a cubit, we set out from a verse in the Mishna describing the steps leading up to the Temple Mount: "All the steps there were half a cubit high and half a cubit in depth." It just so happened that soon after we uncovered the steps fronting the Hulda Gates and the stairs leading from the nearby street to the southwest corner of the Temple Mount, we were visited by a delegation of yeshiva students who were studying the subject of the Temple Mount and asked for permission to measure the height of the steps. Try to visualize the scene as a group of young men clad in long black coats clambered down ladders to the bottom of the excavation shafts with measuring equipment poking out of their pockets. And imagine the depth of their disappointment when they discovered the height of the steps changes from one to the next. The first may be 23 centimeters, the next 21, another 25, and so on. How, then, is it possible to reconcile the Mishna's version with the facts? Our crestfallen visitors derived a bit of comfort from the fact that the Mishna speaks of the steps on the Temple Mount proper, not only those outside the bounds of the compound. In effect, it is possible to extend this observation to the gates, as well, and argue that since their dimensions do not concur with the version given in the Mishna, the text there must have been referring to gates on the esplanade proper, not the five gates built into the retaining walls.

Grounds for optimism about solving this discrepancy — and food for new thought — can be found, I believe, in the dimensions of Barclay's Gate. According to both Barclay and Warren, who continued his work, the dimensions of the gate were 5.6 × 8.8 meters, while the size given in the Mishna is 10 × 20 cubits. Regardless of the exact measure of a cubit, we know that the ratio between the gate's height and width should have been 2:1. Yet this ratio did not emerge from the measurements taken by Barclay and Warren. In digging up the area south of Barclay's Gate, we uncovered the paved street from the Second Temple period, and it helped us arrive at a new view on this issue, for it turned out that the threshold seen by Barclay and Warren was from the early Moslem, not the Second Temple period.

Like the Hulda Gates, Barclay's Gate served as an entrance to the Temple Mount compound during the early Moslem period. We know this because we uncovered a sewage channel outside of the Temple Mount wall that runs close to the threshold of Barclay's Gate under the street that was level with that threshold. Since both the pavement and the channel dated to the early Moslem period, we concluded that the gate's original threshold must have been considerably lower than the level deter-

left: The lintel of Barclay's Gate and the blockage of the gate below it with small stones

opposite: Barclay's Gate — the street level and the gate's threshold in the Second Temple period, the Omayyad era, and at present

mined by Barclay. And indeed, if we were to go down another 2.5 meters, we would reach the pavement and the square from the Second Temple period and find that the original height of the gate, from threshold to lintel, was slightly more than 11 meters. The ratio between this height and the gate's width — 5.60 meters — is thus 2:1, making a cubit equal to 56 centimeters. Lest this conclusion sound too pat, I should note that there were at least two measures for the term cubit, and it may be that the one we have deduced here — the royal cubit — held true for gates, while another obtained for the Temple itself or other components of the Temple Mount's structure.

As the opening quote of this chapter shows, the Mishna also made passing mention of the Tadi and Shushan gates in the north and the east, respectively. The Tadi Gate was not in use at all and the Shushan Gate was used

for the ritual associated with the ash of the red heifer (Numbers 19). Most of the gates to the Temple Mount were located in the south and the west. The gate in the north was not in use apparently because it had been blocked. One of the gates in the east took its name from Shushan, the capital of the Persian kingdom, probably because its shape or the ornamentation on its ceiling or walls was typical of the style prevailing in Shushan — though some interpret the gate's name as an expression of gratitude to the Shushan community for donating the money to build it. One way or another, the Shushan Gate was the one through which the red heifer was carried out to the Mount of Olives, where it was burned to make the ashes that played a crucial role in the Jewish purification rite. Without those ashes, there was no way for a Jew to be purified after coming into contact with the dead; and without using a bit of existent ash, it was impossible to prepare a new batch of this prized commodity.

One day the crusade being conducted against our excavations by a number of ultraorthodox circles in Jerusalem came to a head when a malicious rumor spread through the Meah Shearim quarter that we had uncovered a jar containing the ashes of a red heifer and were hiding it because we did not want anyone to be able to make more of the precious ash, which would purify them and enable them to set about rebuilding the Temple! It is difficult to imagine how quickly this perfectly groundless rumor spread, how seriously it was taken, and how much effort was required to dispel it. A Hebrew proverb has it that "A lie has no need of legs." This particular lie took flight with jet speed, and the lesson we learned from it was that the more fantastic a rumor, the better its chances of being credited!

The Gates Above the Overpasses

As we have seen, the Temple Mount compound was connected to the street below by three overpasses affording access to certain public institutions on the esplanade. Two of these three overpasses were on the west side of the mount (Robinson's Arch and Wilson's Arch); the third was built into the southern section of the eastern wall, in the extension between the "seam" and the southeast corner. And leading off each of these overpasses was a gate.

Robinson's Arch supported a broad street that led through the gate into the Royal Portico. When the arch was destroyed, the upper part of the western wall went along with it, so that no trace of this gate remains *in situ*. But in excavating the ruins of Robinson's Arch on the street below, we found a few stones from its gateposts and lintel. They were carved with moldings characteristic of gates in the classical period, and it is from these moldings that we are able to calculate the width of the gate as 5 meters. Since the width of the overpass was 15.20 meters, we cannot know whether it was a single, double, or triple gate. Similarly we are at a loss to decide whether the gate served as the entrance to a corner tower or a plaza fronting the Royal Portico (the basilica) or whether, indeed, it was itself a kind of vestibule leading directly into the basilica.

The width of Wilson's Arch is 15 meters, effectively the same as its counterpart to the south (Robinson's Arch). Here, too, the gate atop the arch may have been anything from a single to a triple one. But in the case of the entryway over Wilson's Arch, we do not even know where the gate led to — the western portico of the Temple Mount or a more defined structure in that area. We are likewise completely in the dark about whom the overpass and the gate were designed to serve.

A third gate stood at the top of the eastern overpass, and as we have noted it may have been the starting point of a ramp on which the scapegoat was sent from the Temple Mount out into the desert. This gate is also difficult to reconstruct for lack of data uncovered in the field. It is clear, however, that it led into the vaulted area under the Temple Mount esplanade, not to the plaza itself. Exactly why it should have been necessary to go to the lengths of building an overpass for the purpose of dispatching the goat to the desert is far from clear, so that this matter still requires serious investigation.

Warren's Gate

About 40 meters north of Wilson's Arch, buried deep in the earth, was a blocked gate that led to the Temple Mount at what was originally street level. Today it is possible to see a bit of it, mostly parts of its lintel (which is essentially an arch built of stones). This gate was discovered by the members of the British expedition that worked in this area and on the Temple Mount compound a century ago, but they failed to report any details about it — not even how they knew of its existence! Named after its discoverer, Charles Warren, who headed the expedition, the gate has been a challenge to research ever since.

The excavation of Wilson's Arch by Israel's Ministry of Religious Affairs (under my supervision) led to a reunion with this gate. Even now we can see only a small portion thereof, and the rest remains to be revealed. From the little known to us today, however, it is clear that the structure uncovered by the ministry's dig dates to the early Moslem period (the seventh–eighth century A.D.), though it is not entirely the product of the Moslem era. In fact, it is a Moslem reconstruction of the gate from the Second Temple era. The arch of the lintel, for example, is definitely Moslem, but as far as we can tell the gateposts are from the original Herodian gate, so that the lower portions of the gate, still to be exposed, undoubtedly belong to the original structure as well.

Warren's Gate conforms to Josephus' description and is the last of the four gates he mentions in the western retaining wall. Some scholars have identified it with Coponius' Gate, but the problem here is that this northern entryway was situated in close proximity to the Temple and was probably used for bringing in sacrifices, wood, and other materials required by the rites held in the Temple's courts, whereas Coponius' Gate served the public at large for the purpose of entry and exit and would therefore have led onto an area of the esplanade that was not considered sanctified — or, to be more precise, to an area accessible to non-Jews. We know that signs warning non-Jews against entering the Temple's precincts were posted on the balustrade separating the "secular" areas of the esplanade from the "sanctified" area surrounding the Temple proper. And since Warren's Gate led directly to the Temple's courts or the immediately adjacent area (through a tunnel rising up from the street level), logic dictates that it could not have been Coponius' Gate of old. Additional investigation of this site is difficult right now, but perhaps more will be learned about it at some future opportunity.

Secret Passages

A group of volunteers from Scandinavia and France were working in the vicinity of the Triple Gate (eastern Hulda Gate) when we uncovered a large hall hewn out of the bedrock. It consisted of the remains of a spacious vault that had been carved under the staircase leading up from the Hulda Gate. Meager though the finds in this hall proved to be, the

The *mesibot*, secret tunnels carved out of the rock under the Temple Mount's gates to enable ritually contaminated priests to leave the Temple Mount

quantities of earth and detritus were more than ample. Suddenly one of the volunteers noticed that the dirt was sliding downward and disappearing into the unknown. With the humor particular to this group of volunteers, its members pronounced that they had found a solution for removing the dirt! And with this revolutionary piece of news on their lips, they summoned the archaeologist responsible for the area. What our volunteers had found was hardly a cut-and-dried affair. "We are standing over some sort of void," the archaeologist explained to the eager volunteers, "and the shock of the digging is causing the dirt to flow into it." Despite the burning heat of August and the skepticism visible on the faces of many of these volunteers, his explanation inspired most of the others to step up their labors.

Two hours later, revealed before them was a serpentine tunnel that had been carved out of the bedrock. It could be negotiated standing perfectly upright and appeared to continue in a northerly direction but was deliberately blocked at the end of 20 meters. Since we had established a rule not to undertake any excavations on or within the bounds of the Temple Mount proper but only to study what had been found *as* it had been found, rather than try to penetrate the blockage we called it a day and summoned our surveyors and photographer to take over from there. They came posthaste, equipped with candles, but then the question was where to place these candles, for the walls of the tunnel had been carved smoothly. It was our photographer, Avinoam, who came up with the solution when he noticed that small niches had been etched into the sides of the tunnel. They alternated from side to side at regular intervals and were perfectly suited for holding candles. It took us very little time after that to deduce not only that the ancients had likewise placed candles in these niches but that they had carved them for precisely this purpose.

With the candles in place, the tunnel was lit by a dim glow. And while the volunteers who had been working in the area completed their tour of the tunnel, I walked down to the pottery wash to scrutinize the shards collected on the previous day in the hope that these vessels — few though they were — would help determine the identity of the last people to use this narrow passage. All the pottery collected in the tunnel dated to the end of the Second Temple period, leading us to the conclusion that the passage had been blocked at the time of the destruction of the Temple and was a Herodian feature. When I told Menachem Magen, the archaeologist responsible for registering and classifying the finds, about the resourcefulness of our photograper and the magnificent sight of the tunnel with the candles flickering to the left and right, my description rang a bell to him. "Listen," said Menachem, whose fantastic memory and familiarity with the Mishna were renown, "that reminds me of a section in one of the tractates of the Mishna," and he immediatley went off to look up the copy of the Mishna kept in our office. When he returned, we began to read together:

[If] one of them suffered a pollution, he would go out and go along the passage that leads below the Temple building, where lamps were burning here and there, until he reached the Chamber of Immersion. There was a fire there and a privy, and this was its seeming use: if he found it locked he knew that someone was there; if open he knew that no one was there. He went down and immersed himself, came up and dried himself and warmed himself before the fire. He returned and lay down beside his brethren the priests . . . (Tamid Tractate 1:1).

The laws of ritual purity were followed scrupulously on the Temple Mount, and more than anyone else it was the priests who adhered to them to the letter, for they were responsible for the rites and general maintenance of the Temple. If one of the priests became ritually contaminated, he had to leave the Temple Mount immediately and purify himself by means of a ritual bath. To avoid contaminating the Mount itself and anyone he might encounter along the way, tunnels were carved out of the bedrock to lead the priest out of the bounds of the Temple Mount. The tunnels were excavated in successive curves, which is evidently the source of their name, *mesibot*, meaning curving tunnels. Naturally such tunnels were pitch dark, so that small niches had to be carved into the walls for the placement of candles.

Was the tunnel we found one of these *mesibot?* The conclusion seems to be unavoidable. Later on in the dig we came upon another *mesibah* under the western Hulda Gate. The two *mesibot* met south of the Temple Mount, and at their junction were remains indicating that a special ritual bath fed by a lead pipe had once been located there. We can assume that there were a number of such *mesibot* in the Temple Mount. The work of carving these tunnels required an enormous investment of energy and funds, and they were just one of many details in which the planners and builders of the Temple Mount went out of their way to ensure that the entire structure would meet the most stringent demands of Jewish ritual law.

9 Daily Life in the Second Temple Period

Our excavations proved that residential buildings were situated as close as a dozen meters from the walls of the Temple Mount. Still, the area immediately surrounding the mount was designated for public use, meaning thoroughfares and squares as well as public and commercial buildings. It was on the slopes of the western hill and to the north of the City of David that we uncovered the remains of residential neighborhoods. Their buildings were constructed very close together, reminding us again that Jerusalem of the Second Temple period was both a heavily populated and highly prosperous city whose economy was nourished by the steady traffic of pilgrims and a burgeoning network of commercial ties. Although we also know that the city supported crafts and industrial enterprises, as well, to date no sign of such installations has been unearthed within its bounds. The ancient sources help us on this point by noting how the city fathers made sure that petty-crafts workshops were located outside the walls. They seemed to have been aware that ovens and other industrial apparatus pollute the environment and must therefore be kept well away from residential neighborhoods. This precaution was all the more apt in a city as crowded as Jerusalem.

The lively trade in real estate for building purposes, particularly in the areas closest to the Temple Mount, made it necessary to exploit every patch of land to the utmost. As we have seen, shops were even built into the piers of Robinson's Arch and Wilson's Arch. The residential quarters that began near the commercial center adjoining the Temple Mount extended southward and westward, growing into densely built neighborhoods. In essence the streets were no more than narrow alleys that threaded their way between the houses — when, indeed, these buildings did not actually touch up against each other or share common walls — according the city the look of a typical ancient metropolis. Yet despite the intense exploitation of the real estate and crowded effect on the outside, the houses themselves were relatively spacious inside. The format of a typical residential building in Jerusalem was of a patio house, namely, a set of rooms built around a central courtyard. These enclosures were not in themselves very large, but they allowed for relative privacy in a densely populated city. Sometimes the enclosed courtyards contained no special architectural features; sometimes they were rather like peristylar courts in that they had a few pillars in the center supporting a thatch of vineleaves. In any event, the houses in Jerusalem during the Second Temple period, though planned with care, were modest in size compared to the villas in the country's rural areas, for the sheer dearth of space and exorbitant price of land prevented even the wealthy from building in a manner commensurate with their economic standing.

The houses were constructed out of stone, sometimes well dressed, sometimes only partially so. Their walls were plastered both inside and out, while the interiors were also whitewashed and decorated with simple frescoes and other artistic embellishments. One of our more interesting finds related to art and decoration came to light during the excavation of a multi-roomed structure south of the Temple Mount on the slope of the

Residential Buildings

opposite: Steps leading to a ritual bath from the Second Temple period

below: A residential neighborhood of the Second Temple period on the slopes of the western hill; model at the Holyland Hotel

left: Stucco molding — among the decorations used in residential buildings in the Second Temple period

opposite: Reconstruction of a detail from the stucco decoration

Ophel. One summer morning a woman student was cleaning the rooms of this building before they were to be photographed (she later confessed to me that she never cleaned her room in the dorm with such devotion or care), and while working on the floors she noticed some pieces of plaster that had peeled off the walls. We decided to postpone the photography session and carefully collected the remains of this plaster. In doing so we discovered to our delight that the side of the plaster that had been facing down on the floor was both molded and illustrated with geometric designs characteristic of the art of the period. But the real surprise was that interspersed among the geometric patterns and floral motifs were figures of animals. The stringent observance of the commandment "Thou shalt not make unto thee any graven image," so conspicuous in the monumental buildings on the Temple Mount, evidently did not extend to private homes; Jerusalemites permitted themselves the vice of adorning their dwellings with scenes from the animal kingdom. The technique employed here was the stucco method, essentially a simple one: plaster of paris was poured into molds etched in reverse with decorations or figures of the desired animals, and the resultant reliefs were then painted and affixed on the walls.

All the residential buildings of the period were characterized by the common use of vaults as the answer to the structural problem of roofing. This practice was introduced into the region a few decades before Herod's reign and was evidently borrowed from Rome, where builders were well versed in constructing vaults but did not necessarily use them for ceilings (which they preferred made of wood). In Herod's day the barrel vault became almost the exclusive form of roof in Judea. It required considerable engineering skill, auxiliary equipment for building forms, and scaffolds for constructing the vaults — not to mention a good deal of work to dress the stones that would ultimately make up the vaults. When vaults were first built, they were fashioned exclusively out of dressed stone, which required precision chisel work at angles that aligned with the structure of the arches. Nevertheless, barrel vaults proved to be an unparalleled structural solution to the problem of ceilings and roofs in an area where wooden rafters were a highly expensive commodity. The stone vaults also made it possible to construct multi-story houses — and, indeed, many of Jerusalem's houses in that period rose to a height of two or three stories, which was a boon for coping with the pressures of a burgeoning population.

Although houses from the Second Temple period have been unearthed in all parts of today's Old City, we shall address ourselves only to the remains found on the eastern slopes of the Upper City, which lay outside

Ritual Baths

the present Old City wall. The walls of these ancient houses were devastated by builders of later generations — especially during the Middle Ages and the Ottoman period — who used their stones to build the city wall. Nevertheless, enough of these structures remained for us to map out their floor plans. One of the hallmarks of these buildings — an element found in almost every one of them — is the *mikvah* or ritual bath. Since they were carved out of bedrock, these baths survived almost intact despite the subsequent destruction inflicted on other parts of the houses.

Every generation has its social classes, and from this point of view the Second Temple period was no different from any other. Yet rather than be based on economic or social standards, classes then were defined on the basis of a religious-halakhic guideline. Some were very strict in observing the religious precepts of the *halakhah*, others were less rigorous. The more fastidious in their observance of the commandments were called *haverim* ("comrades"), while their less exacting counterparts were called *amei aratzot* ("the uninitiated" or "common folk"). Yet we should note that the commandments in question are not the religious precepts whose observance or violation distinguishes between religious and non-observant people today, such as the Sabbath and the dietary laws of *kashrut*. Those commandments were universally observed in the Jewish community during the Second Temple period. What distinguished between the *haverim* and the *amei aratzot* was a rigorous observance of halakhic practice — most particularly the laws of impurity and purification — sometimes well beyond the demands of the *halakhah.* Hence the abundance of ritual baths.

According to the *halakhah*, the water used in a ritual bath must either be rainwater or come from a constantly flowing source such as a spring. In places where there was no water source in the vicinity, rainwater was used. But that gave rise to problems of its own, for when the water in the ritual bath had to be changed in the summertime, it was necessary to draw water from cisterns. The sticklers of the day felt that drawing water from

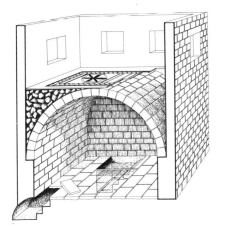

above: Ritual baths carved into the rock on the ground floor of a residential building

right: A ritual bath on the ground floor of a residential building

a standard well did not meet the demands of the *halakhah*, because it was "drawn water" rather than rainwater. In order to make the water fit for use, the following solution was arrived at: a receptacle with a minimum capacity of 40 *seah* (about 800 liters) was built alongside the ritual bath. Referred to as the "treasury," this reservoir was used to store rainwater, and its contents could not be used for any other purpose. The "treasury" and the ritual bath were connected by a pipe two fingers in diameter — "like the width of the tube of a wineskin," as the Mishna puts it. Whenever a householder wanted to clean his ritual bath and change its water, he plugged up the pipe, cleaned and rinsed the bath, and then refilled it with water drawn from a cistern. Afterward the pipe was unblocked and contact was made between the fresh water already in the bath and the water of the "treasury." This blend purified the water of the *mikvah* and made it fit for bathing according to halakhic demands. These three components — the ritual bath itself, the "treasury" beside it, and a cistern from which the water was drawn to fill and change the bath — were found in every one of the houses uncovered on the slopes of the western hill. In cases where there was not enough room to build the three components side by side, or for the sake of conserving space, the "treasury" was sometimes built under the steps leading into the ritual bath, and occasionally the cistern was cut into the rock below them both.

The ritual baths were coated with a gray-colored plaster to prevent seepage. In addition to lime and sand — the standard ingredients of the plaster — olive oil was added to strengthen it and enhance its impenetrability. The ritual bath was entered by at least six steps that were covered by water and were considered an integral part of the bath. Anyone who entered the *mikvah* would descend these steps impure and ascend them cleansed. To ensure that the purified bather would not come into contact with the part of the step he had tread on while descending into the *mikvah*, a number of baths had railings to divide the steps and indicate one side for descent and the other for ascent (we have evidence of this convention in the Mishna). We also uncovered other kinds of ritual baths within the residential quarters, including "seeded" baths that did not draw upon a "treasury" and baths cut into the rock like caves. So far, forty-eight ritual baths have been uncovered by our excavation.

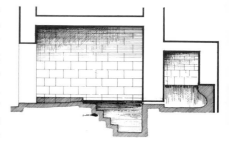

Section and view of a ritual bath on the ground floor of a residential building

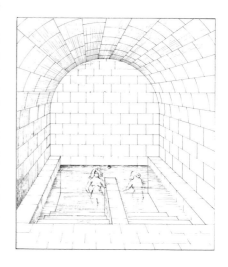

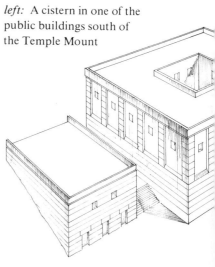

left: A cistern in one of the public buildings south of the Temple Mount

The abundance of ritual baths in the area of the Temple Mount, compared to their relative scarcity in the Upper City and other quarters of Jerusalem, prompted scholars to formulate a number of theories. Some posited that the residents of the neighborhoods adjoining the Temple Mount must have been more pious than the members of the aristocracy, who lived in the Upper City and were less zealous in their adherence to the *halakhah.* From the standpoint of strict observance of the laws of ritual purity, it is hardly necessary for everyone to have his own private *mikvah*, especially as public ritual baths definitely satisfied the need. Then why this abundance of ritual baths in the houses built near the Temple Mount?

As we have seen, a prerequisite for entering the Temple Mount was purification in a ritual bath. We know that many pilgrims lodged in hospices and public hostels, but the custom of renting rooms existed back then, too. Imagine the attraction of a notice tacked up on a street corner were it phrased to the following effect: "Rooms for rent. Reasonable rates. Private *mikvah* on premises." That is how I would explain the profusion of these baths, for many of the householders living near the Temple Mount made a living from renting out rooms. Incidentally, as the pilgrim traffic swelled, rents naturally soared. The city fathers passed regulations putting a ceiling on these prices and preached against the exploitation of pilgrims by declaring that no one had the right to take money for lodgings in Jerusalem because the city of God belonged to everyone. But realistically speaking, who would provide the service for free? So instead of sanctioning rent, they permitted the receipt of "expenses." In effect, they practiced a form of price control.

ls and Community rs

The remains of densely populated quarters were unearthed both west of the Temple Mount and to its south in an extension of the honeycomb of streets and piazzas (where large structures were discovered). Despite the extensive destruction suffered by the latter area due to building activity in later periods, ample remains attest to the layout of this southern part of the Ophel.

The cisterns uncovered in these buildings are huge, accommodating some 150 square meters of water. What's more, five such cisterns were found in a single building! More than anything else, these cisterns convinced us that the structure we had uncovered must have been a public building of some sort, and this assumption was reinforced when we dug 100 meters southwest of the building, close to the main road that crosses this sector today. Our aim in digging there was to enable our own city planners to widen the new road between the Jerusalem–Jericho route and the Dung Gate. The results of our initial investigation, following the method of sinking small experimental shafts, indicated that there were no impressive or important finds in the area — which was consonant with the findings of Kathleen Kenyon, who had excavated here before us. Yet once again, we decided to stick to our own agreed-upon method, which essentially meant digging up the entire area. And this time our results dealt a stinging slap in the face to the advocates of the shaft system — or the "square method" in the jargon of the discipline. For in order to extract the maximum information from any one area, one must dig it all up, rather than make do with small shafts. An excavation shaft could be sunk into a large courtyard, in which case the conclusions it suggests about the nature of the area and its structures would be thoroughly misleading. This is precisely what happened to Kathleen Kenyon when she excavated the area

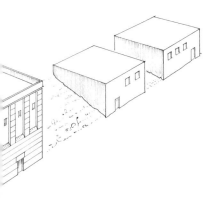

Reconstruction of a public building south of the Temple Mount

under discussion. To her great misfortune, her probes missed the walls of the buildings, and she came to the understandable but erroneous conclusion that the area contained no structures at all.

In contrast, our work exposing the entire area revealed a mammoth building with some ten rooms, five water cisterns, and three ritual baths! Its state of preservation, relative to Jerusalem buildings of the Second Temple period, was excellent. In a number of places vaults were unearthed fully intact, as were doorways from the threshold right up to the lintel. The foundations of this structure were hardy walls from the First Temple period. Although our excavation of the building is not yet complete and we still have not compiled all the information on it, clearly we

above: To the right, the city wall from the Byzantine era; below and to the left of it: a large public building of the Second Temple period

below, left: Covered cisterns in the basement of another public building of the Second Temple period

below: Cistern in a public building from the Second Temple period

have come upon a multi-roomed building of at least two stories.

Josephus' descriptions and archaeological finds of the past decades indicate that there were public buildings in this sector of the city. Some of them were community centers, synagogues, and the palaces of Queen Helena of Adiabene and her family, kings from a distant land in the vicinity of the Euphrates River who converted to Judaism and came to live in Jerusalem. They built their palaces in the rather run-down City of Dàvid, rather than in the exclusive quarters of the city, in something resembling a revival of the "old city" of Jerusalem. It seems that little has changed in the world: neighborhoods that were the equivalent of slums two thousand years ago suddenly attracted the attention of wealthy and exclusive circles — "high society," as it were, just as the older quarters of many of the world's cities are being restored and resettled today as provinces of the rich and bohemian crowds.

Dedicatory inscription in Greek commemorating the contribution of the Jews of Rhodes to the restoration of the flooring in some sort of public building

In addition to the palaces of the nobility, we found community centers in this older but "up-and-coming" part of the city. Pilgrims who streamed into Jerusalem from all over the known world, like tourists in our own day, felt most comfortable in hostels where the language was understood to them, the atmosphere was tailored to suit their sensibilities, and the cuisine was pleasing to their palate. Written sources tell us that a center of this kind existed in Jerusalem for the Jews of Alexandria, and we know that such hostels sometimes contained a synagogue for the use of their guests.

Though we lack sufficient evidence to determine the exact nature of the two buildings uncovered south of the Temple Mount, ample testimony to their luxurious décor emerges from the molded plaster (stuccowork), and their high standard of construction is evidenced by the large number of rooms and the remains of the delicate mosaic floors. One is tempted to speculate that perhaps the western building was one of the palaces belonging to the kings of Hadiab. We have more illuminating information on the eastern structure. One of the ritual baths excavated in this building has a stone plaque bearing a Greek inscription; and although the plaque is broken, and part of the inscription is missing, what remains of it enables us to puzzle out that it has something to do with a contribution made for the flooring of the building by the Jewish community of Rhodes in the second year of the tenure of one of the high priests. The inscription even spells out the sum in drachmas (the Greek currency). It is therefore possible that this donation was a gift of the Jews of Rhodes to their community center in Jerusalem during the first century A.D. At least we can say that the inscription apparently belongs to the building in which it was found.

The Pottery

As a rule archaeological excavations uncover finds of two types that complement each other: architectural discoveries (meaning structures of various kinds) and smaller finds (on the scale of individual artifacts). An excavation of public areas such as plazas and promenades naturally does not yield personal or household effects, as these are usually not found lying about in the streets. On the other hand, when excavating residential areas, the chances of turning up personal and household effects are far greater, for they served as part of the furnishings and tools of daily life. This rule holds true for the excavations near the Temple Mount.

In the ancient periods, pottery and ceramic vessels were the most common of the everyday articles, especially because the raw material for this industry was cheap and ubiquitous and the amount of energy invested in producing pottery was relatively meager. Most of the housewares were made of ceramics. They included storage jugs for liquids (wine and oil), grains (wheat and barley), flour, and the like; cooking pots, plates, bowls, cups, and serving pieces; earthenware lamps; ewers for dispensing wine, oil, and vinegar; and perfume vials. Of this entire array of objects, however, the most distinguished pieces are the soupspoons, which resemble the Chinese variety in being flat and short-handled.

The exception to the rule, stylistically speaking, are the very fine ceramic vessels decorated in color. They somewhat resemble contemporary pieces uncovered in the south of the country, within the area inhabited by the Nabateans. We refer to this style of work as "painted Jerusalem ware," because such pieces have been found circulating in Jerusalem only. Ornamentation, rendered in tones of red and black, are based on floral motifs, and the artist worked in bold, light strokes; yet despite its unassuming style, the product is highly artistic. These vessels are also something of a departure from the conventions of Eastern art in that the Jerusalem artist did not decorate the entire body of the object and was not disturbed by the empty spaces he left behind. Perhaps these pieces are evidence of Western influence on Jewish art of the period.

Most of the pottery we found turned up in residential buildings, especially in their cisterns. After razing the city, the Roman soldiers sacked it, carrying off everything of value as booty, but pottery vessels were left ignominiously behind. Both the soldiers' sense of fun and their appetite for havoc were evidently behind their habit of tossing pottery into the cisterns. This is why the excavation of a house's cistern is likely to yield dozens of undamaged pottery vessels of every shape and kind. The refuse pits are another rich source of pottery. One morning as I passed by one of these pits, I picked up snatches of a conversation between the archaeologist in charge of the site and his team of excavators. One after another, cooking pots of light-red pottery were being extracted from the pit. They looked brand new and probably had hardly been used. "Would you please be more careful," the archaeologist chastised his crew. "Every pot that passes through your hands has a hole in it!"

"We're digging up those pots with our bare hands!" the excavators replied almost in unison. Their indignance was quite justified, for although each and every one of the pots had a small hole in it, that wasn't because the excavators were careless. The holes were in the pots when they found them, having been made after the vessels were used.

Centers for producing pottery sprang up around temples all over the ancient world. Their purpose was to provide vessels for both the sacrificial ceremonies and for cooking the portions of the votive offerings, for after a sacrifice was made its edible meat was divided up between the officiating priest and the person who had supplied the animal. The rulers of the day found that if they gave the temple priests a monopoly on the production of those vessels, it could provide an appreciable supplement to their meager income. Since priests were considered public servants, their "wages" came from donations and tithes, which evidently didn't stretch far enough to provide a living. They were therefore treated to various "perks", among them a monopoly on the vessels required for the temple rites. This practice extended to the Temple in Jerusalem, as well. In order to augment their income even further, the priests tacked on another regu-

The Mystery of the Perforated Pots

A selection of pottery pieces from a Second Temple period house: cooking pots, table implements, cosmetic jars, and oil lamps

lation: the pots for cooking the sacrifices were to be used only once and then had to be broken. In the course of time, as the standard of living rose in Jerusalem, it was difficult to find craftsmen to work in the pottery industry, and the shortage of workers led to a concommitant shortage of vessels. As a result, the production of pots for growing plant seedlings — a common method of agriculture at the time — was severely curtailed. There was a glaring contradiction between the wanton waste of pottery after use in the Temple and the shortage of pottery for agricultural purposes, so the sages of the day decided that rather than shatter the used pots, a hole was to be made in the side of each vessel. That would disqualify it for cooking the meat of the sacrifices but leave it intact enough to serve as a seed pot. This compromise is referred to obliquely in the *halakhah* and our discovery of cooking pots with hardly any trace of soot on the bottom — for they had been used only once — but with a small hole in the side brought that ancient regulation to life for us.

Alongside the craft of pottery-making, Jerusalem developed an industry for producing stone vessels and our excavation unearthed hundreds of

objects made of different kinds of stone. They included salon furniture such as small, round or square stone tables with a single pedestal leading down to a broad base and decorated (as were the sides of the table top) with geometric forms and floral designs; some of these tables were even adorned with mosaics. One of them, found among the ruins of a shop, was inlaid with a simple but lovely mosaic that endowed it with a special grace. "Imagine how many goblets of wine were quaffed beside this table at the climax of business deals," mused the volunteer from France who uncovered it. Most of the stone artifacts we found consisted of more prosaic articles: measuring cups, stoppers for pottery vessels, ink pots, and storage jars, the last being the most interesting of all. Our wonder grew as we realized that they were fashioned by means of lathes. It is well known that lathes were in widespread use throughout the Roman world, even in the stoneware industry; but the fact that Jerusalem's artisans managed to produce vessels as large as storage jars was a genuine surprise.

above: A selection of stone vessels, the pride of the Jerusalem stone industry in the Second Temple period: storage jars, measuring cups, and stoppers

We found one of the stone storage jars while excavating the northernmost store in the pier of Robinson's Arch. It was a very large vessel that had been fashioned on a lathe. The weight of the original stone block must have been half a ton, and the technical ability displayed by the artisan was indeed impressive. In a chance conversation, I learned of a craftsman in Bethlehem who fashions stone vessels on a lathe, and I delegated one of our archaeologists to look into the matter. His findings were fascinating, not to mention instructive, and again showed how much we can learn about the past from examining tangible artifacts. When we invited the Bethlehem craftsman to see the stone receptacles we had unearthed, he clapped his hands in amazement and murmured, "The Devil must have had a hand in this! Otherwise I cannot imagine how they succeeded in making vessels as large as these!" I tend to think the ancients operated a lathe with the aid of gears or water power, rather than the Devil. An aqueduct passed by this area, and it may have served precisely this purpose. It's also possible that one of the objectives of building the aqueduct was to harness water power for other crafts and industrial equipment, including the apparatus for dressing and polishing the massive stone columns in the Temple Mount's colonnades.

We asked ourselves why our forefathers invested so much effort in the stonework industry. Why did they bother to hoist such huge blocks of stones onto a lathe and expend so much physical effort in actual labor? The answer lay in the importance of stone vessels in the *halakhah*, which is what spurred the development of this art. According to the halakhic tradition, a pottery vessel that has been defiled must be broken, but this rule does not hold for stone. Stone vessels were neither disqualified for further use nor broken when they were considered polluted, and herein lay their importance for the laws of purification. The Mishna goes into these laws at length, and they are even echoed in the New Testament in the verses on the miracle of the wine at the wedding in the Cana: "And both Jesus was called, and his disciples, to the marriage . . . and there was no wine . . . And there were set there six waterpots of stone, after the manner of the purifying of the Jews . . ." (John 2:2–5).

A few fragments from these stone vessels bore inscriptions. One of them was "Yehosef," the name of the vessel's owner; another was the word "sacrifice" above two upside-down birds — apparently signifying

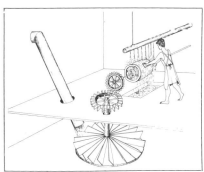

Reconstruction of an installation for producing heavy stone vessels. The lathe was run by water power, with the water supplied by an aqueduct

top and right: Details of the ornamentation of a stone table

far right: A decorated stone table, the *pièce de résistance* of the stonework of the Second Temple period

The handle of a stone jar inscribed with the word "sacrifice" and two upside-down birds

that they were a sacrificial offering. In ancient art, a figure drawn upside down indicates that it was dead. We cannot know to what kind of ritual vessel this fragment belonged, but we do know that the Mishna says: "Take a vessel and inscribe sacrifice upon it . . ." (Second Tithe 4–10), and fragments such as these from the Second Temple period are fairly common in Jerusalem. Finding the remains of ritual implements was not unusual in our dig, and we set down special rules for handling them, for a hint of sanctity still clings to these fragments.

Stone also served as the basic raw material for fashioning weights. In fact, the concept of weights began with stones, as the term "stone weights" implies. Most of the advanced cities of the ancient world, Jerusalem among them, appointed officials to supervise the markets. Their task was to supervise the gates and maintain control over prices and weights, and in this capacity they would inspect and mark scales and issue a permit for their use. We turned up several stone weights incised with inscriptions in Greek. In a number of cases, the king Agrippa I was mentioned by name, together with a year of his reign (A.D. 41–44). Agrippa was an economist *par excellence*, and in his day imaginative and far-ranging commercial activities were carried on in Jerusalem — reminiscent of the enterprises of his grandfather, Herod the Great.

The ruins of stores and the rubble of the streets at the corner of the Temple Mount yielded some rather unusual stone vessels, including a delicate household instrument designed to produce small quantities of oil (evidently cosmetic oil) from seeds. Especially fascinating were the sundials — "hour stones," in the language of the Mishna — that were installed at the top of the Temple Mount wall. One of these is exquisitely decorated and leads us to suspect that the European tradition of placing clocks at the top of towers may have traced back to walls and towers of the Temple Mount in Jerusalem.

Metal Artifacts, Coins, and Safes

The most common and characteristic finds to come out of archaeological excavations are pottery, stone artifacts, and the like, while the chances of finding metal objects are relatively slim, for a number of reasons. First, most of the implements in daily use during antiquity were made of pottery or stone. Second, once broken, these relatively cheap articles were discarded as rubbish and so remained until archaeologists unearth them — and are glad of it. In contrast, a metal implement continued to be of value even if it were broken, for it could always be melted down to produce an alloy. Thus whether intact or damaged, metal objects were always marketable items. perhaps that is why an army plundering a conquered city would pounce on every piece of metal as prize booty. We sensed this very keenly in our excavation, and the discovery of a metal object always elicited a cry of triumph that reverberated from one end of the dig to the other. Everyone dropped what he was doing and came bounding over to gaze at the latest treasure salvaged from the sheltering earth. Bronze objects are most resistant to the ravages of nature, primarily oxidation, whereas iron is most vulnerable to the rust that corrodes these artifacts. Nails, carpentry tools, stone-cutting implements, and other tools, alongside minting instruments and housewares, were the most common pieces to emerge from the strata of the Second Temple period.

A stone sundial

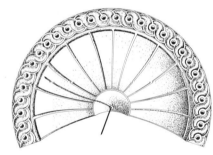

During one afternoon consultation, when we traditionally drew up the work schedule for the following morning, we decided to reassign a group of volunteers from Germany who had put in three weeks of hard work clearing away detritus from large cisterns of the Second Temple period without turning up anything of consequence. In their place, we decided to slot in a team of our regular diggers. The volunteers hadn't complained about laboring away in the cisterns, but we sensed their growing dismay. In return for their efforts, they hoped to find something, while our laborers — for whom digging is a vocation — don't especially care where they work. What's more, because the cisterns are shaded and cool, they're a good place to work during the summer, especially since a suntan — so coveted by the volunteers from Europe — is not particularly in demand among the native laborers. At any rate, this arrangement continued for three days, and then came the surprise: close to the bottom of a cistern, under a heap of stones, one of our veteran laborers found a collection of bronze objects. They led us to speculate that the beleaguered Jerusalemites had placed them there during the last days of the siege and covered them with stones to conceal their treasure from the Roman soldiers. Evidently the owners hoped to return and recover their belongings at some time in the future. They never did, though, and this collection found its way into the hands of their distant progeny, Israeli archaeologists and laborers in search of Jerusalem's glorious past. And a glorious find these vessels were, though they reached us in an advanced state of disintegration. Unfortunately, only a few of the objects were salvageable, but they included a ewer with a high handle, a skillet whose handles were fashioned like duck heads, two jugs and, best of all, an oil candelabrum whose three legs were fashioned in the shape of animals and merged into a ½-meter-high rod topped by a stand for the oil lamp. Metal objects of this type have been found in other excavations in Jerusalem and help illustrate the city's thriving economy during the Second Temple period by attesting to the high standard of living on the eve of Jerusalem's destruction by Titus. A strange mixture of joy and consternation could be felt around that cistern. Only those who have worked on an archaeological dig and have stood up to the trial of week upon week of painstaking labor without turning up a find can appreciate the effect of a discovery like this while off to the side stood the group that had done almost all the work with their bare hands and, in the final days of their stint, were "rewarded" by being transferred to a "more promising area."

This set of bronze pieces were hidden in a cistern to preserve it from the loot-hungry hands of the Roman Legionnaires. The discovery prompted us to wonder where the burghers of Jerusalem kept other valuables, such as their jewelry, money, and important documents. We found an answer in

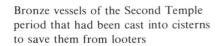
Bronze vessels of the Second Temple period that had been cast into cisterns to save them from looters

four of the houses from the Second Temple period, and no simpler one could there be: they stored their valuables in safes. On the ground floor of each of those houses, small subterranean chambers had been hollowed out of the bedrock. They were not plastered with a waterproof sealant because they were not cisterns. The openings to these chambers were in the walls or the floors and were covered by a slab or tile that blended perfectly into the original flooring or wall stone, so that a stranger standing in the room would not be able to distinguish them. To further compli-

Painted Jerusalem pottery, some of the finest ceramic ware of the Second Temple period

cate access to these safes, they were usually built next to the ritual baths on the ground floor, that is, near installations to which entry was restricted or at least modesty precluded the free flow of traffic. Unfortunately, the soldiers of the Roman Legions made a point of searching out these safes, and the four we came upon were empty. As the fall of the city approached, many Jerusalemites hid their valuables in places not designed for that purpose, like cisterns. But one of the householders living on the slope of the western hill, outside the Dung Gate, had a more pedestrian solution: he hid his treasure of 42 silver shekels from the period of the First Revolt in a cloth sack under the floor. Amazingly enough, the Roman soldiers who looted the area failed to discover this treasure. Nevertheless, by a painful twist of fate, it has not made its way into our hands — at least not *in toto*. The treasure was found by a temporary worker from a village near Hebron who had been with us for two weeks, and unbeknown to us he simply stole it. We finally learned of its existence because someone blew the whistle on him and we managed to redeem 10 shekels of the treasure — though not without a protracted court battle.

Most of the coins we found did not come from treasures that the ancients had stashed away but from constant and consistent collection out of the earth and rubble. To that end we sifted thousands of square meters of dirt through strainers. For the most part, the coins we salvaged by this painstaking method were bronze — though some were of silver — and so far more than 2,500 of them have been found from the Second Temple period. They include a variety of both Jewish and Roman mint, imperial coins as well as local ones issued by the procurators. Even when the date on a coin is unmistakable, it does not necessarily enable us to date the building or installation in which it was found, for the coin may

A selection of bone implements of the Second Temple period: combs, dice, pins, cosmetic instruments, and needles

have been in circulation for quite a while (its lifespan being 200 years or more). As one example, the coins of the Hasmonean king ·Alexander Jannai, minted at the beginning of the first century B.C., continued to serve as legal tender up to the destruction of Jerusalem by Titus.

Mayor Teddy Kollek, in his frequent visits to the excavation site, would regularly ask us, "How come you find ancient coins? Is money floating around the streets today, too?" It's a question to which we have yet to supply a definite answer, but we can say with conviction that for periods marked by inflation, when the value of the currency was low, coins have turned up in substantial quantities. Compared to the 2,500 coins unearthed from the Second Temple period (essentially just the last 250 years thereof), we found more than 20,000 coins from the end of the Byzantine era (all told less than a hundred years, from the close of the sixth through the early part of the seventh century A.D.), a time when rampant inflation heralded the decline of Christian rule.

The Jewish coins uncovered in our dig represent the "basket of currencies" known to us from all the other excavations carried out in this country. They range from the coins of Alexander Jannai and his heirs of the Hasmonean dynasty to those of Herod and his successors and coins

A "safe" under the floor of one of the Second Temple period houses

from the time of the Great Revolt. Characteristic of them all is the absence of the king's profile (with the exception of the coins ascribed to Agrippa). The illustrations that do appear on the coins are popular symbols or floral elements, the same motifs that recur as decorations on the Temple Mount. Thus miniature art, like the monumental art of the period, eschewed any representation of human or animal figures.

Glass, Bone Objects, and Jewelry

Glass, bone objects, and jewelry round out our array of finds from the houses of the Second Temple period. Because of their fragility, the glass pieces were found smashed to smithereens. The artifacts we find on display in museums were, as a rule, retrieved from graves, where they served as votive objects. No one had opened these graves until antiquities became a prime item and dealers began to plunder them or, at best, archaeologists began to excavate them. It is rare to find glass intact in residential structures, though we did find a few small perfume vials whose size had protected them against breakage for 2,000 years. In antiquity glass was considered a sophisticated and respected industry. Our paucity of knowledge on this subject is a function of both the reticence of the sources and the dearth of finds even from the excavation of graves. Bone, on the other hand, has proved to be a hardy substance that served as raw material for the manufacture of a wide variety of cosmetic-related objects,

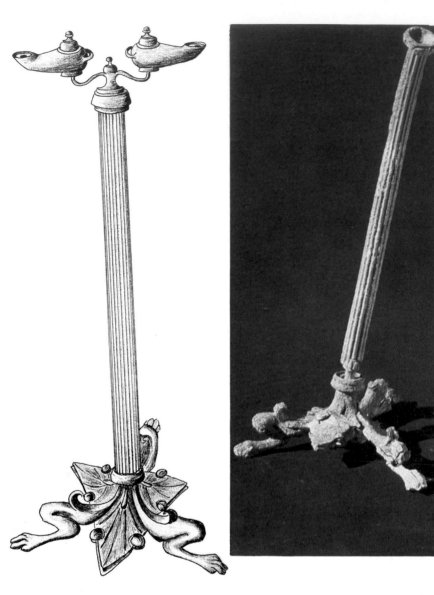

opposite, above: Silver shekels from the time of the First Revolt

A bronze pedestal for an oil lamp

A bronze vessel

opposite, below: A silver shekel from the second year of the First Revolt

such as jewelry, combs, sticks for applying kohl eyeliner, cosmetic bottles, spoons for mixing cosmetic (or medical) concoctions, and the like. Also among the more attractive products of the bone industry are buttons, belt buckles, brooches to fasten capes and togas, needles, spindle weights, and dice. These objects were fashioned with care and decorated with geometric designs, primarily circles. The degree to which they were in constant use can be seen by the polish of wear that makes for the effect of a shiny, transparent varnish.

Jewelry was made out of semi-precious stones set in earrings and rings, most especially seal rings. Somtimes the latter were carved with a figure or other design — in reverse of course. The stone was often raised in a setting for a finger ring or pendant worn around the neck, and its owner used it to stamp his personal seal on documents. One of the more impressive stones from the Second Temple era shows a table laden with produce flanked by two horns of plenty. What better symbol of Jerusalem's prosperous state during this period?

10   Public Buildings and Institutions

Like every large city in the Roman Empire, Jerusalem was graced with public buildings and institutions of various kinds. The largest and most imposing of them, and perhaps unique in the entire world, was the Temple Mount with its full array of structures. But there were also quite a number of other public buildings in the city, including palaces, fortresses, cultural institutions, law courts, a city archive, and sports and entertainment facilities. In the other cities of the classical world, these institutions were traditionally concentrated around the temples, which were considered the *pièce de résistance* of the public buildings, and many of the institutions were used in connection with the festivals celebrated in the temples. We are able to learn about some of these structures in Jerusalem of the Second Temple period, and especially of Herod's day, from the descriptions provided by Josephus and scattered through the Mishna. These sources cite the exact location of only a few of the structures, but because Jerusalem was perceived by scholars as a *polis* (a Hellenistic-Roman metropolis), it was generally assumed that most of the public buildings and facilities were found in the vicinity of the Temple Mount.

For that reason, we placed great hopes on our excavations in the areas adjoining the Temple Mount and fully expected to uncover at least a few of the public buildings shown on the maps of Jerusalem drawn by various scholars. Yet for the most part, these expectations were disappointed. Directly adjacent to the Temple Mount in the west, for example, we uncovered Tyropoeon Valley Street running through the heart of the Lower Market; southwest of this area we found residential buildings climbing up the slopes of the hill to form the so-called Upper City; and about 60 meters south of the Temple Mount's southern wall we exposed the complex of plazas, staircases, and shops that comprised the approaches to the Temple Mount. Only to the south of this area did we find the remains of large buildings — one the basement floor of an imposing structure, the other a multi-roomed structure of which large parts are preserved — and although we cannot define the exact nature of these structures, we can say that they were apparently designed as living quarters.

The Complex of Wilson's Arch

More than a century ago the Palestine Exploration Fund expedition discovered under the eastern side of the Street of the Chain a series of remarkably well-preserved arches and two stories of vaulted rooms that were still intact. Some of these rooms were built on the bedrock or on the slope of the western hill; above them were a number of additional vaults flanking a long and similarly vaulted corridor. The entire complex culminated at the western wall in a huge arch that was subsequently named after its discoverer. C. W. Wilson. The expedition headed by Charles Warren was carrying out the work of measuring and studying one of the loveliest of these vaulted rooms on the ground floor on a day when the Freemasons happened to be holding their convention in Jerusalem. In honor of that event, Warren christened the room the Freemasons Hall, and so it has been known in the scholarly literature ever since.

opposite: The entrance to a large cistern found southwest of the Dung Gate. Built over this cistern was a large public building

overleaf: The southwest corner of the Temple Mount on a winter's day

Immediately after the Six-Day War, we went out in search of Wilson's Arch and found that access to it was a complicated affair, though we finally got through via the narrow area alongside the Wailing Wall where the British had penetrated the arch in their day. The rest of the vaulted rooms, including the Freemasons Hall, were nowhere to be found, as though they had been swallowed up by the earth. On the other hand, our meeting with Wilson's Arch was like a reunion with an old friend. The arch was completely intact (as were the two shafts sunk by the British excavators), and we found it exactly as they had drawn it before blocking the opening below it. Later on representatives of the Ministry of Religious Affairs, which had jurisdiction over the area of the Wailing Wall, began to search for this "missing" complex of vaults. After much hard work and a display of near-heroic fortitude and resourcefulness, the vaults were uncovered again. At the request of the Ministerial Committee for Jerusalem Affairs, I was appointed supervising archaeologist of this project, and as one who followed the work at close hand, I can testify that it bore the distinction of being one of the most malodorous episodes in archaeological history.

Almost as soon as we began digging, it became painfully clear to us why the vaults that had been discovered and measured by the Warren expedition — and that could be entered at the time — had disappeared. At the start of the British Mandate over Palestine in the early 1920s, pipes were laid to carry water to the Old City, and this in turn led to the installation of modern plumbing and made sewers necessary. The problem was that a modern sewage system was not laid, and every householder was responsible for digging his own cesspool. The residents living along the segment of the Street of the Chain above our network of vaulted rooms found this ready-made underground system convenient to use for this purpose. So for close to half a century sewage flowed into these vaults until they simply filled up and not a trace of them remained.

The workers from the Ministry of Religious Affairs, who devoted themselves to the Herculean task of clearing out these vaults, worked like men obsessed by a labor of love. Both the laborers and their supervisors believed they were fulfilling a holy mission. Indeed, it is difficult to imagine the venture succeeding without the irrepressible enthusiasm and driving faith of those teams and their directors. When they began working, the sewage system was still operating as it had for the past half century, so that whenever any one of the residents living on the streets used a toilet, the workers below got a revolting shower of fresh sewage poured down on them. The Jerusalem Municipality soon joined in the effort to relieve the situation by laying a modern sewage system in the area, and eventually the houses of the area were linked to the main sewage network — to the immense relief of the workers below.

Wilson's Arch rests up against the western wall and today, along with sections of the adjoining vaulted rooms, serves as a place of prayer supplementing the plaza in front of the Wailing Wall. Standing under it you can see an enormous intact arch constructed of large ashlars. The members of the Palestine Exploration Fund expedition dated it to the Byzantine era (sixth century A.D.) but noted that its pier was the original one from the Second Temple era. Their dating of the arch to the Byzantine era was quite definitive and somewhat odd, for the expedition's members identified many architectural remains of the Temple Mount as ancient structures, some going as far back as the First Temple period.

Wilson's Arch

Archaeologists naturally try to date back to the most ancient eras, yet here they arrived at a relatively late determination. Indeed, the scholars who followed the British expedition took exception to this dating and instead ascribed the entire arch to Herod's reign on the basis of its overall appearance, the size of its stones, the high standard of construction, its point of exit, and the precise join to the wall itself. And it must be said that these are indeed impressive reasons.

Why, then, did the British expedition arrive at a very different conclusion? No reasons were given in their scholarly report, but it appears that they were guided by the knowledge that lying under the arch, on the pavement dating to the Second Temple period, was the debris of the original structure. Its stones had remained untouched until being found by Warren's excavators, but at some point in history someone had come

Everyday objects from the Second Temple period

right: An iron javelin head
left: A bronze key to the lock of a box

An iron stonemason's hammer

along and reconstructed the arch using stones from a later period. The British learned this vital detail from the shaft they had sunk alongside the arch's pier. The level of the street under the reconstructed arch runs above the debris of the original structure, whereas the Second Temple pavement lies under the debris and is composed of large stones. Shops lined the eastern wall, and the pier of the arch — containing stores closely resembling those in Robinson's Arch — delineated the arch in the west.

opposite: Glass cosmetic bottles

Our excavation at Wilson's Arch taught us that the first investigators of the structure were indeed correct in concluding that its present incarnation postdates the Second Temple period. The primary evidence for this finding is that stones matching the type used in Robinson's Arch are found on the pavement from the Second Temple period, and it simply doesn't stand to reason that if the arch had been reconstructed in its present form during the Second Temple era, the debris of the original structure would have been left lying on the pavement below it. Moreover, during the early Moslem period a new street was paved 4 meters above the Second Temple pavement, and this street is identical in its characteristics to the one paved over the ruins of Robinson's Arch. Yet another piece of weighty evidence is that a reconstruction of Robinson's Arch has enabled us to determine the height of the southern part of the Temple Mount during the Second Temple period. Wilson's Arch in its present, complete form, with the Gate of the Chain above it, is 3 meters lower than the top of the Temple Mount's wall from the Second Temple period, and it is out of the question that the southern part of the western wall was 3 meters higher than its center section. On the other hand, the present height of the Gate of the Chain corresponds to the height of the Temple Mount's platform since the beginning of the Moslem era.

The Temple Mount, Wilson's Arch, and the *Xystus* at the end of the overpass in the Second Temple period

Another reason for concluding that Wilson's Arch is a reconstruction has to do with its style. We know of the remains of three arches adjoining the Temple Mount — Robinson's Arch, Wilson's Arch, and what we have termed the Arch of the Scapegoat in the east — and we are quite sure that the two of them (Robinson's Arch and the eastern arch) date to the Second Temple period. In both cases the stones in the last layers of their piers, at the springline of the arch, were highlighted by protruding "teeth" (dentils). These dentils are absent in Wilson's Arch, testifying that the arch, together with the top courses of its piers — including the layer of dentils — was totally destroyed.

The Temple Mount, Wilson's Arch, and the *Xystus* at the end of a multi-arched bridge in the Second Temple period

The spot where the *present* arch vaults outward from the wall was originally an intact section of wall. In order to rebuild the arch, stones were removed from two to three of its courses along a 15-meter stretch, which is exactly the width of the facing pier. The stones of the Temple Mount's retaining walls in Herod's day had the characteristic marginal dressing. Immediately to the south of the present arch, one can see two stones dressed in this marginal style on three of their sides; the fourth side, which touches the arch itself, has no such margin, so that these stones must be the southern portions of the original ashlars (most of the Herodian ashlars having been cut exactly to fit the space designated for the arch).

The Temple Mount and Wilson's Arch restored and serving as a bridge during the Ommayad period

All this evidence — the presence of huge arch stones in the debris on the Second Temple period pavement, the height of the present arch (which is lower than the Temple Mount's walls), the absence of dentils at the point where the arch begins to curve out, and the stones in the Herodian wall broken to fit the present arch — is sufficient to indicate that the arch indeed dates to some period after the destruction of the Temple and is a reconstruction of the original. If we add to this evidence the presence of small stones at the place where the arch begins to vault outward from the pier — stones that could not possibly have been from Herod's time — the picture is complete. I should also mention that although the stones in Wilson's Arch are large ashlars, they are smaller than the stones of Robinson's Arch and the rest of the Herodian construction throughout the Temple Mount. In fact, they are only one-eighth the size of the stan-

The Temple Mount, Wilson's Arch (no longer in use), and the public buildings constructed over it, from the time of the Crusaders onward

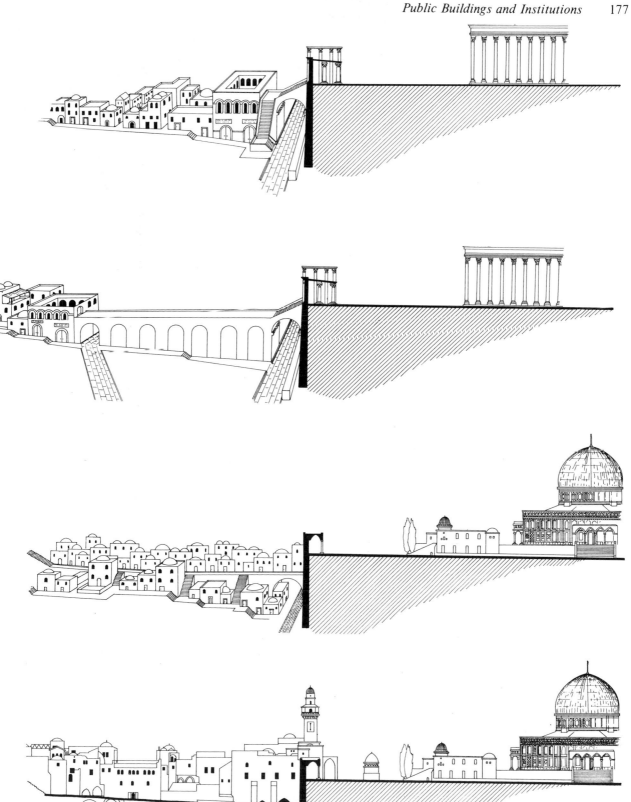

dard stones used in Robinson's Arch, the arch found in the Herodian vault within Solomon's Stables, and the arch on the eastern wall used for releasing the scapegoat.

This being the case, it is pertinent to ask when Wilson's Arch was rebuilt: during the Byzantine era or at the onset of Moslem rule in Jerusalem? Further excavation is required if we hope to answer this question accurately, but I am willing to venture that the reconstructed arch was a Moslem undertaking, since the Moslems were the first to engage in extensive restoration and building activities in the area of the Temple Mount.

Wilson's Arch connected the Temple Mount with structures to the west and ultimately with the Upper City. Many scholars of the city's past have portrayed it as the first link of a bridge that extended about 100 meters westward and linked the Temple Mount with the lower slopes of the western hill in the Second Temple period (today's Jewish Quarter). But we have not found any hard evidence to support this theory. On the contrary, the series of vaults built under the Street of the Chain postdates the Second Temple period. We know this because stones from earlier eras were used in its construction, and one of these stones bears the remains of a Latin inscription, so that the structure must have been built after the Roman era. The conjectured bridge of the Second Temple period was therefore only a single arch built over the paved street at the foot of the western wall (Tyropoeon Valley Street), and it led to a staircase exactly like the overpass of Robinson's Arch. This conclusion is based on the fact that the structure exiting from the Temple Mount connected the western portico with a building called the *Xystus*.

The Hall of Capitals, popularly known as the Hall of the Hasmoneans, west of Wilson's Arch

The Hall of Capitals and the Xystus

As we have noted, in the course of Warren's excavation at the time when the Freemasons were holding their convention in Jerusalem, a large hall built of stone was uncovered deep in the earth just west of the pillar of Wilson's Arch. In our own day, the people from the Ministry of Religious Affairs invested backbreaking labor in clearing this hall, and it is due to their efforts that we are able to study its plan and structure. This hall was undoubtedly one of the loveliest structures in Jerusalem of the Second Temple period. Its walls were constructed of perfectly smooth stones and were lined with exquisitely etched columns crowned by Corinthian capitals. Only a trace of one of these columns remains, in the northeast corner of the hall, and it too was badly scratched at some later date, so that it appeared to the members of the British expedition to be a column representing a tree. The eastern wall had a double opening (graced with a lovely lintel) that connected the hall with others to the east of it. The southern and western sides of the hall also contain indications that other halls were connected to it, so that what we have here is evidently the remains of a multi-halled structure of which only sections of the ground floor remain. All we can do is imagine how magnificent the upper stories of this building must have been when it stood intact.

The vaulted ceiling of the hall was originally supported by columns, and if for only that reason the room deserves to be called the Hall of Capitals. The ceiling was destroyed and then reconstructed at some later date, probably early in the Moslem era during the surge of building activities in this area. Then the reconstructed ceiling was itself damaged during an earthquake (which left it cracked) and was repaired and reinforced with the aid of two arches supported by a central pillar that is still standing. The floor that resulted from this reconstruction work was more

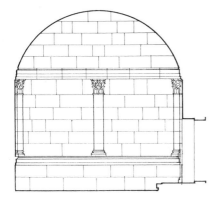

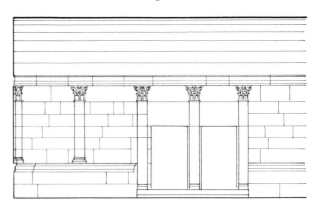

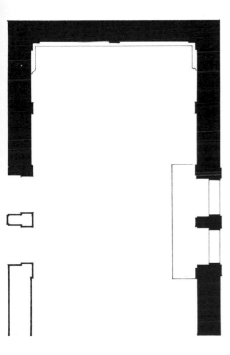

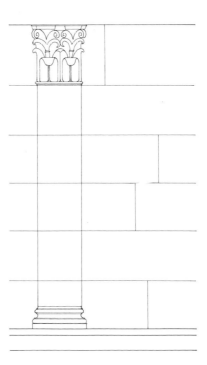

The Hall of Capitals — plan, section, and elevation

than a meter higher than the original flooring of the Second Temple period.

In relating the history of the war against the Romans, Josephus speaks of a bridge that spanned between the central section of the western retaining wall and the structure he called the *Xystus*. In fact, he mentions this building no less than six times as the last structure on the slope of the Upper City and adds the detail that it was connected to the Temple Mount by a bridge topped by a gate. In classical architecture the term *xystus* usually denotes a structure that consists primarily of a large paved plaza. It is possible that the Hall of Capitals was the ground floor of such a structure and that the plaza comprised its second or third story, on the same level as the Temple Mount esplanade, with a bridge connecting it to the Temple Mount. In weighing the merits of this theory, we should keep in mind that Jerusalem was a very densely built city, so that it is difficult to imagine the *Xystus* being located in what is today the Jewish Quarter as this' would imply that a 100-meter strip west of the Temple Mount was absolutely vacant and that the city's built-up area ended somewhere on the slope of the western hill. Moreover, wherever we dug south of this area, we found remains from the Second Temple period very close to the retaining wall, which would tend to refute the reading of a long bridge and open space by the central section of the wall.

The Gymnasium, the Archive, and the Council Building

What function, then, did the *Xystus* serve? We have no definitive information about it, and although we know that in classical architecture the term *xystus* is often associated with a gymnasium, there is no indication that such an institution existed or was built in Herodian Jerusalem. What's more, such a building should not be confused with the gymnasium that was indeed constructed in Jerusalem during the period of Greek rule. Hellenistic culture, which made great inroads among the people of Jerusalem, prompted the construction of such cultural institutions as a gymnasium during the heyday of Greek influence; and the belief that there was a gymnasium in the city during the Herodian period probably crept into Jerusalem lore because of the term *xystus*. Yet it is highly probable that this Greek concept came to mean any broad plaza paved in stone. Thus in using the word *xystus*, Josephus may well have meant a structure with a broad, stone-paved plaza in its center but not necessarily a gymnasium at all.

In contrast, the sources are very specific about the nature of a number of public institutions located directly west of the Temple Mount in this central sector. One was an archive for promissory notes and other documents critical to the city's commercial life. This building — or perhaps it is more accurate to say its contents — were burned during the First Revolt (A.D. 66) by the Zealots, who were fired by the vision of social reform. Another building found in this part of the city housed the equivalent of the city council of the day and was referred to as both the Council Building and the Committee building. It is difficult to decide whether these terms refer to two separate institutions or a single one with two names. However, it is clear that Jerusalem, like every other metropolis of the time, boasted some kind of an institution that ran municipal affairs, including supervision of the markets, prices, cleanliness, law and order, and the safety of the pilgrims. Thus we know that some of the most important buildings in Jerusalem, all built with great splendor, were located on the slope of the western hill facing in the direction of Tyropoeon Valley Street. To which of these buildings did the magnificent Hall of Capitals belong? Only time will tell.

A Theater, Amphitheater, and Hippodrome

In Herod's day the land of Judea reached new heights of power and political and economic status, and all of this was naturally reflected in the spiritual life and religious institutions of the Jews, which likewise flourished. The Temple was of course the heart of Jerusalem for the Jews of Judea and the Diaspora alike, but slowly the city began to attract non-Jews as well, for the reputation of Jerusalem and its Temple had spread throughout the civilized world. Yet in order to furnish Jerusalem with an international standing that would make it a magnet for tourists of all lands and outlooks, Herod felt constrained to build cultural and sports institutions, for without them the city would not rate as a metropolis. Josephus mentions the existence of such institutions incidentally, and because he does not write about them in their own right, we are not at all enlightened about where they were located.

Important as a thriving tourist trade was to Jerusalem's economy, not everyone was pleased about the introduction of these "worldly" institutions into the city. Statues, for example, were placed in the theaters of the day as part and parcel of their structure and décor, but since they violated the prohibition against graven images, the observant Jews of Jerusalem could not abide them. Once, when a rumor took flight that cloth-draped statues had been placed in the city's theater, Herod had to invite the head of the "opposition" to see for himself that these were not statues at all but weapons wrapped in lengths of cloth (it was customary to display arms taken as booty in the lobby of a theater). Not until the rumor was thoroughly quashed did the unrest in the city die down.

The reconstructions of Jerusalem drawn by various scholars and the model of the Second Temple by the Holyland Hotel in Jerusalem place the theater on the slopes of the western hill facing the Temple Mount. Since Josephus gave no indication of the theater's location, any scholar is entitled to speculate where it might have been. The slope of the western hill was a popular supposition because one of Josephus' descriptions of the Upper City as viewed from the Temple Mount speaks of the area having "the shape of a theater." He meant that it was composed of rows of houses terraced one above the next, but some scholars interpreted this passage literally and concluded that the theater stood opposite the Temple Mount. Another point advanced to justify this reading is the fact that in Greek cities the theater was usually built close to the temple, and this custom was probably carried over to Jerusalem. Finally, the topography of the city added additional weight to this premise, as there is a small depression in the eastern slope of the Upper City that could well have accommodated a building such as a theater.

The problem is that excavations both inside and outside the present city wall have failed to turn up the slightest trace of a theater on that slope. What has been unearthed are the remains of residential buildings so constructed as to give the city a terraced look that could well have resembled the audience of a theater — just as Josephus suggested. Moreover, this spot was an unlikely setting for a theater both because it would have required the expropriation of land and evacuation of many residents (in addition to the property that had already been expropriated to extend the Temple Mount) and because it would have roused vigorous opposition on the part of the observant population: since the dramatic arts are not exactly consonant with the spirit of the *halakhah*, what more offensive place to site a theater than facing the Temple itself? In short, what conformed to the needs of a classic Hellenistic city was not necessarily appropriate for Jerusalem, and these are the reasons leading us to believe that the theater was probably located outside the city walls.

Most of the reconstructions of Herodian Jerusalem also show the hippodrome to be one of the most impressive buildings in the city and place it near the foot of the Temple Mount's southern wall. Since we were digging in just that area, we hoped we would be lucky enough to find the remains of one of Herod's most glorious feats of architecture. But our excavations turned up nothing even vaguely resembling a hippodrome. On the contrary, the area yielded the network of streets, plazas, and markets that comprised a monumental "open foyer" of the Temple Mount. The hippodrome would therefore have to be sought elsewhere.

The spacious cistern under the public building southwest of the Dung Gate

But where? If we return to Josephus' writings, we find that the hippodrome is mentioned twice in his works, both in the same context. In one case it is noted in passing in an account of the rebellion that broke out during the reign of Herod's son Archelaus. The rebellion erupted at a time when pilgrims from all over the country had gathered in Jerusalem for celebrations. Most of the pilgrims were put up in the municipal parks or "camping areas," of which there were three in Jerusalem. Then, as now, these areas were specially laid-out sites outside the city where regular services were provided by the municipal authorities and one could obtain water and other facilities in addition to space for putting up a tent or booth. Josephus mentions one of these three parks as being west of the king's palace, meaning in the area of Mamilla or the Ben Hinnom Valley today. The second was northeast of the Temple Mount, somewhere east of what is now Herod's Gate (which was outside the city limits in that period) or, according to a different version, further east on the slopes of the Mount of Olives. In either case it was outside the city walls of that time. The third park was south of the Temple Mount, close to the hippodrome, and is mentioned in Josephus' writings only once: "Distributing themselves into three divisions, they formed three camps, one on the north of the Temple, and another on the south, adjoining the Hippodrome, and the third near the Palace on the west" (*The Jewish War*, II, III, 1, 40–46).

In this quote the hippodrome's relation to the Temple Mount is given only in terms of direction, not of distance. Similarly, when Josephus mentions the northern park, he notes that it is located "north of the Temple" but does not say whether or not it was close to the compound. Logic dictates that Jerusalem's hippodrome was located outside the city, for if we take into consideration the density with which the city was built and the disposition of its inhabitants, it is highly unlikely that horse races would be held close to the Temple Mount. Moreover, building a hippodrome in such close proximity to the sanctified mount would have been out of character for Herod and is certainly not consistent with his reputation for political finesse. Incidentally, in writing about the Rogel Spring in the Kidron Valley, south of the Siloam Pool, a number of scholars have drawn attention to what appears to be the remains of stone "bleachers" that may have been part of a theater or hippodrome. It therefore appears that many of the scholars who located the hippodrome close to the Temple Mount were misled by a biased view of Herod as an arbitrary ruler who was hostile to the Jewish religion and disposed toward quarreling with and humiliating the Jews by forcing them to build such a flagrantly profane institution as a hippodrome near the entrance to the Temple Mount. Josephus' casual remark that this structure was located south of the Temple Mount merely confirmed their prejudice.

Another sports arena mentioned by Josephus was the amphitheater, a round structure containing two adjoining rings (like the Colosseum in Rome) and used primarily for sports events and competitions in which gladiators pitted themselves against each other or wild animals. Josephus also speaks of heavily attended celebrations held in these arenas, of renowned athletes being invited to take part in these competitons, and of the lavish prizes awarded to them. He mentions the amphitheater once without citing its location but does provide the clue that it was in "the lowland," meaning some kind of plain. Areas of flat terrain can be found in the north of Jerusalem, in sectors that were included within the bounds of the city after the construction of the Third Wall. To date, however, no orderly excavations have been undertaken in those places.

Yet Another Public Building

Outside the Dung Gate we uncovered a street dating to the Byzantine era, and under it are some very impressive-looking ruins that we have yet to study in depth. Further excavation of the area is conditional upon reaching an accommodation with the owners of the property and the opening of access roads. But even now, with the meager work we have invested there, it is possible to discern an imposing building constructed alongside an enormous water cistern carved out of rock. The dimensions of this cistern are about 20×7 meters, and it was originally coated with a black-gray plaster characteristic of the Second Temple period but was replastered a second and third time in later periods (it was last in use during the Middle Ages). A side entrance (dating the Byzantine era) leads into the cistern, and its lintel bears inscriptions in Greek mentioning Jesus. According to the tradition of the Byzantine period, this site was an object of pilgrimage or served some other ritual purpose. Nearby are the remains of a large building, and a bit farther off we can see what is left of a white mosaic floor. Without further investigation, it is impossible to date these structures accurately. All we can say now is that built among the ruins is a sewage canal whose contents — pottery vessels and about thirty coins — come from the late Roman period (third century A.D.).

I discussed this discovery with Father Bargil Fixner from the Dormition Abbey, whose main occupation at that time was identifying Christian holy sites of the Byzantine era, and he believes that the cistern was visited by pilgrims of that age who identified it as the prison into which the prophet Jeremiah was cast by order of King Zedekiah. This determination has still to be researched in depth, but while visiting the area Father Bargil Fixner noticed the inscription ακρα (Acra) on one of the cistern's walls. Is it possible that the Byzantines identified the remains of this impressive building as the ruins of the Hellenistic fortress? Or perhaps they believed it was the citadel of the kings of Judah and associated it with the prison into which Jeremiah was cast but mistakenly referred to it as the Acra. One way or another, the remains of this huge public building hold great promise for future excavators.

An imperial Roman coin with a
likeness of the Emperor Nero

11 Roman Jerusalem

The most vivid and dramatic description we have of Jerusalem's destruction comes from Josephus' *The Jewish War* and opens as follows:

And the dawn of the eighth day of the month Gorpiaeus broke upon Jerusalem in flames — a city which had suffered such calamities during the siege that had she from her foundation enjoyed an equal share of blessings she would have been thought unquestionably enviable; a city undeserving moreover of these great misfortunes on any other ground, save that she produced a generation such as that which caused her overthrow (VI, VII, 5, 407–415).

The book goes on to describe scenes from the war, its disastrous consequences, and the great destruction wreaked upon the city. Josephus informs us that Titus ordered his soldiers to raze the Temple and the city to the ground — except for the citadel alongside the king's palace. The ruin was so devastating that anyone entering the area thereafter would not have suspected that a thriving city had once stood there, and the destruction of the Temple was so traumatic an event for the Jewish people that it left an indelible impression on succeeding generations all the way down to our own day. The anguish that emanates from Josephus' description is understandable. A native of Jerusalem who was intimately acquainted with the city, loved it, and witnessed the wrack and ruin that overtook it — not only or even primarily at the hands of the Romans but due to the wars between the rival Jewish factions and as a function of the corruption and immorality that preceded the revolt — Josephus Flavius was steeped in sorrow as he raised his quill and wrote of the fate of Jerusalem in the darkest possible colors.

We came upon signs of this devastation almost as soon as we had begun to dig. It came in the form of the stones that had been cast down from the top of the Temple Mount wall onto the pavement below, and over the years our work repeatedly brought us face to face with the remains of such debris. The street in the vicinity of Barclay's Gate, for example, was piled high with huge stones — ashlars from the western wall that had toppled down into a heap and remained as mute testimony to what had happened there almost two millennia ago. I made it a custom to visit our excavation on the eve of the 9th of Av, the date on which the Temple was destroyed, and on which it is a centuries-old tradition to offer prayers and read Lamentations beside the Wailing Wall. Since the Six-Day War, this day of remembrance has taken on a special aura as thousands of people gather in the broad plaza by the Wailing Wall and the strains of Lamentations echo in the night. Standing there on a street from the Second Temple period with the ashlars of Herod's monumental walls at my feet — stones that had been torn out of the wall by rampaging soldiers — I could almost feel the horror and savagery of those days of destruction when Jerusalem and the Temple Mount, the jewel at its center, were laid low.

As our excavations proceeded, we uncovered stones in the area of Robinson's Arch whose special dressing immediately indicated that they had come from the pilasters or imaginary pillars that had decorated the exterior façade of the Temple Mount's porticoes. Working quietly and quite alone near the spot where some of these stones were uncovered was a volunteer from Germany by the name of Egon Less. Much as we urged him to join in the labors, and the company, of one of the groups, he insisted on working alone, digging by himself, filling his wheelbarrow, and emptying it all alone, over and over again. He wouldn't even hear of receiving help. In fact, single-handedly he did everything that a group of four workers was doing. Egon would collect pottery shards with meticulous care, and from time to time, when I passed through the area where he was working, he would ask me to date them and teach him how to classify them. In one of these talks, held in the vicinity of the spot where the pilaster stones had been found, I realized that the pottery shards belonged to vessels from the Byzantine period — or, more precisely, from the sixth–seventh centuries A.D. — which was rather surprising. After I explained this to Egon, he rallied all his strength and as many mechanical tools as he could commandeer. Two days later, all the debris had been moved and a considerable area had been cleared for an orderly dig. The results of this excavation confirmed that we had, indeed, come upon a surprising find: without exception the pottery and coins gathered from under the stones of the pilasters dated to the end of the Byzantine period. Hence large sections of the Temple Mount's walls must have been standing up to an appreciable height right up to the end of the Byzantine period.

In the course of time, additional information corroborating this conclusion came in from other areas of the dig. Consequently, we are now able to state with certainty that the destruction to the Temple Mount for which the Romans were responsible was not as grave as Josephus would have had us believe — and as early scholars did believe because they took him literally. Although the Romans destroyed the Temple and severely damaged the compound surrounding it, the Temple Mount proper continued to stand as an impressive structure; in fact, its walls rose to an appreciable height for centuries thereafter. Most of the decorative stones that had evidently belonged to the Triple Gate (the eastern Hulda Gate) were found in secondary use in Moslem buildings but never in structures that preceded them (from the Byzantine era), leading us to conclude that the walls from the Second Temple period were still standing up to the height of their decorations during the Byzantine period. And we know that during the war between the Persians and the Byzantines at the beginning of the seventh century, the compound served as a redoubtable fortress that proved very difficult to vanquish.

In the Footsteps of the Tenth Legion

Much of the population of conquered Jerusalem was executed, marched off to be sold as slaves in the marketplaces of Palestine and the neighboring lands, or shipped off to Rome to meet their fate as gladiators in the city's circuses. the rest were banished from Jerusalem, leaving the city a mutilated ghost town, at best a monument to desolation and ruin. The seat of imperial Roman rule was transferred to the port city of Caesarea, which became the country's capital, and the Tenth Roman Legion (the Fretensis or Legion of the Boar) was posted to stand guard over Jerusalem lest Jews steal back into the city and attempt to rebuild it. It has been a widespread assumption that the legion established its main camp on the western hill, where the king's palace and the citadel once stood, and further to the south in what was formerly the residential quarter of the Jerusalemite aristocracy and priestly oligarchy. Very little is known about this camp, however. What we do know is that the Tenth Legion remained in Jerusalem for over 200 years before being transferred to Elath toward the end of the third century. Bereft of a war to fight, its soldiers engaged instead in crafts and industry, public-building ventures, and production for the needs of the free market. Among the crafts in which they specialized was the manufacture of the baked-clay bricks used widely in the construction of bathhouses and industrial ovens (because they were fireproof), pipes for carrying water, and clay pipes for carrying steam from the furnace room to the *caldarium* or hot room of the bathhouse, which served as a sauna. The talents of the legion's soldiers at this craft earned them such renown that they stamped their distinctive hallmark on all their products. Consequently not every building that bears the mark of the Tenth Legion on some component of its construction was necessarily used by the soldiers of the legion; it may be that the structure was merely built of materials marketed by the Tenth Legion. What's more, the fact that a facility is made out of brick, including the bricks manufactured by the Tenth Legion, is not a criterion for dating it, since the inventory of bricks could have been drawn upon for quite a long time. In other cases facilities were pillaged and their bricks used in the construction of buildings. For example, bricks bearing the hallmark of the Tenth Legion were found in a large bathhouse from the Moslem period near the western wall.

Among the most outstanding volunteers working on our dig were students from Ambassador College in Pasadena, California, who returned annually in groups of 100 and spent six weeks in arduous and

Fragments of Hebrew inscriptions engraved on stones from the Temple Mount

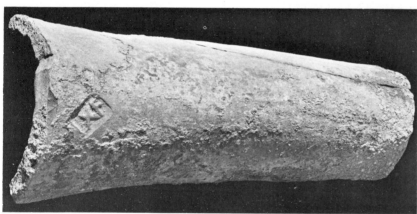

energetic labor. Because of their remarkable fortitude and energy we often assigned them to particularly difficult projects. One was to uncover what could be found under the remains of the Moslem palace south of the Temple Mount. A group of Ambassador students set to work among the foundations of the building, which sometimes extended as far down as 7 meters and included parts of columns from earlier buildings placed in secondary use by the Moslem builders.

The year was 1970 and we were approaching the 9th of Av — when one of the members of this group came running toward me flushed with excitement. "I've been looking all over for you!" he shouted. "What's up?" I asked, though it seemed pretty clear from the state he was in that he had found something interesting. "There's an inscription down there," he told me, and I accompanied him back to the area and climbed down the ladder to find that a column that the Moslems had incorporated into the palace's foundation walls bore a clear inscription in Latin letters. Even at first glance I could tell that this was a royal inscription, though most of it was still not visible. After a few hours' hard work we managed to free the column from the wall of which it had become a part — without

above: Hallmarks of the Tenth Roman Legion on round clay bricks and on a pipe

opposite: Hallmarks of the Tenth Legion on tiles

damaging the wall itself — and cleaned off the remaining plaster that still clung to it. Then came our startling discovery that it was a dedicatory inscription of the Tenth Legion mentioning none other than Titus himself. We were filled with emotion because of the uncanny symbolism of the find. Here we were on the eve of the 9th of Av. One thousand nine hundred years ago to the day, Titus had briefed his troops on the storming of the Temple Mount. And now, in the renewed State of Israel, standing in Jerusalem, digging alongside the Temple Mount, we had come into tangible contact with Titus and his legions. What more could an archaeologist ask for?

Aelia Capitolina

In A.D. 117, almost half a century after the destruction of Jerusalem, Hadrian ascended to the throne in Rome. Roman historians portrayed him as a benevolent and beloved emperor who did much for the benefit of his country, but in Jewish history he is remembered as one of the most monstrous of Israel's enemies. The primary reason for this harsh judgment was Hadrian's determination to rebuild Jerusalem as a pagan city and rededicate the Temple Mount not as a place sanctified to the God of Israel but as a monument to the Roman god Jupiter.

Hadrian's first move was to redesign Jerusalem's network of streets and commercial center. His blueprint encompassed the area of the Temple Mount and the western hill — to be more precise, the area extending from today's Damascus Gate southward to Mount Zion — and was drawn almost precisely along the lines of the former Upper Market and the Lower Market, Jerusalem's main commercial centers at the end of the Second Temple period. He also began planning the construction of a classic Roman forum at the heart of what was formerly the Upper Market. But the crowning innovation — and affront to the Jews of Palestine — was the bestowal of a new name on the city: Aelia Capitolonia, in honor of its founder, Aelius Hadrianus. It was an appellation that stuck for centuries.

If Hadrian's plan was to restore the ravaged city to glory, it was doomed from the start. For Jerusalem is surrounded by mountains, and access to it is difficult. It is not noted for its natural resources, and all its

features dictate that it remain a small city. Throughout its history, Jerusalem has known many periods of florescence, but only when it was a spiritual center for the country's inhabitants. Without spiritual inspiration as its backdrop, it never developed to the stature of a metropolis. In his desire to build a temple to Jupiter on the ruins of the Jewish sanctuary, Hadrian only exacerbated the mood of rebellion already rife among the Jews of Palestine, thereby undermining Roman rule in the country. For the construction of the temple to Jupiter, on top of his harsh treatment of the Jews, led to one of the fiercest rebellions Rome ever faced: the Bar Kokhba revolt. Although this determined uprising ended in a Roman victory, the bloodletting on both sides was so costly that from the viewpoint of the Romans, their victory was a Pyrrhic one, at best.

After suppressing the Bar Kokhba revolt, the Romans scaled down their plans for rebuilding Jerusalem. It appears that Jupiter's temple was finally erected, but it never gained a very exalted standing, as Roman temples go. Emperors came and went, some hostile to the Jews, others developing friendly relations with the Jewish leadership of the day; but none allowed the Jews to return to Jerusalem and restore the city so central to Jewish life. Jerusalem of the second and third centuries A.D. remained a small Roman settlement whose importance lay in its unexceptionality, in the denial of its greatness.

The curious thing about research on Aelia Capitolina is that although

A stamp for marking loaves of bread belonging to the Tenth Legion

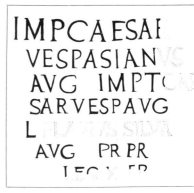

A stone column engraved with a Latin inscription mentioning Titus

the documentary material on it is very sparse, and even the archaeological investigations of the past century have added little, the number of research papers on the Roman city seem to run in inverse proportion to the meagerness of the finds. We were therefore very curious to see how our dig at the foot of the Temple Mount and on the slopes of the western hill might advance, if only by inches, the knowledge of Aelia Capitolina, the Roman city of Jerusalem.

Did Aelia Capitolina Have Walls?

There is hardly a single written source about the establishment of Aelia Capitolina or the city's plan and institutions, and the little known about them comes from references to a number of public buildings in Byzantine literature (written a few centuries after the Roman period). Yet in speaking of an ancient city, one naturally assumes it was encompassed by a wall. Was Aelia Capitolina surrounded by a wall? And if so, where did it run? Earlier students of Jerusalem generally posited that since the Roman soldiers razed Jerusalem to the ground after the First Revolt, as described by Josephus, Hadrian and his contemporaries must have rebuilt the city walls from scratch. Consequently, they conceived Aelia Capitolina as a small city whose walls followed a completely new course. All scholars agreed that the course of the walls in the west, north, and east followed the lines of the present Old City wall (which was built in the sixteenth century by Suleiman the Magnificient), for they knew that Suleiman's wall

A bronze coin mentioning Simeon Bar Kokhba

was built on older foundations. Thus the ancient and splendidly built gate under the present-day Damascus Gate, was identified as one of the structures of the Roman city of Aelia Capitolina. Yet there is no proof for this assumption, and we believe, on the contrary, that this gate is fundamentally a structure built by Herod that continued to serve Aelia Capitolina — if, indeed, the Roman city was surrounded by fortifications at all.

In view of these earlier scholars, the biggest change in the course of the Roman wall, compared to that of predecessors, found expression in the south and was a function of the startling reduction in the city's size. Whole sections of the Herodian city of Jerusalem fell outside the municipal boundaries of Aelia Capitolina. Therefore the Roman fortifications in the south followed an entirely new course, namely, the line of today's Old City wall. Departing from the Temple Mount's southern wall by the Al Aqsa mosque, the present-day wall climbs up the western hill (leaving Mount Zion outside its boundary) until it meets the city wall in the east. The belief that this course was determined as far back as the time of Aelia Capitolina was reinforced by surveys indicating the remains of fortifications under Suleiman's wall. Also contributing to this view were the descriptions written by travelers in the early Byzantine period and particularly a piece by an anonymous pilgrim from Bordeaux who visited Jerusalem during the early half of the fourth century.

What emerges from these testimonies is far from unequivocal, however, and can be interpreted in a number of ways. If you study the corner of Suleiman's wall near the Al Aqsa Mosque, you will notice that it is built over a wall of large ashlars that now serves as its foundation but was once part of a structure in its own right. Earlier scholars assumed that it was none other than the wall of Aelia Capitolina. Furthermore, a small excavation conducted by Kathleen Kenyon by the outer corner of this wall showed that it was built over cisterns from the Second Temple period, thereby bolstering the premise that it was a Roman structure. But the excavation we conducted on *both* sides of this wall proved that it was actually the corner of a large building — a palace from the early Moslem period — that stands on remains from the Second Temple period. We know that the order of strata in a dig does not necessarily follow a consistent historical chronology, especially since the foundations of some buildings were dug through a number of earlier strata and destroyed all trace of them. Thus even if we posit that the wall of Aelia Capitolina followed the general course outlined above, it certainly should not be identified with the foundations of the present city wall, which contain stones from the lintels of a huge church decorated with crosses.

Further evidence refuting the possibility that the conjectured wall of Aelia Capitolina should be identified with the remains under the present-day wall came from the excavation along Suleiman's wall in the form of two finds, one "positive," the other "negative." The "positive" discovery was a line of ancient fortifications under Suleiman's wall. They comprised segments of a wall, a few towers, and some gates. After being destroyed, these fortificaitons served as the foundations for the Ottoman wall. However, they were built in the Middle Ages (the eleventh–twelfth centuries) and therefore cannot be the presumed wall of Aelia Capitolina. The "negative" find was the remains of structures under the medieval fortifications — some outside the medieval wall, others inside or under it. A number of these structures date to the Second Temple period; others are from the Byzantine and early Moslem periods. But characteristic remains

Silver imperial Roman coins

of Aelia Capitolina, either inside or outside the wall, are very sparse indeed.

So once again the question arises: if the course of Suleiman's wall is not identical with that of the wall surrounding Aelia Capitolina, where did Aelia Capitolina's wall run? Yet before embarking on a search, it may be pertinent to backtrack somewhat and ask a different question: was Roman Jerusalem actually surrounded by a wall of its own?

Our investigations enable us to offer the following answer. Josephus' description of the destruction of Jewish Jerusalem, which he claims was so thorough that no trace of the city survived, is indeed a moving literary rendition but did not accurately reflect the situation. For not only did the towers of the royal fortress survive the Roman rampage, the ravaged Temple Mount continued standing up to an appreciable height, as did the remains of other structures now being uncovered by archaeological excavations. A decade before the Six-Day War, Professor Avi-Yonah wrote of the yields of the archaeological excavations in Jerusalem that: "... The house whose foundations were dug alongside these steps dates to Herod's time, and if so it is the *only* private home from that period of which there are any remains." Today, however, this statement has been superseded by a very different reality. Many buildings of the Herodian and Second Temple periods have been uncovered in various places in Jerusalem, some of them still preserved to a height of two stories! Evidence of the destruction is obvious everywhere; nevertheless, buildings remained standing all over the city. And if this is true of residential buildings, it must have been all the more true of fortifications. Although Jerusalem's fortifications were breached and damaged, far more survived than were destroyed beyond repair. Thus if the builders of Aelia Capitolina wanted to enclose their city, they could simply have repaired the breached Herodian wall. Even with the city's population drastically reduced, it was still more sensible to restore an existing line of fortification than build a new one from scratch. Another theory has it that the fortifications of Aelia Capitolina surrounded only the Tenth Legion's camp in the Upper City, but this conjecture likewise lacks corroboration by either the written sources or finds uncovered in the field. So it may well be that when the Aelia Capitolina was built, what remained of the Herodian city wall was restored to serve as its fortifications. One thing is certain, however: the conjectured line of Roman fortifications in the south following the course of the Ottoman wall — which became a "fact" in every historical atlas of Jerusalem — never actually existed.

A City of Soldiers

In building Aelia Capitolina attention was paid primarily to restoring the commercial quarters of the Upper City. The forum, designed as the heart of the city's new commercial center, was to be built in the Upper Market on the main street running between the Damascus Gate and Mount Zion. The remains of Aelia Capitolina found in our dig by the Temple Mount show that its inhabitants were mostly the soldiers of the Tenth Legion garrisoned in Jerusalem, and as we have said, the usual presumption is that the legion's main camp was in the Upper City, in the vicinity of the royal palace and Mount Zion. But a very interesting find from the Aelia Capitolina period turned up near the southwest corner of the Temple Mount.

One of the ironies of searching for and preserving the remains of the past is that the archaeological endeavor entails destruction. The brutal fact is that if you want to know what lies under a certain stratum, you have no choice but to destroy it. This decision is sometimes a difficult one. Imagine having found a beautiful room with fine walls and handsome stone floor. It has taken you days on end to excavate the room and expose it all, but hour by hour you can see another small section of the wall emerge as a result of your labors until you have finally uncovered the floor, cleaned it, and gathered up all the finds on it. By then you feel almost as if you've lived in that room, that you are a part of it and it is a part of you. Suddenly the surveyors and photographers arrive, surrounding you and your room, measuring it, sketching it stone by stone, shooting it from every angle. Sensing that something drastic is about to happen, you try to push all thoughts of the inevitable out of your mind. But finally the fateful moment arrives: dig we must, and that means ripping up the floor to find out what happened on this spot before "your" room was

Three seals of semi-precious stones from seal rings belonging to Roman soldiers

built. The first days are really tough. There you stand with huge quantities of dirt confronting you again. The work is hard, often tedious, and again you ask yourself: where is all this leading to? Sometimes there's a surprise awaiting you, however: the stratum under "your" room has other treasures in store, some even better than what you have already found.

This is what happened to us near the southwest corner of the Temple Mount. A lovely room belonging to a Moslem palace came up in the "lottery" for destruction. Photographs, measuring, sketches, and dismantling of the floors all accomplished, the difficult road downward began. As the detritus of ruin was systematically removed, the color black began to show through, and we knew we had come upon ashes. The further down we went, the more of it there was, and it covered the entire area. Obviously we were digging into the remains of a great conflagration. Tragic though this fire was to the people who inhabited the building, a sight of this kind augurs well for archaeologists. For if a building went up in

A bronze Celtic cavalryman found in the Legion camp on the banks of the Thames River, now on display in the British Museum
left and right: A bronze Celtic cavalryman found in the legion camp at the foot of the Temple Mount in Jerusalem

flames, there was probably no time to salvage its contents, and the finds usually present in the layers of ash on the floor enhance our knowledge of the past. In the room we uncovered, these finds included Roman coins from the second and third centuries A.D., a small wooden box whose contents survived, and some finely fashioned bronze figurines. One of the figurines was of a Celtic rider bearing a shield in one hand and a spear in the other, a memento of the unit of Celtic cavalry that served in Jerusalem. A similar figurine (the only similar one found to date) emerged about a century ago in the excavation of a Roman camp alongside the Thames River in London. Next to the figurines we found a bronze mask and dice made out of bone. The overall contents of this room suggest that it probably served the garrison's priests, whose duties included foretelling the future before the unit went out to battle. Had it not been for that fire, we would not have had any direct archaeological evidence from the second and third centuries in the area of the Temple Mount, for the few other Roman remains that turned up in the area were found in secondary use and we have no way of knowing how they got there.

Other remains of Aelia Capitolina that emerged from our dig were first and foremost pottery vessels, particularly oil lamps with various decorations on them — including pornographic poses. The camps of the Roman army are rich in these finds, together with bronze, silver, and gold imperial coins scattered at random among the ruins. Coins from the Roman period also came up in the fill of later construction that had been hauled to this area from all over the city. No Roman era buildings other than the remains of the burned one were uncovered by the Temple Mount, but there was one other find that may be related to this period — though we have no definitive proof.

below: Pottery oil lamps with a pornographic engraving from the legion camp

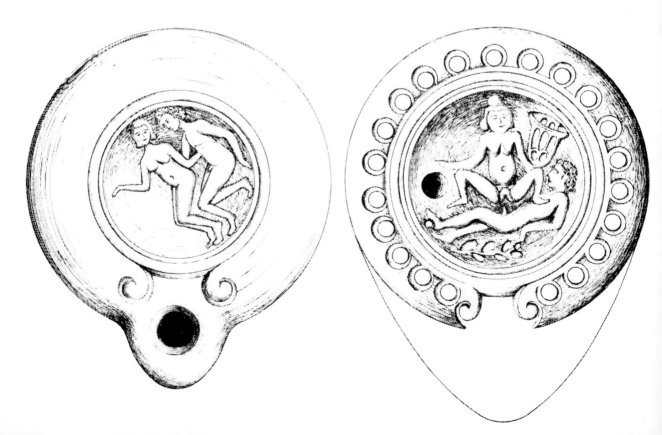

A pottery oil lamp engraved with the figure of Helios, the sun god

In the vicinity of the Triple Gate, we uncovered the remains of a grave carved out of the bedrock. At a later period (sixth–seventh centuries A.D.), this grave, whose contents had been removed, served as the basement storeroom of a Byzantine building. Did the grave originally date to Aelia Capitolina? This is a difficult question to answer, for its layout resembles that of a Jewish burial cave but Jews were not buried in Jerusalem, and certainly not in proximity to the Temple Mount. It is possible that a connection exists between this grave and the remains from Aelia Capitolina scattered around the area, especially because the artifacts found among these remains are characteristic of the ritual offerings placed in graves — oil lamps, cooking pots, glass vessels, coins, jewelry, and seal rings — while there were no finds characteristic of daily life, such as storage jars, spoons, and the like. Before becoming the basement of the Byzantine building, the cave was cleared of all its contents, and only its shape remained as possible testimony to its past. Perhaps it served the Judeo-Christian sect that lived in Aelia Capitolina at the time.

One indisputable token of Aelia Capitolina found in various sites around the city are the Latin inscriptions found on Roman tombstones. One of these was engraved on a stone pillar that today serves as the base of a streetlamp in the Old City. It is a burial inscription that reads: "In memory of the soul of the blessed Lucius Magnus, a soldier of the Tenth Legion, Fretensis, a man of rights. He served 29 years. He lived 39 years." Another find from the period of Aelia Capitolina is a collection of lovely though broken marble statues that were likewise found not *in situ* but in collections of marble fragments that the Moslems collected at the begin-

opposite: A bronze mask from the legion camp alongside the Temple Mount

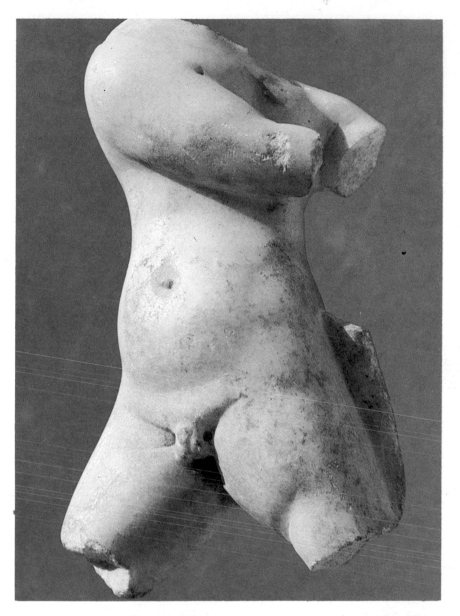

above: A marble statue from the Roman period

right: A foot from a marble statue of the Roman period

left: The head from a marble statue of the Roman period

ning of their rule and set aside for use in mosaics. Among these pieces are the foot from a statue of a man, the heads of men and animals, and other parts of the body. They undoubtedly belonged to elaborate statuaries placed in various parts of the city or on the Temple Mount when the Emperor Hadrian began building the temple to Jupiter.

We should note, however, that Hadrian was not the only one to build in Jerusalem during the Roman period. A fragment of a dedicatory tablet found in our excavation (along with other inscriptions known from various parts of the city) indicates that building continued in Jerusalem during the reign of Hadrian's successors throughout the second and third centuries. While uncovering the foundations of the Moslem palace, for

Part of the head and torso of a marble figurine from the Roman period

A stone tablet bearing a Latin dedicatory inscription mentioning the Emperor Septimius Severus

example, our laborers' spades hit a pavement stone from the Herodian era, and in the course of cleaning this slab we found a Latin inscription engraved on it. This was one of three stones that made up the full inscription. After being deciphered by Professor Avi-Yonah, the inscription led us to conclude that what we had come upon was a structure that the city council and the inhabitants of the city had dedicated to the Emperor Lucius Septimius Severus at the end of the second century. Once again we were witness to a phenomenon characteristic of excavations in Jerusalem, especially in the vicinity of the Temple Mount: a pavement stone from the Herodian era that had been removed from its place and served as a dedication plaque for a public building in the late Roman period went or

to be used as a building stone in a palace constructed during the Moslem period.

A dedicatory inscription mentioning the name of Emperor Hadrian is also found alongside the lintel of the Double Gate. It was discovered and deciphered back in the middle of the nineteenth century, and in its present state it is upside down and appears to be just another one of the stones in the wall that was repaired by the early Moslem builders in the seventh-

Fragments from Roman pottery vessels ornamented with human heads

eighth centuries. This, too, is a fragment of a long inscription, and its purpose is far from clear. It reads: "To [the Emperor] Titus Aelius Hadrianus Antonius Augustus Pius, father of the fatherland, pontifex, augur. By decree of the Decurions." Could it have belonged to a statue of Hadrian placed on the Temple Mount? We simply have no way of knowing.

12   Jerusalem Under Christian Rule

On September 18, 324, the Roman Emperor Constantine defeated Licinius, emperor of the Eastern Roman Empire, in a battle fought by the city of Byzantium. With Licinius' downfall, the Byzantine Empire, including Palestine and therefore Jerusalem, passed into Christian hands. Keenly aware of the importance of the East for the political and economic stability of his empire, Constantine transferred his capital and seat of rule to Byzantium, then a small city on the shores of the Bosporus, and later renamed it Constantinople after himself. No less important, Constantine the Great, the most brilliant statesman of his day, gave priority to the defense of the eastern marches of the empire. Palestine and Syria, two of these outlying areas, had to be reinforced from the standpoint of fortifications, roads, and especially populace. Above all, these provinces would have to be inhabited by subjects whose loyalty to the regime was beyond question. One way to ensure such loyalty was by converting the inhabitants to Christianity. At first this objective may have been perceived as easily attainable, for many peoples throughout the Roman Empire were embracing the new state religion with alacrity. There were, however, a number of recalcitrant peoples within the boundaries of the Byzantine Empire, including the Jews and the Samaritans, that zealously clung to the faiths of their forefathers, spurning both economic temptation and heavy political pressure. For this reason, Palestine could not be regarded as a Christian country even though almost half of its population had adopted Christianity. And under these circumstances, Constantine found it prudent to encourage European Christians to at least visit the country in numbers.

To this end, the emperor resolved to build an infrastructure that would serve the pilgrim and tourist trade and, of course, be thoroughly Christian in character. This plan happened to coincide with the emergence in Palestine of a strong desire to seek out the sites related to the life of Jesus, the members of his family, and his apostles, along with sites associated with the Old Testament prophets and kings. The authorities supported this local initiative, and soon churches and monasteries began to spring up throughout the country and helped attract the faithful to settle and build communities around them. Once pilgrims began to flock to these sites, the country again found itself on the world tourist map — this time by virtue of its attraction to Christans.

Queen Helena, Constantine's mother, who was possessed of a deep religious fervor, can definitely be counted among the most important of the early Christian pilgrims to Palestine. Dedicated to searching out sites connected with the life and death of Jesus, she retrospectively earned herself the honor of being considered the first Christian archaeologist. The queen mother was particularly preoccupied by the search for the site of Jesus' crucifixion and burial, and in the course of her travels she designated sites that are honored in Church tradition to this day. In the wake of these discoveries, Jerusalem experienced a renaissance as a new wave of construction created landmarks everywhere. At the beginning of the fourth century, Aelia Capitolina was therefore a city on the threshold

Residential buildings from the beginning of the period of Byzantine rule in Jerusalem. In the foreground is a peristylar court. Directly above the buildings is a wall from the Ommayad period

A Jewish oil lamp from the fourth century A.D.

above: A wine jug from the fourth century

left: A marble statue of a figure dressed in a toga with a Greek dedicatory inscription on the base, third–fourth centuries A.D.

opposite: A small pottery cruse for holding holy water, among the souvenirs popular among Christian pilgrims to Jerusalem

of a new life — a civilian and spiritually directed life, in contrast to its former incarnation as little more than a military camp.

In A.D. 333 Jerusalem was visited by an anonymous traveler from Bordeaux (known only by his pen name "the pilgrim from Bordeaux"), and portions of his travelogue have come down to us. They include a number of vivid descriptions of Jerusalem mentioning both the ruins of the Temple Mount and two statues of Hadrian that were still standing when he arrived. The vaults of what are now referred to as Solomon's Stables, the entryway to the Temple Mount, and the Double Gate also remained standing, and the Frenchman marveled at their splendor. His description shows that the city's southern wall ran close to the Siloam Pool, and here is what he has to say about it:

As you leave Jerusalem to ascend Mount Zion, on the left side below in the valley, alongside the wall, there is a pool called Siloam, and it has four rows of columns as well as a large pool outside it ... (M. Ish-Shalom, *Christian Travelers to Palestine* [Hebrew], p. 214).

This description tallies with the course of the southern wall running through the area of the Siloam Pool during the fourth century. The pilgrim from Bordeaux also speaks of churches and other structures built by Constantine but makes no mention whatever of building activity in the vicinity of the Temple Mount.

Its transformation into a holy city of Christendom breathed new life into Jerusalem. In point of fact, whenever the element of religious feeling has been associated with it, Jerusalem has prospered and grown, for in the wake of religious inspiration came economic growth and the consequent hustle and bustle of city life. The picture of this development during the early Byzantine period became quite tangible as a result of our excavations.

The area immediately adjacent to the Temple Mount compound, which in the Second Temple period had been designed in the form of broad plazas and market streets, was deserted and desolate at the start of the Byzantine period. Now the public areas at the crest of the western hill took over the spotlight. For it was there, in the vicinity of the Roman forum, that Queen Helena had fixed the site of Jesus' crucifixion on the hill of Golgotha and the place of his burial nearby. Hence it was there that the most important church in the Christian world and the largest church in Jeursalem, the Church of the Holy Sepulcher (or, as it was known then, the Church of the Resurrection), was built.

The Temple Mount proper continued to stand in desolation, an enormous ruin containing a mixture of the remains of the destroyed Second Temple and uncompleted structures begun by Hadrian. In contrast to the momentum of building on the western hill, no attempt was made to take the Temple Mount in hand. On the contrary, it was important to the Byzantines that the compound remain in ruins as tangible evidence that Jesus' prophecy of the Temple's destruction had been borne out. The numerical ratio between Jews and Christians in Palestine at the time tended slightly in favor of the Christians, and the ideological struggle between Judaism and Christianity was at its height. It is against this background that Christianity ascribed such great importance to the Temple Mount remaining a ruin, for its destruction was one of the cornerstones of the new faith. Moreover, the regulations passed in Hadrian's day forbidding Jews to so much as enter Jerusalem (not to speak of

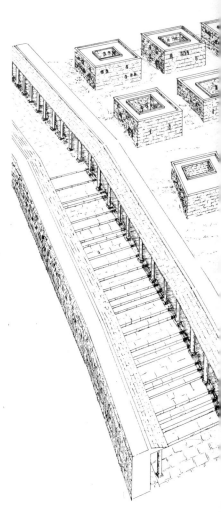

The Temple Mount in the Byzantine period. The southern wall is partially destroyed, and a residential quarter has been built below it

settling there) remained in force during the Byzantine era. On one day each year, however, the 9th of Av, the authorities permitted the Jews into the city and onto the Temple Mount to mourn the fate of their Temple. We can also assume that Christian missionaries took this opportunity to circulate among the mourners and try to convert them to their ascendant faith.

In the early days of research on the Temple Mount, a number of scholars tried to prove that churches had been built there. These claims are groundless, however. For much to the contrary, as we have already noted, keeping the Temple Mount in its destroyed state was a salient tenet of the Christian world view. Today some scholars still hold that there was

a church on the Temple Mount during the Byzantine period. The only
thing we know about this church is its name, the Church of the Corner;
and those who believe that it stood on the Temple Mount submit that it
got this name because it was located at the southeast corner of the esplanade. But the name could have been equally applicable to a church built
in the Kidron Valley, by the outer corner of the Temple Mount. What's
more, while it is highly unlikely that a church would have been built on
the Temple Mount, the Kidron Valley is associated with a number of
Christian traditions about events in Jesus' life, and churches were known
to be located there in the past — just as they are today.

What became of the public areas adjoining the Temple Mount, which
had been plazas and markets during the Herodian period? As the Temple
Mount lay abandoned, their original character was no longer pertinent.
Instead, it was in these areas that the new settlers of Jerusalem began to
build their homes.

Residential Buildings

Our excavations uncovered a number of residential buildings from the
early Byzantine period. We first began to come across them as far back as
1968, during the opening year of the dig, when we were engaged in studying a large structure from the early Moslem period close to Robinson's
Arch. Under this structure we found remains of a building from the late
Byzantine period (sixth–seventh centuries) with a set of facilities for small
industry. And no sooner had we finished measuring the apparatus and the
remains of the building than we dug down under its floors and were
amazed to find yet another residential building, this one built over the
ruins of the Herodian street and the vaults south of the pier of Robinson's
Arch. At first glance it was possible to assume that the lower building was
a Roman one from Aelia Capitolina, but we could not determine that
decisively, since there were no finds within the structure. Only afterward,
when we found other buildings laid out in a similar manner, likewise
located under structures from the sixth and seventh centuries, and containing indisputable chronological evidence, were we able to determine
that this structure dated to the fourth century A.D. For us it was the first
sign of renewed civilian construction in Jerusalem.

The dig outside the Old City wall near the Jericho road, in the heart of
the area once known as the Ophel, yielded fine results, including a large
residential building from the Second Temple period. We therefore decided to extend the excavation westward up to that building so as to fill in
details about its construction. Almost as soon as we set to work, just
below the surface (in this area we had already removed a considerable
amount of detritus using a bulldozer), the tops of stone walls began to
peek through. Had we once again discovered structures that postdated the
Second Temple period? We feared that if such structures were found here,
it would mean that the Second Temple buildings preceding them had been
totally destroyed and were lost to us. And indeed, our worst fears came
true. But in our loss we nonetheless came out ahead, for what we did find
here was a number of residential buildings from the fourth century, all
with a similar floor plan. Like the large building further to the west, these
structures were devoid of objects. Evidently their inhabitants had deserted
them, taking along everything of value. All we found were pottery shards,
coins from the third and early fourth centuries, and the hallmarks of the
Tenth Legion on the ceramic floor tiles; and even these meager artifacts
were associated with the roofs that had collapsed and filled the rooms, so

that we could not use them to determine the exact date of the structure. As luck would have it, the roofs had been made of beaten earth, so that the artifacts they contained had come from the place where the detritus originated.

To remove all doubt in establishing the date of these buildings, we decided to look for finds in the fill under the floors, which would naturally have predated the structures. In this particular case, pottery vessels and shards would not have helped us, for the dates to which they attest cover a good span of time, whereas we were looking for a rather exact definition of the period. Put more precisely, we wanted to find out whether these buildings dated to the Roman era or the start of the Byzantine age, whether they were constructed as part of Aelia Capitolina or were a product of the municipal planning that began in Constantine's day. Coins — present in the fill under the floors — would furnish us with a more accurate determination, for the date on a coin is definitive. We had become very sensitive to the importance of coins, especially after an incident in which a number of them were stolen from the dig by one of the laborers, and volunteers began reporting that antiquities dealers in Jerusalem were trying to tempt them into furnishing finds by promising lavish remuneration.

Be that as it may, we decided to assign a group of volunteers from Germany and Holland to excavate the fill under the floors of these buildings, and they did not disappoint us. In fact, their efforts proved to be most "lucrative." As usual, pottery shards turned up in abundance, but most of the finds in the fill were coins, and one day even a gold coin was uncovered. This was a special boon because over the years bronze coins become coated with a green patina that must be cleaned in a laboratory before they can be identified, but gold coins remain preserved as if they had just come out of the mint. The gold coin our volunteers found was an imperial mintage whose inscription could be read without difficulty. It had been issued during the reign of the Roman Emperor Tacitus, who — to his misfortune but our gain — had ruled for only a few months in A.D. 275–276 before succumbing to a heart attack while on a campaign in the East. During this brief period, coins bearing his name reached the legion camp in Jerusalem. Before leaving the city, the Romans dismantled their camps, and the remains thereof later served as fill under the floor of this Byzantine building. Evidently, this is how the gold coin made its way into the fill. Its discovery bolstered our premise that the foundations of the residential quarter had been laid in the days of Constantine and his successors. In the course of time, we cleaned the bronze coins and found that they further reinforced this assumption. Of the dozens of coins found in the fill, not a single one dated later than the reign of Constantine the Great, most of them coming from the early years of his reign. Hence these buildings had been constructed after the age of Constantine, for his coins could already be found under their floors not as buried treasure but scattered at random throughout the fill.

Plans and Finds

At first these Byzantine structures were built 10–15 meters from one another; later on, when the density of settlement increased, other residential buildings were wedged into the open spaces between them. The original buildings were constructed according to strictly defined floor plans. They were usually peristylar houses, meaning structures with an open inner court and two rows of columns down the center, usually in the form

of a horseshoe (the plan of such buildings being well known from classical Greece and Rome). During the Herodian period, a number of villas based on this plan were built in various places throughout the country, though never in Jerusalem. One reason was that a building of this sort takes up a good deal of space and precious land, reflecting a sense of prodigality that would have been entirely out of place in a crowded city. At the beginning of the fourth century, however, Jerusalem was a city with an abundance of open space, and the construction of such lavish villas was natural under the circumstances. The floor plan was of a series of rooms built around the peristylar court. The main entrance led into the courtyard, which in turn gave access to the various rooms. Occasionally one of the wings would be composed of two adjoining rows of rooms, while the others had only one. One room on the ground floor exiting onto the courtyard was used as a kitchen (so identified by the ovens and cooking implements found inside). These buildings were constructed entirely out of stone, primarily small unhewn stones laid in an attractive pattern, one on top of the other, with the spaces between them filled with even smaller stones — testifying to a high standard of construction.

The early Byzantine structures were two stories high with the ground floor being sunk into the earth, so that the rooms had no windows or doors in the exterior façade and entrance to the building was through either the court or the upper story. On one side of the court was a corridor with a staircase leading up to the upper story. The ceiling of the ground

The tops of walls from the early Byzantine period as they began to be excavated

The same buildings after being excavated

floor was made of wood, but since there was a chronic shortage of long and strong wooden beams in the country, the rooms were divided in two by a stone arch and their ceilings were constucted of short beams laid from the wall to the arch. This method of construction was also used in late Byzantine and early Moslem buildings, in contrast to the stone vaulted ceilings of Herodian architecture.

The floors were made of beaten earth or stone slabs (not of mosaics like the floors found in the sixth–seventh century houses). The water supply was based on the storage of rainwater in 20–100-cubic-meter cisterns carved out of the rock under the ground floor and coated with high-grade plaster. (Sometimes these cisterns dated back to the Second Temple period.) Rainwater was channeled to them by pottery pipes whose remains were found during the excavation of this neighborhood. Each house had one cistern, on rare occasion two.

The structures from the early Byzantine period (fourth–fifth centuries) were devoid of any of the facilities for crafts or cottage industries that marked each of the buildings from the late Byzantine period (sixth–seventh centuries). Another difference between them — and a substantial one, from the technical point of view — is that the walls dating to the earlier period were built of unhewn stone, at least at the corners and doorposts. Despite their being partially subterranean, the exterior walls of the earlier buildings were not covered with any insulating material to protect them from dampness, while those of the later buildings were.

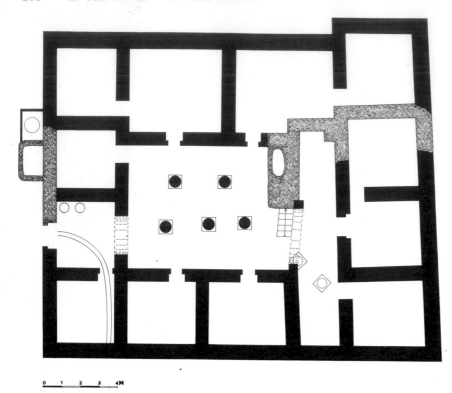

Plan of a residential building from the Byzantine period

The inhabitants of these buildings devoted much attention to the décor of their homes. Sometimes the stones at the point where the ceiling arches began to curve outward were engraved with lovely patterns. Remains of the plaster that had fallen off the walls contained proof that they had been decorated with colored drawings (frescoes). A particularly beautiful example of stuccowork (molding in plaster) was found on the ground floor of one of these houses. It was a painted bust of a man found *in situ* on the wall in the corner of a room. However, most of the remains of the wall plaster were found in the debris on the floor.

Since these buildings had been evacuated by their inhabitants, we found them void of everyday objects — a realization that was greeted with more than a tinge of disappointment. Nevertheless, it seemed impossible to come up entirely empty-handed, for close to one of these buildings we found, quite intact, a lovely pottery receptacle for wine decorated with drinking scenes.

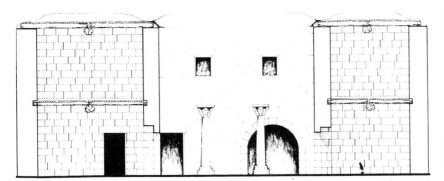

Section and elevation of a residential building from the Byzantine period

opposite: Perspective of the court of a residential building from the Byzantine period

Julian and the Jewish Problem

After the destruction of the Temple, the spiritual leadership of the Jewish people succeeded in meeting the challenge created by the traumatic blow to the national morale and the mass carnage perpetrated in Jerusalem. Sixty years later, the Jews found themselves facing another mortal crisis in the form of the Bar Kokhba revolt. But once again, despite the harrowing results both in demographic and spiritual terms, the leaders of the Jewish people were able to lead the remnant of Jewry in Palestine to national recovery. No other people in history had known such great tragedies and yet overcome these crises to survive and gather strength for the future. Barred from Jerusalem, the Jews organized for a new life in towns and villages all over the country. Bereft of the Temple, the nation's sages and rabbis found creative alternatives of ritual and spiritual practice that enabled the Jews to maintain a national and religious identity even far beyond their native land. One manifestation of this surrogate system was an ideological formula whereby the desire to approach and bring the Heavenly Jerusalem to fruition on earth became a sustaining ideal for the Jews — an ideal that took root at about the time of a great if shortlived turnabout in the history of the earthly Jerusalem during the fourth century.

In February 360 the Byzantine army proclaimed Julian, a subordinate of Emperor Constantinius II bearing the title of caesar (the equivalent of heir apparent), to the rank of augustus (emperor). Unable to accept this challenge to his rule, Constantinius took arms against his young rival. But when the emperor met his death in 361, Julian was recognized as the sole ruler of the entire Roman Empire, east and west. The young emperor (he was not yet thirty) differed from his predecessors in that he believed the alliance between Constantine the Great and the Christian Church had been a fiasco for the state. A disciple of Hellenism, he wanted to restore the glory of classical Rome to the empire. Yet even in his desire to nullify the inroads made by Christianity and restore religious freedom to the empire, Julian moved slowly and deliberately. He even had a plan but never succeeded in implementing it completely for on June 16, 363, he was killed in a skirmish with the Persians (a later version has it that he was done in by a Christian assassin). Julian was succeeded by Jovian, a loyal Christian, and the wheel of history turned back again.

Julian regarded the Jews as allies in his policy of stripping Christianity of its official and preferred status. But his supportive relations with the Jews were also motivated by a military consideration: the emperor was preparing to mount a campaign to the east, and he hoped to acquire the cooperation of the large Jewish community within the rival Persian Empire. Consequently, he not only permitted the Jews to return to Jerusalem and rebuild their Temple, he even urged them to do so quickly. Needless to say, his death put an end to that venture as well. Contemporary Christian sources relate that the abrupt halt in the preparations to rebuild the Temple was an instance of *force majeure*: the warehouses containing the wood set aside for that purpose unaccountably went up in flames. In any event, it is clear that the recently begun work came to a halt, and the relationship between the Jews and Jerusalem reverted to its former state. Yet although this episode in Jerusalem's history was a fleeting one, it left silent testimony on the ground.

Archaeological Evidence

Our first find from this period turned up in the very first days of our work at the southwest corner of the Temple Mount while we were searching for the pavement from the Second Temple period. After we had penetrated the early Moslem and late Byzantine strata, we arrived at the remains of the early Byzantine period (the fourth century). Close to the corner of the retaining walls, on the beaten-earth pavement of an alleyway, we found a decorated oil lamp. Both its style and the archaeological stratum in which it was found attested to its dating as the fourth century. Out of the ordinary, however, was the ornamentation that was visible once the lamp had been cleaned, for it consisted of a seven-branched candelabrum — the characteristic symbol of the Jews of Palestine during that era. Was this merely a coincidence, or could this lamp be related to the Jewish activity concentrating on the Temple Mount during the reign of Julian?

When questions like that arise, archaeology can often proffer a reasonable answer but not a definitive one. In this case, a year passed before we were again dealing with the strata from the fourth century, and this time our attention was concentrated on the western wall under Robinson's Arch. A colleague, who was then digging in the Old City, happened to visit us at the time, and as we were touring the site I noticed him squinting at something. "Unless my eyes deceive me," he said, "I see an inscription on one of the stones in that wall in front of us." And so he had. In a fairly shallow etching that was visible when sunlight hit it from the side, it was possible to make out Hebrew letters, and it didn't require very much effort to read the two-line inscription: "And when you see this, your heart shall rejoice, and their bones shall flourish like an herb ..." (part of a verse from Isaiah [66:14] with a slight difference in rendition, which I will elaborate on below).

The obvious questions were: when did this inscription date to, and who had engraved it on the Temple Mount wall? As to the date, we found that the level of the fourth-century street running by the wall would have placed the inscription at approximately eye level for an average-sized man — though in all fairness it must be said that the level of the sixth–seventh century street was not appreciably different. The shape of the letters, which sometimes provides clues for dating an inscription, was less helpful in this case because changes in the rendering of the letters evolved over scores, sometimes hundred of years, and our knowledge on this subject is not developed enough for us to determine a precise date based on shape alone. The shape of the letters indicates that the inscription may have been written in the fourth century, but this is not the only possibility, as the same writing continued to obtain as late as the seventh and eighth centuries.

Our next tack was to try to decipher the significance of the inscription. From the fourth century onward, we found, chapter 66 of Isaiah was interpreted as a reference to the End of Days, the resurrection of the dead, and the national resurrection of the Jewish people with the reconstruction of the Temple. What could be a more promising realization of that vision than the Julian era, a time when it seemed that the interpretation of the verses from Isaiah were actually coming true before one's eyes? Earlier I noted that there is a slight difference in wording given in the Bible and the formula engraved on the wall. In the Bible the wording reads: "And when ye see this, your heart shall rejoice, and your bones shall flourish like an herb," while the version on the wall reads "their bones." The explanation seems quite logical: "And when ye see this" refers to the people who will behold the inscription, whereas "their bones" are those of the dead about to be resurrected.

Reconstructing the City's Walls

Near the southeast corner of the Temple Mount is a strong wall that branches out from the southern retaining wall, using it for support, and then proceeds southward. This wall was noticed by the earliest students of Jerusalem and was determined to be an ancient structure; some even believed it to be of Jebusite construction. But the very fact that it leans up against the southern wall of the Temple Mount implies that it postdates that wall. It has long been customary to identify it as the city wall of the Byzantine era, and so it is — a fact that has become ever clearer as a result of the excavations conducted on the inside of the wall. Our dig uncovered the remains of buildings from the late Byzantine period and showed them

overleaf: The remains of the Byzantine residential quarter south of the Temple Mount; aerial photograph, 1980

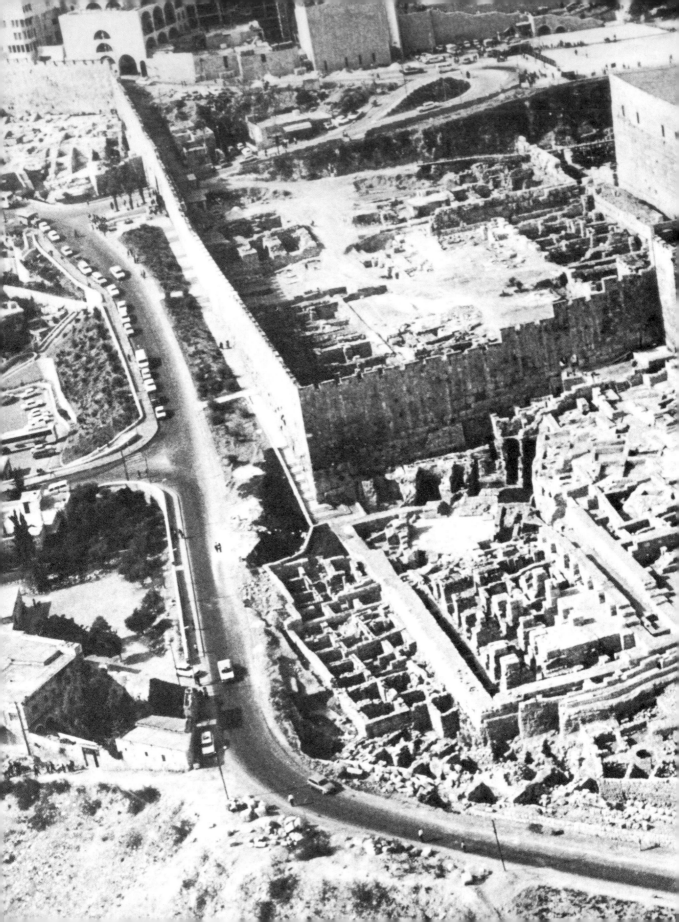

to be architecturally coordinated with the wall. We also learned that the early Moslem city availed itself of sections of the Byzantine wall.

As we dug down deeper we found another wall, fortified with towers, under the wall of the late Byzantine–early Moslem period. Having found its continuation about 150 meters to the southwest, we decided to dig along a relatively extended section thereof. The following picture emerged from this dig: the wall under the later Byzantine structure is constructed out of two façades of finely hewn stones with a fill of earth and small unhewn stones sandwiched between them. It was some 3 meters thick and had towers protruding on the inner and outer sides along its entire length (at least two of which we uncovered). All the building stones were in secondary use, most of them being pavement slabs or stones taken from buildings of the Second Temple period — another indication that this wall postdates the Herodian one. Further reinforcement for this premise came from the course followed by the wall, which ran inside the Herodian city wall. We got down as far as about 4 meters and found that the Byzantine wall was built on top of a large building from the Second Temple period. Moreover, vaulted rooms, ritual baths, and cisterns were found intact under and adjoining both sides of the wall. The early Byzantine wall was therefore "trapped" between structures that sealed it off from above and below — above it a wall from the late Byzantine period, below it structures from the Second Temple era. However, this still leaves a rather large span of time for dating its construction.

It should be noted that we did not find any pavements or houses touching this early Byzantine wall or integrated with it in any way. Houses of the early Byzantine period can be found very close to it, but any definitive connection suggesting to their contemporaneity has yet to be found. The wall can therefore be one of three possible structures: a wall whose construction slightly preceded the buildings of the early Byzantine period uncovered in this area; one contemporary with the neighborhood of the early Byzantine period; or one dating slightly later than the construction of the residential neighborhood. It may well be that the last possibility is the correct one, for after the residential neighborhood was built it was natural to want to fortify the city.

Who built this wall? It's difficult to say, since from the time of Con-

A Hebrew inscription on one of the stones of the western wall under Robinson's Arch

 וראיתיושוה לבבכ
ועמותה ברה כראש

stantine the Great to Justinian (who built the later Byzantine wall) a number of emperors displayed interest in contributing to the glory of Jerusalem. Most eager of all was the Empress Eudocia, the divorced wife of Theodosius II, who worked energetically for the cause of building Jerusalem. It is even said that she reinforced the city's fortifications in the first half of the fifth century.

One way or another, a number of questions about the fortifications of Jerusalem remain unanswered, at least in this sector. Why did the builders diverge from the line of the Herodian fortifications? Was that earlier line eradicated, or was it simply too far south to meet the needs and fit the dimensions of the Byzantine city? No less intriguing is the question of why the early Byzantine wall went out of use so quickly and a new wall, following a slightly different course, was built over it. (As far as we can tell, this newer wall dates to the reign of Justinian in the sixth century.) All these questions, together with the riddle of dating the wall exactly, are a formidable challenge to future students of this Jerusalem. Sometimes a fragment of wall is found (it may not be a wall at all) and its finders date it so precisely that we wonder if they unearthed a plaque declaring its date. On the other hand, sometimes the earth yields up not only a large section of a wall but whole parts of the city within it, yet it is nevertheless difficult to date them with certainty. Every scholar has his own outlook and his own reasons for hesitating. But no matter how you look at it, it's better to leave the matter open and hope to find more precise evidence in the future than to hastily base a dating on some conjecture about the city's history that will later have to be shattered by much hard work.

13   The Age of Byzantine Splendor

The Justinian Era

Jerusalem grew and flourished under Christian rule, for as we have noted, whenever Jerusalem has enjoyed the stature of a holy city from which lofty ideas have emanated and upon which the feelings of countless believers have been focused, the city has prospered materially, as well. The Byzantine emperors wished to reinforce the standing of Christianity in the outlying provinces for more than just religious reasons. They hoped to imbue the Christian masses with a strong sense of the sanctity of Palestine, and what better place to cultivate such a feeling than in Jerusalem, the city where the prophets of Israel spoke the word of the Lord, that served as a stage for the most important events in Jesus' life and as the site of his crucifixion. The seed planted in the days of Constantine the Great grew, blossomed, and reached the height of its florescence during the first half of the sixth century during the reign of one of Jerusalem's greatest benefactors, the Emperor Justinian. It was due to Justinian's efforts that Constantine's dream came to fruition in the form of churches, hostels and markets to serve pilgrims, monasteries, and houses of healing throughout the city.

Construction changed the face of Jerusalem and its surroundings, with the city's center of gravity shifting to the Upper City, near the Church of the Holy Sepulcher and Mount Zion. One area emphatically not touched by the building boom, however, was the Temple Mount, which still lay desolate. Even the remains from Hadrian's time, which were still extant at the beginning of Christian rule, were slowly vanishing. Archaeological excavations in Jerusalem, as well as incidental excavations to save or repair specific structures, have turned up many remains from the late Byzantine period. It is also fortunate for us that Justinian employed as his court historian an intellectual named Procopius who wrote with great facility and made a point of detailing many of the emperor's building projects (even though he was deeply contemptuous of Justinian, and his feelings often rose to the surface in his writings). From our professional standpoint, Procopius' descriptions of buildings have proved to be accurate and reliable, and they tell us much about Jerusalem's splendor in the days of the Emperor Justinian.

The Walls of Jerusalem

During Justinian's reign the city wall, built in some places over sections of the wall that preceded it and following a different course in others, was repaired and reinforced. The eastern wall of the Temple Mount once again comprised the eastern wall of the city, as well; however, it now continued southward beyond the corner of the Temple Mount and was built over the ruins of the Byzantine wall that had been constructed over a century earlier. Circumventing the area known as the City of David, the eastern wall continued across the top of its slope. Sections of the wall and towers that were originally believed to be the remains of Jebusite fortifications, and were subsequently thought to be remains of Hasmonean and Herodian fortifications, evidently date to the late Byzantine era. There are structures known to be from the Second Temple era beyond this line of fortifications, but those of the sixth and seventh centuries A.D. reach down

The Cardo valensis as it was first uncovered

only as far as this wall, and to date no remains from the Byzantine period have been found anywhere beyond it.

Both literary descriptions and archaeological discoveries in the vicinity of the Siloam Pool indicate that the line of fortifications passed through that area and continued up the western slope of Mount Zion toward the Jaffa Gate. This would mean that the city's southern and western walls in Justinian's day followed the course of the city wall from the Second Temple period. From the Jaffa Gate northward, however, the city followed the course of the so-called Third Wall from the Second Temple era, turning eastward at the Tower of Goliath by the city's northwest corner and continuing on to the present-day Herod's Gate. The Justinian city wall therefore integrated the remains of the Second and Third walls from the Second Temple period and added new sections. The Damascus Gate from the Second Temple period continued to serve as the wall's main gate in the north. From there the wall turned southeastward until it touched the northeast corner of the Temple Mount, and north of the Temple Mount the city's eastern wall coincided with the city wall from the Second Temple period.

This description of the city wall is confirmed by the Madaba map, a mosaic map of Palestine and Jerusalem that was uncovered in a sixth-century church in the town of Madaba, Jordan. The sources at the disposal of the artist who created the mosaic included a map and a contemporary guidebook for tourists, and from the results we can see that whoever drew up these sources was well acquainted with the city's appearance. The Madaba map cites the walls, the gates, and the main streets, together with the principal holy places in the city.

Various digs conducted north of the Damascus Gate have uncovered the remains of both churches and other public and private buildings that date to the sixth century and boast some of the most beautiful mosaic floors ever unearthed in this country. These finds indicate that when the walled city filled up with dwellings and public buildings, Jerusalem began to expand beyond its walls in a process similar to the growth that characterized the Second Temple period. It seems that the reserve of land for the development of Jerusalem has always been in the north. Unlike the situation in the Second Temple period, however, the new neighborhoods of Byzantine Jerusalem were not enclosed by a wall (though some scholars believe that the wall identified by most of their colleagues as the Third Wall of the Second Temple area actually dates to the Byzantine age).

The Cardo in the Valley

After digging down a few meters outside the present city wall, we were somewhat dismayed to find ourselves still facing the detritus of centuries when suddenly the tops of a few small structures began to show through. We continued digging until our spades hit upon a floor made of large paving stones or stone tablets. At first glance there seemed to be a remarkable resemblance between these paving stones and those of the Second Temple period. But then, coming from under the paved street we could hear the sound of running water, and the odor emanating from the area left no room for doubt: we were making our way down toward the main sewage line of the Old City, known popularly as "the Turkish sewer" as a testament to its antiquity. The paving stones could therefore not have been from Herodian Jerusalem — unless they were in secondary use. This sewage system, it turns out, was responsible for the original discovery of the street, for it had suffered blockages due to an earthquake in the 1920s.

One such blockage affected a section of the sewer near the Dung Gate, about 100 meters north of the place where we were working. It was during the repair work that the stone pavement was unearthed, and the British archaeologists then at work in the area identified it definitively as dating to the Herodian era. Their dig was conducted about 100 meters north of ours, inside the sixteenth-century Turkish city wall by the Dung Gate. Yet the resemblance between the stones they studied and the slabs revealed before us indicated that we were dealing with one and the same street.

Extending our excavation enabled us to uncover additional data about the street. The sections we uncovered were all part of a single section that extended more than 100 meters northward and was composed of large and medium-sized paving stones that had probably been removed from a street laid in the Second Temple period. At the southern end of the street is a junction with one branch leading on toward Mount Zion, over the western hill, and the other descending southward toward the Siloam Pool as a stepped street. The northern part of the street, found near the Old City wall, was destroyed by the construction of a fortified tower. In time we realized that this tower dated to the eleventh–thirteen centuries, meaning that the street was no longer in use at that time. It must therefore have dated to sometime between the Second Temple period and the eleventh century A.D.

Later on in our excavation we found whole rooms from the Second Temple period under this street, shoring up our premise that it postdated the Second Temple period. We also unearthed coins and pottery from the third century A.D. in the immediate vicinity, leading us to conclude that the street must have postdated that century as well. At first we believed that the street dated to the third century and belonged to Aelia Capitolina. We had arrived at that conclusion because we unearthed coins and pottery in what we thought was a sewage canal under the street, confirming the last date of its use; afterward, however, we realized that it was not a canal at all but the fill under the street between the remains of two huge buildings resembling towers. Hence the street was to be dated later than the third century.

Every additional day of digging brought with it many new details about this street, its plan, and its construction. It was 12 meters wide and lined with broken columns and the bases of others, including a few bases found *in situ*. Three meters away from the columns, a row of structures had been built parallel to the street. In time we understood that what had begun to take shape before our eyes was one of the two main thoroughfares of sixth-century Jerusalem shown on the Madaba map. The finds unearthed in a trial probe under the street confirmed this conclusion definitively.

Justinian's Jerusalem essentially elaborated upon the master plan of Aelia Capitolina, which in turn inherited its fundamental layout from the Jerusalem of Herod's day. The resemblance — and often identity — between the city's layout during various periods is rooted in the necessarily similar approaches adopted by Jerusalem's planners, for their thinking was guided primarily by the city's topography. Two main streets ran across the city from north to south. One, the "Cardo valensis," meaning "the Cardo in the valley," emerged from the Damascus Gate, passed through the lower quarters of the city in the vicinity of the destroyed Temple Mount, and reached the junction that led to Mount Zion and the Pool of Siloam, respectively. The other, the "Cardo maxi-

ma," emerged from the Damascus Gate and proceeded southward toward the church of the Holy Sepulcher in the direction of Mount Zion, serving the upper quarters of the city. Perpendicular to these two was a third thoroughfare, the Decumanos, or the street crossing the city from west to east, approximating the course of today's David's Street from the Jaffa Gate up to the western wall by the Gate of the Chain. The two streets running the length of the city from north to south are shown on the Madaba map and were described as broad streets lined with arcades — covered pavements whose roofs were supported by columns. The street we uncovered was the lower of the two, the Cardo valensis. By coincidence, however, soon after we discovered the Cardo valensis, the upper main street (Cardo maxima) was likewise uncovered in excavations conducted in the Jewish Quarter. It too had columns supporting its arcades, and its width — 12 meters — was the same as the lower street.

When the continuation of the Cardo valensis was unearthed during the work of laying sewage lines under Hagai Street in the Old City, the section previously excavated by the British proved to be precisely the missing link between the stretch we excavated and the sections uncovered on Hagai Street. Recently M. Magen excavated some lovely sections of the Cardo valensis at the top of Hagai Street, and as a result of all these finds we have been able to amass a wealth of details about the main streets of the Byzantine city. The Old City's sewage system — misnamed the "Turkish sewer" — ran under the Cardo valensis. The fact is that sewage systems built during Justinian's reign (in the sixth century) are still operating in a number of cities. However, now that a new, alternate system has been built along the Cardo valensis, the Justinian system, which served the population of Jerusalem for almost fifteen hundred years, is an archaeological exhibit.

The Route of the Cardo

During the Second Temple period, Jerusalem was served by two main arteries, one in the Upper City and one by the Temple Mount. The Lower Market (Tyropoeon Valley Street), which ran from the present-day Damascus Gate south to the Siloam Pool, was 10 meters wide. The section that passed by the Temple Mount was laid close to the western wall and was lined by shops. The paving of the Upper Market, Jerusalem's other main artery, was dictated by the city's special topographical structure, built as it was partly on the higher, western hill and partly on the lower, eastern one. The Upper Market likewise originated in the vicinity of the Damascus Gate (the main entrance to the city from the north) and ran southward to Mount Zion.

These two streets generally ran parallel to each other (though not by strict geometric standards, since they both emerged from the same place), and between them lay a network of streets running west–east. In the classical world, an ancient city built on a plain was planned so that its two main streets crossed each other at the center, with a ramified network of lesser streets running parallel to them. The place where the two main streets crossed became the center and focus of the city. This plan harks back to the Roman army camps and a similar, more ancient layout of Greek cities. But this master plan was not appropriate to Jerusalem, whose special topography required two streets running north–south and a perpendicular street crossing them both. The principle of the planning was classical, but the actual layout was dictated by the city's topography.

above: The Cardo valensis, a view northward with the Tanners' Tower from the Crusader period in the background

below: Bases from the colonnade *in situ* at the sides of the Cardo

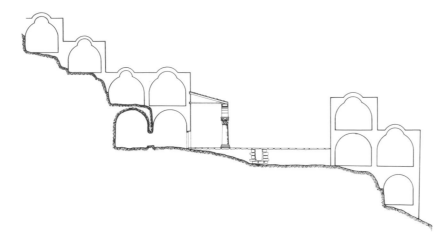

A reconstructed east–west section of the Cardo valensis

This master plan was also adopted in Aelia Capitolina and essentially did not change in the Byzantine period. Yet despite the basic resemblance in the layout of the streets during Second Temple and Byzantine periods, there are considerable differences as well. At one point, the Cardo valensis, built along the Lower Market of the Second Temple era, veered about

A reconstructed elevation of the Cardo valensis looking westward

80 meters west of its predecessor, the detour having been caused by the presence of debris from the Roman destruction of Jerusalem near the western wall. Clearing away this debris would have required a considerable effort, so the planners simply chose a new course for the street. We should also note that where the debris of the western wall covered the Lower Market, the paving stones from the Second Temple period remained *in situ*. Thus it was the debris that saved the street of the earlier period intact, whereas south of the Temple Mount, where heavy ashlars had not piled up on the pavement, the paving stones were removed for use in laying the Byzantine street. This is undoubtedly why the section of the Byzantine street south of the Temple Mount is composed of large Herodian paving slabs in secondary use, while the northern part of the street is built of smaller paving stones.

The major difference in design was far more substantial, however. Whereas the Second Temple street was of a piece and made no differentiation between the "sidewalk" and the "road," the streets of the Byzantine period boasted colonnaded sidewalks — an arcade — between the shops and the street proper. The width of the sidewalk was about 3 meters, and its roof served as protection against the rain. Doing business in a central market calls for displays of wares — the shop windows of our own day, which are even illuminated at night, being a development of this same

Section and perspective of the Cardo valensis looking northward

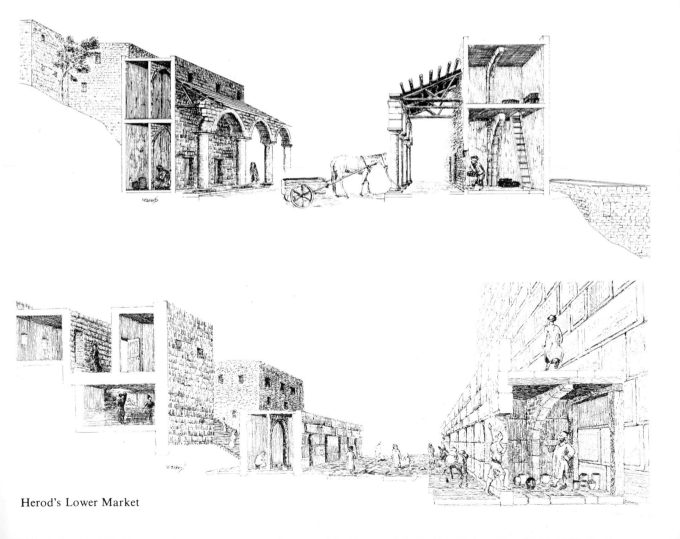

Herod's Lower Market

idea. In countries where it rains all year round or the rainy season is long, there is an advantage to providing protection from the rain if you want shoppers to brave the weather to come out and buy your goods. This idea was widely adopted in Europe — Rome, Greece, and Asia Minor — but in Jerusalem it was superfluous, for the relatively few rainy days each year hardly justify such a great investment or the waste of space for arcaded sidewalks. The Herodian street was planned according to the needs of the time and place, while the Byzantine Cardo drew upon a European design. (An interesting exception to this situation is the Herodian city of Sebaste, in Samaria, whose central market had arcaded sidewalks. Perhaps Herod assigned the planning of this non-Jewish city to foreign architects or men who had studied city planning abroad.) In the course of time, the arcaded street in the East developed into the covered bazaar, though here, too, changes have been introduced over the centuries. Known to every self-respecting Middle Eastern city, the bazaar has become very narrow, and the stalls that line it are covered by a single roof, making stalls and sidewalk into a single unit. This change may have achieved great economy in building space on the ground floor, but it did so at the cost of making the transport of goods to the stalls very problematic, as wagons cannot negotiate the market. It also limits recourse to the use of pack animals, since they are a source of annoyance to the pedestrians. This form of market developed in the East not out of a need to provide shelter from rain but in order to construct living quarters above the market's roof as a way of exploiting the limited space available in ancient Eastern cities. The covering also made it possible to close the market at night and place it under guard.

At the start of constructing the Byzantine city wall in the south, the course of the wall changed slightly (compared to that of its predecessor from the Second Temple period), veering inward toward the city. This shift was only natural, since the later the date of a wall, the closer it runs to the center of the city because earlier ruins raise the level of the residential houses in the following strata, and with that rise comes a gradient that always retreats inward in the classic fashion of a tell.

The City Wall in the South

Remains from the First Temple period can be found on the slopes of the Kidron Valley; above them are remains of structures from the Second Temple period; and it is above these ruins that Jerusalem's city wall was built in the fourth century. One strata above this line of fortifications, near the southeastern corner of the Temple Mount, are the remains of a strong wall that still stands up to an appreciable height. This is the sixth-century Byzantine wall, which, with a few additions, served the city in the early Moslem period as well. A 30-meter section of the sixth-century wall has survived but its continuation is missing. Yet even in places where remains are lacking, the course of the wall is clear, and whoever digs anywhere in the Ophel, including the City of David, can find remains of sixth-century buildings, How did it happen that such a strong wall simply vanished in certain spots? It appears that the wall was destroyed at some point, its stones were pillaged for use in new buildings, and what remained of its foundations was washed down the slope of the Kidron Valley by the rains. This was indeed the fate of many walls in Jerusalem. Nonetheless, the few sections that have survived, supplemented by information from other structures, have enabled us to reconstruct the course of the wall.

The Enigma of the Nea Church

Among the grand buildings built by the Emperor Justinian was a magnificent church known as the New Church of Mary, or simply the Nea (Greek for "new"). The Nea's major distinction was that ever since the inception of archaeological research, finding the remains of this church has been one of the discipline's greatest and most persistent challenges. In this case we faced exactly the opposite of the usual problem posed by the archaeological endeavor: in most instances the archaeologist uncovers structures he did not know existed until they were revealed, but here we had a wealth of information about a structure but were unable to find it.

Procopius described the Nea at length, writing as follows:

And in Jerusalem he dedicated to the Mother of God a shrine with which no other can be compared. This is called by the natives the "New Church"; and I shall explain what sort it is, first making this observation, that this city is for the most part set upon hills; however these hills have no soil upon them, but stand with rough and very steep sides, causing the streets to run straight up and down like ladders. All the other buildings of the city chance to lie in one group, part of them built upon a hill and part upon the lower level where the earth spreads out flat; but this shrine alone forms an exception. For the Emperor Justinian gave orders that it be built on the highest of the hills, specifying what the length and breadth of the building should be, as well as the other details. However, the hill did not satisfy the requirements of the project, according to the Emperor's specifications, but a fourth part of the church, facing the south and the east, was left unsupported, that part in which the priests are wont to perform the rites. Consequently those in charge of this work hit upon the following plan. They drew the foundations out as far as the limit of the even ground, and then erected a structure which rose as high as the rock. And when they had raised this up level with the rock they set vaults upon the supporting walls, and joined this substructure to the other foundation of the church. Thus the church is partly based upon living rock, and partly carried in the air by a great extension artificially added to the hill by the Emperor's power. The stones of this substructure are not of a size such as we are acquainted with, for the builders of this work, in struggling against the nature of the terrain and laboring to attain a height to match the rocky elevation, had to abandon all familiar methods and resort to practices which were strange and altogether unknown. So they cut out blocks of unusual size from the hills which rise to the sky in the region before the city, and after dressing them carefully they brought them to the site in the following manner. They built wagons to match the size of the stones, placed a single block on each of them, and had each wagon with its stones drawn by forty oxen which had been selected by the Emperor for their strength. But since it was impossible for the roads leading to the city to accommodate these wagons, they cut into the hills for a very great distance, and made them passable for the wagons as they came along there, and thus they completed the length of the church in accordance with the Emperor's wish. However, when they made the width in due proportion, they were unable to set a roof upon the building. So they searched through all the woods and forests and every place where very tall trees grew, and found a certain dense forest which produced cedars of extraordinary height, and by means of these they put the roof upon the church, making its height in due proportion to the width and length of the building.

These things the Emperor Justinian accomplished by human strength and skill. But he was also assisted by his pious faith, which rewarded him with the honor he received and aided him in this cherished plan. For the church required throughout columns whose appearance would not fall short of the beauty of the building and of such a size that they could resist the weight of the load which would rest upon them. But the site itself, being inland very far from the sea and walled about on all sides by quite steep hills, as I have said, made it impossible for those who were preparing the foundations to bring columns from outside. But when the impossibility of these tasks was causing the Emperor to become impa-

overleaf: The southeast corner of the Nea Church and the southern apse

tient, God revealed a natural supply of stone perfectly suited to this purpose in the nearby hills, one which had either lain there in concealment previously, or was created at that moment. Either explanation is credible to those who trace the cause of it to God; for while we, in estimating all things by the scale of man's power, consider many things to be wholly impossible, for God nothing in the whole world can be difficult or impossible. So the church is supported on all sides by a great number of huge columns from that place, which in color resemble flames of fire, some standing below and some above and others in the stoas which surround the whole church except on the side facing the east. Two of these columns stand before the door of the church, exceptionally large and probably second to no column in the whole world. Here is added another colonnaded stoa which is called the narthex, I suppose because it is not broad. Beyond this is a court with similar columns standing on the four sides.

Hence by courtesy of Procopius we have a colorful and accurate description of the structure to which Emperor Justinian devoted so much of his attention. Also built in the immediate vicinity of the church were such public buildings as hostels, hospitals for the poor, and even a library. However, the church was subsequently destroyed, and there was no trace of even the auxiliary buildings around it. This was the great enigma of Byzantine Jerusalem.

Understandably, then, finding the location of the Nea has been an archaeological and historical quest of the first order. Some early scholars tried to identify the Al Aqsa Mosque on the Temple Mount with the Nea, claiming that it had originally been a church that was later converted into a mosque. Their premise was based primarily on the mosque's floor plan, which is that of a multiporticoed basilica with capitals on its columns in classic Byzantine style. They drew additional support for this view from the report that the Caliph al-Walid (ruled 705–715) built the Al Aqsa Mosque, for it was al-Walid who converted the large Byzantine church of St. John the Baptist in Damascus into a mosque. Consequently, they argued, the Nea in Jerusalem must have suffered a similar fate, though no written source makes any mention of such a transformation. The fact is that few scholars subscribed to this premise, and in the course of time it was abandoned altogether. One reason was that the Christians would not have wanted to build a religious structure on the Temple Mount for ideological reasons. Another equally important consideration was the existence of a large and strong Jewish community that the Byzantines surely would not have wanted to offend, especially since the memory of the Bar Kokhba revolt — which had broken out because of an attempt to establish a non-Jewish (in that event pagan) religious institution on the Temple Mount — was still fresh. Even more pertinent is the point that a close reading of Procopius clearly indicates that the church was built on a hill other than the Temple Mount, and to this testimony we must add the evidence of the Madaba map, which shows that the Nea was built on the western hill. Two outstanding scholars of Jerusalem, Père Vincent and Professor Avi-Yonah, suggested that the church was located somewhere on the slope of what is today the Jewish Quarter, but the enigma of its exact location prevailed, because not a single section of any wall that could possible be ascribed to the church was ever found. Père Vincent postulated that the remains of a Byzantine mosaic floor uncovered in 1914, while excavating the foundations of the Porat Yosef Yeshiva facing Robinson's Arch, belonged to the Nea; however, it later emerged that they belonged to an ordinary house from the Byzantine period.

opposite: Remains of a public building south of the Nea Church

A stone lintel from the door of a church (the Nea?) in secondary use as a building stone in a palace from the period of the Omayyad dynasty

The archaeological excavations that began after the Six-Day War were the first to come up with finds related to this architectural jewel designed by Justinian. While digging foundations for new houses in the southern part of the Jewish Quarter, the laborers uncovered a wall made of enormous stones. It was later seen to contain a large recess, which proved to be an apse. The first premise advanced at the time was that they had indeed hit upon the traces of the Nea, and a while later excavations conducted some 100 meters west of that spot unearthed additional re-

left: Broken piece of a marble decoration belonging to a magnificent church (the Nea?) found in secondary use in a palace from the period of the Omayyad dynasty

right: Detail of a decoration on the church's lintel

mains of the same structure — sections of floor and walls belonging to the front court or atrium. But the most fascinating and important find, in terms of identifying the structure as the Nea, turned up outside the Old City wall. There, in excavations conducted prior to establishing an archaeological garden around the Old City wall, the church's southeast corner was uncovered. It proved the accuracy of Procopius' description, for on this steep cliff of the western hill the excavation yielded a strong foundation made of large (5–15-ton) stones. The southern of the church's three apses was found eleven meters from the corner, on its eastern wall; the other two apses were inside the city wall under the buildings known as Batei Hamahaseh. Fortunately, half of the southern apse lay outside the sixteenth-century Turkish wall, for otherwise we probably would not have found it. Once redeemed, however, the apse enabled us to solve a number of long-standing questions.

First, it proved that the church's three apses were of the exterior type and protruded from the eastern wall, as was customary in large Byzantine churches. (This was in contrast to claims made by the scholars who studied the Mount Zion Church, the Nea's twin, and posited that only its central apse was exterior. We should note, however, that the Mount Zion Church, which was likewise built during the Byzantine period, has not yet been uncovered, so that the study thereof is purely theoretical.) The apse in the Jewish Quarter, likewise part of the Nea, is an internal one. Taking the evidence of these two apses, we can say that the Nea had five apses, three external and two internal. They were situated at the end of the five rows of internal columns that divided the church into a high central hall or nave with two aisles on each side. The distance between the southeastern corner and the southern apse is 11 meters, and the diameter of this apse is 7 meters, measurements that make it possible for us to reconstruct the length of the cross wall as 50 meters. This same figure emerges from measuring the eastern cross wall from its southern corner to the internal apse found under Batei Hamahaseh Square in the Jewish Quarter. Based on the eastern wall and the walls of the atrium in the west, the church's length can be calculated from the ratio between the length and the width of churches of this kind.

A multi-roomed building unearthed close to the Nea, outside the Old City wall and adjoining the church's southern retaining wall, is apparently the ruins of one of the structures described by Procopius as part of the complex of auxiliary buildings built alongside the church. West of this building, inside the Old City wall, enormous cisterns were uncovered, but their original use was undoubtedly as the vaults built to level out the slope for building purposes. This structure, which was discovered by the British expedition headed by Warren and subsequently cleaned by N. Avigad, remains almost intact, while the buildings that once towered above it were totally destroyed. Its construction is typical of sixth-century Byzantine public buildings, as its masons had used both stone and bricks. Later a young bulldozer operator named Hussein, who was bitten by the archaeology bug, happened to be working on the area and was thrilled to find on one of the plastered walls of these cisterns an inscription mentioning the Emperor Justinian. The enigma of the Nea had been solved.

While the remains uncovered in the excavation of the Nea were impressive in their dimensions, we could see that the main body of the church had been destroyed with a thoroughness that suggested zeal. There is no

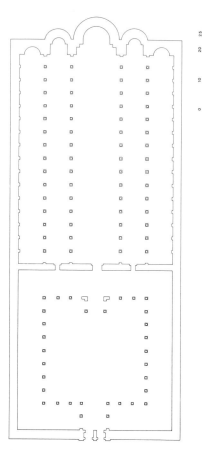

A reconstruction of the Nea's plan

The Terrible Destruction of the Nea

information on the fate of the church in the written sources. A few scholars believed that it was ravaged over the centuries in the waves of conquest that afflicted the country; though most assumed that it was destroyed by the powerful earthquake that struck Jerusalem in the middle of the eighth century (which also took a toll of many of the Moslem buildings in the city). But in our excavations by the Temple Mount, we uncovered finds that, together with the discovery of the Nea's southeastern corner, led us to draw different conclusions about the actual chain of events.

Especially interesting in Procopius' description of the Nea is the attention he devoted to the "treasure of the columns." In fact, as we read it, it sounds rather like an attempt to provide a literary and religious "cover" for an incident that the Byzantines would have liked to suppress. The description of the site involved makes it difficult to avoid the conclusion that Justinian's builders dismantled the porticoes of the ruined Temple Mount and hauled off their columns to build the church. In our excavations we found remains of the columns of the Royal Portico, and some were fashioned of a local red-colored stone — the same stone that suggested the color of flames to Procopius. The pillage of these columns was evidently a deed that the builders tried to conceal from the Jews of Palestine and the Diaspora. Yet even though the prohibition against Jewish residence in Jerusalem was still in effect, we can assume that the removal of the columns from the Temple Mount did not remain a secret, and the authorities may have feared a wave of violent demonstrations both in Palestine and in the Jewish communities abroad. An interesting detail attached to this incident further bolsters this conjecture. As the columns were being dismantled and the Byzantines were picking through the ruins of the Temple Mount, they apparently found a number of fine

A reconstructed section and view of the Nea

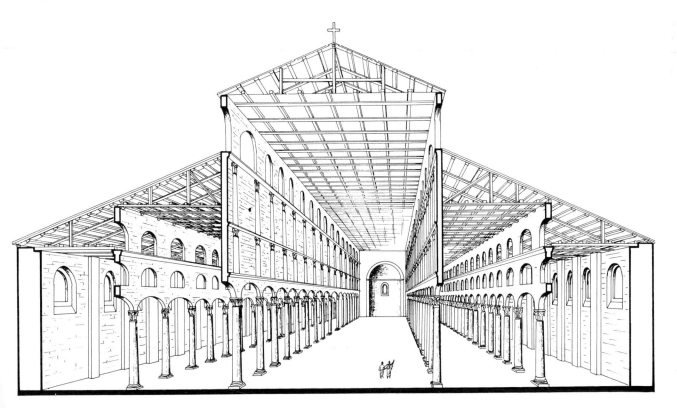

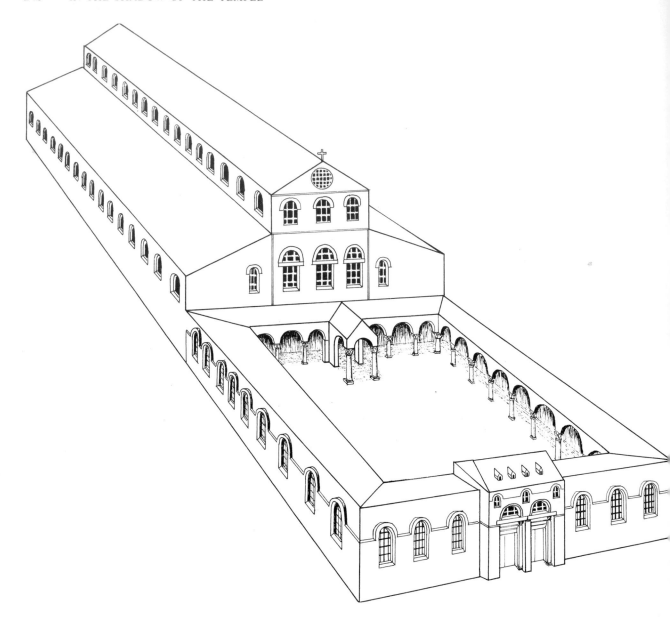

An isometric reconstruction of the Nea

metal implements, and the laborers of the day assumed that they had belonged to the Temple. Procopius, at any rate, makes mention of this detail in two of his histories by relating that the Temple's treasures, originally transferred to Rome, were later carried off by that city's various conquerors — Goths and the Vandals — but were subsequently recaptured by Justinian and returned to Jerusalem to be kept in the great Nea Church. The story sounds rather outlandish, not to say tendentious, and seems designed to legitimize the presence in the Nea Church of what the Byzantines took to be implements from the Temple. This was no act of thievery, the moral went, but precisely the opposite: the restoration of plundered treasure to its right place — in this case the return of the Temple's instruments to Christianity, as the heir of Judaism. Viewed on a simple human level, the impulse to fabricate such tales bespeaks the fear and shame that was attached to the pillage of the Temple Mount for the sake of building the church. The emperor, through the auspices of his court historian, may have tried to cover his tracks, but the Jews remembered the deed and wreaked their vengeance at the first opportunity.

Alongside the Temple Mount we found the ruins of a palace and a number of other impressive buildings from the early Moslem period that contained the remains of a splendid church in secondary use. Some of these remains were stones that had definitely been taken from the Nea. In fact, the southeast corner of the Moslem palace is built of stones that are identical to those in the corner of the Nea (and are not to be found in any other building in Jerusalem). To this find we must add fragments of a stone lintel decorated with floral designs and a cross (which once belonged to the large entry door of a magnificent church) plus a few dozen columns and other architectural elements bearing crosses, inscriptions, decorations, and broken marble latticework characteristic of Byzantine art in the sixth-century churches of Palestine and Syria — all in secondary use in the Moslem palace. We are therefore forced to conclude that the church from which the stones were taken must have been destroyed before the Moslem structure was built at the close of the seventh century. If so, the Nea could not have been destroyed by an earthquake during the eighth century. Yet assuming that our premise about the date of the Nea's destruction is correct, we must ask ourselves how it was destroyed or, more to the point, who destroyed it and why.

In 614, when the Persian armies conquered Palestine and Jerusalem, many Jewish soldiers, particularly Palestinian Jews, took part in the battle. These fighters viewed their participation in the war as a requital for the oppression of the Jews during the reign of the Byzantine emperors. Their vengeance found expression in the destruction of many churches and the slaughter of Christians. Especially severe was the damage wreaked in Jerusalem. It appears that a number of churches were destroyed there, but most of the wrath — and the devastation — was directed at the Nea, the church that had caused a deep affront to the most sacred of Jewish holy places. The Jews could not overlook the fact that the stones used to built it had been taken from the Temple Mount, and their anger raged to the point of massacre. This must have been the reason for the enormous effort invested in destroying the Nea, which was far more heavily damaged than even the Church of the Holy Sepulcher. Afterward, at the end of the seventh century, when the Moslems began to construct a complex of buildings below the Temple Mount, they hauled off stones from the ruins of the Nea, which the Christians had not been permitted to restore.

The vicissitudes of history are truly a matter to ponder: a Byzantine emperor used the remains of the Temple Mount to build an enormous church and did his best to cover the fact; the Jews of the country destroyed the church at the first opportunity; the Moslems built in the area of the Temple Mount using the remains of that same destroyed church; and after hundreds of years of silence, Israeli scholars redeemed this intricate tale from the depths of oblivion. That is the way of archaeology in Jerusalem.

14. The Byzantine Residential Quarter

The Temple Mount lay in ruins, and the focus of public activity had shifted to the hilltops, where the important churches were built. It was in the course of the Christian settlement and repopulation of Jerusalem that the area south of the Temple Mount was transformed into a predominately residential neighborhood. One of the first features we noticed about the buildings there was an appreciable difference between the first houses built in the fourth century and those built in the sixth century, which remained standing until the onset of the ambitious building enterprise of the Moslem period. These differences came out in both the floor plans of the houses and in the technical details of their construction, the earliest Byzantine houses being characterized by a layout and construction technique imported from abroad while the sixth-century buildings evince planning and construction to meet the specific needs of the residents and prevailing way of life in Jerusalem. What's more, the locally designed construction was an improvement over the imported variety, both in its approach to structural problems and in a number of technical details. Another prominent feature that distinguishes the construction of the sixth century from the earlier Byzantine method is the intense exploitation of space. Houses actually touch up against each other as they had in the Second Temple period, or at best are separated by narrow alleyways. Our first encounter with residential buildings from the late Byzantine period was at the southwest corner of the Temple Mount, and their discovery helped us determine the time frame of the buildings from the subsequent Moslem period.

The more we worked on this stratum, the more we realized that the picture of Byzantine construction that emerged from the excavations was incomplete. The magnificent Moslem buildings yielded up the remains of structures from the Byzantine period when the Byzantine houses happened to be at a level lower than their floors. But where the Byzantine buildings extended higher than the level projected for the floors of the Moslem structures, they were destroyed beyond recognition, and other than conjecture we have no way of knowing how they looked and, indeed, whether or not they actually ever existed. The point is that one must be doubly cautious when discussing the destiny of settlement during the Byzantine period, for our information is based on what survived after the Moslem builders wreaked havoc in this area.

The Floor Plan of Residential Buildings

opposite: A residential building from the age of Byzantine rule

overleaf: Living quarters on the ground floor of a structure from the Byzantine period

We were in the midst of our first season of excavations, and our "victim" was a simple, milky-gray, marble-mosaic floor in one of the rooms of a seventh- or eighth-century Moslem building when we were again confronted by the same unavoidable fact: if you want to know what's below you, you must "operate" on and remove the upper stratum. So by the same well-worn process, the room was cleaned, photographed two or three times, and re-checked one last time. Yet one could sense how painful it was for archaeologists to destroy the floors they had uncovered with such painstaking labors. But the upper floor was soon forgotten, and our undivided attention was applied to the earlier building coming into view.

On the day this mosaic floor was removed, the tops of walls had already begun to show through the detritus. It later transpired that the building found under this floor was a two-story structure, one-and-a-half stories of which were still preserved. The Moslem planners used to determine the height of a mosaic floor in advance, noting it in their master plan. In this case, the floor was set at a level equivalent to one and a half stories of the extant Byzantine building, so only half a story was demolished, the rest of the building was filled with soil and rubble, and the new floor was laid. So much for floors. We must remember, however, that the foundations of the Moslem buildings were sunk very deep, and it was in the course of laying them that the walls of Byzantine structures were broken or wholly destroyed. This is also why some of the remains of the Byzantine buildings were found *in situ* while others turned up elsewhere. Sometimes one room of a Byzantine house was uncovered on one side of a Moslem foundation wall and a second room on the other side, but there were also occasions when we found the foundation of a wall from the Moslem period going smack through the center of a room from the previous era. When we tried to conjure up a picture of the Byzantine buildings on the basis of their remains, we found that we were able to visualize their floor plans. It was as if the houses were standing there before us like models, open to our scrutiny.

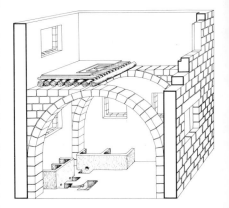

A room on the ground floor of a Byzantine structure with a tanning apparatus inside it

This was our experience excavating under the floors of Moslem buildings in the southern sector. Yet we were forced to ask ourselves why it was true here, of all places. The answer seems to lie in the fact that the Byzantines were content to build on the slope, but the Moslems wanted to put up massive buildings on a uniform level. Like their predecessors in Herod's and Justinian's day, they first built high support walls for this purpose and then filled in the interior space with earth so that they could lay floors. In a number of cases, whole residential buildings of the Byzantine period were part of this fill, which is why we found them intact. The same was not true on the western slope, however. There the Moslems often found it necessary to destroy all trace of the structures of both the Byzantine and Second Temple periods, for they wanted to lay their floors level with or occasionally even lower than the floors of those earlier buildings.

After some three years of excavating, we had a stroke of genuine luck when we reached the eastern sector of the southern wall. The construction of the Moslem era came to a halt there, for the monumental building enterprise had ended with the fall of the Omayyad dynasty and the succession of the Abbassids. Consequently, entire buildings from the Byzantine era were found intact in this sector. Not only were these structures undamaged and in no way affected by the foundations laid in subsequent ages, they had actually been inhabited by the Moslem builders. Needless to say, the construction of the Moslem period constitutes a special chapter in the history of Jerusalem, and we will take it up at length later on in these pages.

We uncovered the remains of eighteen residential buildings in the area of our excavation, while another four buildings were unearthed outside the city wall by the Dung Gate. These structures had almost identical floor plans following the model of patio houses, meaning rooms built around the four sides of a courtyard with their doors and windows facing on the enclosure. The plan was predicated on the need to built houses very close to each other while nevertheless maintaining a sense of privacy, for each building was effectively sealed off from the outside and light and air

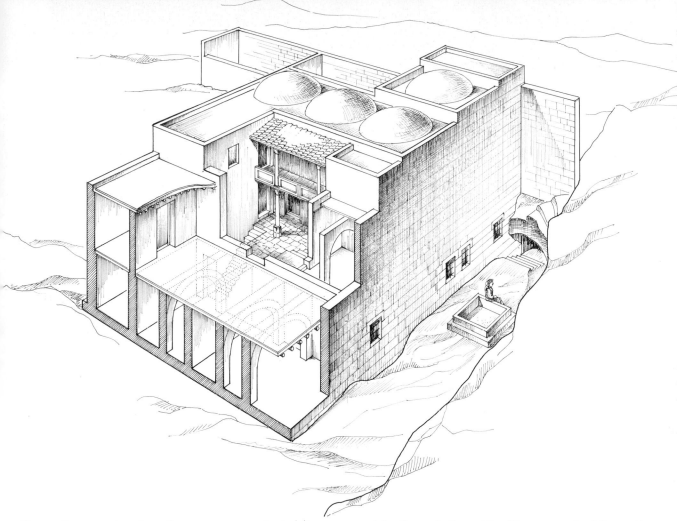

Perspective reconstruction of a
residential building from the
Byzantine era

penetrated its rooms solely through the patio. The concept of the patio
house is especially functional in a city whose alleys were as narrow as a
meter and a half.

   The Byzantine patio houses were two-and-a-half stories high, the half
story being the basement built into existing depressions in the rock, hewn
out of the bedrock, or exploiting the remains of earlier cisterns. These dark,
cool places contained larders where the householders kept their food and
wine. The ground floor was used for storage or extra living space but pri-

Section of a residential building from
the Byzantine era

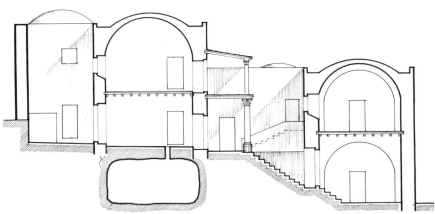

marily for workships. Every last house in this neighborhood contained some kind of installation for crafts or light industry, which was a major feature of life in Jerusalem during the Byzantine period. These appurtenances stand in stark contrast to the rule during the Second Temple period, when workshops and industrial facilities were located outside the city limits. Unlike their predecessors, the Byzantine-Christian inhabitants of Jerusalem seem to have been oblivious to air pollution and ecological concerns. The upper story of these houses comprised the living quarters and was reached by a stairway, usually ascending from the courtyard. As we noted earlier, the patio was always enclosed, but part of it was covered over by a wooden ceiling supported either by stone columns or wooden poles. This covering shielded the entrances to the rooms and the stairs to the upper story against sun and rain. The courtyards of the sixth-century structures were not modeled on the peristylar court so typical of Jerusalem buildings from the early Byzantine era, whose columns were designed primarily for decoration. In this case the columns served the obvious structural purpose of roofing over part of the courtyard; this is likewise why only two columns are found in these courts, rather than the five or six in the courtyards of the fourth-century buildings.

Almost every one of the houses from this sixth-century quarter contained industrial installations of one kind or another in the courtyard or in one of the rooms on the lower story. Some of them were readily identifiable, while the nature of others still eludes us. Among the appliances we have been able to identify is equipment for tanning, for dyeing and finishing cloth, and for refining copper and other metals. At the time, the petty crafts in Jerusalem were geared mostly toward the pilgrim and tourist trade, as souvenirs and other mementos were in great demand. Yet the

The toilet in the outhouse of a Byzantine building

opposite, above: The cistern of a Byzantine building

opposite, center: The stairway from the ground to the basement floor of a Byzantine building

opposite, below: The ground-floor rooms of a Byzantine building

city also boasted a cloth and leather industry that was acclaimed far and wide.

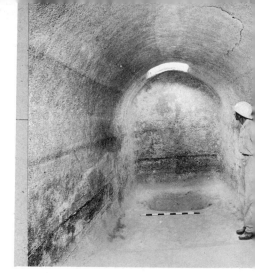

Other than serving for storage space, crafts installations, and the few animals owned by the family, the ground story also housed the kitchen, as attested by the fact that ovens, pottery ware, and other cooking equipment were found in a number of buildings. Sometimes, in addition to the central patio, the houses had backyards that were reserved for such home-making tasks as washing. In one building we even uncovered an outhouse — a small room off the backyard with a seat built to hold a pottery chamber pot. (Pots of this kind were found in a number of other houses as well.) This particular toilet did not flush, but in other houses we found the equivalent of flush toilets with pipes leading directly into the sewage system.

During the Byzantine period, Jerusalem's water supply was channeled to the city by one aqueduct leading from Solomon's Pools, near Bethlehem, and another to the south of it. Essentially, these were Herod's waterworks still in operating condition, after repairs and refurbishing, centuries after they had been built. The water brought by aqueduct served the needs of the public and government buildings, while the supply of water to private homes was still effected by collecting and storing rainwater. Pottery drainpipes leading down from the roofs at the corner of each courtyard, and occasionally in the corners of the interior rooms, channeled the water into cisterns via filtration pools, where the silt, sediment, and other impurities settled to the bottom. The cisterns were well coated with a reddish plaster whose color derived from the pottery shards that had been pounded to a powder for use as one of its ingredients (in contrast to the cistern plaster of the Second Temple period, which was gray-black due to the addition of an appreciable quantity of ash).

The cisterns had a capacity of 25–80 cubic meters each, and there were at least two per house, for in a city where the water supply is dependent upon the rainfall one must always take care to have an ample reserve. One cistern was used for drinking water; the other served a variety of purposes and had holes in its ceiling so that the water could be poured back in after being used to wash floors or for other household or personal needs. In writing of Alexandria at a later age, the Jewish traveler Meshulam of Volterra mentioned patio houses whose water supply came from cisterns: "You will find a courtyard in every house with a brick floor, a tree, and a cistern in the center. And every house has two cisterns, one for fresh water, the other for used water."

The architects of these houses tried to set them on bedrock, and toward that end they readily destroyed the structures of earlier strata. Their zeal grieves contemporary archaeologists, because of the heavy damage it inflicted on the remains of the past. Still, it is difficult to condemn these builders, for their decision was an architectural imperative, and their buildings have stood the test of time by virtue of their rock foundations. More important from a contemporary point of view, the firm foundation made it possible to build the walls to a considerable height — as much as three and even four stories. Compared to the fourth-century houses, these later buildings also display noteworthy improvements in the standard of construction. The walls of the earlier buildings contained many rough stones and few dressed ones (the latter sometimes present only at the corners of the building), while dressed stone was on its way to becoming the standard in the sixth-century structures — though

there was no dearth of rough stones used then, either. The walls were as much as 60–80 centimeters thick and thus easily able to stand the weight of a few stories. Mortar usually made of a mixture of lime and local soil, though sometimes out of lime and sand, was the adhesive used in constructing the walls. The lime-and-sand mortar was very hard and durable; the lime-and-soil variety was weaker and in time disintegrated altogether.

Once completed, the walls were coated inside and out with thick layers of plaster produced from lime and sand (the proportion of lime was generous, particularly on the second layer, giving the wall its bright white color). To ensure that the second layer of plaster adhered to the base coat, grooves were incised in the latter or small stones or pottery shards were inlaid on it. There is no inherent or chronological difference between the groove system and the inlaid stones. In one room we found both methods used together on the same wall, and the second coat of plaster was perfectly smooth. Sometimes the top layer was left a natural white tone; sometimes it was decorated with a second color. The embellishments found in the houses of this quarter were very simple designs: a few stripes, either straight or wavy but always drawn in a profusion of colors and tones. An entire wall was never painted in color, however. For the most part, these buildings were plastered on the outside as well. A few of them, whose dressed stones were of exceptional quality, remained exposed to the elements and lacked any protective coating whatever. As is customary in the Mediterranean lands, the outer walls were plastered in white and whitewashed anew every few years to ensure adequate protection against the sun's strong rays.

The builders of this quarter exhibited an inordinately high level of professional skill in plastering the outer walls. We had assigned a group of teenagers organized in the army's paramilitary program (the Gadna) to dig in an alleyway between two sixth-century houses. On one side of the alley was a house whose floors were exactly level with the street. As the young people were digging away, they came upon a strange phenomenon that, hard as we tried, we could not explain. I should add that we spent a good deal of time engaged in explanations, and judging by the sheer quantity of questions they dreamed up, queries were these youngsters' forte. Some of them were genuinely interested and seemed to know no rest until their curiosity was satisfied; others simply caught on to the fact that

Details of Byzantine construction:

right: A mosaic floor with a Greek inscription reading "Blessed be they who dwell in this house"

left: Stairs carved out of the rock leading from the ground to the basement floor

right: A white mosaic floor decorated simply in black and red

left: Apparatus used in crafts and light industry found on the ground floor

left: A water filter carved into the stone at the entrance to a cistern

far left: Pottery pipes for channeling water to the cistern

even the simplest of questions would elicit a long, detailed answer. And what could be more welcome than an involved intellectual analysis — to which it is doubtful that anyone was listening — so long as it enabled them to take a break from their back-breaking labor in the merciless heat.

The question at hand this time was a formidable one, however. While digging we uncovered the exterior wall of the building whose floors were below street level, and it turned out to be coated with red plaster, like the sort used in water cisterns. "Is this really a street we have here?" the volunteers asked. "And if so, why has it been treated like a cistern?" We were stumped. But the solution emerged when we reached the bottom of the alleged cistern and found that the red, waterproof plaster was present only on the wall and did not extend on to the bottom — ruling out the possibility that it was in fact a water reservoir. Later on we noticed that this phenomenon recurred on a number of exterior walls, and further scrutiny taught us that the coat of plaster was actually a sophisticated technical solution to a structural complication. As I have said, we were dealing with the wall of a residential building whose floor was below street level. The same was true of all the other apartments and houses that had the red plaster on their exterior walls. To prevent the moisture that builds up in the exposed alleyways and seeps into the fill beneath them from penetrating into the rooms, the exterior walls were coated with the same plaster used in cisterns, which is more expensive but has the vital quality of being fully waterproof. This is how the builders achieved protection against dampness. Nowadays it is common to weatherproof subterranean walls with tar. It turns out that the sixth-century builders of Jerusalem were so well versed in their craft that they were able to cope with even these thorny problems of construction.

The streets and alleyways of the day were simply beaten earth or were paved in stone, while within the courts and houses the floors were always tiled or stone-paved. We found a whole assortment of flooring techniques used in this quarter. The courtyards were always done in paving stones or tiles. Stone floors were sometimes found in the rooms as well, but in this case the floor was smooth, requiring a higher level of technical skill in laying it. Another kind of flooring consisted of tiles of fired pottery — essentially ceramic floor tiles. These were light red in color, like the standard pottery of the day, and each was 25×25 cm in size. Laid with great care, the tiles created a highly attractive floor. Even more common as a form of flooring were mosaics. The Byzantine mosaics found in synagogues, churches, and other public buildings are among the most beautiful ever to be uncovered in this country, and there is hardly a public building from that era in which a fine specimen of mosaic flooring has not been found.

The reasons for the widespread use of mosaics during this period were the availability of a large number of low-paid artisans and the cheap means of production. Mosaics, after all, are made up of small colored cubes of stone cut with knives and chisels, and the more mosaic stones one could produce, the lower their price.

Hardly a single one of the houses we unearthed did not have a mosaic floor in one or another of its rooms. Usually the mosaics were created in a pattern; a few, however, were plain, made exclusively of white stone cubes. Among the decorative designs were inscriptions in Greek (including verses from sacred writings), simple geometric patterns, and basic floral motifs. The dominant colors, in addition to white, were red and black. In each case we are talking about the floors on the ground level, for

Reconstructed courtyard of a
Byzantine house

we have found only a few sections of broken floors from the upper stories
(the rest having been destroyed with the collapse of the ceilings). Nevertheless, from the sparse remains we can see that the flooring in the living
quarters was richer in design and color. For example, we have come
across areas with depictions of waterfowl.

As to the ceilings, even though they buckled and collapsed, enough of
them remains for us to reconstruct how they, and the roofs above them,
were built. For the most part, the ceilings of this period were made of
wood, and this is a major departure from the rule in the Second Temple
period, when ceilings were constructed as stone vaults. Earlier we made
reference to the shortage of wood in this region and how stone was
adopted as a substitute. The builders in Jerusalem applied the techniques
of building in stone then prevailing in the Negev and the Golan to the raw

left: Reconstructed backyard of a Byzantine house

right: Hallmark on a ceramic pipe

right: Hallmark on a ceramic roof tile

material at their disposal: wood. This approach may be evidence of an architectural influence from abroad; it may attest that the residents were not natives of the area.

In any event, only short beams could be manufactured from locally available wood. To make the work of roofing economical and efficient, a stone arch was constructed in the center of each room, thereby reducing the span between the walls by half and making it possible to use short beams. These were laid side by side, one from the wall to the arch, the next from the arch to the opposite wall. On top of these beams the builders put down a layer of dirt fill; and on top of that they laid the floor of the next story, fashioned of mosaic stones or ceramic tiles. If a room exceeded the standard length, which was 3–4 meters, one or more additional arches were built at equal distances. In some cases we discovered that instead of the room being divided by the rib of a stone arch, a thick wooden beam was laid from wall to wall as a support for the shorter beams laid perpendicularly to each of the opposite walls. This technique is very similar in principle to the stone-arch approach, except that instead of an arch, a straight wooden rafter was used for support.

What advantage was gained by such widespread use of wooden ceilings instead of the stone vault of earlier periods? Did the builders of the

Second Temple period also prefer wooden ceilings but found themselves forced to resort to stone for the sake of thrift? We know that regardless of whether the ceilings were of stone or wood, the roofs of the Byzantine buildings were finished in stone — as is still true of the houses in the Old City today. Stone finish was a pragmatic necessity, since the roof served as an area for collecting and draining rainwater into the cisterns. This process is likewise the reason why the roofs were paved on a gradient and had a small rise or dome in the center. Yet our excavations also turned up shards of pottery tiles, indicating that they too were used for roofing. Tiles of this kind were among the most popular forms of roofing material in the countries of the northern Mediterranean Basin. In Palestine, due to energy limitations (meaning a scarcity of combustible material for firing ovens), tiles were a less viable option. Nevertheless, we did find a few roofs — usually verandas — that were laid with these tiles, because their support columns were apparently not strong enough to bear the weight of stone. The tiles were produced in factories close to areas with high-quality clay. The ones we found bore the hallmark of some ten different factories. To date we have not been able to ascertain definitively whether these factories were Palestinian or whether the tiles were imported from Byzantium or elsewhere, though the relatively large number of factories suggests that the tiles were not of local manufacture.

Despite the difficulties of transport and the great distances involved, there was a lively trade in imported building materials during the Byzantine era. Especially noteworthy was the import of marble in large, commercial quantities for private construction and even more for public buildings. Local archaeologists used to call the marble found in digs in this country Italian marble or "Carrara," after a region in Italy rich in choice marble (its use in this country is mentioned in sources of the period). We had an interesting experience with a group of Jerusalem building contractors who had donated funds to our excavation. As one expression of our gratitude, we took them on a private tour of the dig, and

left: Hallmark on the rim of a large pottery bowl used for kneading dough

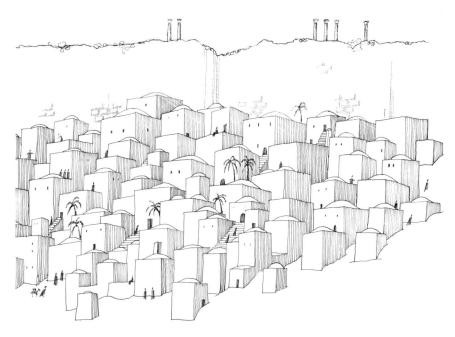

right: Reconstructed view of the neighborhood south of the Temple Mount in the Byzantine era

as we passed by a collection of marble columns I told them about the import of marble from Italy. Suddenly one of our more laconic guests turned to me and said, "Excuse me, sir. I haven't understood very much of what you've told us up to now, but I'm an importer of marble, and this much I can tell you: these columns — as anyone who knows anything about marble can see from their gray color and their veins — come from Turkey, in the vicinity of Istanbul." And very right he was. As an importer he was familiar with the marble quarries of the Mediterranean Basin and their characteristic features. On second thought, we were forced to admit that there was a good deal of logic in importing marble from the Constantinople region, the heart of the empire, both because of its relative proximity to Palestine and because the royal quarries were located there.

As might be expected by now, our excavation of the residential buildings yielded an array of objects in daily use. Though they varied in shape and were designed for different purposes, once again most were made of

A selection of ceramic bowls and dishes from residential buildings of the Byzantine era

pottery, for during this period clay continued to be the basic raw material for manufacturing household articles. Among the finds worth mention are a jug attached to a brazier (which served as a heating element) to form something akin to a samovar. We should also make mention of the cooking implements, for the advances that had taken place in this realm were nothing short of revolutionary. Alongside the standard cooking pots, which narrowed toward the rim, were pots that more closely follow our own modern design. Their sides and necks were fashioned as a single unit, so that the upper portion of the vessel remained open. We also found pottery skillets and a full range of tableware and serving pieces, including bowls, plates, cups and goblets, ewers and spice containers, pitchers for water, wine, oil and vinegar. Their shapes recall the ancient traditions of design, even though they have assumed a new look both from the aesthetic and technical standpoint.

The storage jars of this period reached a capacity of as much as 50 liters. Usually round and made of high-grade pottery, they were etched with deep rib-like grooves, which may have been designed both for decorative effect and to increase the area of their outer surface, thus rendering them more stable. These jars were used to store oil, wine, honey, and basic foodstuffs such as wheat and barley. Among them was a unique jar with a small "railing" around its rim and holes drilled at the base of its neck. It had undoubtedly contained a more expensive liquid, for after its contents were drawn out, the instrument for ladling it was laid across the rim and the remains of the liquid drained back into the jar.

Most of the pottery lamps we found were simple and practical and of local manufacture. Yet we also uncovered imported lamps, the Coptic pieces from Christian Egypt being of special interest because they are decorated with lovely drawings, and the remains of similar pieces found in other parts of the country are limited to isolated shards. Since Jerusalem provided tourist services to countless pilgrims, we were not surprised to come upon small decorated pottery flasks used for keeping holy water from the Jordan — souvenirs to be taken back to friends and family throughout the Christian world.

Stone vessels, which were so common during the Second Temple period, seem to have vanished without trace in the Byzantine era, and the reason is clear: their manufacture was both difficult and expensive, while

opposite: Reconstruction of the courtyard of a two-story structure from the Byzantine era

the reason for taking the trouble — anchored as it was in the demands of the *halakhah* — no longer applied in this Christian community.

The articles made of bone that turned up in the excavation attest to the durability of ancient traditions. Brooches, needles, combs, dice, spindels, and decorative handles for knives and walking sticks are examples of this exquisite art that developed substantially during the Byzantine era.

The most common find of all from the Byzantine period was coins. As I pointed out earlier, since the end of this era was marked by rampant inflation, it is hardly surprising that the number of coins dating to this time extends into the thousands. Although the discovery of other metal objects was rare, we nevertheless managed to turn up a fine collection of bronze pieces in one of the buildings that we know was subsequently inhabited by Moslem construction workers of a later period. Thus the discovery of these bronze vessels is not directly related to the house in

Pottery vessels from residential buildings:

above: A "samovar"

above, left: Jugs

below, left: A storage jar

below, right: A jar for liquids

Pottery vessels from residential buildings:

above, right: An oil lamp

above, left: A decorated rim

below, right: Pipes

below, left: A hanging oil lamp

which they were found, and chances are good that they were transferred there from elsewhere.

Even though the inhabitants of Byzantine Jerusalem left their homes to the south of the Temple Mount in an orderly and organized fashion and took most of their belongings with them, the majority of our small finds in this era were household articles. Scattered throughout various wings of the buildings, they shed a good deal of light on the daily life of the period.

15   Between the Cross and the Crescent

The Persian Wars and Moslem Conquests

At the height of the Byzantine era, the region encompassing Syria, Transjordan, and Palestine was the eastern march of the empire. To the east thereof the Persian Empire, the other great power of the day and Constantinople's chief rival, was gathering strength; and for the centuries that these two superpowers existed side by side, fierce wars raged between them, with the Persian forces reaching Antioch (close to the heart of the Byzantine Empire) no less than four times and the Byzantines reaching Ctesiphon (the capital of Persia) three.

At the start of the seventh century, yet another war broke out between these two empires, with massive forces swelling the ranks on both sides. Untold resources were invested in the war effort, and every possible ally was mobilized for the fight. In contemporary terms, one could call this confrontation a world war. Under the leadership of King Khosrau II, the Persian army broke through the Byzantine lines into Syria and kept on marching with the aim of reaching and taking Constantinople. Within a few years the Persians had conquered all of Syria, Palestine, and Egypt and were standing before the gates of the Byzantine capital. Of the great empire established by Justinian, only Constantinople and its European hinterland remained. But there the momentum of the Persian thrust was broken, and after fifteen years of fighting Emperor Heraclius succeeded in pushing the Persians back out of his territory, while a brilliant outflanking maneuver via the Armenian mountains enabled his forces to close in on the Persian rear. The old border between the two powers was restored. Tens of thousands of lost lives and the harrowing damage to the world economy had brought the sides right back to where they had started. With one major difference: the economic turmoil of the age, particularly among the peoples inhabiting the ravaged outlying areas, and the weakness of the exhausted rival armies practically invited the rise of yet a new rival — the Moslem Arabs. So it was that the Moslem Empire rose in the wake of the relentless clashes between two older, declining powers.

The Persian breakthrough to the region now known as the Near East came at the beginning of 603, during the rule of the Byzantine Emperor Phocas. In 610, following a revolt against the faltering emperor, Heraclius, the talented commander of the Byzantine forces, ascended to the Byzantine throne. Yet even with a military leader at their head, the Byzantines failed in defending themselves. The war wore heavily on them, and in 614, as a sign of their weariness, Jerusalem fell to the Persians. One reason for the Persian success in this region may have been the message conveyed by the invading forces to the Jews of Palestine. The Persians asked for their aid and were rewarded with Jewish support in the form of funds, food, and primarily manpower, as many young Jews flocked to join their forces. In addition, appreciable assistance was proffered by the Jewish community within the Persian Empire itself. The Jews participated in this war not as mercenaries but as a nation with its own stake in the victory, since they regarded the war as a struggle for national liberation. Khosrau II was perceived as a latter-day Cyrus, the Persian monarch who had permitted the Return to Zion after the destruction of the First Tem-

The cross carved into the stone lintel of a building from the Byzantine period. After the Persian conquest of Jerusalem, the lintel was plastered over, covering the cross, and seven-branched candelabra were painted over it

ple. It seemed almost as if the Messiah's tread could be heard in the distance, and the entire nation dedicated itself to the battle. When Jerusalem fell to the Persians in 614, the hammering of the stonemasons who would reconstruct the Temple was already echoing in Jewish ears.

The Christian community of Palestine suffered greatly at the hands of the Persians (as had the Christians of Syria and the other conquered lands), and of the many Christians who were put to the sword, particularly vulnerable were men of the cloth. For Christianity, the official state religion, had been used to advance the political aims of the empire, and the Persians chose not to distinguish between the political regime in the strictest sense of the term and the religious functionaries who had incidentally served its ends. The damage to the Christian community was particularly notable in Jerusalem, where two forces joined to wreak havoc: the Persians, who rightly believed the city to be one of the underpinnings of Christianity and of the empire's strength in the East; and the Jews of Palestine, who harbored a deep grudge over the Byzantines' general hostility toward the Jews throughout the empire, no less than for the deeds of Justinian and his successors in Jerusalem — and particularly

Silver coins of the Persian Empire bearing the image of King Khosrau

on the Temple Mount. Hence the chronicles of the day are replete with acts of murder, plunder, and wanton destruction.

During the battle for Jerusalem, the Byzantines, in an ironic twist, made their last stand on the Temple Mount. Thus in 614, the walls of the Temple Mount were still high and strong enough to serve as the basis for a defensive deployment. Jerusalem nontheless fell to the invaders, and for the first three years thereafter the city was effectively ruled by the Jews. Then the wheel of history turned again, and the Persians reneged on the promises they had made to the Jews in exchange for their support and participation in the war. The turnabout came as a function of the Persian desire to reap the benefits of their victory by making their conquests "official," as it were. Their partners to the negotiations on this issue were naturally the Byzantines, and the Persians wanted to reach an accord that would obviate further fighting. Seen from this perspective, the Jews were no longer coveted allies; and to avoid affront to the Christians and their creed, the Persians were quite willing to violate their promises, or at least place them in abeyance.

The respite was only temporary. For fifteen years hence, in 629, Heraclius mounted a second campaign against the Persians and succeeded in breaking through the Armenian mountains to the heart of the Persian Empire. In a relatively short time, all the conquered territories — Jerusalem included — were back in Byzantine hands. The return of the Byzantines was a heavy blow to the Jews of Palestine, and even more devastating than the wave of murder and destruction that afflicted entire communities was the emotional setback suffered by the Jews. Here the stage had been set for a national and religious revival. The Jews could almost see the restored Temple standing before them — and all that it implied. And then, so quickly and abruptly, everything had been reversed. Jewish families that had clung to their faith for generations, despite a policy of bloody persecution and attempts to convert them to Christianity, now abandoned Judaism and converted out of sheer despair. One such apostate was the head of the Jewish community of Tiberias, who accompanied Heraclius on his victory march to Jerusalem. The Temple Mount was subjected to another round of destruction — this time, it appears, to disabuse the Jews of the last of their crumbling illusions about the restoration of their Temple.

The Persians, having been roundly beaten, lived in terror of the victors. Yet Heraclius had little time to rest on his laurels, for on the breached borders of the empire the cavalry of the ascendant Moslem Empire was already on the march. In face of this latest threat, the Byzantines invested most of their energy and resources in defending their frontiers. Restoration work began on the important churches in Jerusalem, but it was limited to only the most vital operations. The Nea Church, for example, was not rebuilt because it had been so thoroughly devastated that it was beyond restoration. What's more, considering the unstable security situation, Heraclius was hardly eager to precipitate a confrontation with the Jews. His policy was to placate them, even attract them to Christianity by gentle persuasion, rather than allow their bitterness to fester at a time when his empire was again vulnerable to attack.

By 636 the armies of Islam had reached the borders of Palestine. The Byzantine forces were still reeling from the blow they had sustained at the second battle of the Yarmuk River in 638 when the Arabs entered Jerusalem and received the surrender of the city from the local patriarch, Sophronius. At first the capture of Jerusalem, which was a rather modest military achievement, made little impression on the world of Islam. But twenty-two years after the fact, when Muawiyah wrested control of the caliphate and the entire Moslem Empire, all that changed.

The military commander of Syria and Palestine, Muawiyah was a scion of the Omayya clan (the last of the families of Mohammed's tribe to embrace Islam) and the first caliph to establish the principle of dynastic rule, rather than elections for the caliphate. This change did not come easily, however. For years the empire was racked by a savage struggle against Omayyad rule. But once in control, the Omayyad caliphs proved to be among the greatest of the Arab rulers. During their tenure Spain fell under the sway of Islam and the borders of the empire extended as far as India. Because he governed an expansive empire whose geographical center was Syria and Palestine, Muawiyah recognized the benefits of transforming Jerusalem into a religious and political center. He also appreciated the importance of Jerusalem to the Byzantine world and feared that the reconquest of the city might become a cause capable of uniting the forces of the Christian world — which in fact came to pass a few centuries later, during the age of the Crusades. It was therefore to bolster the defense of Jerusalem that he wished to accord the city a Moslem religious character. He even entertained thoughts of making it into his capital and seat of rule in place of Damascus, though upon becoming caliph he decided that Damascus was a more suitable capital after all. Jerusalem was therefore to become a religious center second only to Mecca and Medina.

The campaign to make Jerusalem into a Moslem holy city centered primarily on the Temple Mount — which was a massive ruin at the time — and did not meet with resistance from the Jews. On the contrary, the return of the Byzantines to Jerusalem in 629 had crushed the Jews of Palestine, both politically and emotionally, and left the community in no condition to resist the new conquerors. Then again there was little reason to oppose the advent of Islam, as the Jews tended to perceive the new religion as a heavenly wand that had been waved over the enervated Byzantine Empire and caused it to collapse. Even more auspicious was the fact that at the beginning of the Moslem era in Palestine, Jews were permitted to return and settle in Jerusalem. This turnabout is the background to some of the most intriguing finds that turned up in the vicinity of the Temple Mount.

I have already discussed the removal of a mosaic floor in one of the rooms of a Moslem building and the discovery of a structure from the Byzantine period below it. The fact is that uncovering residential buildings from the Byzantine period under these Moslem-era floors was common occurrence, but when we cleaned out one such building near the southwest corner of the Temple Mount we were treated to a few piquant details about its history. Fortunately, an outstanding group of volunteers was working on this site — members of the group from Ambassador College — and they had developed something of an emotional attachment to the Byzantine building. "For a few days now I've been arguing with myself about whether I'm seeing straight or should have my eyes checked," one member of this group remarked to me on a bright summer morning. "It seems to me that I can see drawings in red paint on the debris lying on the floor of the room. But I've been embarrassed to tell the others about it because sometimes I can see them and sometimes I can't. Like a mirage. Come solve the mystery," he said. The story sounded queer but still worth checking out. So we climbed down to the floor of the room and found before us a long stone — the fallen lintel of one of the doors to the building — coated with a layer of white plaster. It was on this plaster, the young man told me, that he could see drawings. Actually, I too could see some spots of red paint on the plaster, making his tale sound much less far-fetched. "Let me have your canteen," I said and proceeded carefully to pour water over the white plaster and wash off the layer of dust covering it. Suddenly we could clearly see drawings in red paint of seven-branched candelabra and a small scoop, a *lulav* (palm branch) and probably also a *shofar* (ram's horn) and an *etrog* (citron) — common

Seven-Branched Candelabra

Drawings of seven-branched candelabra on the walls of buildings from the Byzantine era that were seized by Jews at the time of the Persian or Moslem conquest

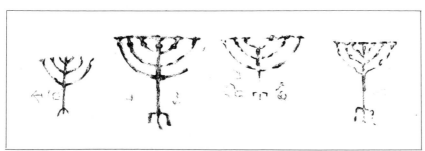

symbols of Jewish art of the Byzantine period found in embossing work and in the ornamentation of ancient synagogues.

Naturally we began to scrutinize all the walls of the building thoroughly and systematically and were rewarded by finding an additional drawing of a red seven-branched candelabrum. All these drawings were in a very poor state of preservation, and it was difficult to discern them. In our desire to photograph them successfully, we went as far as the Department of Criminal Identification of the Israeli Police, whose photographers, with the aid of highly sophisticated equipment, duly shot the drawings and developed prints that helped us decipher them. Later we found a notch carved into the doorpost of one of the buildings. This kind of indentation was known to us from contemporary Jewish houses as the spot carved to hold the parchment of the *mezuza*. Now there was no question that the building had been inhabited by Jews. The date of its last use was likewise clear: sometime before the Moslems embarked upon their monumental building enterprise at the end of the seventh century. All we had to do now was raise the lintel stone and turn it over to a museum. We lifted it with great care but nevertheless failed at our task, because most of the plaster flaked off. Our sole comfort was that we had photographed the stone beforehand. Still, it seems that there is some good in almost everything and no end to surprises in an archaeological dig, for under the shedded plaster we found a cross engraved on the stone!

This purely coincidental find clarified a chain of historical events that can be summed up in the following picture: the building began as one of the houses of the Byzantine neighborhood built south of the Temple Mount at the start of Justinian's reign. One of its residents took it upon himself to carve a cross on the lintel of one of the rooms as testimony to his faith. With the Persian conquest of Jerusalem and the effective transfer of rule to Jewish hands, the houses of the Christians who had died in the fighting or been deported from the city were expropriated by the new regime, and Jews moved into these buildings — the same Jews who had assisted the Persians and were now preparing to rebuild the Temple. Discomfited by the sight of a cross on the lintel, they covered it with plaster and painted their own symbols over it. These Jews also carved notches for *mezuzot* on the doorposts of the rooms. Other remains of that period consisted of silver coins of the Persian king Khosrau II and a lovely seal made out of a semi-precious stone fashioned in a typical Persian style.

When we uncovered the lintel in this building, I recalled a particular piece of information mentioned in an ancient Jewish manuscipt in the Cambridge University collection. It recounts the experiences of the Jewish community in Jerusalem following the Moslem conquest, informing us that the caliph instigated the transfer of Jews from Tiberias to Jerusalem because he needed experts in professions associated with the Jews. The document ascribes the negotiations on the resettlement of Jews in Jerusalem to the Caliph Omar, but this is a standard (and unreliable) attribution; all the deeds of the early Omayyad caliphs, who built Jerusalem and its mosques, are usually credited to Omar as a way of glorifying the dynasty as a whole. Here is what the documents tells us:

The Jews came to Omar and [asked] him: How many members of the Jewish community will the emir of the [Moslems] have transferred to the city? [The caliph consulted with the patriarch of Jerusalem, since Christians comprised the majority of the city's population.] The patriarch said: Let fifty (families) be transferred, and

A marble tablet engraved with a seven-branched candelabrum, probably from a synagogue near the Temple Mount dating to the seventh century

the Jews replied: We will not be fewer than 200 households [evidently the minimum number necessary to maintain a community and its institutions]. The bar-
gaining between them wore on and on until Omar decreed that seventy
households should be transferred, and [the Jews] agreed to it. Then he asked:
Where will you wish to live in the city? And they said in the south of the city,
which is the Jews' market. The point of their request was to be close to the Temple
and its gates, as well as to the waters of Siloam for immersing themselves . . . (S.
Assaf and L. A. Meyer, eds., *Sefer Hayishuv*, Vol. II [Hebrew], p. 18).

The document indicates that in the early Moslem era the renewed
Jewish community settled in a quarter south of the Temple Mount. Is it
impossible, we asked ourselves, that we had come upon the remains of
that quarter in the form of the homes of Christians that had subsequently
been inhabited by Jews? Or were these buildings the remains of the Jewish
quarter dating to the fourteen-year period of Persian rule? We cannot
answer these questions without qualification, but there are grounds to
believe that the buildings date to the earlier, Persian era. For among the
ruins of the Byzantine houses with the drawings of candelabra is evidence
of a new phase of construction that was probably the beginning of the
Byzantine restoration of the area of Heraclius' reconquest of Jerusalem.
This phase is followed by the monumental public construction of the
Omayyad era, ruling out the possibility that the area should be identified
as the Jewish quarter ascribed by the Cambridge manuscript to the beginning of the Moslem era. That neighborhood was probably located slightly
south of our excavation, as suggested by its proximity to the Siloam Pool.

Phases in the Life of a House

We uncovered no less than eighteen houses in the Byzantine neighborhood south of the Temple Mount, though not every one of them contained late remains or additional phases of construction implying their
existence throughout the seventh century. Some were destroyed at the
beginning of the century, evidently during the Persian Byzantine wars;
others stood sturdily for many years and evidence additional phases of
construction, enabling us to trace their history.

One impressively preserved building was uncovered in the eastern
sector of the area near the Triple Gate. At first glance it appeared to be a
typical Jerusalemite courtyard house of sixth-century design with a central court fronted by rooms along all four of its sides. In this case, its
northern wing contained another court and its southern one had a small
open plot that served as a garden. Later we saw that the residents of the
buildings had sealed off its southern wing by blocking the door between
the courtyard and the rooms with a heavy stone. In so doing they created
a new courtyard house whose rooms faced onto the open plot to the
south. This courtyard was a long, narrow one with rooms along only
three of its sides, and access to it was via an alley on the western side. In
essence, the building had changed shape before our eyes: instead of a
multi-roomed villa with a garden at the side, it was now two adjoining
apartments of more modest dimensions fully exploiting the area of the
garden. Archaeologists call a change of this sort a "phase." As a rule
these phases are interpreted as a function of major historical events. You
have a ruined building before you, and immediately you tend to assume
that its destruction is associated with a significant happening. An altera-
tion in the structure of the house or in the way a door closes seems to
signal a change in regime or an upheaval in international policy. Yet here
we had an example of change whose significance was undoubtedly related

to the sphere of domestic relations, which is probably how most of these changes should be understood. For reasons beyond our knowledge, the owners of the house were moved to seal off part of the building. Perhaps it was because their son married and received a portion of the property for his own household. We can speculate, for example, that his wife did not get along well with her mother-in-law, so the young couple "detached" their wing from the main building by sealing off the door. As their family grew, they built on extra rooms in the garden until a whole new building took shape. The array of explanations that could elucidate an incident of this sort is as broad as the imagination, and there is little point in our trying to exhaust it. I merely wished to show how difficult it is to establish an absolute link between changes in the layout of a structure and concomitant political events as a way of demonstrating the need to keep the implications of an archaeological find in proper perspective.

This particular building, being extraordinarily well preserved, became the Mecca of our dig, drawing countless visitors and fellow-archaeologists. On one of the "tours" led by members of our excavation team, Ron Gardiner, an archaeologist with a particularly sharp eye that had already "spied" quite a few obscure inscriptions, detected some engravings on the plastered walls of the building's courtyard. Copying these engravings with the aid of strong flashlights — that were shone at an angle to cast shadows in the slits of the etched lines — showed them to be depictions of seven-branched candelabra. Once again we had found classic Jewish symbols in Byzantine-period houses built alongside the Temple Mount. And once again we began to scour the walls of all the buildings and found engravings of symbols in yet another of the houses. This time, however, they were Christian symbols: engravings of crosses and a drawing that resembled a church — perhaps the Church of the Holy Sepulcher. Clearly, however, these engravings had been made during the third phase of the building's existence.

This latest phase was particularly manifest in one of the structures we uncovered intact. In its third incarnation the building assumed the form of a hostel. By closing apertures and sealing off doors, an entirely new set of separate rooms was created. No longer were they the rooms of a family apartment but something closer to a singles' dorm. It is to this phase that the engravings of the Christian symbols belong and that most of the finds — in fact all of the artifacts uncovered in the building — are to be traced. When a building is destroyed, the artifacts therein always belong to the last inhabitants, in this case the residents of the third phase. In the event that the finds are actually accessories belonging to the structure of the house — door hinges and the like — we assume that they come from the last phase of the building's life, though nothing prevents us from positing that they come from an earlier one. In this case the artifacts and accessories found in the buildings had been brought to it from elsewhere, which was fortunate for us since that is prcisely what made it possible to date the third phase in the building's life.

Rare Bronze Objects

Finding pottery shards and coins are routine in excavations alongside the Temple Mount, but finding objects of another sort was cause for celebration. When we reached the floor of one of the rooms in the building under scrutiny, green-colored implements — the tone of the patina that covers bronze objects as a result of prolonged oxidation — began to show through under the debris of the upper story. Such artifacts must be handled very carefully, for they are highly fragile due to the harsh conditions they have endured for centuries. After photographing them we turned them over to Anna Hasson, our expert in the laboratory treatment of such artifacts, and once she had submitted them to the appropriate treatment we were able to view the objects in all their glory. That particular room yielded a large number of pieces, and additional finds came out of the room next to it. They included a large bronze crucifix (about 60 centimeters long and 35 centimeters wide) that still bore the iron nails by

A selection of bronze objects belonging to a church but found in a room of a Byzantine-age building converted into a dormitory and inhabited by construction workers. Among the objects: a door knocker and lamps for illumination and for the candles used in religious rites

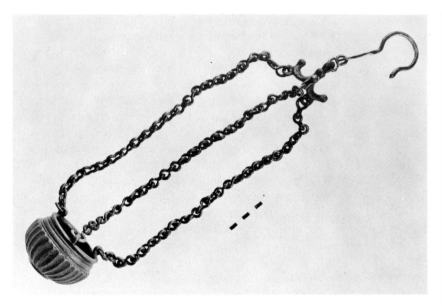

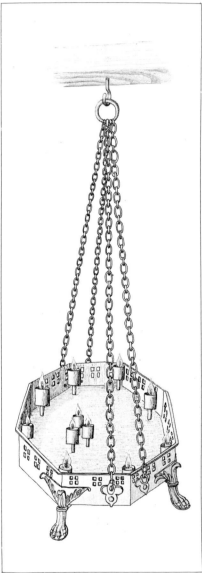

which it had originally been affixed to a wooden door or larger wooden cross, probably of the kind carried in a procession. No door of the building in which it was found was large enough to have accommodated an ornament of that size, so we assumed that it must have come from a considerably larger door, perhaps that of a church. On the other hand, if it had decorated a large wooden cross meant to be carried in processions,

The bronze lock of a wooden box

it definitely belonged to the accessories of a church. The other bronze objects retrieved from the building — hanging lamps, chandeliers, the arm of an illumination lamp bearing a dragon's head, and the rings of door knockers attached to crosses — likewise appear to have come from a church. We also found metal accessories in a wooden box, the box's lock, and the stone cover of yet another box engraved with a cross. These wooden and stone boxes were originally reliquaries and were usually kept under the altar at the front of the church, the relics being shown to worshippers on special days. Altogether, these finds seemed to have little relation to the residential building in which they were found, during either the first phase of its life, as a beautiful villa, or its last phase as a hostel-type structure. Thus our conclusion that they must have come from one of the grand churches of Jerusalem.

We know that the Moslems built a palace and network of accessory buildings in this area early on in their rule and that to do so their builders

Large bronze crucifixes and a conjectured reconstruction of the entry doors of the Nea Church

evacuated the residents of the Byzantine residential quarter. The houses of this quarter ultimately became part of the fill under the floors of the subsequent Moslem structures. But the Moslem construction stopped short of the eastern sector of the quarter, so that the surviving Byzantine houses there were in far better condition than the houses preserved under the floors of the Moslem buildings. Among the finds yielded up by these houses were pottery and coins from the early Moslem period, indicating that the buildings were still in use at that time. They were not inhabited as apartments, however, but as single rooms. And as we have noted, it is to this phase that the Jewish and Christian engravings, as well as the rare and very special objects, belong.

All this evidence led us to hypothesize that this building, like the others that evinced signs of a third phase after the evacuation of their inhabitants, served as housing for the laborers working on the Moslem construction project. These laborers were Jews and Christians from both Palestine and abroad. They had moved into the houses of the abandoned quarter and took measures to ensure their privacy by closing off the rooms. I saw a parallel phenomenon during the restoration of the Jewish Quarter in the Old City of Jerusalem not long ago. Some of the apartments in the quarter that had been purchased from their former inhabitants and temporarily remained empty were inhabited by the Arab construction workers who hailed from outside Jerusalem. These apartments were similarly transformed into collections of single rooms, each laborer jealous of his privacy in his own room. What's more, the construction workers scratched slogans and drawings on the walls of their rooms.

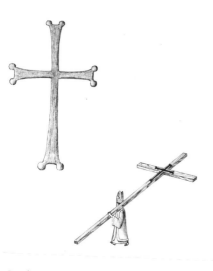

Conjectured reconstruction of a large bronze crucifix affixed to a wooden cross and carried in a procession

Let us return to the laborers of our own day, who were engaged in dismantling dilapidated buildings in the Jewish Quarter and hauling off the debris. In doing so they sometimes found objects in the buildings and took them back to their rooms either to keep or to sell at the first opportunity. If we think back to the construction workers 1,300 years ago, they too were engaged in dismantling buildings and must have found an array of objects and accessories that could have been sold or kept as a kind of "perk". Architectonic remains of the Nea Church, which had been destroyed by the Persians and had never been restored, were found integrated into later Moslem buildings. We can therefore assume that the construction workers dismantled its ruins and hauled building stones off to the new construction sites. In doing so they undoubtedly found the bronze objects and the remains of boxes that had belonged to the church.

The fate of the building containing the bronze artifacts (and others exhibiting a third phase) was identical to that of the Moslem buildings in the area: all were heavily damaged by an earthquake in 747. Their ruins yielded up the objects that originally belonged to a large church, and although the connection between the Nea and the finds of our excavation is admittedly conjectural, one thing is clear: the remains of a large church were found in both Moslem structures (in the form of masonry) and in the Byzantine buildings used during the Moslem period as dormitories for construction workers (in the form of artifacts), and the Nea Church had already been destroyed by the time of the Moslem conquest of Jerusalem. The cornerstones of the Moslem palace, for example, were taken directly from the ruins of the Nea, as attested by the type of stone, its source, size, and dressing. It is therefore reasonable to conclude that the bronze objects came from the Nea as well.

16 The Start of the Moslem Age

A Huge Moslem Building

In our early surveys of the area around the Temple Mount, before actually beginning to excavate, we noticed the remains of some rather sturdy walls in two small shafts that had been sunk near the southern wall by members of Kathleen Kenyon's expedition. Miss Kenyon's excavations were conducted on behalf of the Jordanian Department of Antiquities and were designed to ascertain whether or not a school could be built on the site. In her book *Jerusalem: Excavating 3000 Years of History*, she speaks of remains belonging to a large Byzantine structure and goes so far as to identify it as the public buildings — hospitals and hospices — that Justinian had build adjacent to the Nea Church. Her judgment on this matter was very wrong because it was based, among other things, on the premise that the Nea stood on the Temple Mount. Moreover, neither the plan of these allegedly Byzantine buildings nor any other architectural details were elucidated by the expedition because Miss Kenyon's squares were simply too small to yield sufficient information. Her dig was followed by another, under the supervision of Père Roland de Vaux, one of the leading archaeologists of the Ecole Biblique et Archéologique in Jerusalem and a veteran of Miss Kenyon's team. It also uncovered a number of walls but was otherwise essentially fruitless, as Miss Kenyon notes in her book. The sad fact is that not only did these scholars fail to define the plan of the structures because of the limited scope of their excavations, even their dating of the remains was wrong, and they never published an explanation of how they arrived at their chronological conclusions. When King Hussein was told that the buildings they uncovered were from the Byzantine era, he gave his permission to build a school on the site.

And so things would have remained had history not intervened in the form of the Six-Day War and all that followed — specifically, of course, our dig. From my own past experience, I realized that our excavation in the vicinity of the Temple Mount would have to be conducted very differently from the approach taken by Kenyon and de Vaux. The only way to achieve reliable results would be to dig up the whole area. After having worked at the Crusader castle of Belvoir, overlooking the Jordan Valley, I knew that the systematic excavation of an entire site opens up myriad possibilities for solving architectural and archaeological questions. For one this comprehensive approach makes it possible to trace sewage and drainage systems — which, being under the floors of buildings, were usually not damaged by the wreckers of ancient structures in their relentless pursuit of building stones of the raw materials for the plaster and whitewash industries — and such systems are usually a rich source of information for archaeologists.

So slowly but consistently we began to expose the area by conducting the excavation on two planes. One was horizontal, meaning the investigation of broad, single-stratum areas. The other was vertical by means of sinking a shaft at the periphery of the area and going down through several strata in order to tentatively identify them and plan the continuation of the dig downward. Based on this thinking, and thanks to the experience acquired at Belvoir, I called in a bulldozer and put it to work.

The Double Gate, or Prophet's Gate, one of the entrances to the Temple Mount during the early period of Moslem rule

With the heavy equipment backed by the efforts of hundreds of laborers and volunteers, within a relatively short time we had opened up the western area below the southern wall and realized that it was occupied by a single immense building. All the exposed walls, including the sections discovered by Kenyon and de Vaux, belonged to one and the same structure: an almost perfectly square 2-acre building that was flanked on the north by a broad paved street. Once we had mapped out the building's floor plan, the next question was a historical one: who had built it and when? The initial answer presented itself after we had dismantled the paving stones of the adjacent street and, through a careful sifting of the detritus, painstakingly collected the finds therein. They comprised a substantial quantity of pottery and coins, including coins from both the end of the Byzantine era and the second half of the seventh century, following the Moslem conquest. At first we were genuinely surprised by this haul, yet the initial conclusion was obvious: the street and adjoining building had to be contemporary with or later than the artifacts found in the fill. A technical examination of the building showed that we were speaking of a structure with an enclosed central court and exedras surrounding it on all four sides backed by rooms extending to the outer walls of the building. This architectural plan was associated with palaces and other luxurious buildings throughout Syria, Transjordan, and Palestine during the early days of the Moslem era. Had we indeed come upon a magnificent Moslem structure here at the foot of the Temple Mount?

The question was not an ordinary one, and we had to overcome some admittedly ingrained resistance before arriving at the correct answer. I clearly recall that at about the time we unearthed this huge building, Professor Mazar took ill and was confined to his bed for a month or so. I made it a custom to visit him every evening and report on the day's finds. By pure chance, on the day that the Byzantine and Moslem coins were identified, I found him sitting with the engineer-archaeologist Emanuel Dunaevsky, who had been my mentor and was Mazar's personal friend. Seizing the opportunity to air my theory before two such distinguished archaeologists, I laid forth my tentative conclusion that the building steadily emerging before our eyes dated to the beginning of the Moslem period. Their reaction was surprise followed by unabashed scepticism. After all, a large corpus of scholarly literature on Jerusalem, written over several generations, repeatedly stated that the Moslems had built only two major structures in the city: the mosques of Al Aqsa and the Dome of the Rock. And even these, the scholars said, were essentially Christian buildings reconverted for the use of the Moslems. Yet, now, just beyond the Temple Mount, we found an enormous building that seemed to display every sign of being a Moslem creation. Mazar was unconvinced, but we agreed to meet again the next evening and pursue the arguments.

The next morning I spent a good deal of time sorting out the evidence for and against my premise that the building was indeed of Moslem vintage. Fortunately, decisive evidence was not long in coming. For under the floor in one of the rooms we came upon the building's sewage canal, and the finds therein were abundant. Calling upon our best excavators, we opened up a section of the canal and removed everything that had been thrown into the sewage system and had settled to the bottom by virtue of its weight. While the building was inhabited, its occupants had had the sewage system cleaned out whenever it became blocked. Then they would go right back to discarding their refuse into it. The

The remains of the Omayyad palace at the foot of the Al Aqsa Mosque and the southern wall

system finally went out of use shortly before the building was destroyed, and fortunately for us it had not been cleaned too recently before that. In fact, it was almost full and blocked again, so that the vessels we salvaged from it dated to the final years of the building's existence. Moreover, there was no mistaking the date of these vessels, for they were light-colored and decorated with molded designs characteristic of "Khirbet Mafjar ware," so named after the place they were first discovered in the remains of an Omayyad palace near Jericho. They dated to the first half of the eighth century, which in this case was the final stage of the building's existence.

Returning to Professor Mazar's home that evening, I brought along samples of the shards. Dunaevsky, who had visited the dig that morning and was won over by the evidence before him, accompanied me. Faced with these latest exhibits, Mazar agreed that we had indeed uncovered an extraordinarily large building from the early Moslem period just outside the Temple Mount.

right: The floor and columns of the bathhouse within the palace complex from the Omayyad era

left: The corner of a room and a column from the palace from the Omayyad era

The Early Moslem Era in Jerusalem

Early in the development of Islam, Mohammed, from his perspective in Medina, established that the direction every Moslem must face while praying was toward Jerusalem. Some scholars believe this was a gesture to the Jews of the Arabian peninsula, whom he hoped to convert to the nascent religion. Shortly afterward, however, the city of Mecca fell to Mohammed's supporters and the compound known as the Kaaba, which contained the sacred Black Stone became the center of religious activity. Consequently the direction of prayer (*qibla*) was finally determined as Mecca, rather than Jerusalem.

The mutual decline of the great powers of the day, Persia and Byzantium, opened the way for the ascendant religion of the Arabian Peninsula to penetrate both empires. One aim of the Moslem conquests was to restore a sense of order and cope with the world economic crisis that had been precipitated by the dissolution of the empires and was particularly severe in the geographical interface between them, the region of Syria and

Palestine. The advanced debilitation of the powers quickly led to their collapse, and following the battle of the Yarmuk in 636 almost all of Syria and Palestine fell to the Moslem troops led by the second caliph, Omar.

In 638 Jerusalem fell too, but the sources do not ascribe great significance to the battle for the city from either a military, political, or religious standpoint. It was only in retrospect, after Jerusalem had grown in importance as a religious center, that the Moslems upgraded the city's "image," and legends ascribing the conquest of Jerusalem to none other than Omar himself became widespread. Jewish documents of a later period also cite Omar as the caliph who dedicated himself to transforming the Temple Mount into a Moslem place of prayer, but these documents did not necessarily place historical authenticity above all other considerations. The Jews were, after all, concerned with protecting their rights, many of which were anchored in the promises made to them during the reign of Omar. The truth is that we have no clear-cut evidence that Jerusalem enjoyed a high standing as far back as Omar's day. But a change in the city's status definitely did take place after the reign of the first four caliphs, in 660, when the Caliph Ali was murdered and Muawiyah, the governor of Syria and Palestine, wrested control over the entire empire and made the caliphate into a dynastic institution.

As we saw earlier, since Damascus was Muawiyah's base of power it became the new capital of his dominion, thereby shifting the empire's center of gravity to the area of Syria and Palestine. As part of this geopolitical shift, the Omayyads were interested in creating a holy city in the region associated with their dynasty, not to replace Mecca and Medina but to supplement them. Since the tenets of Islam required the faithful to go on a pilgrimage to a holy place, it made eminent sense to establish a religious center somewhere in the vicinity of the empire's political capital. The choice fell on Jerusalem, the city holy to Jews and Christians (many of whom now converted to the new religion out of either conviction or strong economic pressure). And within Jerusalem, no place could be more suitable for the cultivation of a religious center than the destroyed Temple Mount.

Still, geopolitical needs were not enough to bring about this metamorphosis. It was necessary to furnish a religious justification for selecting the site, and such legitimization would be all the more convincing if it could be tied to a legend about the prophet Mohammed himself. Every tale in the Koran relating to Mohammed's life has a specific address; every major event is attached to a distinct place, making it quite impossible to change any of these settings to Jerusalem. The sole exception to this rule was the tale recounting Mohammed's dream and Night Journey on the back of a wondrous animal — half horse, half man — named al-Burak ("Lightning"). Mohammed was ordered to ride to the "outer" mosque, where the Angel Gabriel raised him up to heaven to meet Moses, Elijah the Prophet, and Jesus. This tale and its varied explications and interpretations became an important motif in Islam, and since the location of the "outer mosque" was not precisely defined, it was possible to identify it as the Temple Mount in Jerusalem — though many scholars of Islam believe that the original object of the tradition was the outer mosque in Medina. Here, then, was a rationale for constructing in Jerusalem the mosque that quickly won renown as Al Aqsa (Arabic for "the outer").

Students of Jerusalem's history cannot help but remark on the striking parallel between this exercise in creating a holy place and the approach adopted over a millennium earlier by David and his son Solomon. When it was decided, for various political and geographical reasons, to make Jerusalem the capital of the twelve tribes of Israel, the obvious corollary was to build the focal religious institution of Judaism there. But first it was necessary to enhance the religious import of the city in the eyes of the people, and a suitable event from the lives of the patriarchs — "the fathers of the nation" — was sought for this purpose. Like the events related in the Koran, those in the Bible are ascribed to specific places. But there was one loophole, as it were, in the story of the Sacrifice of Isaac — a milestone in the development of the Jewish faith. It was alleged to have taken place on Mount Moriah, but no one knew exactly where the honored mountain was. The powers that be therefore pronounced the mountain north of the Davidic city of Jerusalem to be the very same Moriah, and there, on the hill that was later converted into the Temple Mount, David built an altar and his son Solomon built the First Temple. (The Samaritans, by the way, have preserved the tradition of the northern Kingdom of Israel that Mount Moriah is Mount Gerizim above Shechem [Nablus], which goes to show that the determination of the site was not consistent in the First Temple period.)

The Dome of the Rock and Al Aqsa

Once the Temple Mount was decreed as the setting of Mohammed's ascent to heaven, the work of building began. First the breaches in the Temple Mount's walls were sealed. Then the compound was adorned by the lovely buildings of the Al Aqsa Mosque and the Dome of the Rock — two jewels and among the earliest achievements of Moslem architecture.

The clouded origin of the Dome of the Rock results from a quirk of history that has required scholars to indulge in some genuine detective work. The Omayyad caliphs were among the towering figures of Moslem history, but as conquerors and empire builders they naturally tended to cultivate the martial arts, and the leading personalities of their age were men of the sword. Thereafter, when the Abbassid dynasty came to power, it devoted most of its attention to pouring content into the political and social frameworks established through the efforts of their Omayyad predecessors. Pride of place in the social hierarchy went not to military men but to artists, philosophers, scholars, and physicians. Understandably, then, it was under the Abbassids that the first Moslem historians began writing the chronicles of Islam. Since cultural pursuits were under the patronage of the caliph, the history of the previous dynasty was deliberately neglected — when it was not ignored altogether — in favor of the achievements of the Abbassids. In fact, the Abbassids practically blotted the Omayyads out altogether, both by their pursuit and persecution of every last member of the dynasty and by their attempt to obliterate all reference to the Omayyad contribution to Moslem civilization, including their monumental achievements in architecture and construction. This is why such a critical chapter in the early history of Islam, spanning almost a century, was all but lost to posterity.

Since the building activities of the Omayyad dynasty were conveniently deleted from the historical literature, faint echoes in documents and archaeological finds are the only clues we have to go on in attempting to reconstruct the true course of events. Take the Dome of the Rock, for example. Moslem history books from the tenth century onward inform us that it was built by the fifth and one of the greatest of the Omayyad caliphs, Abd-al-Malik (reigned 685–705), but he is not mentioned in any source contemporary with the time of its construction. To confuse the matter even further, the mosque contains a long dedicatory inscription mentioning the name of the seventh Abbassid caliph, al-Mamoun (813–833) as its builder. The fact is, however, that al-Mamoun was born more than a century after the mosque was built. How, then, do we know that Abd-al-Malik was the builder of the mosque, despite the evidence of the inscription? If one scrutinizes the inscription carefully, it becomes clear an act of fraud was perpetrated here — and a rather clumsy one, at that. Al-Mamoun's men simply erased the name of Abd-al-Malik and placed their master's name in its stead. If you read the inscription to the end, however, you can see that while changing the name, the forgers neglected to change the *date* of the original version, which takes us back to the year 70 of the *hegira* or Moslem era (A.D. 691) and fell during Abd-al-Malik's reign. This inscription is the sole evidence to the effect that the Dome of the Rock was built in 691 (and therefore by Abd-al-Malik), and I have cited the incident to show how meager is our information about the achievements of the Omayyads. Later on we shall take a look at the archaeological discoveries and show how the excavation by the Temple Mount has enhanced our knowledge of Omayyad history and endeavor in Jerusalem.

The Dome of the Rock was built close to the site of the Temple, apparently near the holy of holies (which Jewish tradition credits as being the foundation stone from which the world was created). In this case, however, the site was chosen because of its association with Mohammed's ascent to heaven, whereas the "outer mosque" was constructed at the south of the Temple Mount (in the vicinity of what was once the Royal Portico), above the tunnel leading up from the western Hulda Gate. We know that the Dome of the Rock was built by Abd-al-Malik, and that Al Aqsa was built as a stone structure by his son and heir, al-Walid (705–715), though this rendition is not what emerges from the written sources. The Christian pilgrim Bishop Arculf of France, who visited the country in about 680, toward the end of Muawiyah's reign, related that a large house of prayer made of wood stood at the southern end of the Temple Mount. This was the earliest incarnation of Al Aqsa. Thereafter Abd-al-Malik built the Dome of the Rock and al-Walid rebuilt Al Aqsa in stone. Bishop Arculf's account leads us to understand that the first caliph to foresee the central role that the Temple Mount would play in Islam and to forge it as a Moslem holy place was in fact Muawiyah. For it was Muawiyah who rebuilt the destroyed walls of the Temple Mount compound and put up the temporary mosque; his successors enlarged and improved upon his seminal work.

Arab scholars of the tenth century debated the question of why their forefathers chose to build on the Temple Mount. The renowned historian and geographer al-Muqaddasi, a resident of Jerusalem, believed that the Dome of the Rock was meant to compete in splendor with the Church of the Holy Sepulcher and thus serve as a symbol of Islam's victory over Christianity. In contrast, the ninth-century historian Ya'qubi believed that the Dome of the Rock was built to draw the pilgrim traffic away from Mecca and Medina to Jerusalem. Nineteenth-century scholars tended to accept Ya'qubi's view, but today most scholars believe that his reading was colored by factional rivalry: Ya'qubi bore allegiance to the Shiite faction of Islam, whereas the Omayyads were adherents of the rival Sunni sect — which was reason enough for him to spread the libel that their intent was to have Jerusalem compete with Mecca. It seems to me that both interpretations are probably correct and need not be mutually exclusive. The idea of transforming Jerusalem into one of the holy cities of Islam was undoubtedly spawned by the complex of political, social, and economic problems confronting the Omayyads on both the domestic and foreign fronts. Yet that does preclude the possibility that an architecturally superb and artistically adorned building such as the Dome of the Rock was conceived as a monument to Islam's triumph over the religions of which it regarded itself as heir. Building a mosque on the ruins of the Temple Mount and designing its form and height so that it would dominate the main church in the city — the Church of the Holy Sepulcher — served this purpose to a T.

From the standpoint of their form, the two mosques are a product of Byzantine-Christian architecture. The Dome of the Rock is an octagonal building topped by the semblance of a round drum supported by columns and covered by a dome. This architectural form served Christian architects in the building of churches. But these were not standard churches, whose main purpose was to enable people to gather for prayers and religious ceremonies. Instead, they were "commemorative churches," like the octagonal church built by the Byzantines atop of Mount Gerizim after suppressing the revolt of the Samaritans in the sixth century. To mark their victory, they destroyed the Samaritan temple and built the octagonal "commemorative church" in its stead.

Recognizing this similarity of form, a nineteenth-century scholar by the name of James Ferguson proposed that Abd-al-Malik's Dome of the Rock was essentially a Byzantine church that had been converted into a Moslem building. But there is no evidence for this assertion. On the contrary, Jewish literary sources relate that prior to the construction program begun in the early Moslem era, the Temple Mount was strewn with garbage and otherwise in an advanced state of neglect. At the same time, it is true that as Moslem buildings go, the format of the Dome of the Rock is wholly unique.

We could hypothesize — though it would require extensive research to prove — that with the return of the Byzantines to Jerusalem in 629, during the reign of Heraclius, the Christians chose to build an octagonal "commemorative church" on the Temple Mount as an act of retribution for the damage and humiliation they had incurred at the hands of the Jews. If so, the church would have been similar in format to the one on Mount Gerizim. We could further posit that due to their preoccupation with incessant wars in the outlying areas, the Byzantines never managed to complete the structure, and coming upon its foundations, the Moslems picked up where they had let off and accorded the building its final form as a mosque. Moreover, the mention of refuse being strewn about the Temple Mount should not necessarily be taken litertally and might indeed be the misconstruction of a pun. The name of the Church of the Holy Sepulcher at the time was the "Church of the Resurrection," which is rendered in Arabic as *Kenisat al-Kayamah.* But we know that local punsters of the day dubbed it *"Kenisat al-Kumamah,"* meaning the "Church of the Rubbish." If the Byzantines had begun building a church on the Temple Mount, it could well be that the Jews, in their anger, referred to it by the derogatory term "rubbish," thus explaining the reference to the refuse. This is pure conjecture, however, and should be appreciated as such.

The building known as Dome of the Rock was destroyed and restored a number of times, always in its orignal format, while the Al Aqsa Mosque —

which also went through a number of incarnations — was not reconstructed along its original lines. The studies of K.A.C. Creswell, one of the great scholars of early Moslem architecture, and R.W. Hamilton show that the original mosque of Al Aqsa built in al-Walid's day, was considerably larger than the present structure. Its plan resembled that of a basilica, the central hall being flanked on each side by seven arcaded aisles, so that the building's dimensions resembled those of the Great Mosque in Córdoba, Spain. Moreover, its width was consonant with the dictates of the Moslem rite: the *imam*, who leads the prayers, stands opposite the *mihrab* (or prayer niche facing Mecca) in the middle of the southern wall (or *qibla*, literally the direction of prayer), and the worshippers stand ordered in long rows behind him. This format called for a wide structure so that the many people standing abreast in each row could be as close as possible to the *qibla*. But since this plan is very similar to that of a basilica, it is conceivable that it was borrowed from Christian architecture and tailored to the needs of the Moslem prayer rite.

Despite the relative paucity of information about the Omayyad period, we do know of a number of sources attesting that the Omayyads drew liberally upon the know-how of Byzantine-Christian architects and craftsmen in the various fields of construction. The caliphs even called upon the Byzantine emperors to supply them with special materials and professionals. Architectural finds in the field add another dimension to our knowledge. For example, some remains found in a palace of the Omayyad dynasty near Jericho — Hisham's Palace or Khirbet Mafjar — suggest that Jewish and Christian builders took part in the main Moslem construction enterprise. Jewish sources also speak of the involvement of craftsmen specializing in various fields but particularly in cloth dyeing, which was more or less the exclusive province of the Jews who served on the Omayyad building project. Until recently scholars of Jerusalem's history believed that the sum of the Moslem contribution to the city's architecture consisted of the Al Aqsa Mosque, the Dome of the Rock, and a few other small structures on the Temple Mount. What's more, such ostensibly meager construction activity at a time when the Omayyads were known to have engaged in extensive building elsewhere in their empire prompted certain conclusions about Jerusalem's importance in Islam that were in sharp contradiction to the Omayyads' desire to enhance the city's standing. Our excavations, and the studies they inspired, now show that the picture drawn by generations of scholars was sorely inadequate. In this and the following chapter, I shall elaborate upon our contribution toward correcting this picture.

The Golden Gate — or the Gates of Repentance and Mercy

The eastern wall of the Temple Mount contains a magnificent gate that appears from the outside to be composed of two arches but is actually a complex structure built into the wall. Its main element is a large hall, half of which is occupied by columns bearing capitals. The roof is a collection of domes supported by the walls and central columns. The ornamentation on both the inside and outside of the gate is embossed on the stone with great imagination and skill. But in contrast to the ornamentation on the inside, which includes the work on the capitals and was fully executed, the embossing on the gate's exterior was never completed. Both façades, facing inside and out, have geometric and floral reliefs carved on their capitals. In contrast, the exterior wall to the north and south of the gate has been marked with lines seemingly in anticipation of being embossed, but the work was, for some unknown reason, never executed.

The earliest identification of this gate can be found in the writings of tenth-century Arab historians and geographers who referred to it by two names, one for each of its arches: the Gate of Mercy and the Gate of Repentance. The Jews referred to the two arches by a single name, the Gate of Mercy, and a folktale had it that the Messiah would enter Jerusalem and the Temple Mount through this gate. The name used by the Christians (and translated into all the languages of Europe) is the Golden Gate, and Christian tradition associates it with Heraclius' entry into Jerusalem after defeating the Persians in 629. The tale appears to draw upon and reflect many legends and is an attempt to glorify Heraclius' entry into the city by suggesting a parallel with Jesus' entry from the Mount of Olives. One way or another, from the earliest days of Jerusalem scholarship up to our own time, scholars have believed that the gate was built during the Byzantine era — a view reinforced by the growing body of research on Byzantine art. In fact, both the gate's plan and the technique used in engraving its ornamentation all but certified that it was indeed to be regarded as a Byzantine creation.

Yet we have come to a very different conclusion. The discovery of major Moslem finds alongside the Temple Mount, pointing out the true extent of the early Moslem building enterprise and establishing the comparative significance of the Temple Mount in the Byzantine-Christian and Moslem world views, leads us to conclude that the Golden Gate is not of Byzantine vintage and could only have been built at the outset of the Moslem building campaign in Jerusalem, meaning the Omayyad era. We arrived at that conclusion by some rather straightforward logic. First, we know that the Christian rulers made a point of leaving the Temple Mount in desolation as an ideological statement. Why, then, should they suddenly have taken an interest in building such a magnificent gate on the destroyed mount? And what would have been the point of a gate that led to a desolate ruin? In contrast, during the early Moslem era the Omayyads brought the Temple Mount to life again. There is not very much of a difference between Byzantine and Omayyad architecture, especially since the architects, artisans, and masons used by the Omayyads — Christians and Jews alike — were students of Byzantine culture. The art of sixth- and seventh-century Byzantine construction differed little from the art of seventh- and eighth-century Moslem building, and in the absence of patently unique characteristics, it is impossible to date finds from these periods precisely.

Faced with this historical paradox, we had to examine the ornamentation of the gate scrupulously to see whether it bore any element that might contradict our premise, such as a cross worked into the decorative motif. To study the gate, we first had to turn to the *waqf*, the recognized authority on the Temple Mount and nominal owner of the property, and obtain its permission to do so. The results of our study, which included a precise measuring of the gate, again indicated the Omayyad origin of the structure. Needless to add, the directors of the *waqf* were delighted to hear that another architectural element on the Temple Mount could be traced to their ancestors.

We visited the Golden Gate a number of times with cameras, measuring instruments, and ladders, and scrutinized every square centimeter of it. At the end of this meticulous examination we were satisfied that it bore no hint of any Christian symbol or any other element that might run

above: The Golden Gate viewed from outside the wall

right: The frieze on the inside of the Golden Gate

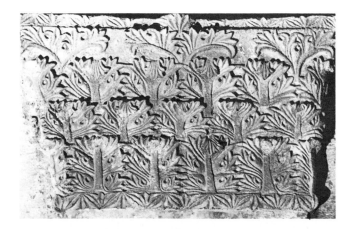

right: A capital from a pilaster inside the Golden Gate

opposite: The interior of the Golden Gate

counter to the spirit or tenets of Islam. We also verified that a certain ornament which appeared as a cross in a drawing made over a century ago was in fact an entirely different motif: a knotted rope. Hence there was no reason to deny the possibility that the gate had been built during the Omayyad era.

What did remain outstanding was the matter of a motive. Whatever possessed the Omayyads to build a gate in this sector of the Temple Mount? In considering this question we must keep in mind that at the time this was the *only* gate in the part of the Temple Mount wall that doubled as the city wall; all the other entrances to the Temple Mount were on the south, west, and north, undoubtedly because access from these directions was more convenient. The gate's size and ornamentation are also quite out of the ordinary, in comparison to all the others. For that reason I believe that the Golden Gate was not designed primarily for traffic but was first and foremost a monument, like the gates of triumph designed to commemorate a certain virtue or event.

Thinking along these lines, the gate could well have been designed to commemorate Mohammed's miraculous arrival on the Temple Mount on the back of al-Burak. In fact, support for this reading can be found in the works of Mujir a-Din, a fifteenth-century Jerusalem historian who informs us that the steps leading from the Dome of the Rock eastward were called the al-Burak Steps. Other sources from the Middle Ages likewise quote traditions connecting al-Burak with the eastern side of the Temple Mount. Of course there is the counter-tradition of the so-called al-Burak Gate (now identified as Barclay's Gate) being in the western wall. But this tradition did not emerge until as late as the nineteenth century, when the Wailing Wall, in addition to being a Jewish religious symbol, became an emblem of Jewish nationalism. It was probably no coincidence that about the same time a number of Moslem traditions were suddenly "re-ascribed" to the western wall. In point of fact, the Moslems attached no importance whatever to the western wall until Suleiman the Magnificent officially turned the section known as the Wailing Wall over to the Jews — and even encouraged them to pray there.

Be that as it may, still in quest of the origin of the Golden Gate, we took note of the fact that as far back as the tenth century it was known by its two names: the Gate of Mercy and the Gate of Repentance. It therefore occurred to us that perhaps if we solved the riddle of the gate's two names, we would understand why it had been built. Did the double structure symbolize that Mohammed had entered through one side asking for mercy and left through the other with his answer? And is it possible that the gate was the main entrance to the Temple Mount at the time? Unfortunately we remain with many more questions than answers. However, we can say with certainty that whatever lay behind the construction of the Golden Gate, it was built during the Omayyad era and is not a gate in the usual sense but a commemorative monument of some kind.

With the permission and aid of the *waqf*, we also reinvestigated the two gates in the southern wall — the Double Gate and the Triple Gate — and had some interesting findings to report. The eastern Hulda Gate, which was originally a triple gate, had three arches of equal size during the early Moslem period as well. Since it had been heavily damaged by the Byzantines, the Moslems had to rebuild it almost from scratch. On the other hand, the western Hulda Gate was restored by the Moslems using the

The capital atop a column by the gatepost of the Double Gate

The Double and Triple Gates

The ornamentation of the arched
lintel of the Double Gate

original structure, which remained almost intact. The inner side of the
gate, with its domes, retained many elements from the Second Temple
period. The right gatepost had to be repaired because its stones were worn
down; the left gatepost and the central pillar that supports the lintel
evidently date to the Second Temple period, though further examination
must be undertaken before we can determine how much of the original
gatepost survives. During the early Moslem period, columns were placed
alongside the gatepost to enhance the gate's design. Sometime thereafter,
though still during the early Moslem period, two decorative elements were
added above the lintel: two arches adorned with floral designs identical to
those in the Golden Gate, and an ornament reminiscent of dentils that
was also decorated with floral engravings like those on the Golden Gate.

All who entered the Temple Mount through the Double Gate made
their way up to the esplanade under the Al Aqsa Mosque. During the
Omayyad era, the Double Gate was called Bab a-Nabi, or the Prophet's
Gate, and we toyed with the idea that it might signify some connection
with the legend of Mohammed's arrival on the Temple Mount after his
Night Journey to Jerusalem. One way or another, since access to the
Double and Triple Gates was through the complex of royal buildings that
stood south of the Temple Mount during the Omayyad period, it is dif-

ficult to believe that they were used by the public at large, and they probably served the members of the court alone. Hence the Golden Gate (or al-Burak Gate), in addition to being a monument, was probably the main entrance to the Temple Mount at that time.

In the chapter dealing with the northern of the two overpasses by the western wall, I described Wilson's Arch and the data that led me to conclude that it was built in its present form by the Omayyads. We can now add some details about the underground structures adjacent to the arch. Since they were built on ruins from the Second Temple period, we have concluded that they postdate that era. Occasionally we came across stones with barely legible Latin inscriptions from the Roman period in the structures, and our experience has been that Roman inscriptions can be found in secondary use *only* in buildings from the Moslem and post-Moslem eras, so that the buildings of Aelia Capitolina must have remained standing until the end of the Byzantine period. If so, the network of structures built west of Wilson's Arch, which rest up against the arch, must be dated later than the time of its restoration by the Omayyads.

Moving backward in time from clear-cut evidence, we know that most of the houses on the Street of the Chain, the nearby bazaar, and the Gate of the Chain at the entrance to the Temple Mount, all of which are built above this network of structures, date to the Crusader and Mameluke eras. Thus the network under them must have been built before then, or the twelfth century at the latest. We therefore found it logical to date its construction to some time between the eighth and twelfth centuries, when Jerusalem was under Abbassid and Fatimid rule. And given these outside dates, it is reasonable to assume that the structures were built during the Fatimid era because the Fatimid caliphs made the development and greater glory of Jerusalem one of their chief priorities.

The network adjoining Wilson's Arch is composed of at least two units of long, multi-roomed buildings. Each centers on a long west–east-oriented corridor with a row of rooms to the north of it, both the corridor and rooms being constructed of vaults of hewn stone. The corridors begin at a multiarched structure in the west — which lies in a north–south orientation and serves as a passage for pedestrians under the Street of the Chain — and end at the street paved along the western wall. One of these corridors (which was excavated in its entirety) is about 80 meters long, 2.5 meters wide, and 2.5–3 meters high. Two stages of construction can be distinguished in the central unit, which was recently cleaned. At some point the structure suffered heavy damage and was restored in almost its original format. But the partially collapsed ceiling of the corridor, which had originally rested on the arches of the rooms, was now rebuilt strictly perpendicular to the rooms' walls, rather than over arches. In the course of time, and after yet another round of collapse and restoration, changes were made in a number of the rooms. Their roofs were built as vaults, but rather than being semicircular or barrel vaults, they assumed the shape of pointed arches.

The floor plan of these units is very reminiscent of the plans of military barracks in Egypt during the days of the Fatimid caliphate. Evidently Jerusalem's importance during the early Moslem period made it necessary to station a military garrison within the city. The city's governor and military commander lived in the fortress near the Jaffa Gate, as did a select military unit; but it appears that in addition to them a garrison was

Wilson's Arch

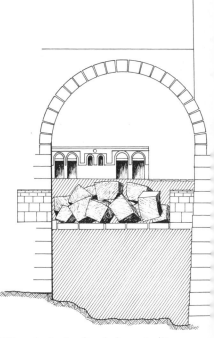

Wilson's Arch after being rebuilt during the reign of the Omayyad caliphs. The street, paved over the debris of the arch from the Second Temple period, is only 4.30 meters wide

opposite: A vaulted corridor at the center of a multi-roomed structure built west of Wilson's Arch — looking westward

quartered permanently in the area of the Temple Mount, which was traditionally a focus of incitement and riots. The network of structures adjoining Wilson Arch was therefore probably the barracks of the Fatim-id army in Jerusalem. During the subsequent Crusader period, these barracks were not needed, since the knights of the Order of the Templars held the Temple Mount, living together with their squires and horses within the enclosure and in the Al Aqsa Mosque. And during the later Ottoman period, the government and military buildings, known as the

The Golden Gate viewed from the east.

saraiyya, were again constructed close to the Temple Mount (about 200 meters northwest of Wilson's Arch), so that these barracks fell into further disuse and were eventually lost under the buildings of the Street of the Chain and the bazaar.

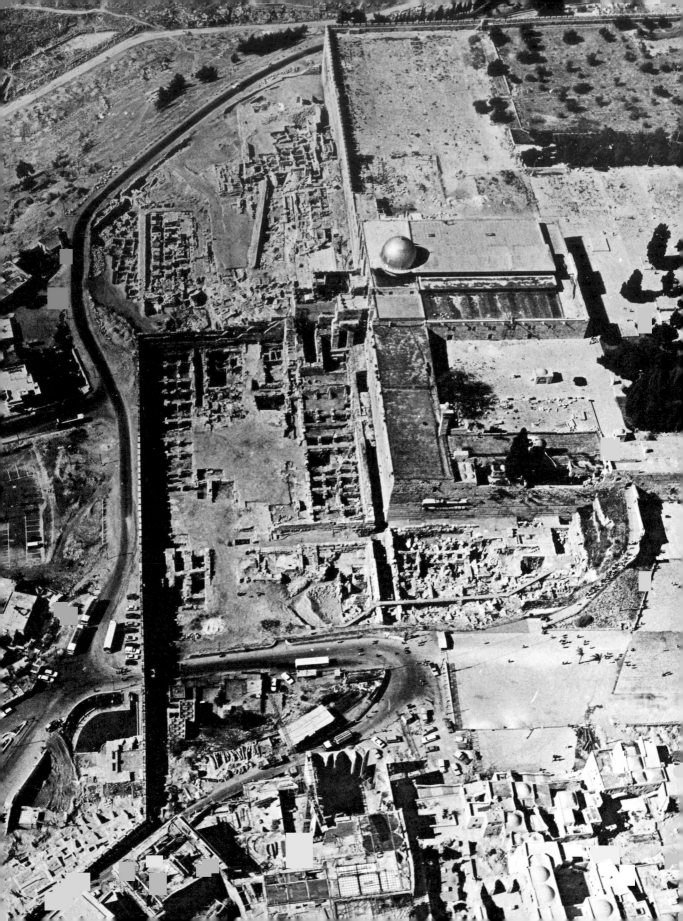

17   The Omayyad Era

The Caliph's Palace in Jerusalem

I have already mentioned the discovery of a large building south of the Temple Mount and its identification as dating to the Omayyad period. The further we extended our dig south of the Temple Mount, the clearer the plan of this building became. We could see how strikingly similar it was to that of palaces throughout the Moslem Empire and especially in the central portion thereof, which had long been under the sway of the Omayyads. The most salient feature of the building was a broad, enclosed, stone-paved courtyard surrounded by exedras that rested on the walls of the recessed rooms and on a line of columns facing on the court. Behind the exedras were rows of long rooms, of which only the foundation walls survive. But from these remains (and the ruins of a similar building uncovered later on) we were able to learn that these long rooms had been further subdivided into smaller ones. Since the dividing walls did not support the ceilings above the ground floor, they were not built on foundations, so that we were able to find only meager traces of their existence.

Together with the building's extraordinary size, the finds that began to turn up within — arch stones coated with white plaster and painted with lovely frescoes, beautifully embossed stones, and the like — indicated that it must have been an edifice of unusual splendor. Could it have been a royal palace from the Moslem era? Answering that question in the affirmative required much serious thought, not because of any bias to be overcome but because of an obvious paradox: if it really was so grand a building as a palace, how could we explain the fact that its existence has been suppressed for centuries?

The answer lay in the rabid prejudice of the Abbassid caliphs and the historians under their patronage, who, as we have seen, went far out of their way to obliterate all reference to anything Omayyad. Curiously enough, together with our spades, it was an almost forgotten and long-enigmatic document that finally salvaged this splendid palace from oblivion.

The document had surfaced in excavations at Aphrodita, in Egypt. It was one of the papyri ascribed to a wealthy landowner who lived at the beginning of the eighth century, during the reign of the Caliph al-Walid. Fortunately for us, this landed gentleman was a highly organized and meticulous man who kept lists of the slaves he sent as a tribute or to do forced labor throughout the Omayyad empire. Among others, two carpenters are mentioned as having been sent to work on the construction of the "palace" in Jerusalem. Yet amazing as it may seem, this document, found at the beginning of the twentieth century, failed to convince scholars that the Omayyads had indeed built a palace for the caliph in Jerusalem. They simply didn't take it seriously, despite the fact that it was clearly an original. Now we can state with confidence that the man knew what he was writing about, and slowly everyone got used to the idea that what we had dug up south of the Temple Mount was none other than an Omayyad royal palace!

Later on we saw that this structure was one of a complex of buildings

The remains of the Omayyad palace and auxiliary buildings, aerial photograph, 1977

A fresco in a floral motif from the palace

opposite: Another fresco in a floral motif from the palace

build adjacent to the Temple Mount. In part, this discovery was a fluke. One morning I was sitting on the northern wall of the Omayyad palace gazing idly up at the southern wall of the Temple Mount when a chirping bird caught my attention. It was standing on a stone that protruded from the wall some 8 meters above the level of the Omayyad street. Slowly it dawned on me that this was not just any stone but the first curving stone of an arch, and later on we found another one like it. Together they were evidence enough that an arch must have extended from the Temple Mount's southern wall to the northern wall of the large Omayyad building, or presumed palace, and a conjectured reconstruction of that arch taught us that it connected the Temple Mount to the roof of the two-story building. The gate supported by this arch must have led onto the Temple Mount compound. But it was not situated at random; it was at the western end of Al Aqsa's southern wall, or *qibla* (a wall that was much longer in the Omayyad period than it is today), so that the gate must have led directly into the mosque. Since the entrance to a mosque can be in any one of its walls *except* the *qibla*, an aperture in the southern wall here suggests that it could only have been made for the use of a very eminent

opposite: View and reconstruction of the courtyard of the Omayyad palace

left: A plaster of Paris model of the Omayyad palace and its auxiliary buildings

personage, such as a caliph. Thus we had very convincing evidence that the elaborate building to the south was indeed a royal palace.

The Great Breach

If you stand facing the southern wall of the Temple Mount, even without a trained eye you can see that the southwest corner, which survives from Herod's day, rises up to an appreciable height but that a little way to the east someone had opened a breach in the wall. This breach was subsequently sealed with square stones about 80 square centimeters in size, and the repair can be discerned easily both because of the variant size and dressing of the stones and because of the unequal courses of the original ashlars and the ones used for the repair. Before our dig, scholars believed that this breach was one manifestation of the destruction wrought by Titus' soldiers and that the repair had been done by Hadrian's masons at the start of his building program on the Temple Mount. However, our excavations below this break pointed to a very different version of events.

The first clue came from two finds of Byzantine vintage. All along the southern wall, we were able to follow a channel that had been fitted with pipes for carrying water, and under the paved street from the Omayyad era we uncovered a sewage canal. Both these channels — one for sewage, the other for fresh water — dated to the Byzantine period (sixth century) and had been destroyed by whoever breached the wall. The breach therefore postdated the Byzantine era and could not possibly have been the work of Titus' rampaging troops. In fact, since it had been created sometime after the sixth century, the Persians were the more likely candidates for this dubious distinction, having destroyed the wall during their war with the Byzantines. We happen to know that the Byzantines fortified themselves on the Temple Mount, making it eminently reasonable that

the gaping hole was the result of an assault on their "fortress." On the other hand, it is equally possible that the wall was destroyed by the Byzantines themselves upon their triumphant return to Jerusalem in 629, in an outburst of anger at the Jews for having collaborated with the Persians. What better way of mocking and humiliating the Jews, who had entertained visions of rebuilding the Temple, than by causing further destruction to the Temple Mount?

One way or another, the repair of the breach was undoubtedly the work of the Moslems as preliminary to or part of their building activities on the Temple Mount. This supposition is backed by a combination of references in Jewish commentaries of the Omayyad period and archaeological evidence, leaving little doubt that the breach in the southern wall was not made by Titus and rectified by Hadrian but was effected by either the Persians or the Byzantines and repaired by the Omayyads.

Water, Greenery, and a Pretty Face

As our excavations moved steadily southward from the Temple Mount up to the present Old City wall, we systematically uncovered the large palace — 94 × 84 meters large, to be exact. The city wall had subsequently been built over the remains of its eastern and southern walls, so that what survived was mostly the palace's foundations and a few sections of walls belonging to the ground story, including several exterior walls. From these remains, however, we were able to trace its plan in detail and even draw a reconstructio of its upper storey. We have already remarked that the palace's plan very much resembled that of several other royal residences uncovered in Syria and Palestine. Fortunately for us, two such Omayyad palaces were uncovered in Israel and the West Bank — Hisham's Palace (Khirbet Mafjar) near Jericho and al-Walid's palace near

the Sea of Galilee — and have been thoroughly studied. Like these two prototypes, the Jerusalem palace consisted of an enclosed courtyard surrounded in the first instance by arcaded exedras and further back by a series of rooms. These palaces were further characterized by a single entrance gate on one side, round towers at each of their outer corners, and semicircular towers in the middle of their exterior walls.

Scholars believed that this plan was influenced by or actually copied

The Dome of the Rock and the Al Aqsa Mosque on the Temple Mount in Jerusalem

from the layout of Byzantine frontier fortresses, the successors of the Roman fortresses built in the outlying areas of Syria and Palestine. It is easy to understand why the Arabs of the early Moslem period adopted this master plan. The first imposing structures they came upon in their penetration of the Byzantine Empire were these border fortresses, which housed the military commanders (the troops being relegated to tents around these "forts"). Thus the conquered fortresses became the first

A reconstruction of the Omayyad palace, view northward toward the Al Aqsa Mosque

living quarters to be occupied by the Moslem commanders, who were eventually promoted to the rank of military governors and thereafter became the civilian rulers of the defeated lands. Having grown accustomed to the martial format and being familiar with its pragmatic advantages, the new governors chose it as the plan for their palaces. The plan was copied in its entirety, including the towers and a single gate — a perfect job of duplication displaying not the least understanding of the pragmatic functions of the building's various parts. Or so scholars believed, though most of these palaces were not uncovered inside walled cities and were thus built as independent units that had to be defeated.

left: Excavating at the southwest corner of the Temple Mount

right: Painted shards, royal ceramics from the Omayyad palace

However, the structure before us, while identical to the other palaces
in its internal layout and principles of construction, shows evidence of
having been adapted to meet special needs. Clearly it was not simply a
mindless copy or imitation of anything. For example, the Jerusalem palace did not have towers and did have multiple entrances in almost every
one of its sides, since there was no need for a strictly defensive posture.
Another reason for doing away with the towers in Jerusalem is related to
the close proximity of the auxiliary buildings. Due to the problems of
evacuating the houses of the Byzantine neighborhood, only a relatively
small area was cleared — sufficient for the construction of a few build-

Capitals and embossed stones, architectural elements from the Omayyad palace

ings. To streamline the construction process and facilitate the building of large structures, the royal buildings were built a mere 5–8 meters from one another! Considering these crowded conditions, adding towers would have been out of the question, as they would have required distancing the buildings to extend the open space between them.

An ancient Arab proverb has it that "A princess' honor is carried within her." The veil worn by observant Arab women translates this concept into a social practice, and it also came to expression in the architecture of the early Moslem period. One of the outstanding characteristics of the Jerusalem palace, based as it was on a cold and rigid military plan, was that it maintained an external appearance that belied its royal nature. That was true only on the outside, however. The walls facing on the inner courtyard were adorned with a mixture of reliefs and frescoes drawn in warm and bold colors. The décor in Jerusalem was confined to geometric and floral motifs and was conspicuously devoid of any human or animal figures, whereas other Omayyad palaces had a wealth of reliefs, embossings, and frescoes featuring animal and human figures — even half-naked people! Perhaps the reason for the artistic restraint in Jerusalem was the palace's proximity to the Al Aqsa Mosque and the consequent demand for a decorous approach to ornamentation. At any rate, the Jerusalem palace's strong and simple, almost spartan appearance on the outside (notwithstanding its attractive ornamentation on the inside) had a highly practical aspect to it: a fear of provoking the caliph's subjects, who labored under a heavy yoke of taxation to fund

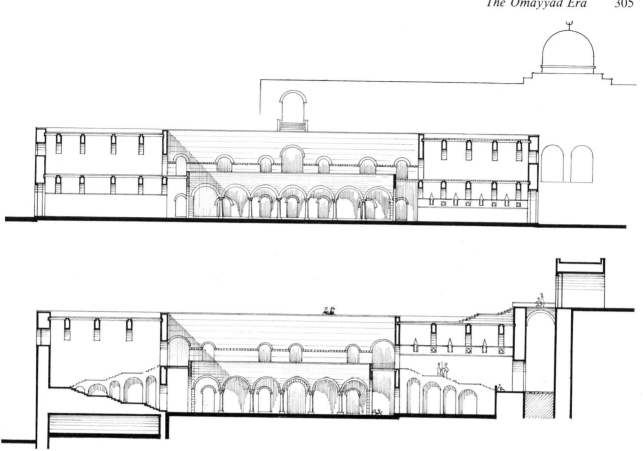

Reconstructed sections of the
structure of the Omayyad palace

their ruler's life of luxury. (This was evidently a very sensitive issue, for ultimately the gap between the living standards of the rulers and the ruled was successfully exploited by the Abbassids to cull public support for their struggle against the Omayyads and to eradicate the surviving members of the dynasty.)

Returning to the palace proper, among the hallmarks of its architectural approach was the unique use of the water system and the role of the foliage associated with it. Drawing on the existing aqueducts that carried spring water to Jerusalem, the Omayyads added a new system of pipes and channels that led the water into the courtyard, where trees and other foliage were planted. This detail was a borrowing from Persian architecture, and a few decades later gardens were planted in the courtyards of Omayyad palaces, and even of mosques, as far away as Spain. Thereafter the idea was copied by churches, whose gardens — *patios de los naranjas*, or Spanish citrus gardens — were characterized by orange trees. The motif of a citrus tree, with its deep-orange fruit, is known to us from the beautiful mosaic floor uncovered in the Jerusalem palace. These were evidently bitter-orange trees (*citrus aurantium*), a wild orange whose skin has a light-green tinge and whose fruit is neither deciduous nor pleasing to the palate, so that it is gladly left on the tree and can remain there for up to half a year. The bitter-orange tree is not particularly large, and when in bloom its scent carries for quite a distance. Planted among the bitter oranges were olive, pomegranate, and palm trees, giving the courtyard the look and feel of a lush garden. The flow of the water in the canals also contributed to the atmosphere through the soothing effect of its rippling sound, the soft drone of bees and other insects attracted to the water, the foliage, and finally the subtle scent of the water grasses that sprouted at the edges of the channels.

Omayyad architecture was essentially the combined product of the Byzantine architecture so prevalent throughout Palestine and Syria and classic elements imported from the East (India and Persia) whose guiding principle was to engage the senses — sight, sound, and smell — with pleasurable stimuli. Together they made for a delicate aesthetic harmony that was quite innovative in Jerusalemite architecture — which had always been marked most of all by the sense of sturdiness that comes from building in stone — and revived something of the sensuous atmosphere of the East that had not been known in the city since Herod's day. The general effect was, in the words of another Arab saying, "A taste of the good life: water, greenery, and a pretty face" — that "pretty face" being a metaphor for the design and ornamentation of the building.

Our main source of information on the structure of the Omayyad palace was its foundations, for in the course of time the palace itself was severely damaged and then heavily plundered by builders hungry for lime (some fifteen lime-producing ovens were found among its ruins). The result of this double scourge was extensive destruction, but we were nevertheless able to reconstruct the building's plan and saw that it had been a two-story structure. How could we ascertain that? I have already noted that by excavating the entire area, we were able to trace the palace's drainage and sewage systems and found that they had channels of two sorts: the first brought in water for daily use, drawing either on an aqueduct or on the rainwater that had collected on the roof and pavement. This water was then stored in two enormous (500-cubic-meter) plastered cisterns in the northeast corner of the palace. Originally dating to the Second Temple period, they had been replastered for their present use. The channels that

A Two-Story Palace

The southern wall of the eastern building, under which are structures from the Byzantine era and, below them, a public building from the Second Temple period

above, left: A niche in the southern wall of the palace built to hold a sewage pipe descending from the second story

above, center: A sewage canal under the western street from the Omayyad era

above, right: A sewage canal under the floor of a room in the Omayyad palace

below: A drainage pipe from the building east of the Omayyad palace

carried the water were coated with a high-quality waterproof plaster designed to prevent the seepage of so much as a drop of the precious liquid. The second system comprised the sewage pipes that carried refuse out of the building. They were laid in channels that had purposely not been plastered because the planners wanted some of the sewage to be absorbed by the soil. A few of the channels that carried sewage water were well plastered, of course, but that was because they ran close to the floor, and the architects wanted to ensure against seepage for fear of offensive odors. So if we find a well-plastered channel leading into one that is not plastered, we can assume that it belonged to the sewage system. Pottery pipes lead down from the roof into the water system. But the pipes of a drainage system do not tell us anything about the height of a building, for we have no way of knowing whether the rainwater they carried came from the roof of the ground story or a higher one. On the other hand, if the pipes leading downward enter the *sewage system*, the building must have had at least two stories, for plumbing of this kind implies the existence of kitchens and bathrooms, and they would hardly have been situated on the roof!

We found not one pipe descending into the sewage system but seven — and that speaks for a highly advanced lifestyle requiring the disposal of

large quantities of water. In two-storied buildings the ground floor served as the servants quarters, stables, and storage rooms while the upper floor comprised the main living quarters, which were well endowed with lavatories and sophisticated plumbing facilities. Judging by the quality of the systems we found, the Omayyads were well versed in sanitary and drainage engineering. In fact, the builders of this particular system showed themselves to be expert plumbers, and the solutions they devised to overcome various problems were perfectly consonant with the principles of modern sanitary engineering, in terms of both siphoning techniques and the sanitary traps necessary for proper disposal of wastes.

By systematically uncovering all of the palace's foundations, we were able to appreciate the superb technical ability of the builders as well as learn something about the problems that preoccupied the people of the day. We found, for example, that the foundations of this building were laid using no less than five different methods of construction. It is almost axiomatic in archaeology that a change in the nature or style of finds signals a change in period, even though sometimes we can trace the difference to a specific reason and conclude that the finds come from the same era or, contrawise, we know that they date to the same period and we're totally stumped by the reason for the change. Take, as an example, an abrupt and blatant decline in the quality of foundations. The reason might be as momentous as a change of regime or a natural disaster that affected economic or labor conditions. On the other hand, it could equally have been something as mundane as a foreman quitting his job or simply walking away from a specific area of the construction site, leaving the

Arches of the western building served as the foundations for the structure above it

Finds Under the Floor

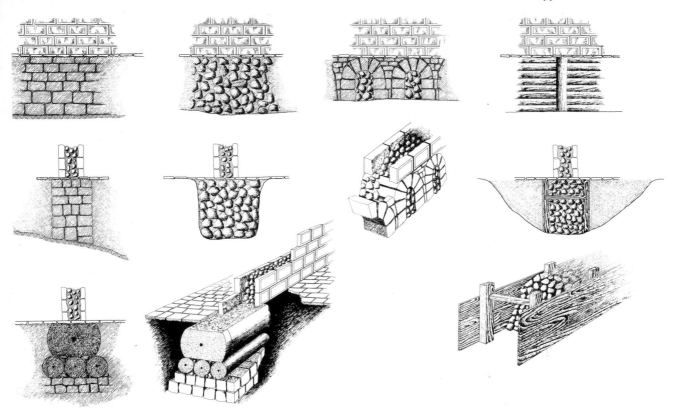

Various methods of laying the foundations of the Omayyad palace

laborers — who knew that the foundation would be covered by a layer of dirt and not be visible anyway — to take the path of least resistance.

In laying the foundations of this particular building, which sometimes went down as far as 9 meters — for the building was at least two stories high, each story being 6.5 meters — the builders encountered a number of topographical diffculties. Sometimes the terrain was exceptionally low, making it necessary to built foundation walls and cover them with fill. (Since these walls were constructed of dressed stones, the contemporary excavator could well arrive at the erroneous conclusion that they were the lower courses of the building's walls, and we had to be especially wary of this pitfall.) In other places, however, the terrain was particularly high — the projected height of the floors, in fact — and then trenches had to be dug and filled with undressed stones and mortar to create the foundations. Our exposure of these foundations revealed that the stones had seemingly been laid haphazardly. Frequently we found a foundation that looked like the negative imprint of the wooden frame used to hold it until the mortar had set because the trenches had been dug into unstable detritus. This detail taught us that the builders believed it worthwhile to invest in the wooden frames as a way of saving on stone and mortar. And evidently it was especially important to economize on mortar, which was made of sand and lime and took considerable amounts of water to produce. Once covered over, the wood eventually rotted, leaving a negative impression of the form on the sides of the foundation. The Omayyads, not being natives of the country, were not particularly concerned about conserving its forests and cut them down mercilessly both to produce these forms and as a source of energy for the lime industry. This is no petty plaint,

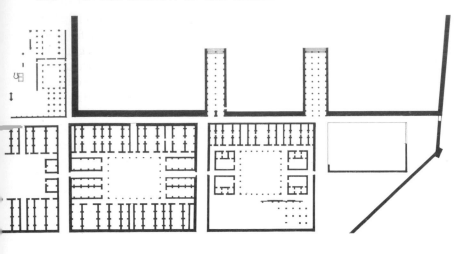

Plan of the Omayyad palace and its auxiliary buildings

for it wasn't long before the country had been practically shorn of its forests and took on a rather desolate appearance.

After the foundations were laid and the infrastructure was built over it, the laying of the building's floors did not necessarily follow. Today, too, the laying of floors is among the last jobs done in a construction project. In the case of the Omayyad palace, first the space between the foundations had to be filled in almost up to the floor level. The fill was composed of refuse building materials and the detritus that had piled up as a result of digging the foundations. And as detritus it naturally contained pottery shards and the remains of other artifacts — material from

A room in the eastern building fronting the Double Gate

many and varied periods, depending upon which strata the builders had excavated to lay the foundations. Also found in this type of fill were broken vessels dating to the brief span from the time of digging the foundations up to the time of laying the floors. Once the infrastructure had been erected, the laborers often used the shell or half-finished building as their living quarters. To meet their needs, certain amenities were installed (as were certain construction facilities, such as an appliance for mixing mortar and the like), and when the floors were laid these facilities were covered over. Thus even though from the standpoint of stratigraphy (the order of the strata) these remains are found under the floors, they are contemporary with the stratum above them. At the risk of belaboring the point, I must stress that these highly relevant details of stratigraphy can be ascertained only by conducting an extensive excavation of any one area, because the fill might be as much as a few meters thick and may have been built up layer by layer at varying intervals. For this same reason, our standard procedure called for excavating only half of the fill, leaving the rest untouched until we could verify that we were indeed working our way down through a single stratum. Proceeding in this manner, we slowly got a cross-section of the fill, which was admittedly very colorful but quite void of any archaeological significance, since it was the random result of the way in which the laborers had cast the rocks, ruins, and detritus over the foundations.

The flooring on the ground story of the Omayyad palace and the adjoining buildings was for the most part made of stone, though we did come across instances of mosaic floors created out of relatively large cubes set in plain designs. Between the fill and the stone flooring of all the rooms and the exedras, the builders had put down a 15–20-centimeter layer of red earth (terra rossa), which had been carted in from quite a distance. Was the purpose of this layer of earth to serve as a kind of platform for stabilizing the floors? Actually, it was exactly the opposite. The slightest seepage of water through the stone flooring would cause the terra rossa to expand and thereby place pressure on the stones, so that there is nothing *worse* than having terra rossa under stone flooring. Could it be that the builders had made a crude mistake? It doesn't seem likely, for there was no layer of terra rossa under the street pavements or the mosaic floors, which were laid over and into a dark, heavy mortar that acted as a strong adhesive. It would therefore appear that the great pains taken to lay the stone flooring over a bed of terra rossa meant that the flooring was temporary and ultimately destined to be dismantled in favor of a mosaic floor. In order to pull up the floor more easily and be able to use its stones again, the builders took the trouble to cart in and spread the layer of terra rossa precisely because of its instability. I have cited this detail out of literally scores of telling details regarding the Omayyad construction technique to show how carefully the builders of the day calculated their every move.

Some of the mosaic floors found in the Omayyad buildings were composed of 2.5-centimeter marble cubes. For whatever reason, these marble mosaics were preferred by the Omayyad builders, and to lay them they collected fragments of marble latticework from destroyed Byzantine churches and placed them in special storage receptacles on the construction site. We discovered one of these receptacles containing a haul of fragments, some with decorations characteristic of Byzantine church art, others carved with crosses or bearing inscriptions in Greek.

The ambitious building program inaugurated in the days of Abd-al-Malik was never fully consummated, so that several details of the Omayyad buildings — including the final flooring — were never completed. It may be that work stopped a few years before the fall of the dynasty because the last of the Omayyad caliphs ran into severe financial difficulties. Testimony to that effect can be found in the declaration of one of the last caliphs before his council. As a condition for accepting the throne, he stipulated that: "In my time no stone will be built upon another, or brick set upon brick . . . anywhere in the caliphate."

Other than the above-mentioned girls' school, there was no building standing in the proposed area of excavations south of the southern wall when we began our dig. Most of the area looked like a big empty lot, and in the course of time, after the residents of the adjoining Moghrabi Quarter had been evacuated and their dilapidated houses were razed, this open area grew even larger. We extended our excavation into the former Moghrabi Quarter, seizing the opportunity to dig in the vicinity of Robinson's Arch and study the nearby strata of structures dating to the Second Temple period. But almost as soon as we set to work, we began to encounter the remains of huge walls built out of ashlars resembling the stones of the Omayyad palace. Extending the excavation further revealed that there were indeed another two large buildings in the vicinity, one west of the palace, the other west of the western wall. And as we continued to dig, we discovered that to the west of these buildings was yet a fourth structure. The task of dating these buildings was not difficult, for the fill under their floors incorporated the remains of whole structures from the late Byzantine period. At first the remains uncovered on the southern slope were defined as belonging to all three of the buildings, but it soon turned out that the walls of what had appeared to be various units actually belonged to one and the same extraordinarily large building (95 × 85 meters) whose plan was identical to that of the palace. To the east of this building we uncovered the start of another structure that was never completed because the construction program came to a halt toward the middle of the eighth century. It was as if time had stopped alongside the Temple Mount.

If we could have photographed the area back in the eighth century, we would have seen the following picture: the destroyed walls of the Temple Mount had been restored and the compound housed the Dome of the Rock, the imposing Al Aqsa Mosque, and the Golden Gate. Immediately to the south of the Temple Mount was a large palace flanked on the east by an identical but unfinished building. Between these two structures was an alleyway leading to the western Hulda Gate, or Prophet's Gate, below Al Aqsa. Further to the east were foundations walls — the start of yet another building whose construction was halted early on, so that its exact plan cannot be determined. The western part of the area had a number of buildings, including a structure composed mostly of an enclosed court whose surrounding rooms were graced with mosaic floors. What makes this structure stand out is the fact that it lacks exedras. To the west thereof, on the slope of the western hill, was another large building that has yet to be excavated. And north of these two buildings, facing Robinson's Arch, was another structure that had a unique plan: two small enclosed courtyards surrounded by halls whose ceilings were supported by many columns and whose floors were of stone or mosaics set in simple

The Auxiliary Buildings

above: Columns and pillars from the bathhouse belonging to the network of the Omayyad palace

below: The remains of the Omayyad palace and its auxiliary buildings

patterns. A study of its plan gave rise to the hypothesis that it was a
bathhouse, and as our investigation continued it turned out to be precisely that. North of the bathhouse was the reconstruction of Wilson's Arch
and the adjoining network of vaulted halls. Thus what we saw before us
was an example of dense construction on a large scale. All in all, these
buildings added up to a dazzling archaeological discovery. For 1,200
years the remains of these Omayyad buildings awaited their redemption.
For 1,200 years the Abbassids succeeded in their mission of wiping out all
trace of the Omayyad enterprise in Jerusalem, but now the archaeologist's
spade had brought them to light. It is one of the ironies of this city's
history that this remarkable discovery was made by Israeli archaeologists,
while King Hussein — a scion of the Hashemite dynasty, which traces
back to the family of the prophet Mohammed — was responsible for
further burying all trace of this glorious palace by building yet another
structure over its ruins in the belief that they were the remains of a
Christian building.

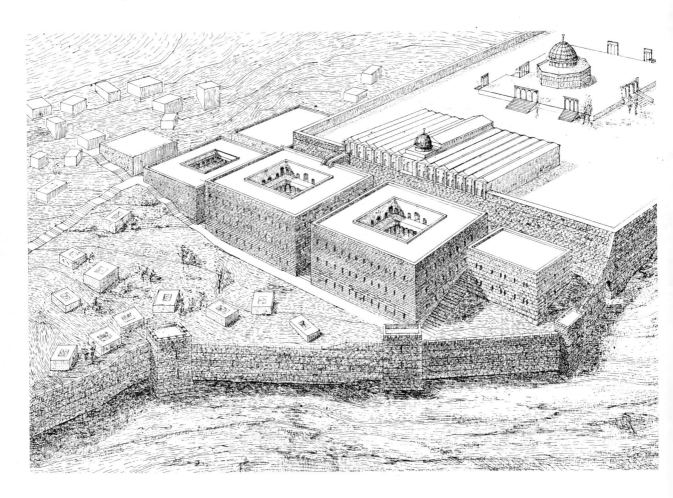

To make room for the complex of the palace and auxiliary buildings,
the Omayyad architects were forced to "rezone" and replan the area
adjoining the Temple Mount. It was necessary to expropriate land and
evacuate whole families from their homes (and for all that, their ambitious project was never fully realized). Yet even though the Omayyads

A reconstructed view (east–west) of
the Omayyad royal complex at the
foot of the Temple Mount

ruled much of the civilized world, they exercised great restraint in dealing with the citizens of Jerusalem. The expropriation of land was kept to a minimum, making it necessary to build with a high degree of density. The result was that these imposing structures bore down on and practically touched one another, the alleys between them being a mere 4 meters across (compared to the 10-meter-wide streets of the Second Temple period). These alleyways apparently served as access streets for frequenters of the palace — the royal entourage, attendants, and servants. Entrance to the Temple Mount was through the gates still extant from the Second Temple period (such as Barclay's and Warren's Gate) and the new gates built in the northern but primarily in the western wall (specifically the Gate of the Chain over Wilson's Arch).

The Royal Bathhouse

The young people who worked on our excavation were volunteers in the fullest sense of the word, since we were unable to provide for any of their material needs. On the other hand, we were truly generous with such

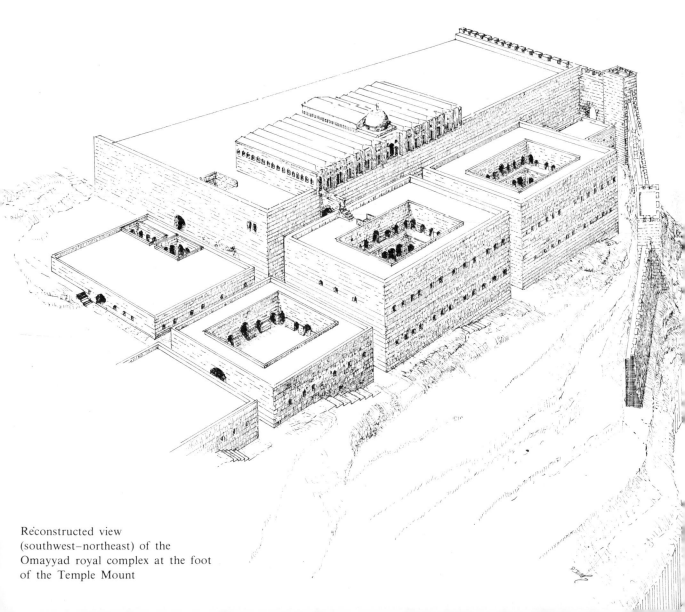

Reconstructed view
(southwest–northeast) of the
Omayyad royal complex at the foot
of the Temple Mount

things as tours of the dig and lectures on the history and archaeology of Jerusalem, both during work hours and at special sessions. As a result, many of our volunteers picked up quite an education, and it was reflected in their work. One morning, for example, a young man assigned to a section at the northern end of the excavation site, near Robinson's Arch, approached me with a very pertinent observation. "You told us that it was traditional to build in stone in the lands of the East and in brick in the West," he prefaced his discovery. "Yet in our sector, we can begin to see the tops of walls made of red, oven-fired bricks." His point was an intriguing one, and I immediately marched off to have a look at what he was talking about. A few more days of careful digging solved the mystery: the red-brick walls comprised the furnace of a bathhouse. Since stone tends to crumble when it comes into contact with fire, and local stone dissolves into lime, it was imperative to use a fireproof material for building furnaces, and baked bricks were just as well suited to the task as anyone could ask.

Yet the technical solution was not the most fascinating aspect of this find. The most exciting thing was the very discovery of the bathhouse. Of course we expected to find one somewhere in the complex of the Omayyad palace, because our knowledge of other palaces of the period and of the role played by the bathhouse in the royal lifestyle made its presence somewhere in this vicinity almost an imperative. The Moslem bath was a social institution, much as a sauna is today. In Omayyad buildings it was common to find it situated close to a large banquet hall, and that explains the special plan of the western building, which was essentially a grand banquet hall with a bath in its northwest wing.

Only part of the bathhouse has been excavated; the rest lies out of our reach under the plaza in front of the Wailing Wall. But from what we do know of its layout, we can surmise that the section containing the furnaces — the hot room or *caldarium* — exended over an area of 1,000 square meters, making it one of the largest such rooms ever uncovered in this country. The furnaces were made out of pillars built out of square bricks and topped by arches (likewise made of red baked bricks) that supported the floors above. From the few remains still *in situ*, we were able to learn that the pottery pipes that heated the room ran along the walls and that the floor was covered with marble in at least a few places; marble benches were also part of the furnishings. The entire setup was very similar to the bathhouse found in Hisham's Palace in Jericho, and its operative principle resembled that of a Roman bath (which was essentially the prototype of the Moslem bathhouse). North of the furnace area is a fairly well-preserved wall with an aperture that led into a lavishly built, small room whose ceiling was made of two large slabs of stone. This small room gave access to other rooms and was in effect only a corridor or vestibule. We could not investigate the rest of the rooms because they are located under the Wailing Wall plaza, and any attempt to excavate them from the side, rather than from above, could be dangerous to life and limb. But we can propound that this series of rooms was the caliph's private lounge, or the *diwan*. The *diwan* in the bathhouse of Hisham's Palace in Jericho is a room with a lovely mosaic floor. The difference here is that we are talking about an entire apartment, not just a single room.

When we cleaned the heat-conducting floors, we came upon another important discovery. I have noted that the pillars of the furnaces were made of square bricks, but parts of the heat-conducting floor and subter-

The ceiling of the royal *diwan* in the bathhouse

Three ways of exploiting columns in the Omayyad palace according to the height of the columns taken from destroyed Byzantine buildings

ranean brick-lined passages were made out of round bricks, some bearing the hallmark of the Tenth Legion. What were these bricks doing in a Moslem bathhouse? There are two possible answers: perhaps the building had originally been a Roman bathhouse that was extended and remodeled by the Moslems to suit their own needs and tastes. In that case, we would expect that it had also been in use during the Byzantine period — an assumption supported by sources on Byzantine Jerusalem that refer to bathhouses in this area, though there is no evidence to the effect that the Moslem bathhouse was Byzantine in origin. Over the centuries, this general area became associated with public baths, and from the time of the Mamelukes and Ottomans up to the present, similar institutions have been located slightly to the north of it. In this context we should recall that the aqueduct running from Bethlehem to the Temple Mount entered the enclosure in this same vicinity, leading to yet another possibility (and one that seems more reasonable to us): it could well be that the Moslem builders dismantled a destroyed bathhouse or a nearby Roman brick building to build the royal bath in this area. Baked bricks were an expensive commodity, making it worthwhile to dismantle old bathhouses in order to build new ones.

Building Materials

I have repeatedly alluded to the fact that the Omayyad buildings in Jerusalem drew heavily upon stones and sometimes whole parts of earlier structures. The example of the bricks in the bathhouse may be open to question, but there is no doubt whatever that the Omayyads dismantled destroyed buildings and "recycled" the stones in their own structures. Much of the destruction had been caused during or following the Persian conquest, though churches remained in ruins even after the city had been retaken by Heraclius because by then the Byzantines were steeped in new and no-less-taxing wars with the Arab tribes to the east. And although the victorious Arabs did not indulge in a wave of destruction, neither did they allow their Christian subjects to rebuild the already wrecked churches.

Instead they used the dismantled ruins in their own construction projects.

This assembling of building materials from various sources, ranging from the Temple Mount to the ruins of the Nea Church, necessarily meant that the finished product would fall short of the splendor expected of a palace and the royal buildings surrounding it. One consequence of the hodge-podge was that the interior walls had to be covered with a thick layer of plaster, and the same may have been true of the exterior ones. But the element most prominently affected by the use of second-hand building materials was the exedra, because its columns were scavenged from ruined public buildings all over the city. Marble columns were in special demand because marble had to be imported. When the Byzantines built their churches, their marble columns were ordered in the necessary quantity and size directly from the workshops in Constantinople. But the Omayyad builders were limited in their ability to acquire raw or manufactured materials overseas, which is why they relied so heavily on what they could find at hand. Many columns from the churches were broken and no longer usable on display. Yet rather than discard them altogether, the builders relegated them to walls and foundations, where they turned up as ordinary building stones. Every column found intact was a cause for celebration. The problem was that because of their eclectic provenance, the columns varied in height and diameter. This difficulty was overcome by placing a short column on a higher base (occasionally supported by a stone) and by sinking a higher column into the foundation, so that it

Marble screen fragment taken from destroyed churches served the Omayyad builders

opposite: A column engraved with a cross in secondary use in the Omayyad palace

opposite: The northern exedra of the eastern building. The height and diameter of the columns differ, as they were taken from the ruins of different buildings

The base of a column in one of the rooms of the Omayyad palace. It was totally sunk under the floor because the column it bore was a tall one

looked as if it were "sprouting" out of the floor. These solutions resulted in something of an abstract style of décor. But the look of the Omayyad exedra was at any rate very different from its Byzantine predecessor, not only because its columns were of different heights and diameters but because some of them still bore engravings of crosses in what was otherwise an Islamic artistic setting. The fact that the builders and residents of the palace were not disturbed by this anomaly is evidence that these buildings were both constructed and destroyed before the Abbassid era, because during that period (beginning in the latter half of the eighth century) Islam became increasingly parochial, and much energy was invested into obliterating all trace of the non-Moslem religious symbols carved into stone.

In addition to the interesting architectural finds uncovered among the ruins of the Omayyad palace — capitals, embossed stones, fragments of frescoes, and the like — we came upon a wealth of objects and accessories from everyday life, many of them preserved in the sewage channels. It's hard to believe the range of things that men are capable of flushing down a toilet or washing down a drain. I can recall a news item about a resident of New York flushing away a new-born crocodile that grew to a length of 3 meters before the sanitation workers tracked it down and removed it from the sewer system. Of course we didn't turn up any crocodiles, but we did find a plethora of animal-shaped perfume vials, pottery containers whose upper half was designed in the shape of an animal head, cruses for oil and vinegar, and small jars for spices and confections. Once broken, these objects were commended to the sewage system, and there they lay until being redeemed by the archaeologist's spade.

Another find that drew a lot of attention was sets of wine glasses and bowls for serving refreshments, including a number of pieces arranged on trays, seven bowls to a tray. You can comfortably hold these glasses in the palm of your hand, but it is difficult to stand them on a table, because their bases are either flat and narrow or rounded. Similar bowls and glasses were found in the Byzantine houses, making it impossible for us to be precise in dating them. There is, however, a striking difference between the vessels found in the houses and those found in the remains of the palace: both have a similar shape and were made the same way, but all the vessels from the palace were decorated on the sides with floral designs, geometric patterns, and even animal figures rendered in black and white. These delicately executed decorations lend a quality of great charm to the vessels. To date vessels of this kind have been found primarily in the Jerusalem palace, though some have turned up in Hisham's Palace in Jericho and in a number of other places in Palestine, especially in churches. This last observation notwithstanding, we can definitely call this group "palace ware" and venture that the artistic influence on these vessels probably traces to the Coptic ceramics of Egypt, whose decoration is similar.

Other groups of vessels were ornamented by the method of pricking or molding (or both) their light yellow-brown clay. Known as "Khirbet Mafjar ware," they included middle-sized containers particularly for liquids and were made by a technique that derives from Persia and was unknown in this area prior to the Omayyad era. Resembling metal in both shape and design, these vessels are floridly decorated and exhibit many motifs that are unusual in ceramic ware. Considering the Omayyads' frugal use of metals, which were reserved solely for arms, it is not surprising that the artisans of this period designed pottery objects such as lamps and candelabra to resemble metal ones. Incidentally, the pragmatic need to conserve metals developed a religious dimension as well, so that during this period Islam viewed the use of metal for daily purposes with a jaundiced eye, and religious propaganda related to metals with unabashed contempt because they were used in the arms industry.

Finally, we also came upon a collection of vessels found in daily use: pottery containers, jugs, cooking pots, cruses, spoons and bowls. From the point of view of their design, they are direct successors of the pottery of the Byzantine era, and the reason for this resemblance is clear: there had been no revolution in the style of daily life, the craftsmen were the same, and the composition and tastes of the local population had not changed very much. Also found in the palace were pottery chamber pots that look as chamber pots have looked from time immemorial. Most of them were glazed (on the inside only) in dark green or dark brown. In addition to the pottery vessels found among the palace ruins were a number of metal artifacts, primarily of bronze. They included small decorated mortars and pestles for crushing spices and bronze coins still bearing the name Aelia — a lasting souvenir of Aelia Capitolina. There was also an ample number of iron objects — including such accessories as door hinges, nails, hooks, and window latches — but their state of preservation was particularly poor. The artisans of the day likewise tried their hand at working in bone, so that we also found bone knife handles carved with reliefs of various kinds. In essence, we had before us a broad array of objects representing daily life, and with their aid we are able to get a feel for the lifestyle of the people who lived in and around the Omayyad palace.

Our excavation of the Omayyad stratum south of the Temple Mount enabled us to fill in many details about a neglected period of local history, and we arrived at the following picture: seized by the urge to build, the caliphs of the Omayyad dynasty embarked upon construction projects throughout the empire, but nowhere more than in Syria and Palestine. This momentum was generated by an encounter with two civilizations (the Byzantine and the Persian) that counted the art of construction as a prominent feature of their heritage. In both these cultures, architecture flourished as an integral part of the empire's intellectual life, and the Omayyads seemed to be captivated by the impressive architectural achievements of the world they had just defeated. They felt dwarfed and humbled by the power of the structures in whose shadow they now stood — particularly the churches — and developed a passion for building on a large, even grandiose scale. At first they were able to indulge this whim to the utmost for they lacked neither funds nor cheap labor, both of which they acquired by plundering the lands and imposing heavy tribute on the people they had conquered. So it was that their building enterprise spread through the new empire. The innovative and particularly the aesthetic achievements of Moslem architecture, which began to come into its own during this age, derived from a synthesis of eastern and western elements of design and construction and accounted for its unique flavor.

History is filled with examples of one society encountering the culture of another, being fascinated (even hypnotized) by it, and trying to emulate it but copying only its external forms, not the essence of its content — the chaff, as it were, instead of the wheat. This is essentially what happened in

above: A bronze bell from the palace

center: A bronze pestle and mortar from the palace

the encounter between the worlds of Byzantium and Islam, and the resultant superficiality was an omen of decline. In the course of time, primarily because of the economic erosion that weakened it at the time of this unprecedented building program, the first signs of a crisis began to appear in the Omayyad empire. Construction came to a halt in Jerusalem, and the shells of buildings stood forlornly alongside completed structures. This rather grim picture began to take shape toward the middle of the eighth century. Then came a massive blow by nature that added destruction to neglect. The earthquake of 747 left a deep mark on an entire generation. Jewish sources refer to it as the "seventh earthquake" and describe it in great detail. Its epicenter was Jerusalem, the Jordan Valley, and Jericho, so that the damage there was particularly severe.

In Jerusalem both holy places and secular buildings on and beyond the Temple Mount were gravely damaged. Our excavations revealed the effect of the quake in the form of cracked walls and warped foundations, fallen columns and sunken floors. It was at about the same time that the Abbasids were plotting their revolt against the Omayyads. Their plan succeeded, and in 750 the Omayyad dynasty fell. When the turmoil surrounding the revolt subsided, life began to return to normal, but Jerusalem was no longer to be the center it had been under the Omayyads. The Abbassids were the progeny of the army commanders who ruled over Iraq and Persia, so once again the center of gravity shifted: Damascus declined from its height of glory, and the capital of the kingdom moved to Iraq, first to Al Kufa and finally to the new city of Dar a-Salaam ("The House of Peace," now known as Baghdad) built on the Tigris, not far from the old Persian capital of Ctesiphon. Economic and architectural activity likewise centered on the new capital, and much of the Omayyad construction in Palestine and Syria fell victim to neglect and deteriorated into ruin.

This was the sad fate of the Omayyad building program in Jerusalem. (The exception to this rule was the Temple Mount proper, for the new regime, still pledged to the sanctity of Jerusalem, rebuilt the structures there.) The Omayyad buildings south and west of the Temple Mount were the last manifestations of large-scale royal construction undertaken in this area. For the first time since the days of David and Solomon, the seat of the royal palace had returned to the vicinity of the Temple Mount; and it was the heirs of David and Solomon who were privileged to find its remains.

above: Painted pottery shards from the Omayyad palace

below: A pottery wine goblet from the palace

opposite: An animal-shaped vessel for storing spices

18 The Days of the Abbassids and the Fatimids

above: A fragment of a monumental inscription from the reign of the Fatimid dynasty hinting at restoration work done on the Temple Mount

opposite: The remains of the "Sulfur Tower" from the end of the Fatimid period

As we have seen, the successful revolt of the Abbassids led to a shift in the seat of rule eastward to their strongholds of support in Iraq and Persia. Considering the Abbassids' deep hostility toward the house of Omayya and all its achievements, it is surprising that the concept of Jerusalem's sanctity, which was relatively new to Islam, survived the subsequent wave of revisionism. Evidently this tenet had become so firmly rooted in the Moslem ethos that it was beyond challenge; otherwise it is difficult to imagine the Abbassids having reconciled themselves to it. It is equally possible, however, that the motivating factor at work here was a desire not to abandon Jerusalem to Christianity. After all, the Byzantines set great store by Jerusalem, whether as a cornerstone of the Christian faith and a center of Christian art or because they appreciated that by keeping an attachment to Jerusalem alive in the Christian consciousness, they were establishing a good "jumping-off point" for whatever political opportunity fate might bring their way. Neither was Western Christendom oblivious to Jerusalem's drawing power; Charlemagne, for one, built pilgrim hostels in the city and went out of his way to establish ties with the Abbassid caliphs.

Whatever their motive, the Abbassids continued to accord the Temple Mount special attention. Its mosques were repaired and, as we saw earlier, in a rather clumsy attempt at forgery the caliph al-Mamoun even tried to take credit for having built the Dome of the Rock. Outside of the Temple Mount proper, however, the products of the Omayyads' grand building enterprise suffered a very different (and very sad) fate. Worse than not being rebuilt after the earthquake, they were actually abandoned to stone and lime contractors, who built ovens in the vicinity of the royal complex and dismantled its stones for use in the construction of other buildings throughout the city or for the production of lime.

It wasn't long before the area assumed the look it had when we uncovered it: the random remains of walls and floors scattered among the foundations that had escaped the wreckers. Hence the role played by the Abbassids in the area around the Temple Mount ranged from abstaining from building activity to outright, deliberate destruction, and the stratum dating to their reign is essentially a negative one from an archaeological viewpoint. Actually, it is not even a distinct stratum, in the strict sense of the word, but rather evidence of the destruction caused to the Omayyad buildings. The layer of ruins that resulted from the deliberate wreckage or incidental collapse of these buildings is as much as 6–8 meters thick and contains whole walls. The "Abbassid stratum" is therefore a collection of heaps of detritus, destroyed walls, pillaged floors, and not a single sign of any constructive activity — which is indeed an unusual state of affairs in archaeology.

The Fatimids and Seljuks

It is the nature of sprawling empires that over the years they begin to suffer from erosion and are steadily undermined until they finally break up and disappear from the world stage. Sometimes the process is slow, sometimes swifter, but it almost always follows much the same pattern.

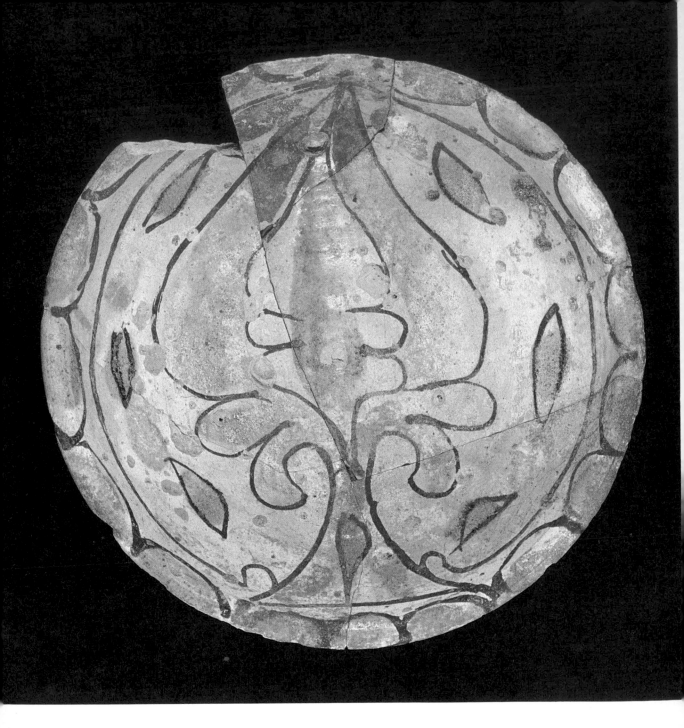

The erosion begins on the marches of the empire, far from the centers of government and culture. Even as the Abbassids wrested control of the Moslem Empire, for example, they lost a large and important chunk of territory, as Spain remained under the rule of the surviving Omayyads. As time went on, their weakening hold reached the eastern Mediterranean, and in 868 the commander of the imperial army in Egypt, Ahmed ibn-Tulun, rebelled against the caliph and took Egypt out of the Abbassid sway. In 877 he proceeded to conquer Palestine and Syria and establish his control there, as well. The Middle East then entered an era of wars of succession in which it repeatedly passed from hand to hand. In a relatively

above and right: Ceramic bowls from the Fatimid era

short time, Egypt and Palestine had gone through a series of upheavals, and each change of regime seemed to be bound up with increasingly brutal wars that spread mayhem throughout the country and took a heavy toll of its population, even though they were only incidentally involved in the political struggle at hand. And of course every successive conqueror appreciated the unique status and power possessed by Jerusalem, so that not a single one of the wars passed the city by.

At the start of the tenth century, a new Moslem state arose in North Africa, and with it came a new dynasty. Sa'id ibn-Husein, the founder of the dynasty, considered himself a descendant of Fatima, the daughter of

A pottery oil lamp adorned with an inscription

the Prophet Mohammed, and his successors became known as the Fatimid line. In 969 one of his descendants conquered Egypt and then Palestine immediately thereafter. The dust of battle had hardly settled when units of a fanatical sect known as the Karmatians marched up from the direction of Persia and penetrated as far as Egypt, passing through Palestine on their way and leaving their mark on Jerusalem. The chaotic situation in the area was exploited by the Byzantines, who once again sent their forces marching into Palestine. But while the Christians were still celebrating their victory, they were ousted by the Fatimids, who struck from Egypt.

I would not have outlined this sad series of events were it not for the profound effect it had on the future of Jerusalem. Despite all the turmoil, the city managed to bear up and function as an urban center within its walls. Commercial trade flourished and Jerusalem's inhabitants con-

above, left: The remains of a residential building from the Fatimid era built on the ruins of the Omayyad palace

below, left: A pottery oil lamp decorated with a floral design

Reconstruction of that same
residential building built on the ruins
of the Omayyad palace

overleaf: A treasure of gold coins
from the Fatimid era

tinued to take pride in their city. The period was described in the work of
a contemporary Arab historian and geographer, Mohammed ibn-Ahmed,
better known as Muqaddasi or the Jerusalemite. From his detailed accounts we are able to gather that the area south of the Temple Mount no
longer played an important role in the city's life and effectively lay in
ruins, but the rest of the city was fully built up. Muqaddasi also tells us the
following about the city's walls and gates: "Jerusalem is smaller than
Mecca and larger than Medina... [It] is surrounded by a wall with eight
iron gates: the Zion Gate, the Wilderness Gate, the Palace Gate, the Gate
of Jeremiah's Grotto, the Silwan [Siloam] Gate, the Jericho Gate, the
Gate of the Column, and David's Gate." These names and the number of
gates indicate that Jerusalem was still a walled city and that its walls
encompassed a large area (similar to their circumference during the Byzantine and Omayyad eras).

In terms of the vicissitudes of the times, the eleventh century proved to
be much like its predecessor, except that in the tenth century Jerusalem

was able to weather the cataclysmic events taking place around it but by the eleventh its fortitude had begun to wane. Particularly trying was the age of the Fatimid ruler al-Hakim (reigned 966–1021), who held the city in terror of his every mood and whim. The unstable, often frenzied al-Hakim ultimately came to regard himself as the incarnation of the deity and, as such, was antagonistic toward and destructive of Christianity and Judaism alike. During his reign the economy and religious centers of Palestine were laid waste. Even Jerusalem felt his wrath when the Church of the Holy Sepulcher, among other religious sites, was reduced to ruins. The city's population began to flee in panic, leaving many areas practically devoid of life. Added to the stress of living in such terror was the fear of marauders who galloped out of the desert and finally the effects of a heavy earthquake that racked the city in about the middle of the eleventh century. Jerusalem had barely recovered from these wicked blows when a new military threat began to loom in the distance.

The main actors on the stage of Jerusalem's history were now the Seljuks, members of a Turkish tribe originating in Central Asia who had been recruited into the service of the caliph, converted to Islam, and slowly undermined the Abbassid regime from within. By the eleventh century the Seljuk leaders were sultans in every way, while the caliphs retained authority solely in the field of Moslem religious law. To mark their ascent to power, the Seljuks marched westward, and once again Palestine was afflicted by a period of political turmoil as rule of the country passed from the Fatimids to the Seljuks and back again. The ravages of war were again a common sight; the economy was crippled, and instability reigned everywhere. Marching back and forth across the wasted landscape, the Seljuk and Fatimid troops only heightened the wrack and ruin. Finally, while the country was back in Fatimid hands, news came from afar that yet another, newer army was on the march, this time from the west. The Crusades had begun. Suddenly Jerusalem was in the throes of fevered preparations to meet the new assault, and we naturally wondered what the city had looked like, especially in the area of the Temple Mount, at the time these events began to unfold.

Bathsheba's Courtyard

As the rooms of the Omayyad palace were slowly being exposed by our volunteers, a group of walls began to emerge close to the southeast corner of the palace's courtyard. As they were smaller and narrower than the rest and were built at angles different from those of the palace's walls, we could see that they were not congruent with the original plan. After excavating the entire building, we understood that these irregular walls belonged to a structure that postdated the palace and had been built over the stone pavement of its courtyard. In fact, its walls incorporated fragments of the capitals that had once adorned the palace's exedras. This building — the only one remaining intact in the area — was characterized by its simple plan and construction. Near its southern wall two small storehouses had been dug into the ruins, and they contained a number of storage jars that had apparently served the building's inhabitants.

These were structures from the Fatimid period build on the ruins of the Omayyad palace. As such, the earliest date we can establish for them is the eleventh century. It is noteworthy that this was the first time we had come across such pitiful buildings in the vicinity of the Temple Mount, and they testify that Jerusalem's history in the tenth and eleventh centuries was incontrovertibly one of hardship to the point of destruction.

Among the ruins of the palace and
the auxiliary buildings of the
Omayyad period are remains of
residential buildings from the Fatimid
period (aerial photograph, 1977)

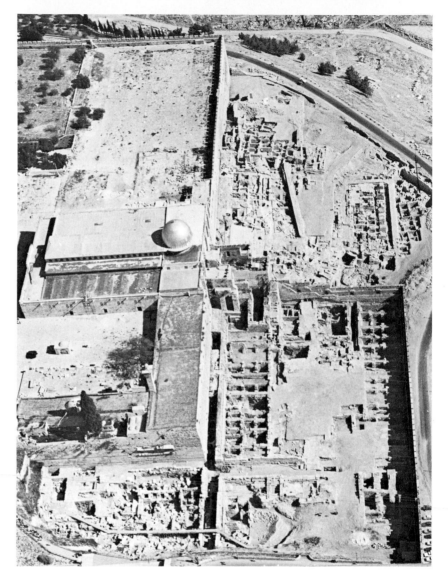

Later on, when we began to dig east of the Old City wall, we uncovered a few other remains of simple buildings from this era, likewise built
on the ruins of a building from the Omayyad period. South of the Temple
Mount, some 50 meters from the western Hulda Gate, a large structure
with stone floors had been erected over the remains of foundations from
the Omayyad building. It had a large central courtyard surrounded by
pillars, and when we removed a section of its floors we were rewarded
with finds (mostly coins and pottery) from the eighth and ninth centuries
in the fill beneath them.

A few years prior to these discoveries, the scholar Y. Braslavy published a document from the Cairo Geniza that was believed to date to the
tenth century and was the equivalent of a guide to Jewish pilgrims visiting
Jerusalem. It tells of the sites frequented by tourists and notes their
traditional places of prayer around the Temple Mount. One of the descriptions hints at a building that we had recently unearthed: "And the
gates in the southern wall, called *Abwab al-Ahmas* and *Dar al-Ahmas*,

Silver bracelets decorated in an Oriental style, a treasure from the Fatimid era

stand before them, and it is called Bathsheba's Courtyard.'' Jews had been serving on the Temple Mount from as far back as the early days of the Moslem era. It was customary to place into service one-fifth of the captives regularly taken in war, and these servants came to be called "*ahmas*", meaning one-fifth in Arabic. Later on the term *ahmas* was used to denote all the servants on the Temple Mount, without relation to their number, and in subsequent periods these servants were no longer Jews. The writer of the document found in the Cairo Geniza related that the *ahmas* lived opposite the gates of the Temple Mount, that the gates in the south were popularly called the Ahmas Gates after them, and that the building in which the *ahmas* lived — a structure with a large courtyard — was popularly called Bathsheba's Courtyard after King Solomon's mother. Could it be that we had found precisely the building cited by this ancient guidebook? The site, date, and plan of the buildings are all consonant with this possibility, but prudence dictates that we not commit ourselves definitively on the issue.

The document that we might well dub "The Guide to the Jewish Pilgrim" suggests that during the Fatimid era the destroyed areas of the Temple

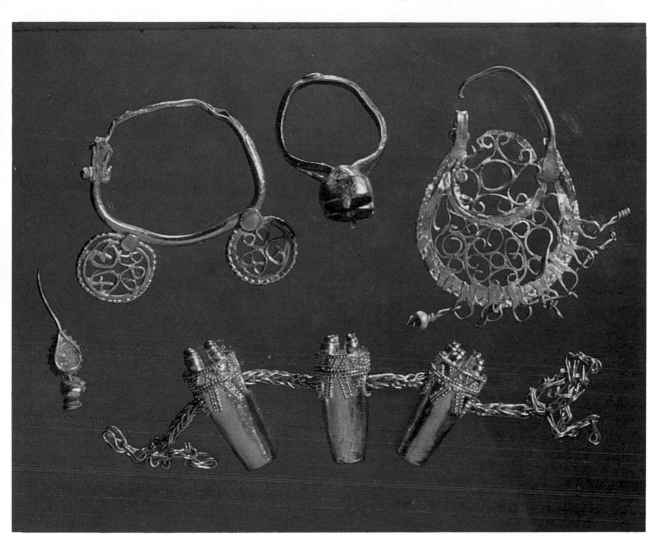

Gold earrings and bracelets, handiwork of the Fatimid era

Mount were among the popular tourist sites for Jews visiting the city. Medieval travelers inform us that the Jews used to redeem their pledges to the community with a pilgrimage to Jerusalem and by praying at the Temple Mount's walls. Some descriptions from the Middle Ages mention the custom of engraving names on those walls, thereby turning them into a kind of guestbook. Investigators before us had discovered various Hebrew inscriptions on the Temple Mount's walls. One instance of graffiti, found within the structure of the Double Gate, was left by a Jewish couple from Sicily, and similar inscriptions can be found near the Triple and Golden Gates as well as by the northern wall. Clearing away the detritus at the foot of the southern wall exposed another Jewish inscription from this period (tenth–eleventh centuries) that reads "Jeremiah son of Gedaliah son of Rabbi Joseph" carved in perfectly formed letters. Who was this anonymous Jewish pilgrim and why did he invest hours of effort in engraving his name on a stone of the Temple Mount's wall? The heart is better equipped to answer such questions than the head.

Above all, a sense of Jerusalem's history in the eleventh century is reflected in a discovery that turned up by the southern section of the western wall. This time it was one of our dedicated laborers, an Arab resident of the Old City named Abu Hassan, who approached me during a lunch break. "Something unpleasant has turned up in the excavation," he warned. "Human bones." As it turned out, these were not bones scattered about at random but a human skeleton laid out in a grave. The skeleton lay on its side in an east–west orientation with its face turned south toward Mecca, as called for in the Moslem burial custom. Not a day went by before another skeleton was uncovered near the first, and before we were through we had uncovered more than thirty skeletons, each laid out in its own grave in the same orderly manner. Actually, it seems we had come upon a cemetery dug into the ruins of the Omayyad bathhouse and the walls of structures dating to the tenth century, including a simple mosaic floor built on the Omayyad ruins (the graves themselves postdate these remains). A massive stone was unearthed over some of the skeletons at the southern end of the burial field, near the corner of the Temple Mount. It was so massive, in fact, that at first we thought it was a section of the city wall, and after a while we realized that it was indeed a wall (though not the city wall) and that it was from the Crusader rather than the Seljuk period. Thus it appears that the Crusaders ignored the fact that

left: The gravestone of a Fatimid soldier from the cemetery at the foot of the western wall

they were building over human graves. They must have noticed the skeletons, because the foundations of their wall were build directly over them, but simply paid them no mind.

What we had before us, then, was a cemetery — albeit a small one — in the heart of the city. The initial identification of the skeletons showed them to be of young men. Moreover, the fact that the graves were arranged in rows and that there were only thirty of them, all dating to the same time, may indicate that their occupants were soldiers who had fallen in one of the many wars that plagued Jerusalem during that period. One way or another, however, it is beyond question that this cemetery was inside the city in an area evidently not inhabited at the time. It may also be possible that these were the bodies of soldiers who had fallen within the city and for objective reasons could not be buried outside in the official cemeteries. Later on we also found the remains of gravestones, two of which had writing on them, but all that remained of the inscriptions were the words "this is the grave" in Arabic. A fragment of one of the gravestones had originally borne a royal inscription. The design and elegance of the Arabic script, together with the place where it was found, suggest that it was an Abbassid or Fatimid dedicatory stone connected with the Al Aqsa Mosque and that its inscription had probably been damaged in the great earthquake that struck Jerusalem in the middle of the eleventh

opposite: "Jeremiah son of Gedaliah son of Rabbi Joseph," a medieval Jewish pilgrim who engraved his name on one of the stones of the southern wall

century, causing extensive damage to the Temple Mount. Another gravestone later found in this area was engraved marble slab unearthed
intact. The engraving was very beautiful and its inscription clear, except
for the name of the deceased, which had deliberately been effaced. Judging by the formula of the inscription, this stone had marked the grave of a
Christian Arab. From the viewpoint of its date, it could definitely have
belonged to the cemetery, but how was a Christian connected to this
graveyard? Could it be that Coptic Christians were among the defenders

above: The Tanners' Gate Tower in
the city's southern wall

opposite: A marble gravestone of a
(Coptic?) Christian officer in the
Fatimid army, from the cemetery at
the foot of the western wall

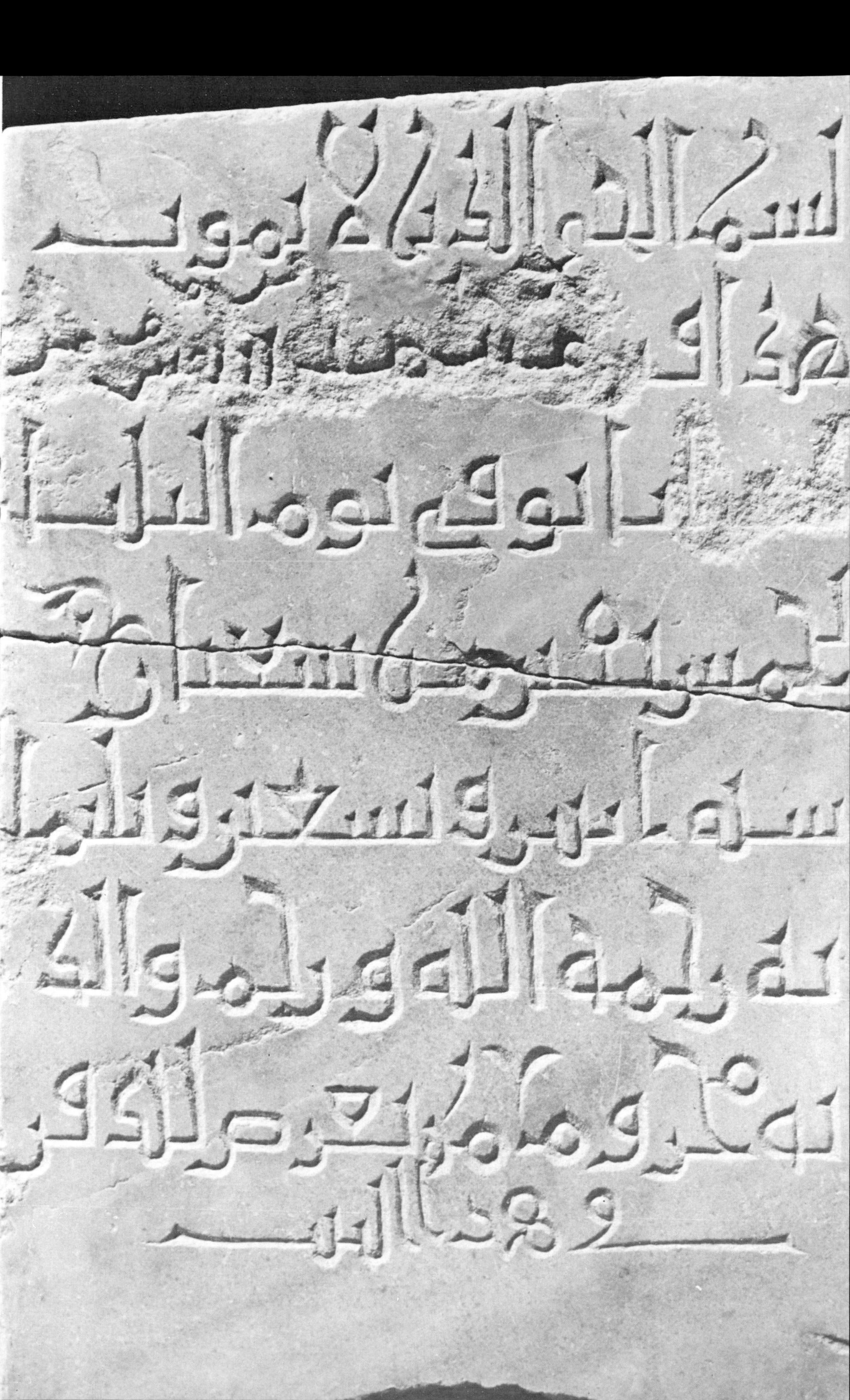

of Fatimid Jerusalem? We know that there were high-ranking Christian and Jewish officers, even commanders, serving in the Fatimid army. Perhaps one of the commanders fell in battle and was laid to rest here beside his soldiers. Near the cemetery we also found a small prayer cell within a burial room and an adjacent plastered pool that may have been used to purify the corpses.

As luck would have it, news about the discovery of skeletons spread through the city like wildfire, and the imagination of some of our citizens began to work overtime. I recall being summoned by a member of the Rabbinical High Court, Rabbi Ovadiah Yosef (who was later to become chief rabbi). The rabbi told me he had learned that we had uncovered the skeletons of the Zealots who had died fighting Titus at the time of the Roman siege of Jerusalem. It is well known that the Jews never buried their dead within the city walls, but during the siege anything was possible. I was sorry to have to disappoint Rabbi Yosef but explained that the graves had been found over the remains of the Omayyad and Fatimid periods. I even accompanied him to the area so that he could see the form of burial for himself. He quickly confirmed that these were not Jewish remains and recommended that we inform the Moslem body authorized to deal with the matter. I asked Abu Hassan, the worker who found the first skeleton and was a denizen of the *waqf*, to handle the matter for us, and in the end the skeletons were transferred to a common grave in the Moslem cemetery by the eastern wall. We were not given any time to study them, so that the accuracy of our observations is necessarily based on the initial impression of the anthropologist who viewed the skeletons *in situ*.

No find could better have illustrated the state of affairs in Jerusalem during the eleventh century than that cemetery south of the Temple Mount. The small buildings of the early Fatimid era had become a mound of ruins, and our excavation among these ruins turned up three treasures of gold coins. Two of them reached us intact, the third had only a few coins left (the rest evidently stolen by the first person to discover it, which alerted us to the problem of our workers helping themselves to small but valuable items). Each of the intact treasures contained fifty gold coins, which may have been the savings of soldiers who put them aside for a rainy day, burying them in jars among the ruins in the hope of being able to return and recover them someday. The coins had been minted all over the Moslem world, from the beginning of the tenth century up to the end of the eleventh. We can assume that they were buried on the eve of the Crusader conquest, which is undoubtedly why their owners never managed to retrieve them.

For a few score years, a basic premise about Jerusalem's city wall in the south was so firmly established in the scholarly literature that it was actually translated into a fact on the maps and plans of the city. This ostensible fact had it that the Old City's southern wall from Mount Zion up to the Dung Gate — built during the reign of the Ottoman sultan Suleiman the Magnificent — had been constructed over the remains of the city wall of Aelia Capitolina. That assumption was erroneous, however, and the results of our dig put it to rest once and for all. Here is how it all came about.

The Dung Gate, as its name implies, served as the passage through which refuse was removed from the city during the Ottoman period. Over

The Tanners' Gate Tower, the predecessor of the Dung Gate in the city's southern wall, was first built during the rule of the Fatimids or the Crusaders

The Refortification of the City

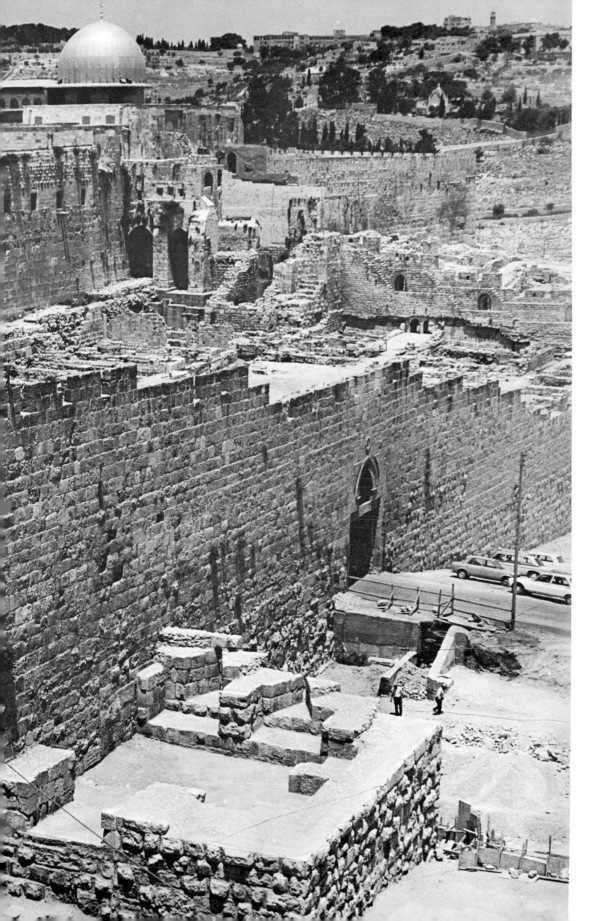

the centuries, the remains of this refuse accumulated alongside the gate in the form of detritus. Together with the remains of buildings that had been carted out to the "city dump," it built up over a span of 400 years to the point where the exterior of the Old City wall was almost totally covered. Thus revealing the full height of the wall entailed, first of all, clearing away all that detritus.

In approaching this task, we availed ourselves of a bulldozer and trucks and found that once a few thousand square meters of detritus had been removed, the remains of a large tower began to show through some 15 meters west of the Dung Gate. It wasn't until we had excavated the tower and its vicinity thoroughly that we could indentify it as a gate tower — not one of the main gates of the city but a postern to be used as an alternate or emergency exit. Since the Dung Gate had retained its original form until being restored in 1953, almost as soon as this tower began to emerge we realized that it must have belonged to a line of fortification predating Suleiman's wall. Later on another tower was discovered 80 meters to the west. We called it the "Middle Tower" because to the west, under the Ottoman structure known as the "Sulfur Tower" (*Burj Kibrit*), we found the remains of a third massive tower; and further west along the continuation of this line was yet another gate tower that belonged to this same network of pre-Ottoman fortifications. This time, however, we also found an inscription dating to the beginning of the thirteenth century regarding the repair of the tower, and we believe that this gate tower is the predecessor of what we now call the Zion Gate, built 100 meters further to the west during the Ottoman period.

It is beyond question, however, that this line of fortifications predated the Old City wall built by Suleiman the Magnificent in the sixteenth century. Its course is described on a twelfth-century map of Crusader Jerusalem and on other maps dating to the thirteenth century, the latter even giving the exact names of the gates. Thus we learn that the wicket found in the tower near the Dung Gate was called the Tanners' Gate — a fitting name since Jerusalem's animal market was located inside the walls, in the area adjoining the Temple Mount's western wall, and it stands to reason that this market was associated with the slaughter of animals and the tanning of their hides. Hence the tanners of Jerusalem probably lived in this area as well, and the gate was named after them.

In the city plan of Crusader Jerusalem, the Tanners' Gate was located at the end of a long street that traversed the city from the Damascus Gate in the north. This was none other than the successor to the Cardo valensis or Tyropoeon Valley Street from the Second Temple period. Who built the line of fortifications shown so graphically on the twelfth-century Crusader map? We found two dedicatory inscriptions in its ruins, but they were the work of its restorers, executed at the beginning of the thirteenth century, and give us no clue as to when the fortifications were originally built. We do know that at the close of the eleventh century, on the eve of the conquest of Jerusalem, the Crusaders invested the city, establishing a number of siege camps around the walls and drawing on sophisticated siege equipment that had been transported to Palestine courtesy of the Italian commercial cities. One of these siege camps — the Provençal camp headed by Raymond of Saint-Gilles — was set up on Mount Zion in June 1099. Hence we are led to conclude that the line of fortifications between the Dung Gate and Mount Zion — or, to be more precise, the line of fortifications that begins under the Al Aqsa Mosque and continues up the western hill toward Mount Zion — was constructed some time before the Crusaders surrounded the city.

Excavating the line of fortifications outside the Dung Gate enabled us to date it more precisely. The technique of construction, the plaster, and the floors of the destroyed buildings found under this wall suggest that they were of Byzantine vintage (though we must keep in mind that the residents of Jerusalem used a similar construction technique during the early Moslem period). The city wall predating Suleiman's wall was found sandwiched in between the Ottoman fortifications and the remains of these presumably Byzantine buildings. Coins and pottery vessels found *in situ* in some of those buildings — jugs with handles bearing Arab inscriptions, a cooking pot on a stove, oil lamps, and the like — indicate that they were still inhabited during the tenth century. Thus the wall must have been built sometime in the eleventh century.

The destruction of the Byzantine wall in the southern part of Jerusalem, near the Siloam Pool, was an extended process and a result not of deliberate devastation but of the decline in the city's size and power. The events of the eleventh century were responsible for that decline. And then — suddenly, it seemed — the beat of the Crusaders' horses could be heard at the gates of the Holy Land. Quickly the protectors of Jerusalem prepared to defend the city by building a new line of fortifications consonant with the city's reduced size — fully half of its former area. The course of these fortifications were dictated by the presence of massive ruins that could serve as a firm foundation. These were the ruins of the Omayyad palace and its auxiliary buildings, and they made it possible to build the new line of fortifications from Al Aqsa southward (over the remains of the palace's eastern wall) and then westward (over the remains of the southern wall of the palace and of the two buildings built beside it). From there the fortifications continued westward on the natural rock over the slopes of the western hill, continuing over the ruins of the Nea Church and its adjoining complex. Due to their sturdy stones, all these ruins proved to be excellent foundations for this quickly improvised wall. Another detail brings us closer to the end of the eleventh century as the date when this line of fortifications was built. The Tanners' Gate Tower has embrasures, which are known in Palestinian military architecture only from the second half of the eleventh century onward since they are associated with the introduction of a smaller, more advanced form of the crossbow.

To sum up, our excavations show that the new line of fortifications south of the city was built on the eve of the Crusader conquest of Palestine. Its course diverged from that of its predecessor (which was built much further south and was based on the natural topography of the Jerusalem hills) and was dictated mainly by the presence of massive ruins that could serve as foundations. The new southern wall continued to serve Jerusalem for centuries thereafter and was the basis for Suleiman's wall, which has been standing for over 400 years now.

19 A Cross on the Temple Mount

The Crusaders in Jerusalem

At 9 A.M. on Friday, July 15, 1099, after a long siege during which the Crusader host managed to put together a formidable collection of siege equipment, their leader, Godfrey of Bouillon, won eternal fame as his siege tower approached the northeast corner of the city wall and his soldiers broke into Jerusalem (the breach, incidentally, being into the quarter inhabited mostly by Jews, who defended it valiantly if unsuccessfully). Shortly thereafter, Raymond of Saint-Gilles and the men of his Provençal camp broke in on the southern side of the city, while Tancred's forces effected the third breach and made directly for the Temple Mount, raising their Norman banner over the Al Aqsa Mosque. Mayhem ensued as the Crusaders embarked on a rampage of brutal, indiscriminate murder. So it was that Jerusalem passed from the hands of the infidel into those of the knights of the cross and became the capital of a new Christian dominion, the Latin Kingdom of Jerusalem.

It was something less than a kingdom in the strict political sense, for the bitter rivalry between the various Crusader camps and the determination of the monarchs of Europe to prevent the emergence of an independent political power in the Holy Land precluded the installation of the first "monarch" of Crusader Jerusalem as "king." Moreover, from an ideological viewpoint it was difficult for the Crusaders to crown a flesh-and-blood, secular monarch in the city where Jesus had borne a crown of thorns. The Provençal chronicler of the day, Raymond of Aguilers, refers to this problem in writing that:

A king must not be chosen in the place where the Lord suffered and was crowned, lest he say in his heart: "I am seated on the throne of David and rule his kingdom," and lest that generation lack faith and morality; for God may destroy him and take out His wrath on the country and the people. And so the prophet spoke in saying: "When the Most Holy comes, all anointment will come to an end" [his interpretation of Daniel 9:24], and it is clear to all the nations that He is coming.

Thus the first head of the Latin Kingdom was known by the rather innocuous title "defender of the Holy Sepulcher" (though his successors ultimately arrogated the title of king), and it was Godfrey of Bouillon, weakest of the Crusader commanders, who was chosen for the role.

Once the initial euphoria of the conquest had passed, life in the Latin Kingdom settled into a more domestic routine. Jerusalem's fortifications were repaired and reinforced, with the crown and various military orders each doing its part in the sector of the city with which it was associated. The royal palace was built near the citadel in the west (by the Jaffa Gate), thereby reviving the tradition established by Herod. The Church of the Holy Sepulcher, which had been the declared objective of the Crusades, was restored — actually entirely rebuilt — according to its original (Western) plan and design and soon became a magnet for pilgrims. The Hospitallers (the Order of St. John), one of the two largest and most aggressive orders of the crusading knights, built their large center beside it, while the men of the other major order, the Templars, took over the Temple Mount and for the first time in Jerusalem's history turned it into a center of Christian activity: the Dome of the Rock was converted into a church, as

The northern apse of the Church of St. Mary of the German Knights on the slope of today's Jewish Quarter was Al Aqsa, and the array of buildings around them housed the members of the order.

Islam never reconciled itself to the Christian invasion of the East, and as a result the Latin Kingdom became the target of relentless attacks. The almost ninety years of struggle between Islam and the Crusader kingdom saw times of both peace and war, tension and calm; but the Moslems' desire to return the situation to the *status quo ante* by eliminating what Islam regarded as an "alien body in its midst" never abated. The Crusaders, for their part, had embarked on a program of almost frantic construction in Jerusalem — mostly of churches — in an effort to accord the city a classically Christian image and thereby ensure unflagging support from Europe. From the intensity and scale of their activity, the Moslems were able to cull an appreciation for Jerusalem's religious and ideological sway and the political importance of the region as a whole. Suddenly the city that had been little more than a provincial outpost during the Abbassid age loomed large at the center of Moslem attention. Taking a page from the Crusaders' book, the Moslems wove a counter-doctrine to the Christian claim to Jerusalem. Reams of literature were written about the city; the Al Aqsa Mosque — much like the Holy Sepulcher before it — was portrayed as a conquered and defiled sanctuary that must be liberated at all costs; and the *jihad* (holy war in much the same sense as the contemporary European crusade) was again emblazoned on Islam's banner.

Almost ninety years after the Crusaders first broke into Jerusalem, in July 1187, the decisive battle between the forces of the cross and of the crescent — between the Moslem army under the command of the talented warrior Saladin and the Crusader host led by Guy de Lusignan — was fought in the Galilee at the Horns of Hittin. It was a pitched and grueling battle that ended in favor of the Moslems, with the better part of the Crusader force, the king, and many of his knights dying in the field or being taken prisoner and almost the entire country falling to the victors. By late September Saladin's forces were closing on Jerusalem. Facing his triumphant army was the remnant of the Christian force beaten at Hittin and a handful of youngsters recruited from among the city's population and the refugees crowded within the walls.

Saladin had vowed to take Jerusalem by force and slay all of its inhabitants in revenge for the wanton carnage perpetrated by the Crusaders when they conquered the city. But the stubborn resistance of its defenders made him reconsider his options, and in the end, under pressure from some of his officers, he agreed to the condition proposed by the Christian defenders, namely, the payment of a ransom to redeem the inhabitants of the city. We should note that this proposal was not arrived at unanimously. Some voices among the besieged Christians opposed the accommodation because it entailed surrender. Instead they demanded that Jerusalem be defended by force of arms even if the price were exorbitant and the inevitable outcome defeat. Here is the plaint of one of the beleaguered Christians:

> How great the pain! Is there any pain to compare with it? Have we ever read that the Jews abandoned the Holy of Holies without bloodshed and bitter battles, yielding it of their own volition? May these fiends who willingly betray the Holy City and the Messiah perish!

But this was the voice of the minority, and on October 2, 1187, the keys to the city were surrendered to Saladin.

The Fall of the First Kingdom

A devotee of the crusading ideal in its Moslem rendering, Saladin set about transforming Jerusalem into a Moslem city *par excellence.* The golden cross that stood above the Templar stronghold in Al Aqsa was torn down and dragged through the streets of the city like an object of common scorn. A special wooden *minbar* (prayer rostrum), fashioned in Damascus at Saladin's request in anticipation of the reconquest of Jerusalem, was placed in the mosque as the sultan's redemption of his pledge. (Unfortunately, this *minbar* was consumed by the fire set by a crazed Australian tourist in August 1969. The most valuable piece in the mosque, it was the only furnishing irretrievably destroyed in that fire.) Churches throughout the city were converted into mosques and religious seminaries or were destroyed by order of the sultan.

A few years hence, Crusader troops again reached the shores of the Holy Land. Led, among others, by the king of England, Richard the Lion-Hearted, they longed above all to redeem Jerusalem and were far from content with holding the coastal strip and its ports. Essentially they made no headway inland but were nonetheless indirectly responsible for a wave of destruction that bore down on Jerusalem. In 1219, when rumors of an unprecedented Crusader assault on the city were rife, al-Malik al-Muazam, the ruling power in Damascus, ordered Jerusalem's fortifications (and for all intents and purposes the city itself) destroyed, so that even if the Crusaders did take the city they would be incapable of defending it. Contemporary sources relate that except for Al Aqsa, all the buildings on the Temple Mount, as well as the Church of the Holy Sepulcher and most of the rest of the city, were reduced to one massive ruin. But just as we have seen that the usually meticulous Josephus exaggerated when it came to describing the destruction of Jerusalem, these accounts are probably also skewed by hyperbole.

Considering the emotional pitch of the conflict between the crescent and the cross, its resolution was surprisingly civilized. The rivalry between Saladin's successors had weakened them all and in 1229 prompted the sultan of Egypt, al-Malik al-Kamil, to enter into a peace treaty with Frederick II, the Holy Roman Emperor and leader of the Fifth Crusade. The agreement provided for Jerusalem to be divided between the warring camps: the Crusaders were permitted to resettle and rebuild the city and its fortifications as they saw fit, but the Temple Mount compound would remain in Moslem hands and under the aegis of a Moslem flag. Christians were permitted to visit the Temple Mount but while there were required to honor the laws and customs of Islam (for example, by removing their shoes when entering its bounds). Of course the treaty also included clauses that were less than satisfactory to either of the sides, but the signatories nevertheless regarded it as an achievement for their respective countries and causes. In its wake, the Crusaders returned to Jerusalem peacefully and began to rebuild the centers recently destroyed by Saladin and al-Malik al-Muazam.

During their second tenure in the city, the Crusaders held Jerusalem for less than twenty years and did their best to develop it, though they came nowhere near duplicating their initial achievements. In 1244 the city fell to the invading Tartars, bringing Christian rule to an end. All in all, however, Jerusalem and the Temple Mount area had witnessed many momentous events during the era of Crusader hegemony, so that we were naturally very curious about the finds from this period that were likely to turn up in our excavations. And we were certainly not disappointed.

As we have seen, at the close of the eleventh century, just before the Crusader conquest, the Fatimids refortified Jerusalem in the south. Curiously, however, their new line of fortifications left some two-thirds of the Temple Mount's southern wall exposed, and ever since then the greater part of the Temple Mount's southern wall has doubled as the city wall. The Triple Gate was sealed, and a fortified tower was built over the Double Gate near the spot where the new city wall branched out from the Temple Mount wall.

On the inner side of the Temple Mount's southern and eastern walls there is a network of vaults that comprise one of the most beautiful and fascinating interiors in Jerusalem. These vaults, originally built so that the Temple Mount's esplanade could be constructed over them, are supported by rows of stone pillars and are essentially a restoration of Herod's handiwork, though on a far more modest scale. The level of the esplanade in this sector is lower than the original Herodian plaza, and the vaults are built of small stones. Inside, however, are the remains of a number of destroyed arches from the Second Temple period, hinting at the beauty and strength of the original structure. Over the years this interior came to be known as "Solomon's Stables." The source of the name traces to the fact that the knights of the Templars used it as stables for their horses. The Templars, as we have seen, made Al Aqsa and its auxiliary buildings their headquarters, calling the mosque *Templum Solomonis* (Solomon's Temple). Many studies on Jerusalem therefore concluded that this underground area was built by the Crusader knights, but as it happens this is not the case.

When the Omayyads built Al Aqsa and repaired the ruins of the Temple Mount, they had to rebuild the compound's southern wall. In doing so they followed Herod's example and built a spacious void, making "Solomon's Stables" a product of the early Moslem period. In the eleventh century, when an earthquake struck the region and heavily damaged Al Aqsa, the vaults were evidently undermined but were then repaired by the Fatimids in anticipation of the Crusader onslaught. For all that, however, the idea of using this network of vaults as stables must be ascribed to the Crusaders alone. They were the first to bring horses onto the Temple Mount, just as they were the first to turn the Temple Mount into a residential area. The entrance to the stables was not through the gate in the southern wall but through an opening on the esplanade, at the end of a tunnel that lead up from the Triple Gate. There, over an earthen ramp, the way led down into the interior of the Temple Mount and the Crusader stables.

The British expedition led by Charles Warren noted that a passage was built under "Solomon's Stables" and that it exited outside the Temple Mount. We were particularly intrigued by this passage and were eager to study it because, judging by its dimensions, it could well have dated to the Second Temple period. The passage was clearly marked on the Warren expedition's plans, so we had no difficulty finding it, and after a few days of excavations we had reached down to its exit. Actually it had two exits, one on top of the other, both having been broken through or carved into the stones of the southern wall. This left no doubt that the tunnel postdated Herod's construction program, even though its walls and ceiling were lined with Herodian-period ashlars. The Herodian dating of the stones was beyond doubt, but since their dressed side was occasionally facing toward the back or on the side, they were clearly in secondary

Solomon's Stables and the Postern

The secret tunnel built by the Crusaders under Solomon's Stables

A silver coin from the Crusader period minted in Chartres, France, in 1200

use, confirming that the tunnel was built later than the Herodian period. Some of us believed that the tunnel was constructed during the days of the Bar Kokhba revolt, which was one way of explaining the breach created in the Temple Mount's wall. The problem with this reading is that in Bar Kokhba's day, the area at the foot of the Temple Mount's southern wall lay within the bounds of the city, so that a passage exiting there would have been to no purpose. Moreover, the tunnel is lined with stones taken from the lower courses of the Temple Mount's walls, which were still intact at the time of the Bar Kokhba revolt. Above all, however, the most important feature of this hidden tunnel was the fact that it enabled its users to leave the city. Thus we can assume that it must have been built at a time when the southern wall of the Temple Mount coincided with the city wall, and that did not obtain until the end of the eleventh century.

The tunnel leads inward for a distance of 30 meters from the southern wall before being blocked by pieces of stone and debris. We know that it continues further, but we had made it a hard-and-fast rule not to excavate within the bounds of the Temple Mount, which is currently under Moslem jurisdiction, without first acquiring the permission of the appropriate Moslem authorities. In this case they permitted us only to measure and photograph the exposed section of the tunnel, not to conduct an excavation of any kind. Upon concluding this work, at the express request of the *waqf* and with the aid of its engineers, we sealed up the tunnel's exit with stones.

Our conclusion from this limited investigation is that the tunnel was indeed built by the Crusaders when they repaired the Fatimid fortifications of Jerusalem. It is supported by a twelfth-century map (the Cambrai manuscript) showing an opening in the southern wall marked *poterna*, or postern. The Temple Mount served as a military headquarters for the Templars, and since they were versed in military architecture, it stands to reason that they would make provision for a postern. Furthermore, the style of construction using large stones need not mislead us, because even though these particular stones are obviously in secondary use, we know of original medieval construction projects in this area that used very large stones — Baybars Tower in the Subeibeh Fortress near the Banias River, for example, or the Tower of Goliath, a feature of Jerusalem's fortifications dating to either the Fatimid or Crusader eras.

Inside and Outside the City

The premise that the Fatimid line of fortifications in the southern part of the city remained in use throughout the Crusader era, with certain improvements, has been confirmed by our excavations. Outside the wall, however, south of the Temple Mount and east of the city wall — meaning throughout the area in which our excavations were conducted — not a single remain of any Crusader building could be found. And within the city, west of the north-south sector of the southern wall, except for part of the wall of a large building constructed over the Fatimid cemetery, not a single trace of Crusader construction turned up, most of the remains coming from the Fatimid period. It was only in the excavation conducted on the slope and top of the western hill (the Jewish Quarter) that any remains of Crusader buildings were unearthed. What emerged from that excavation confirmed what we already knew from the sources: the city's cattle market was located over the ruins of the modest Fatimid residential neighborhood west of the Temple Mount, and alongside the market were structures serving the tanning industry. A small purse containing about fifty Crusader silver coins was found buried in this area, and we are tempted to speculate that it had been lost by one of the cattle merchants.

A strong foundation found near the southwest corner of the Temple Mount led us to posit that we had come upon the remains of the Crusader city wall. But as our work continued, it emerged that this wall belonged to nothing more imposing than a residential building. Unfortunately, a few impetuous visitors who toured the excavations and overheard us musing aloud were quick to take our tentative speculation as law — going so far as to publish it in a book as evidence of the discovery of a Crusader city wall in Jerusalem! Meanwhile we had come to the conclusion that the mooted Crusader city wall in this area was in fact one and the same as the city wall from the Fatimid period.

The plan of the Crusader city followed the basic layout that had served Jerusalem since antiquity: two main streets running north–south crossed by one running east–west. The city was almost square, and of its two north–south streets starting out from the Damascus Gate, one served the upper quarters, running past the Church of the Holy Sepulcher and continuing on toward Mount Zion (which was then outside the city wall), and the other led through the valley toward the Dung Gate, then called the Tanners' Tower or Tannery Postern. The southern section of this street passed under a bridge built over several barrel vaults that has been restored as a result of the excavations (today the tunnel leading under the Street of the Chain from Valley Street to the Wailing Wall Plaza).

Crossing the city from west to east (from the Jaffa Gate to the Temple Mount) was David Street and its continuation, then called Temple Street, today the Street of the Chain. Temple Street was by far the most important of the avenues leading to the Temple Mount; hence the gate at its eastern end became the most important and imposing of the gates on the western side of the compound. Known today as the Gate of the Chain, it was then called the Beautiful Gate and the Crusaders invested much thought (to say nothing of funds) into making it one of the most splendid monuments in Jerusalem. The gate was composed of two adjoining arches with marble columns placed alongside the gateposts. Decorated in a wreathwork design, the columns were topped by capitals worked primarily in a leaf motif, though they also contained instances of human figures. (Under a subsequent Moslem regime, these figures were damaged or effaced, but it is nevertheless possible to discern some of them.) In the front part of the gate are two domes supported by sturdy pillars, and as an architectural unit the gate is light and airy, despite its highly elaborate decoration.

Under this gate (and the Street of the Chain) are the complex of Wilson's Arch and its adjoining vaults (as described in Chapter 10). The western part of this complex contains the arch that simultaneously supported the bridge leading to the Street of the Chain and vaulted the subterranean passage to Valley Street.

The area of the vaults is a mixture of architectural styles, being in part the Omayyad restoration of Herodian structures and in part the Fatimid addition of a military barracks. And alongside this potpourri are eleventh-century structures that continued to be used during the Crusader era.

A pilgrim by the name of John of Würzburg who visited Jerusalem in the 1260s has left us a marvelous description of the city in his book of trav-

The Beautiful Gate

opposite, right: The three apses of the Church of St. Mary of the Germans

opposite, left: Marble capitals of the Beautiful Gate, the *pièce de résistance* of Crusader art on the Temple Mount

els. One short passage that particularly caught our eye goes as follows:

> Following that street [the Street of the Chain], to the right of the gate leading to the Temple, is a passage through a boulevard of columns, and on that street are a hospice and a church built recently in honor of St. Mary but popularly called the German building, for only German-speaking people are accepted there.

This compound, after having been seized by Saladin's men and converted into Moslem buildings, was damaged in the wave of deliberate destruction ordered by al-Malik al-Muazam. But after Frederick II received rights in Jerusalem by virtue of his peace treaty, the Crusaders began to restore their damaged buildings; and since Frederick was a German emperor, the German properties were the first to receive attention. Thereafter, Jerusalem's return to the bosom of Islam under the Mamelukes wiped out all trace of this church, and it remained no more than a faded historical memory for over 40 years.

Based on the writings of John of Würzburg and other pilgrims, scholars knew that this complex of German buildings was probably to be found under the houses of the Jewish Quarter, facing the Temple Mount. But it was not until after the Six-Day War, when the work of restoring the Jewish Quarter was in full swing and the ruins of hopelessly dilapidated buildings were being cleared away, that one of the foremen came upon remains of this Crusader complex. While his workers were hacking away with their spades and pickaxes, enveloping the site in a cloud of dust and plaster, he suddenly noticed a lovely capital balanced on a wall. Immediately bringing all work to a halt, he summoned his superiors, who in turn called me to the site. Even a cursory glance was enough to establish that the building was of Crusader vintage; the style of the capital gave it away immediately. A. Netzer and A. Ovadiah were the first to study the building and correctly identified it as part of the complex of German buildings known to us from the medieval sources. Later on Jerusalem's mayor, Teddy Kollek, asked me to excavate and restore whatever could be salvaged. I knew that the better part of our work was still before us,

and, indeed, it took a considerable research effort to apprehend the plan of the complex. At first we thought it best to dismantle the main buildings and stables in order to study their plan thoroughly. At the same time, we preserved whatever was found worthy of preservation and reconstructed a few walls to buttress adjoining walls that were on the point of collapse.

Our excavation exposed the entire complex and revealed its history as follows: at the start of the twelfth century, shortly after the establishment of the Order of St. John of the Hospitallers, a group of German members of the order began to organize independently and set for themselves a worthy if ambitious goal — caring for pilgrims from Germany, who did not understand French (the lingua franca of Jerusalem at the time). We know that other national and ethnic groups from both Europe and the East founded hospices catering to pilgrims from their native lands — the Hungarian hospice in Jerusalem, for example — so that the establishment of the German hospice was by no means extraordinary.

The church built as part of the hospice was named in honor of St. Mary and may have been something to the effect of a memorial to the New Church of St. Mary (the famed Nea) built in this same area. The new St. Mary's stood at the center of the complex and was flanked by a service wing, dormitory, and a hospital with a small ceremonial hall above it. Contemporary sources speak of the poverty of the German knights, which is reflected in the simplicity of these structures. They also make reference to the Germans' long-standing desire to secede from the French Order of the Hospitallers and found an order of their own with a specifically German national character, but successive popes, under pressure from the Hospitallers, would not permit it. Thus it was not until the Third Crusade (1190) that a German military order — St. Mary of the Teutons — was founded as an independent framework.

A reconstructed view of the Church of St. Mary of the Germans looking westward through the front court

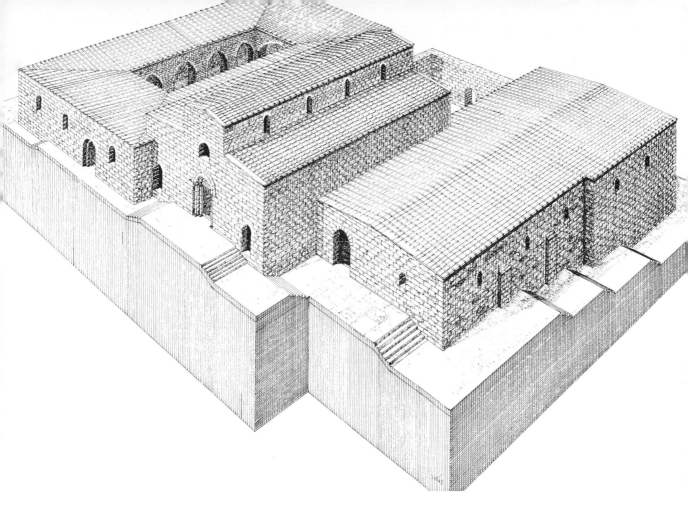

A reconstructed perspective of the
German hospice complex

The church that comprised the heart of its hospice in Jerusalem was
built, in the spirit of the times, in the modest Romanesque style and was
21 × 12 meters large. It comprised three halls — a nave and two side aisles —
and had in its eastern wall three semicircular windowed apses whose
upper sections were decorated with a border of simple geometric patterns.
The entrance to the church was through a gate in its western wall facing
onto the street running northward into the Street of the Chain. Its gateposts were worked in the style of the day and were flanked by windows
facing onto the side aisles. Its northern wall had a decorated recess that
was evidently designed to hold relics or other sacred objects and a door
(in the western part of the wall) that connected the church with the
hospital and ceremonial hall. This wing was two stories high with a
stairwell leading from its ground floor (the hospital) to its upper one (the
ceremonial hall). The plan of the dormitory, which was built on the
northern side of the church, also followed the popular formula of a
central court surrounded by rooms. To the east of the church was another
court and below it was room for storage purposes (we know that it was
not a crypt because there is no direct connection between the church and
this underground room).

Despite the proximity of this complex to the main aqueduct, the hospice contained no less than five cisterns for collecting and storing rainwater. Digging with great care, we cleaned out one of these cisterns and were
rewarded for our pains by finding dozens of pottery vessels, mostly from
the thirteenth century. They were usually glazed pieces, especially bowls

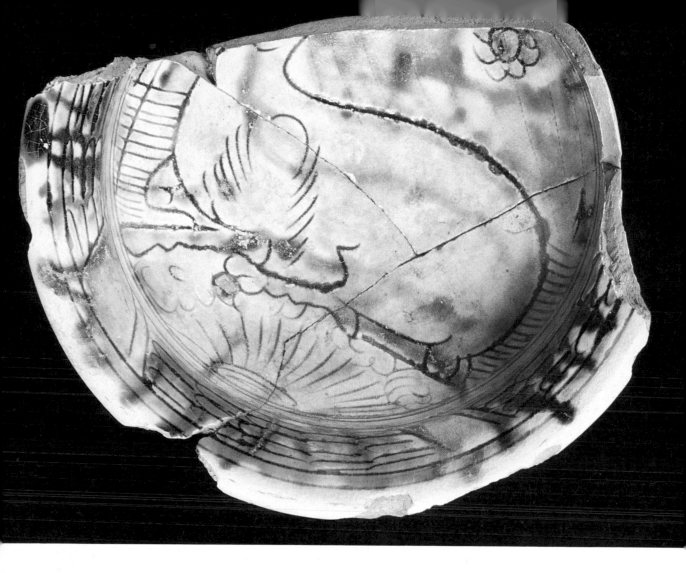

An imported ceramic bowl found in the German complex

opposite: The restored hospital hall of the hospice complex

and other vessels that had been used in the refectory. This haul had apparently been collected and thrown into one of the cisterns when the building was evacuated during the Mameluke period. Most of the pieces were of local manufacture, made by Jerusalemite potters, but we also found vessels imported from the East — though none made in Europe. This phenomenon is well known from Crusader life in Palestine, for the inhabitants of the Latin Kingdom, unlike colonists of later ages, usually bought their household goods in the local market.

Under the floor of the hall that served as a hospital, we found the remains of a Byzantine mosaic floor typical of the sixth century — evidence that the Byzantine residential neighborhood built at the foot of the Temple Mount extended up the western hill. We also found the ruins of a cistern that had been coated in a black plaster — remains of the residential quarter of the Second Temple period. Finally, a superficial and unsystematic check of the four wings of this complex taught us that during the Crusader period it had been surrounded on all sides by other buildings, including houses that continued to host the residents of the Old City until the recent restoration of the Jewish Quarter.

20 In the Shade of the Crescent Again

Mongols, Mamelukes, and Ottomans

Before the Crusaders had a chance to savor the fruits of the peace treaty concluded by Frederick II, Jerusalem was again overrun and victimized by rampaging soldiers. Throughout the latter half of the thirteenth century, parts of Palestine remained a battleground for the Egyptian troops ranged against the Crusader armies — primarily the French, whose forces were concentrated on the Mediterranean coast. Yet while these enemies were preoccupied with each other, Tartars, Mongols, and other Turkic tribes from the heart of Asia, as far away as the edge of China, came galloping out of the East at the Crusaders' backs and swamped the region in a series of daring, long-range campaigns. Crusader Jerusalem, which had yet to recover from the blows suffered at the hands of Saladin and his heirs, fell prostrate to the Khorezmians in 1244, and they knew no mercy. Hardly had they spent their wrath on the city when in 1260 the Mongols broke into Jerusalem under the command of the fierce Hulagu (a grandson of Genghis Khan and a brother of Kublai Khan) and consummated the sack of the city. Testimony to the effect of these shattering events can be found in a letter from the Jewish sage Nahmanides to his son in Spain. A native of Gerona, Spain, Nahmanides was obliged to leave that country after his triumph in a philosophical debate with Christian opponents (forced upon him by the king of Aragon). Making his way to Jerusalem, here is what he found in 1268: "...And what can I say about the country? Much of it is deserted; the desolation is overwhelming. As a rule, whatever is sanctified by the sword is destroyed by the sword, but Jerusalem is more devastated than all else..." This mournful missive faithfully reflects the finds we uncovered in the stratum between the Crusader period and the beginning of the Mameluke era.

The leader of the rebels who overthrew the Ayyubid dynasty and founded the Mameluke sultanate in Egypt — which also cast its hegemony over Palestine and Syria from the latter half of the thirteenth century until these countries were conquered by the Ottoman Turks early in the sixteeth century — was the bold military commander Baybars, who first won fame by defeating the Mongols in battle near the Harod Spring in the Jezreel Valley. The sultans of Egypt had built their army, and particularly its elite units and officers corps, on mercenaries imported from the Balkans and Central Asia (called Mamelukes from the Arab word "slaves"), for fear that locally groomed commanders might aspire to wrest the throne by force. Yet their elementary precaution was insufficient to prevent the takeover by Baybars; and to firmly establish his rule, which was based on the relatively small military elite, the new sultan took great pains to win broad public support. Above all he appealed to religious sects with considerable influence among the people, according them both official recognition and landed holdings. Another salient principle of Mameluke policy was to do away with the last traces of Crusader rule in the form of the armies still holding out along the coast of Palestine. Pursuing this goal to the end, the Mamelukes defeated and evicted the Crusaders from Palestine at the close of the thirteenth century, going on to re-establish Jerusalem as a Moslem holy city and leading religious

Structures from the Mameluke period in front of the Moghrabi Gate, by the entrance to the Temple Mount (Hanna Dejani, Photo Prisma, 1936)

above: A glazed-pottery bowl from the Mameluke period

right: A glazed-pottery bowl from the Mameluke period

opposite: Fragments of ceramic tiles from the Dome of the Rock. Manufactured in Iznik, Turkey, they were designed by Sinan, Suleiman's court architect

center, for they were keenly aware of its potential as a symbol that was capable of serving the monarchs of Europe in their efforts to mobilize men and resources for a new campaign to conquer the Holy Land.

The aura of the Moslem holy city, much like the mystique surrounding Jerusalem in the Christian imagination, contributed to the defense of the country by rallying a broad array of Moslem forces to the cause. Especially important in this context was the Mameluke support for the *qadis* (Moslem judges) and other religious functionaries, whom they wished to draw away from their center of rule in Egypt. Consequently the Mamelukes tried to invest Jerusalem with special drawing power, and their decision to convert it back into a religious center sparked an outburst of construction whose likes had not been seen since the early days of Crusader rule. Whole streets in the vicinity of the Temple Mount were rebuilt, including many public buildings; other structures were renovated to serve as *madrasat* (religious seminaries), monasteries for hermits and dervishes, pilgrim hostels, and tombs and mausoleums for Moslem notables. And all were fashioned with pomp and splendor in the best tradition of Mameluke architecture, which was heavily influenced by the style of building popular in Central Asia at the time. Some of these Mameluke buildings have survived the centuries and are still considered among the architectural jewels of the city.

At the beginning of the Mameluke period, the area south of the western wall retained its character as a cattle market, for the momentum of construction had not yet reached it. But as the development projects around the city multiplied and the population grew, private houses sprouted up in this sector. We uncovered their remains, particularly in the form of plastered cisterns (some of which were still in use until the period of the British Mandate). The Temple Mount was revitalized, with its mosques restored, small commemorative buildings added, and a number of religious seminaries and minarets built on its western side overlooking the residential neighborhoods. As a result of this ambitious building program, Jerusalem re-emerged as a holy city in the fullest sense. The question that remains to be answered is whether or not this vibrant religious center was fortified by walls.

Mameluke hegemony in Palestine was superseded at the start of the sixteenth century by another Moslem regime, once again not native to the country. This time the conquerors were the Ottomans Turks, who had taken up the scepter of the Byzantines in Asia and Europe and were in the process of establishing a sprawling empire. Egypt fell to the Ottomans in 1516, sealing the fate of the Mameluke regime — and of Jerusalem. For the Ottomans were to rule Palestine and Syria for four centuries, but for most of that time Jerusalem would emphatically not bask in the glory of a great holy city, as it had under the Mamelukes. Much to the contrary, in terms of both its political and economic standing, the city lacked all distinction. It was not even honored as a district capital, just another one of the thoroughly undistinguished provincial cities characteristic of Ottoman Palestine. The only attempt to raise Jerusalem from its lowly state and revitalize it in a somewhat different format was made soon after the Ottoman conquest by the son of the conqueror (and ultimately the most famous of the Turkish sultans), Suleiman the Magnificent.

As one might expect, Suleiman's motive was essentially to exhibit a presence in Jerusalem. Throughout its history, the main source of pressure on the Ottoman Empire came from Christian Europe; the East was

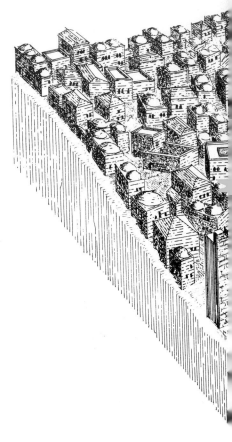

A reconstructed view of the southwest corner of the Temple Mount during the Mameluke period

overleaf: David Roberts' early-nineteenth-century painting of Jerusalem's southern wall and the Al Aqsa Mosque

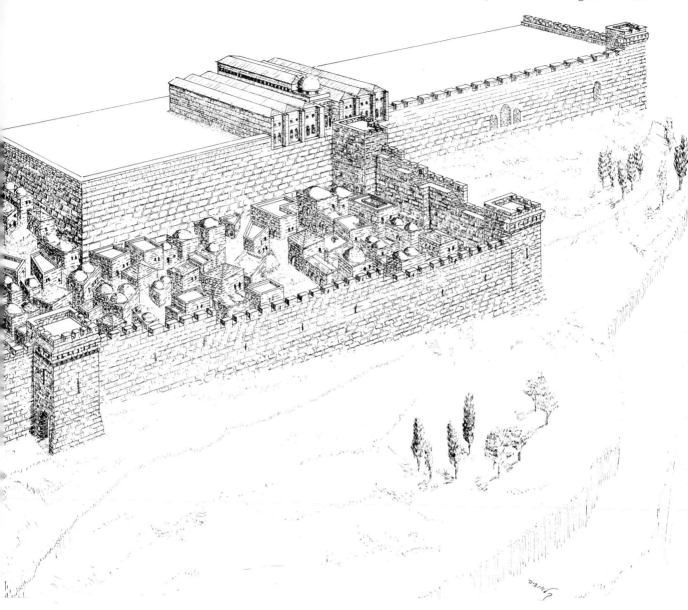

uniformly Moslem by then and had accepted the Ottoman yoke with quiet resignation, if not outright relief, because of widespread dissatisfaction with Mameluke rule. At the same time, Palestine's importance as a bridge to the international trade routes declined after the discovery of America, as the Ottomans joined in the exploration of sea routes circumventing Africa to take their ships to India and the Far East. Thereafter, it was not until the turn of the nineteenth century, after Napoleon's campaign to the Middle East, that Palestine began to draw international attention again; and following the opening of the Suez Canal in mid-century, the region experienced a political revival by becoming the object of rivalry between the declining Ottoman Empire and the European powers — and among the powers themselves. But back during the reign of Suleiman (1520–1566), the economic revolution that would eventually displace the Middle East as a crossroads of international trade was still incip-

ient, so that Palestine and Jerusalem continued to be a focus of attention.

One of Suleiman's most outstanding projects was the restoration of the Temple Mount, with emphasis placed on the Dome of the Rock, whose exterior walls were covered with colorful tiles. Manufactured in the Turkish ceramic center of Iznik, these tiles were glazed in tones of blue, green, turquoise, black, and brown and were tastefully decorated in an array of geometric and floral patterns. Over the years, unfortunately, most of them faded or dropped off the walls, and their shattered remains were cast off the Temple Mount to the foot of the southern wall, which became something of a dumping ground for the city's rubbish. We found a number of these tiles at the outset of our excavations — pale testimony to what had once been the height of splendor. I should add parenthetically that when Jordan's King Hussein had the exterior of the mosque restored in the 1950s, the ceramic tiles were again imported from Turkey — this time from Kütahya, Iznik's successor as a ceramic center — and they followed the patterns from the days of the sultanate.

What was Jerusalem like when the Ottomans first beheld the city? From the results of our dig, it is rather difficult to say. We were able to determine that within that general time frame, the city was marked by wholesale neglect, its buildings dilapidated or in ruins and its cisterns left in disrepair — though some of them were used to irrigate the large open field extending southward from the Temple Mount that for all intents and purposes was one huge vegetable patch. The open cattle market of the Crusader and early Mameluke eras was deserted and had effectively become an extension of that same vegetable dominion running south of the wall. What we cannot determine for sure is whether this neglect began with the advent of Ottoman rule or whether the city was already in a state of decay when the Turks arrived. It does appear, however, that the decline must have begun toward the close of the Mameluke period, when Jerusalem was prey to the attacks of marauding Bedouin sweeping in from the east and was victimized by the strife of the squabbling notables of the Hebron Mountains to the south. The city's pitiful state at that time is reflected in the strikingly meager finds uncovered south of the Temple Mount — with the exception of a brief interlude of florescence during the reign of Suleiman the Magnificent.

Suleiman's Wall

During the 1530s Suleiman the Magnificent not only rebuilt Jerusalem's walls and gates but took special care to place inscriptions at intervals along the city wall to commemorate his initiative. Historical sources also tell of this feat. But in contrast to Suleiman's version of events, a close reading of these testimonies, supplemented by a thorough examination of the wall itself both prior to our excavations and after we had completed our labors, showed that Suleiman's wall, though certainly an impressive structure, had been built on the remains of an older line of fortifications. This older wall was fairly well preserved in a number of places; in others the builders of Suleiman's wall merely used it as a foundation. Either way, however, without detracting from the merits of his enterprise, we are obliged to note that Suleiman's builders did not create this wall where nothing had existed before, as the many strategically placed inscriptions would have us believe. More than all else, those inscriptions attest to no more than Suleiman's astute appreciation of the power of the written word!

At first Suleiman's wall had four gates, one on each side of the city: the

Jaffa Gate in the west, the Damascus Gate in the north, the Lions' Gate (or Jericho Gate) in the east, and the Zion Gate in the south. The openings known today as Herod's Gate (or the Flower Gate) in the north and the Dung Gate in the south were essentially only wickets then, and as such were not suited for the passage of wagons, which made them easy to block against the enemy in time of war. Herod's Gate was originally created in the exterior façade of the wall and was not elevated to a full-fledged gate much later. The Dung Gate was not widened to its current size until 1953, during the Jordanian period, when it became necessary to accommodate military vehicles entering the Old City from the south. The original Dung Gate was located in the tower that protected it and had to be widened even after that tower was destroyed, because it was only 1.5 meters wide. The New Gate, by the northwest corner of the wall, is, as its name implies, a relatively recent creation. It was opened at the end of the nineteenth century, when the security situation was generally favorable, as a way of facilitating the connection between the Christian Quarter of the Old City and the new neighborhoods that were spreading outside the walls. The gaping breach in the wall by the Jaffa Gate was made at the end of the nineteenth century to enable Kaiser Wilhelm of Germany, an honored guest of the Ottoman government, to enter Jerusalem without sacrificing one bit of the pomp and circumstance to which he was accustomed. That, of course, was the official reason, though we should add that the Ottoman authorities exploited the breach to revamp the network of roads so as better to accommodate the needs of modern transport. Turning to the eastern wall, the Golden Gate should not really be counted as a gate in the literal sense of the term because it is blocked.

There is now an eighth gate in the Old City wall, a small opening that we created in the southern wall near our excavations and christened the "Excavation Gate." As we extended our dig outside the Old City wall, we found it necessary to establish a connection between the original site of the excavation inside the wall and its continuation beyond it. As luck would have it, under the section of Suleiman's southern wall that runs north–south for a brief strech, we discovered the eastern wall of the Omayyad palace and noticed that it had an aperture approximately in the middle. This had originally been the palace's eastern gate and was preserved up to a third of its height, before being filled in with stones to serve as the foundation of the Ottoman wall. It was there that we decided to open up our gate. To support the city wall, whose foundation we were removing, we built two arches that rested, respectively, on a central pillar and on the surviving gateposts of the Omayyad gate. So it was that, without much ado, a new gate was added to Jerusalem's city wall in May 1971.

The History of a Wall

Two Jewish travelers described Jerusalem at the end of the fifteenth century as a city without a wall. In 1481 Meshulam of Volterra wrote: "For Jerusalem has no walls, just a bit on the side on which I entered; and even though it has been destroyed [as retribution for our sins], it boasts ten thousand households..." Similar testimony was furnished in 1487 by Obadiah of Bertinoro, who wrote: "Most of Jerusalem is desolate and in ruins, and needless to say there is no wall around it; and the population within, by what I am told, is some four thousand households..."

The very fact that Suleiman the Magnificent built a wall around Jerusalem in the sixteenth century implies that when he embarked on that

above: A glazed-ceramic chalice from the end of the Mameluke period

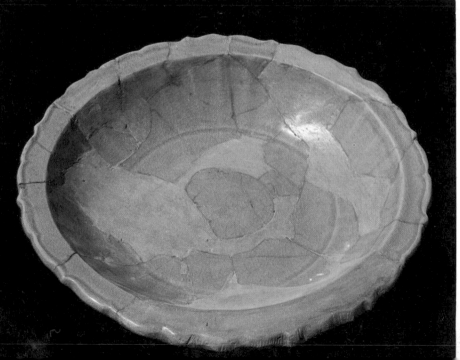

left: A Chinese porcelain bowl imported at the beginning of the Ottoman period

opposite: A selection of pottery pipes from the early Ottoman period

venture, the city's previous wall was in ruins. Yet two questions immediately present themselves: to exactly what extent was the wall destroyed;
and for how long (if at all) was the city devoid of a defensive wall? Many
scholars have taken the testimony of these travelers at face value, and
since there are no sources relating to the city from the time of its destruction by al-Malik al-Muazam in 1219, they accepted the premise that the
city remained bereft of fortifications for centuries.

That was not so, however, as we can pretty much see for ourselves if
we subject the descriptions of these fifteenth-century travelers to more
rigorous scrutiny. Meshulam of Volterra reported that even though the
city was in a state of ruin, it had 10,000 households, which translates into
some 60,000 inhabitants! Consequently, we cannot take the descriptions
of these travelers literally, for a devastated city with so many inhabitants
is a blatant contradiction in terms. All of which suggests that the word
"destroyed" must have meant that there were breaches in the city wall or
that its fortifications were otherwise damaged. The powers that be, for
reasons best known to them, probably deemed it in their interest to have
the city wall remain in a state of disrepair and even permitted the citizens
of Jerusalem to cart off its stones for their private needs. This attitude was
characteristic of the last days of Mameluke rule in Palestine, when the
sultans of Egypt, who had contributed so much to the greater glory of
Jerusalem, began to fear that the Ottomans would overrun the city and
incorporate it into their expanding empire. It was then that Jerusalem
began its sharp decline. The great Mameluke building spree, which had
extended from the latter half of the thirteenth century in the days of
Baybars to the middle of the fifteenth century under Qait Bey (so ramified
and intense had the construction activity been in Qait Bey's time that
many Europeans were convinced he was about to transfer his capital to
Jerusalem), came to an abrupt halt. And in the six years between the visits
by Meshulam of Volterra and Obadiah of Bertinoro, the city's population
dropped by 60 percent, from 10,000 to 4,000 families.

Is it conceivable that a city in which a mighty sultanate had invested so
much thought and care — to say nothing of human and financial resources — was not protected by a wall? That is difficult to imagine. What's
more, the writings of a number of Christian and Jewish travelers, as well
as contemporary Arab historians, indicate, or at least imply, the existence
of a wall. We know, for example, that after the conclusion of the peace
treaty between Frederick II and al-Malik al-Kamil, the Crusaders set to
restoring Jerusalem's city wall (which had been demolished by al-Malik
al-Muazam) and that the Mamelukes picked up where the knights left off.
In addition, the existence of a wall clearly emerges from maps of Jerusalem dating to the end of the thirteenth and beginning of the fourteenth
centuries.

Perhaps the strongest supporting testimony, however, comes from a
Jewish traveler from Spain who visited Jerusalem in 1333 and wrote that
the city had four gates. That alone indicates that Jerusalem must have
been a walled city, for there can be no gates without a wall. Moreover,
when Jerusalem's fortifications were deliberately destroyed by al-Malik
al-Muazam, the gates must have been a prime target, both because it is
difficult to rebuild a gate and because the destruction of a gate leaves a
gaping hole in the network of fortifications. Hence any reference to the
existence of gates is tantamount to a statement about the existence of
fortifications — though I should note that not all scholars see eye to eye

on this point. Père Vincent, for example, one of the greatest of Jerusalem scholars, did not overlook this information but contended that the wall was demolished even though the gates survived. Others have simply ignored this and similar testimony implying the presence of a city wall.

The archaeological evidence obtained by our dig tends to support the reading that the city was still enclosed by a wall, albeit a damaged one, at the end of the fifteenth century. Under the Sulfur Tower in Suleiman's wall, we uncovered the remains of a much larger and stronger tower that had belonged to an earlier set of fortifications. This older tower protruded substantially beyond the course of the Ottoman wall, and over the southern part of its ruins we found the remains of two aqueducts that had carried water from Bethlehem to Jerusalem during the Ottoman period. In contrast, the previous (meaning Mameluke) aqueduct — which was essentially a restoration of its Byzantine predecessor, which in turn had been built on the remains of the aqueduct from the Second Temple period — bypassed this large tower. Since the Ottoman aqueducts were built over the ruins of the medieval tower, they must have postdated it. Similarly, since the Mameluke conduit circumvented the medieval tower, it must have been contemporary with it. Thus we may conclude that this imposing fortification was standing during the Mameluke period and was probably not destroyed until shortly before the onset of the Ottoman era.

Whether or not this evidence is conclusive, it does suggest that Jerusalem's fortifications did not lay in ruins during the Mameluke period. Moreover, to the degree that it is possible to find evidence of their destruction, it applies only to the end of the fifteenth century, when, the sources tell us, Bedouin tribes were able to maraud in the city at will. As a result of the city's vulnerability, many of its inhabitants abandoned Jerusalem. But by then the Ottomans were already closing in on the area, and the Mamelukes, who might have repaired the fortifications, did not want to leave a properly defended city to them. On the contrary, they believed that the more the chaos mounted, the better it would serve their ends.

Jerusalem's Aqueduct

Jerusalem's renaissance as a holy city with public buildings of every kind required a regular supply of water in addition to the rainwater stored in the city's cisterns. Since initially being constructed in the Second Temple period, the aqueduct from Bethlehem to Jerusalem had been repaired or rebuilt several times. Because the flow in this system was due to gravity and the difference in elevation between the springs and the city was negligible, the route of each succeeding aqueduct usually remained identical. At first these aqueducts had entered the Temple Mount via the southern slope of Mount Zion, which lay within the city until the construction of the medieval wall. Thereafter the aqueduct was situated outside the city, running along the southern wall until it entered the city some 100 meters west of the Dung Gate. The Mameluke aqueduct, as we have noted, followed the earlier course and even made use of some surviving sections of its predecessor. Two Mameluke sultans were known to have addressed themselves to the problem of supplying water to Jeruslem. One was Qait Bey, who ordered the construction of an aqueduct that was completed in 1470. To commemorate that event, a lovely fountain, known today as the Qait Bey Fountain, was built on the Temple Mount. (It was also immortalized in an inscription on the Street of the Chain.)

One of Suleiman's projects in Jerusalem was the repair of the aqueduct leading from Solomon's Pools to the Temple Mount. The purpose of

Pottery shards from vessels manufactured in Iznik, Turkey, in the early Ottoman era

this aqueduct was essentially to furnish water to the city's public and royal buildings; as in generations past, the residents of Jerusalem had to dig and plaster their own cisterns to ensure a steady supply of water to their homes. Uncovered in our excavations, the Ottoman aqueduct was an open conduit 70 centimeters deep and 50 centimeters wide coated with a high-quality waterproof plaster to prevent seepage. The flow of water in an open aqueduct is a rather straightforward affair, compared with getting it to flow through a closed pipe. On the other hand, an open system has distinct disadvantages insofar as its water is accessible to anyone who wants to draw it out for his own needs. In times of order and stability, an open aqueduct can be supervised and maintained with relative ease. The open system of the Roman-Byzantine era, for example, bore an inscription forbidding shepherds to advance any closer than 5 cubits from either side of the conduit — and to make sure there would be no misunderstanding, the measure of a cubit was engraved alongside the warning! In less settled times, supervision proves to be far more troublesome.

In the course of time, Ottoman rule in Palestine grew progressively more slack, so that by 1620, a century after the Turks had conquered the country, their hold over it could already be described as tenuous. Bedouin pitched their tents along the aqueduct for the express purpose of helping themselves to its water, and the authorities were powerless to stop them. Their answer to this nuisance was to lay pottery pipes within the open channel. These pipes were made up of individual links, each 50 centimeters long and 25 centimeters in diameter. The problem was that getting water to flow in the closed pipe required a knowledge of hydraulic engineering, which the Ottomans sorely lacked. Within a short time, therefore, the pipe was blocked and the flow of spring water had come to a halt. Later on holes were drilled in the pipe in an effort to ease the pressure by releasing the air bubbles and thereby, presumably, getting the water to flow again. But this stab at a solution came to nought, and eventually the project was simply abandoned.

A Forward Wall in the South

In the area immediately south of the Temple Mount, outside the Old City wall, we thought we could see a line protruding to create something like a cultivation terrace. As soon as we began excavating in this area, we decided to expose and study this mysterious line; and although only its foundations survived, we uncovered enough details to identify it.

It turned out to be a wall, 3 meters thick, that began approximately half way down the north–south section of the southern wall (referred to above in connection with the Excavation Gate), continued eastward, and then turned northward until it met the southern wall of the Temple Mount (which doubles here as the city wall). Replete with two towers, which marked it as a fortification, this wall had been built over the ruins of structures from the Omayyad period, and its western section had been demolished by the Ottoman builders when they constructed Suleiman's wall — considerably providing us with the wall's outside dates. Arriving at a precise dating has proved impossible, because the area fronting the wall has been cultivated for the past century and there were no remains of floors directly associated with it. Before going deeper into the question of its date, however, let us examine its purpose. The wall had apparently been built to provide additional protection for the Double and Triple Gates, which, though blocked, constituted a weak point in the city's defenses. Along its course, this was also reached as far as the only gate in

the city's southern wall and, in the days when it had stood up to its full height, blocked that too, as it did the secret passage built by the Crusaders. This leads us to posit that it must have been built sometime between Saladin's defeat of the Crusaders in the twelfth century and Suleiman's restoration of the Old City wall in the sixteenth. Could it have been Saladin who was responsible for protecting these vulnerable points of the Temple Mount? Inscriptions mentioning other of his activities can be

above: The stone pavement and bases of columns from the old Ottoman market south of the Temple Mount

below: Plan and section of the market from the Ottoman period

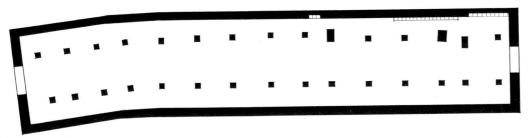

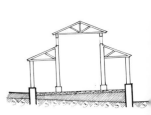

found in Jerusalem, but nowhere is there an allusion to this one. Perhaps, then, it was the Mamelukes who took this extra precaution to bolster the city's defenses in the south. Unfortunately, we are presently unable to offer anything more than reasoned conjecture about the origin of this wall.

A Market in the South

Between this forward wall and the Temple Mount's southern wall, in the section lying between the Double Gate and the Triple Gate, we uncovered the remains of a large structure with a stone-paved floor. Judging by its plan, it had been a structure with three halls — a central one and two narrower side aisles, like a classic basilica — and was similar in design to the Ottoman markets or bazaars. Further evidence to this effect was the small shops on either side of its pavement and the small stone troughs, suitable for feeding sheep or goats, found in some of its stalls. The generalized destruction of both this building and the forward wall made it impossible for us to determine the chronological relationship between them. But although decisive proof is lacking, it does appear that the building dates to the Ottoman period. We know that the medieval (Crusader and Mameluke) cattle market was located inside the city wall. In the last century this market moved outside the Old City and established itself below the eastern wall, near the Stork Tower at the northeast corner. Called *Suk al-Juma*, or the Friday Market, it attracts mainly people wishing to buy or sell sheep and goats, though merchants specializing in other animals and particularly in fowl — pigeons and chickens — come as well. The building uncovered south of the Temple Mount, if it is indeed from the Ottoman era, apparently served the same purpose until the market was relocated outside the city wall.

That probably happened at the start of the nineteenth century, after the southern wall east of Al Aqsa was badly damaged in an earthquake and debris fell onto the bazaar-like structure we uncovered. A lovely work by David Roberts, painted from the vantage of the Mount of Olives, shows this breach in the Temple Mount wall by Al Aqsa, and today you can clearly see the evidence of its repair. Once the market moved eastward, the area south of the city wall turned partly into agricultural land and partly into the city dump.

Troughs from the market of the Ottoman period

In time the piles of refuse at the foot of the Temple Mount's southern wall grew progressively higher, particularly after the compound was struck by fire — and it suffered a number of fires before the one set by Dennis Michael Rohan, a disturbed Australian tourist, in 1969. Decades worth of broken pottery, building refuse, and all the other effects of the ravages of nature, man, and time were cast down into the field directly south of the compound, so that our excavation below the Hulda Gates began by having to remove heaps of ash-black dirt that towered as much as 5 meters high. But within this immense rubbish pile we found a trove of pottery that had originally come from the buildings on the Temple Mount.

One such trash heap included scores of broken vessels from the Mameluke period — some hopelessly shattered, others almost intact — ranging from simple painted vessels to ceramics of the highest quality. Among the latter were lovely chalices made of deep bowls perched on high stands (pieces of this type are still popular for serving sweets, fruits, and other refreshments). The ceramics of the Mameluke period were usually glazed in bold tones of green and orange. They were produced in a form and then decorated on the outside with verses from the Koran. At first scholars believed that these lovely pieces, known from various places in the East, were brought to Palestine from the manufacturing centers of Cairo and Damascus. But we found stone forms for creating them, leaving no doubt that Jerusalem was likewise a center of production. The array of vessels found in the rubbish heaps included everything from cooking and serving implements to cups and goblets and storage jars of varying size. What characterized them all, however — be they graceful serving pieces or mundane storage jars — was the irrepressible drive to ornament them. Typical of the jars are handles stamped with the hallmarks of the potteries that produced them, while other stamps may have signified that the vessels were the property of the sultanate or indicated their contents.

The other pile of refuse we systematically examined dated to the Ottoman period and also contained a wealth of broken vessels, including some that could definitely be dated no earlier than the sixteenth century. Many had been crafted in the Iznik ceramic center, but since they were found alongside pieces from the Mameluke period, they could not be used as a standard for dating. One item that placed us on a firm footing in regard to dating, however, was the pipes, for it was not until after the discovery of America that tobacco and the habit of smoking were introduced in Europe and the East. The most common pipes were made out of a ceramic bowl and a wooden, cane, or bone mouthpiece. They came in all shapes and colors and, being of pottery, were highly breakable. But since they were also cheap, once damaged they were readily discarded — and we found them by the dozens.

While collecting the pottery shards from this second heap, one of our excavators came upon porcelain fragments as white as snow with decorations in blue. To us they bore a striking resemblance to the modern china manufactured in Holland, Czechoslovakia, and Germany and looked as if they had just been discarded yesterday. Because they appeared to be contemporary, we were stumped about what to do with these shards. But then some small markings on the bases of some of the pieces gave us pause to reconsider before dismissing them so lightly. For those marks were Chinese characters, and as soon as we realized it, we called in one of the Sinologists at the Hebrew University to decipher them for us. The learned

Imports from China and New World Influences

professor came, read the inscriptions easily, and told us that they were routine salutations and blessings. Later on a visitor from Britain, one of the many distinguished guests who joined the standard tours of the site, happened to be a scholar of Chinese history and language, and when he heard about these fragments he asked if he might have a look at them. He too read the inscriptions without difficulty but interpreted them as the names of emperors of the Ming dynasty, which had ruled China during the fourteenth–fifteenth centuries. Seeing our surprise at the varying interpretations, he explained that the first reading was also correct, but in addition to being standard blessings they were also the titles of the Ming emperors.

These finds made us more eager than ever to determine the date of the refuse pile. The Ming shards indicated that the original pieces had been relatively small vessels, bowls and cups decorated in bright blue with dragons and other figures. They must have been among the lavish gifts sent to the Ottoman chiefs before the capture of Constantinople. A rare collection of similar pieces, which accompanied the Turks on their migration westward from Central Asia into Asia Minor, can be seen in Topkapi (originally the sultan's palace in Istanbul, today a museum). We know that they continued to be used in the palace until the sultanate was abolished, and it appears that a number of pieces from this set found their way to Jerusalem, probably as a gift from Suleiman the Magnificent to the wardens of Al Aqsa and other religious functionaries responsible for the Temple Mount. Broken during one of the subsequent calamities that struck the compound, they were consigned to the trash heap, and there they remained until we salvaged them.

These samples of Ming ware taught us that it is possible to find artifacts whose date is more or less known without being able to use them for dating the stratum in which they were found. In this case, the vessels had been made about a century prior to their arrival in Istanbul; another century passed before their arrival in Jerusalem; and another four centuries probably ensued before they were discarded in the place where we found them. Together with the Ming ware, we found other imports from China, specifically celadon ware (special stoneware with a dark-gray center and a deep-green glaze on the outside), alongside imports from Persia and Turkey that were poor imitations of the Chinese pieces. The Persians did their best to reproduce Ming ware, but in their ignorance of the Chinese language their artisans painted hallmarks that looked like Chinese characters but lacked all meaning. The technical level of the Persian product was also appreciably lower than the Chinese originals, and many more centuries were to pass before the secrets of the Chinese potters were mastered in Europe and the Near East.

21 An Archaeological Garden

Our excavations confirmed the picture already obtained from dozens of landscape drawings and engravings, and even occasional photographs taken over the past century, showing the field that stretched southward from the Temple Mount's southern wall past Suleiman's wall to be desolate. During this period a number of inconsequential changes took place on the western side of the Temple Mount, such as the addition of a residential wing to a structure built on pillars north of Robinson's Arch, and the construction of a few more buildings in the southern part of the Moghrabi Quarter. But most of the area remained a deserted tract occasionally marked by vegetable plots. East of the city wall, residents of the village of Silwan purchased cultivation rights from the *waqf* and built a few squalid rooms as living quarters and to house their flocks. Their latrines were directly below the Al Aqsa Mosque, leaning right up against the Temple Mount's southern wall. This deplorable situation obtained throughout the period of the British Mandate and the Jordanian administration, though it is difficult to understand why this area was deliberately abandoned to decay. I raised the question a number of times in meetings with the heads of the *waqf* but never received a satisfactory answer.

Only the most modest of archaeological excavations were conducted in this area, even though the history of the place cried out for a major effort. Except for the important pioneering work of the British expedition under Warren in the 1860s and Kathleen Kenyon's expedition in the 1960s, which failed to turn up finds of any importance because of its minimalist methodology, no attempt was made to reveal the wealth of remains buried deep in the ground. On the contrary, Jordan's King Hussein, who regarded himself as the guardian of the Moslem holy places in Jerusalem and invested generously in restoring the structures on the Temple Mount, was responsible for making the remains of the glorious Omayyad palace even more inaccessible by ordering the construction of a school precisely in this area so potentially rich in archaeological finds.

Our work, in contrast, extended throughout the area south of the Temple Mount and spilled over into the sector adjoining the southern part of the western wall. In the previous chapters, I have described most of the important finds that have led so many people — political adversaries included — to acknowledge our signal contribution to the knowledge of Jerusalem's past. In one of his visits to the site, the *mufti* of Jerusalem made a point of telling me, "Above and beyond our differences, and despite the fact that you have carried out your work on the *waqf*'s property without first obtaining permission to do so, I believe that you have contributed substantially to our knowledge of Jerusalem's history. The hidden past uncovered in these excavations is particularly important to us as Moslems; and for me, as a man of the cloth, the clearing of the area at the foot of our holy places and its maintenance as a clean and orderly site is of special value." In contrast to the charges voiced by no less eminent an organization than UNESCO, his words were like a cool breeze on a sweltering summer's day.

Israel's ouster from UNESCO, ostensibly because of our excavations,

A model for the archaeological garden: a reconstruction of the Church of St. Mary of the Germans

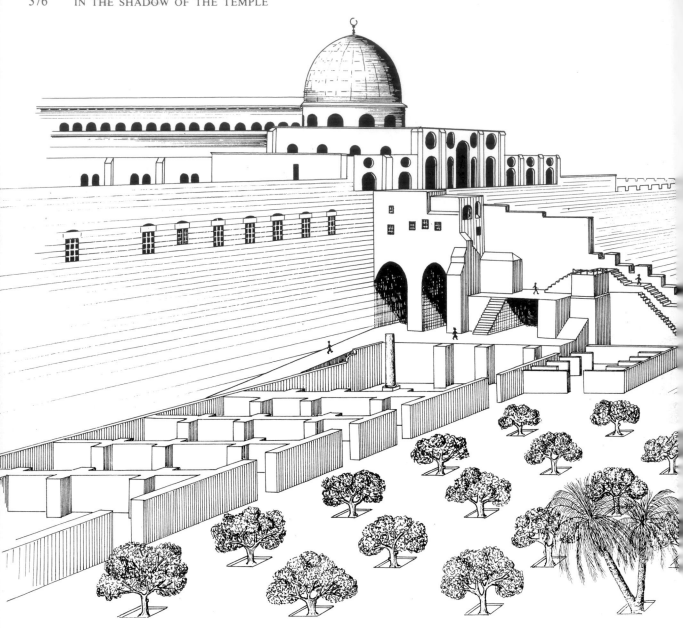

Projected view of the archaeological garden at the foot of the Temple Mount: the courtyard of the Omayyad palace

sent a tremor through the world press and scholarly community, and the astonishment at this decision was all the greater because of the speciously "scientific" reasons furnished to justify it. Yet I believed that it was neither dignified nor expedient to refute these claims, because the UNESCO resolution was so obviously a bald political maneuver. Suffice it to say that among the grounds for the expulsion cited in the resolution was that our excavations deal only with discoveries relating to Jewish history of the Second Temple period, deliberately neglecting all the other periods and cultures. Anyone who has read this far need not be told that this accusation is simply false. The fact that the first and most impressive finds of our venture came from the Moslem period — the Omayyad palace and its complex of auxiliary buildings — and that so striking a find from the Christian era as the Nea Church fell to our lot was not a matter of blind luck but a result of our determination to conduct an objective and exhaustive investigation. Another loudly voiced claim — that the sole purpose of the dig is to undermine the walls of the Temple Mount and bring about their collapse — is so patently absurd that it is pointless to address it at all. We can only hope that the forces responsible for the passage of this cynical resolution will ultimately fail at camouflaging the true purpose of their shameless libel.

A Multi-Era Archaeological Garden

This book has reviewed the major archaeological finds uncovered in the course of twelve consecutive years of hard work alongside the Temple Mount. Although the job is not yet complete and we continue to dig, both downward and outward, most of the work has already been done, and today visitors can see the remains of walls — some substantially destroyed, others still standing up to a considerable height — that tell the story of Jerusalem over the ages. As we approach the conclusion of our dig, we find ourselves deliberating the question of what should be done with these remains once our work is over. When they were buried under tons of detritus, they remained safe and intact, as it were; but now that we have exposed them to the elements, they are no longer protected against the ravages of time. Added to the problem of preservation is the question of reconstruction, as a matter of principle. If you excavate at a place that is of interest to the public at large and attracts many visitors eager to learn from the antiquities uncovered there, you have no choice but to reconstruct parts of the site. For it is easier to apprehend something with a perceptible shape than to conceptualize it from fragmentary and occasionally arbitrary remains. The natural questions are: how much should be reconstructed, should original remains be set off from reconstructed ones, and exactly how should the reconstructions be carried out? These are but a few of the decisions that must be made before we can embark upon the task of reconstruction.

Before we could begin planning the preservation and reconstruction work, another salient characteristic of this particular site had to be taken into consideration. Most archaeological sites are expressive of a single culture or civilization, be it a mono-ephocal site like Masada or a multi-era site like the Forum in Rome. In the latter, to cite just one example, a particular emperor was responsible for the initial construction, his successor respected his work and expanded upon it, and all subsequent rulers followed suit, so that centuries of accumulative culture come to expression over a broad area. But the history of Jerusalem that emerges from our excavation is not one of accumulative construction; it is a saga of war, destruction, and decay.

One generation devoted itself to building and when its successor came along it destroyed existing achievements to reshape the same area according to its own outlook and tastes. The result is that centuries of culture were reduced to heaps of detritus and debris. The history of most ancient cities and archaeological sites is horizontal; Jerusalem's story must be read vertically.

Thoroughly schooled in this problem, we understood that the preservation and reconstruction of the antiquities by the Temple Mount would demand careful thought and planning. First of all, structures from every one of the periods would have to be preserved faithfully to reflect the history of Jerusalem as a saga of different peoples, religions, world views, and creative efforts. This requires a very complex approach to both exca-

vation and reconstruction, for the walls of otherwise dispensable structures must be left standing for this purpose alone, and it is necessary to
dig with great care under their floors and, when the time comes, even to
cover up the finds in certain places so as to preserve the strata above them.
The unique character of our site also required us to arrange the remains of
various eras side by side, so that visitors would be able to appreciate the
difference between one structure and another, one period and the next.

Occasionally the way in which the structures were uncovered promoted us to experiment with approaches that had never been tried on any
other archaeological site. For example, the builders of the Omayyad period buried entire buildings of the Byzantine era as part of the fill under the
floors of their structures. In one case we uncovered a whole building
under the floor of the Omayyad palace and removed all the fill from its
rooms, so that we now have, pretty much intact, the ground floor of what
was formerly a two-story residential building. Over it we can build a thin
but strong cement ceiling at exactly the floor level of the Omayyad palace
and then cover it with the palace's original stone flooring. The result will
represent two distinct historical and archaeological strata, one over the
other, so that the visitor can enter the Omayyad palace; tour its wings,
column-lined courtyard, exedras, and adjoining rooms; and then descend
stairs leading under its floors to visit a residential building from the
Byzantine era. In this way he can see for himself how the different archaeological strata were created. Our site contains the remains of twenty-
five strata from twelve distinct periods. By displaying them with
intelligence and imagination, future visitors will be able to take in the full
story of Jerusalem's past at the foot of the Temple Mount.

Among the more outstanding features of the projected archaeological
garden are a large public building from the First Temple period, the
remains of the Acra Fortress and its cistern from the Hellenistic era, a
number of formidable buildings from the glorious days of the Herodian
era, two strata of residential buildings from the Byzantine era, the

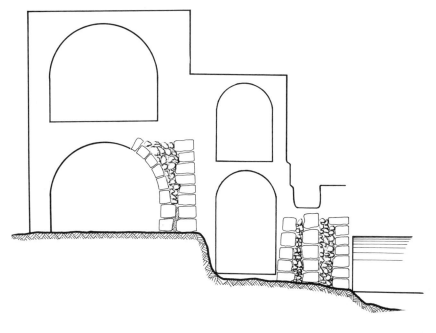

Remains of the vaults from the Second
Temple period built on the ruins of the
walls of a large building from the First
Temple period

Omayyad palace and other remains of this complex, remains from the days of the Fatimids and Crusaders, Mameluke cisterns and, towering above them all, the city wall built by Suleiman the Magnificent.

In speaking of an archaeological garden, naturally we must make it possible for our guests to tour comfortably, so that a network of paths, secure railings, shaded corners, water fountains, and installations for lights — as preparation for sound-and-light shows and for illumination at night — as well as signs and explanations, have been planned. All these require attention to the last detail. For example, should we use some material other than stone for the paths and railings, since stone is the characteristic raw material used for building in Jerusalem? Our plans take into consideration countless details of this kind, so that from this stand-point, too, the archaeological garden is destined to be quite unique among arcaheological sites the world over.

When the various structures uncovered in our dig originally stood in all their glory (or otherwise), they were part of the larger canvas of the city, and we want this fact to be reflected in the archaeological garden as well. Just as the residential neighborhoods and public areas were hum-ming with life, we intend to recreate some of this vitality by reintroducing the foliage that originally grew in the area. The most outstanding aspect of the site will obviously be the construction in stone. The problem is that such a massive quantity of stone is almost blinding, especially in the hot season; but the generous addition of foliage can mitigate that sensation by softening the light color and harsh glare of the stone and aid in highlight-ing essential elements while playing down superfluous ones. It will also create a sense of balance, provide shade for visitors in a city that often seems to suffer from a surfeit of sun and, by stimulating the senses, heighten the enjoyment of visiting the site. The presence of water, the colors and scents of the foliage, and the birds and insects attracted by them will enable us to create something pleasing, multi-dimensional and, above all, authentic. Our approach to the foliage in the archaeological garden is that it must serve as a setting for the stone walls and not cover anything of interest and that it must comprise varieties widespread at the time these buildings stood — meaning the trees and plants reflected in the ornamentation of the day: olive branches, vines, pomegranates, citrus, and palm trees.

The finds we have unearthed over the years range from the remains of buildings to artifacts in daily use. Each complements the other, and to-gether they relate the story of one period or another in the city's long history. Since it is impossible to reinstate the everyday objects in the buildings — for the structures are now in ruins and will expose the smaller finds to perils from both man and nature — an exhibition hall is planned so that we can display all the artifacts uncovered in the dig, provide plans and models of the area, and present aerial and other photographs as background material. Here, too, the exhibits and reconstructions will be presented against the background of daily life, not in glass cases like sterile, lifeless collections.

The realization of all these plans — beginning with the completion of the dig itself, progress in reconstructing and preserving the site (which has already begun), and the construction of an exhibition hall — will bring our extraordinary archaeological endeavor to a fitting conclusion. The Temple Mount, which has long held, and still holds, a focal place in the interest and imagination of hundreds of millions of people all over the globe, will soon be able to offer a vivid and cogent exposition of its glorious history based on our excavation and the reconstruction, preservation, and presentation of its yield. It is our fervent hope that in the days to come, our venture will be able to share its blessings with all who are privileged to visit this site and the countless others who cherish the well-being of Jerusalem, wherever they may be.

Selected Bibliography

Aharoni, Y., and M. Avi-Yonah, *The MacMillan Bible Atlas*, Jerusalem, 1964.

Avigad, N., "Discovering Jerusalem (Preliminary Reports)," *Israel Exploration Journal* 20 (2970), pp. 1–8, 129–140; 22 (1972), pp. 193–200; 25 (1975), pp. 260–261; 27 (1977), pp. 55–57, 145–151; 28 (1978), pp. 200–201.

Ben-Dov, M., "Discovery of the New Church — Jewel of Byzantine Jerusalem," *Christian News from Israel* 26 (1977), pp. 86 ff.

——, "Herodian Jerusalem Revisited," *Christian News from Israel*, 3–4 (1978), p. 138.

Bliss, F.J., and A.C. Dickie, *Excavations at Jerusalem, 1894–1897*, London, 1898.

Buskin, T.A., *Der Tempel von Jerusalem, von Salomo bis Herodes*, Leiden, 1970.

Conder, C.R., *The City of Jerusalem*, London, 1909.

Crowfoot, J.W., and G.M. Fitzgerald, *Excavations in the Tyropoeon Valley, 1927*, PEFA, 1929.

Jeremias, J., *Jerusalem Zur Zeit Jesu*, Gottingen, 1962.

Josephus, *The Jewish War*, books I–VII, Loeb Edition. T.E. Page, ed., London, 1961.

Kenyon, K.M., *Jerusalem: Excavating 3000 years of History*, London, 1967.

——, *Digging Up Jerusalem*, London, 1974.

Le Strange, G., *Palestine Under the Moslems*, Beirut, 1890.

Macalister, R.A.S., and J.G. Duncan, *Excavations on the Hill of Ophel, 1923–1925*, PEFA VI, 1926.

Mazar, B., *The Mountain of the Lord — Excavating in Jerusalem*, New York, 1975.

Moore, E.A., *The Ancient Churches of Old Jerusalem*, Beirut, 1961.

Procopius, *Buidings, V, 6*, Loeb Edition, M.B. Dewing, ed., London, 1954.

Runciman, S., *A History of the Crusades*, Vols. I–III, Cambridge, 1954.

Safrai, S. and M. Stern, eds., *The Jewish People in the First Century*, Vols. I–II, Assen, 1974.

Simons, J., *Jerusalem in the Old Testament, Researches and Theories*, Leiden, 1952.

Vincent, L.H., *Jérusalem Antique*, Paris, 1912.

—— and F.M. Abel, *Jérusalem Nouvelle*, Vols. I–III, Paris, 1914–1926.

—— and M.A. Steve, *Jérusalem de l'Ancien Testament*, Vols. I–III, Paris, 1954–1956.

Vitruvius, *De Architectura*, Books I–X, Loeb Edition, T.E. Page, ed., London, 1962.

Warren, C. and C.R. Conder, *The Survey of Western Palestine: Jerusalem*, London, 1884.

Weill, R., *La Cité de David*, Vols. I–II, Paris, 1920–1947.

Wilson, C.W., Ordnance Survey of Jerusalem, London, 1865.

—— and C. Warren, *The Recovery of Jerusalem*, London, 1871.